TEILHARD DE CHARDIN

A Biography

ROBERT SPEAIGHT

TEILHARD
DE CHARDIN

A BIOGRAPHY

COLLINS

ST JAMES'S PLACE, LONDON

1967

For

JEAN MAMBRINO
vingt ans après

CONTENTS

MAPS

ILLUSTRATIONS

FOREWORD

ANY NEW BOOK about Pierre Teilhard de Chardin requires explanation, if not excuse. When I was invited, in January 1963, to undertake the present work, there was no immediate question of Claude Cuénot's massive and indispensable biography appearing under the imprint of an English publisher; nor was the flood of books by Teilhard, or about him, more than a modest stream. Now, I must confess, I sometimes ask myself—and I can well understand others asking—'Was this book really necessary?' I can only plead in excuse that once having set my hand to a fascinating task, I was unwilling to abandon it; and also that much material, both published and unpublished, is now available which invites collation from a biographer. While Teilhard's thought continues to be examined from every angle, the man behind it is hidden. Between the smoke raised by his critics and the smoke raised by his thurifers his true stature tends to be obscured.

This was sufficiently remarkable, as it seemed to me, to merit a shorter, less technical and perhaps less ambitious biography than M. Cuénot's. The extent of Teilhard's appeal is a dramatic vindication of his own claim to speak to, and for, the men and women of his own time. My own interest in his work was aroused by a reading of *Le Milieu Divin* long before it was published. I met and talked at some length with him in Paris, shortly after he had returned there, in the summer of 1946; and I also knew his close friend and counsellor, Père Valensin. I have never met two men whose acquaintance I felt so privileged to make, or whom I so regretted not to have seen more often. Nevertheless, I cannot pretend to any expertise in philosophy, theology, or—still less—in science. On the other hand I cannot help discussing, although I have no authority to decide, the controversies which have gathered round Teilhard's name. It must be for others to reply to Cardinal Journet or Sir Peter Medawar. Where the replies have been forthcoming, I have not hesitated to quote them; those trained in science or theology must debate their validity. Teilhard has been described as 'scientist and seer',[1] and the seer, if he is suspect to the scientist, is hardly less so to the theologian. But some critics of Teilhard have impugned not only his professional competence but his personal integrity, and to these I hope this book will bring a conclusive answer. It does not, however, claim to be definitive. The relations of Teilhard to his superiors, and of his superiors to the Roman authorities, are still subject to ecclesiastical discretion. This also applies to his own correspondence; he expressed himself freely, and to a wide variety of friends. But enough has now been published, or is available to discriminating research, for the story to be told in its essential outlines. Such a task has seemed to me worth undertaking, at the risk of recapitulating much that is already known.

If Teilhard de Chardin has suffered from his opponents, he has also suffered from his more uncritical advocates. A bold exponent of the Gospel has been treated as if he were the Gospel himself. This is the last thing he would have wanted. Everything he wrote was submitted to the judgment of his friends; more often than not he accepted their revisions. His ordeal was not the heat of public controversy; it was the frustration of enforced silence. If his work had been published and discussed during his lifetime, its impact might have been less dramatic, but it might also have been more coolly appraised. He might himself have been compelled to a greater precision. Audacious in his ideas and firm in his convictions, Teilhard still had the gift—or the grace—of infinite patience. He knew that any idea is contestable, and that the more original an idea the more surely it will be contested. He would have profited largely from such public argument. As it is, he is something of a *cause célèbre* and something of a *casus belli*. There is another book—many books perhaps—to be written on the *après Teilhard*; my present concern is with Teilhard 'in his habit as lived', and my thanks go out to those who knew him—as I had scarcely known him—on the battlements of time.

All I have attempted here is to give a summary and sequence of his thought, and to relate these to the story of his life. It is the story of a dual vocation, and we understand nothing of Teilhard unless we see the formidable abstractions of his synthesis as the expressions of a particular man living in particular places at particular points in time, and

[1] Charles Raven, *Teilhard de Chardin: Scientist and Seer.*

having his roots in a particular social milieu and a particular locality. To say that he transcended these is not to say that he was ever unattached to them. He collected stones as another boy might have collected stamps, and on the single occasion when he met his most implacable theological opponent they talked of Auvergne. For a few brief moments soil was stronger than scholasticism. It has been objected that the sense of tradition was too weak in Teilhard's thought; in his character it was very strong indeed. But he was at once too grandly and simply a *seigneur* to bother very much about the traditions which had made him gentle. You may argue that the Christ of the Gospels finds a too limited place in his teaching, and that his Christianity seems to owe more to the cosmos than the catechism. It was not, however, that he disbelieved in the Gospels or the catechism, or that he thought that either could be dispensed with; it was rather that the dynamism of his faith came from other sources as well. You may object that he made too little allowance for sin and consequently minimized redemption; you may legitimately prefer the more traditional ways of Christian thought. These are the options of piety—or the imperatives of theology, if you insist. What you cannot deny is the fact that Teilhard has brought many people to a belief in Christ who would otherwise have had no belief in him at all.

Apologetics are out of fashion today, but in the right understanding of the word Teilhard was a passionate apologist. He was not concerned merely to explain things to himself, but to explain them to other people. Where a professional philosopher or theologian—and Teilhard claimed to be neither—will elaborate a theory mainly for their own satisfaction, Teilhard was out to persuade. Where a more academic thinker will rarely emerge from his study, Teilhard was constantly coming out of his laboratory—and the windows of his laboratory, metaphorically speaking, were always open. These alternations of mental and physical activity make up the rhythm of his life. The pathos of that life lay in the prohibition to address the larger public that he wanted so ardently to reach, and its heroism in the humility with which he bowed to this refusal. Let no one suppose that it was a humility easily achieved, any more than his optimism was a facile cheerfulness. For all its outward serenity and essential balance, his life was a struggle. But if you set him beside other apologists for the Christian faith in a century which is more and more convinced of its implausibility, and if you separate him from the controversy which his thought has aroused, what will strike you is his common sense. However far he looked, and however deeply he felt, his sense of proportion—which was a kind of intellectual justice—never deserted him.

His robust optimism, which he regarded as 'the secret of all activity and all success',[1] will have to abide the judgment of time; and the judgment is never final. Already, little more than ten years after his death, the conquest of space, the uses of atomic energy, and the development of cybernetics have more than kept pace with his predictions. On the other hand, the decline in manners and morality, and, to some extent, in literature and art, has been precipitous. In the matter of religious belief it has been catastrophic. Yet to the new and acrid secularism of the West the Church in which Teilhard never ceased to believe has replied with a dramatic *aggiornamento*. Nothing that Teilhard said in public or in private—and much that he did not say—was left unsaid at the Second Vatican Council. Much that he had clamoured for was implied or incorporated in its decrees. When he wrote of inspiration that 'it is not limited to the composition of a text, but it envelops that text and *lives* in it to the extent that the Church very slowly understands it',[2] he was stating what is now a theological commonplace. If Teilhard were alive today, he would accept his *réclame* with such equanimity as his modesty allowed; but he would find his optimism vindicated in the popularity and progress of his ideas.

Where others were preoccupied with the consummation of the world, or with its present crisis, Teilhard was equally concerned with its remote beginnings. Within his own province of palaeontology he was an acknowledged expert, never going beyond the facts as science had ascertained them. But from the observation of phenomena to the securities of faith and the adventures of contemplation is a distance which the deductive faculties have no power to bridge. Many who have followed him have been unable to follow him to his own conclusions. But to all who have followed him a certain distance he has given a measure of that belief in life which, for him, was inseparable from belief in God. The words of Père de Lubac, who was his friend, his brother in religion, and the judicious interpreter of his thought,

[1] Letter to Pierre Lamare, 29 March 1932.
[2] Letter to Père Auguste Valensin, 20 October 1919.

excuse whatever some have found defective in his formulations and others have found unacceptable in his faith:

The efficacity of his message lies not so much in a more or less skilful philosophy as in the extremely powerful witness of a man perfectly attuned to the ideas and preoccupations of his time.

Benenden, 28 December 1966

ACKNOWLEDGEMENTS

I MUST FIRST OF ALL express my thanks to Mlle. Jeanne Mortier, and her staff at the Fondation Teilhard de Chardin in Paris. Here, in perfect surroundings, I spent many useful hours working on such texts of Teilhard as have not yet been published, and particularly on his correspondence. I have already expressed my indebtedness to M. Claude Cuénot's biography; it remains to add that M. Cuénot encouraged me to make every use of this, but particularly to include in my own study any new material I could find. Exhaustive as M. Cuénot's work has been, there was fortunately no lack of this.

I had the most willing co-operation from Mlle. Alice Teillard-Chambon, who not only received me most hospitably at Le Chambon and in the Rue de Fleurus, but allowed me to see her copies of Teilhard's letters to Monseigneur Bruno de Solages. I am deeply grateful to Monseigneur de Solages for permitting me to make use of these. At Sarcenat I was cordially welcomed by Mme. Victor Teilhard de Chardin, as I was by the Assumptionist Fathers at Notre Dame de Mongré and by the Diocesan College at Aix-en-Provence, which used to be the Jesuit novitiate.

I am particularly grateful to Teilhard's friends in the Society of Jesus. To Père de Lubac, who has all along aided me in my work and replied to my questions, and with whom I have had many long conversations in Lyon, Paris and Rome. To Père d'Ouince, with whom I talked in great detail, and who kindly let me read his introduction to the volume of letters from Teilhard to two correspondents who prefer to remain anonymous. These had not yet been published when my biography was complete, but Père d'Ouince's introduction was of great use to me. Similarly Père Barjon showed me the MS of his own, as yet unpublished, biography and I profited from several conversations with him. The staff of the library at *Études* was always helpful in finding the material I required. Père Leroy, whom I visited in his laboratory attached to the Collège de France, generously gave me of his time and allowed me to draw upon his memory.

Among the English members of the Society I must thank Father Vincent Turner for unearthing for me a number of critical articles from the library of Campion Hall and Heythrop College, and to the Master of Campion Hall for offering me hospitality while I was at work on them. Father John Russell not only secured for me some photostats from the Heythrop library, but placed his scientific knowledge at my disposal. I was helped in the same way by the Librarian at Farm Street. Father Philip Caraman sent me a photostat copy of a letter from Teilhard to Father Martindale, and I am grateful to Mr. John Guest of Longmans Green & Co. for allowing me to see the page proofs of Father Caraman's biography of Father Martindale, in which there were some interesting details of the Jesuit novitiate at Aix.

In the United States I profited from conversations with Father Gannon and the late Father John La Farge, and from correspondence with Father Christopher Mooney. I am most grateful to Father Mooney for his kindness in reading the MS of the present work, and for giving me his expert advice. And I must thank the Librarian of Gonzaga University, Spokane, for the photostat copies of two important articles.

Among others to whom I am indebted are Dr. George Barbour, the Reverend Vernon Sproxton, Professor T. T. Paterson, Mrs. Joanna Kelley, M. Roger Garric, Mme. Claude de Tovar, M. Georges Beauroy, Mme. Roland de Margerie, Miss Malvine Hoffman, Mrs. K. Croose-Parry, Professor Dorothy Garrod and Mr. Morgan Murphy. I am grateful to M. Claude Tresmontant for allowing me to publish quotations from his letter to Teilhard, printed on page 327, and to Father Herbert McCabe, O.P., for his translation of the passage from St. Thomas Aquinas which stands as an epigraph to the book.

A particular word of thanks must go to Dr. Bernard Towers, whose advice on scientific matters has been as invaluable as his hospitality at Jesus College, Cambridge, was agreeable; to Mr. Bernard Wall for his judicious comments on the book which he read in MS; to Mrs. Priscilla Collins, who was at all times a true partner in the work she was publishing; to Père A.-M. Dubarle, O.P., upon whose just estimate of Teilhard, both as 'scientist and seer', I have greatly relied; and to my secretary Mrs. Pat Brayne for the patience and efficiency with which she has typed a MS which was in constant need of revision.

Everything as it is developed tends to become like God so that it may be perfectly itself; a thing is perfect in so far as it is fully realized and so everything that is still in potency seeks to be realized by development. The later, then, and the more perfect a state of realization is, the more truly we can call it the goal of the original matter. So when we come to the last and most perfect realization that can occur amongst material things, we can say that this is the final goal of matter seeking realization by form. The states of realization effected by forms arrange themselves in certain definite steps. First of all, primary matter can be formed to constitute the elements. Then, though formed to this extent, it is still in potency to actual physical bodies, for such bodies are made out of the elements. Then, though it has reached the stage of physical body the matter is yet in potency to vegetative life, for life is the realization of the possibilities of such a body. In its turn vegetative life is in potency to sensitivity, and sensitivity to the life of understanding. We can see these steps actually being traversed in the course of human gestation; for the foetus begins with a plant-like life, it then develops an animal life and finally a human life. But after this there is no subsequent greater realization amongst things that are born and die; so the ultimate goal of all generation is human life, and all matter strives towards this in its quest for form.

St. Thomas Aquinas III. Contra Gentiles: c. XXII.

Nel suo profondo vidi che s'interna
    legato con amore un volume,
    ciò che per l'universo si squaderna;
Sustanzia et accidenti, e lor costume,
    quasi conflati insieme per tal modo,
    che ciò ch'io dico è un semplice lume,
La forma universal di questo nodo
    credo ch'io vidi, perchè più di largo,
    dicendo questo, mi sento ch'io godo.

Within its depths I saw ingathered, bound by love in one mass, the scattered leaves of the universe: substance and accidents and their relations, as though together fused, so that what I speak of is one simple flame. The universal form of this complex I think I saw, because, as I say this, more largely I feel myself rejoice.

Dante Alighieri, Il Paradiso

A Christ not shut off in history but flowing, concrete, phenomenal – that Unity of Being Dante compared to a perfectly proportioned human body.

W. B. Yeats

God did not create the world and then quit.

Saint Augustine

Simplicity of character is the natural result of profound thought.

Hazlitt

Le succès ne prouve rien, pas même contre.

Émile Faguet

CHAPTER I

THE VOCATION

THE FRENCH have a charming name for a small country-house; they call it a '*gentilhommière*'—a place for gentlemen to live in—and the word accurately describes the home where Marie-Joseph-Pierre Teilhard de Chardin was born on 1 May 1881. The fief and barony of Sarcenat had formed part of the lands made over by Robert IV, Count of Auvergne, to the chapter of Chamalière, and was given by them to Sidoine Savaron in 1652. The Savarons were a family of Clermont-Ferrand, and Sarcenat remained their property until it was acquired by the Teilhard de Chardins in 1820. The Savaron escutcheon of three roses is carved in stone under a window of the second storey. The house, built under the reign of Louis XIII, stands on high ground, three kilometres from the village of Orcines, and seven to the west of Clermont, in the Massif Central. The landscape is austere; two hundred years earlier it had appropriately cradled Pascal. In the near distance the conical summits of the Puy-de-Dôme limit the horizon, and the rocky soil is veined with crystal. The house itself is approached through an avenue of chestnuts, limes and young elms, and backs on to the hillside. It has a pepper-pot tower to one side, and two irregular *pignons*. The façade is intersected with tall windows, framed in grey shutters, and plastered in white. In front the ground slopes away steeply, past a small fountain, to the meadows beyond; and the sprawl of Clermont-Ferrand is rather aggressively visible below. There are scores of such houses in France, unpretentious in style, formal in shape, and casual in upkeep. They are the nurseries of a Christian and military tradition nowhere more tenacious than in Auvergne; and it is easy to recognize in Sarcenat the *loi de naissance* to which Pierre Teilhard de Chardin owed a willing obedience.

A Pierre Teilhard discharged the duties of *notaire royal* at Dienne in 1325, and another was living there in 1816 to whom Louis XVIII gave titles of nobility. In 1841 the grandson, Pierre-Cirice, married Marguerite Victoire Barron de Chardin, and the two families were united not only in nature but in name. Three years later Emmanuel—the father of Pierre Teilhard de Chardin—was born, and in 1875 he married Berthe Adèle de Dompierre d'Hornoy who traced her descent to a sister of Voltaire. They had eleven children of whom Pierre was the fourth. The family motto was comprised in a single prophetic hexameter: *Igneus est illis vigor et celestis origo*.[1]

Emmanuel Teilhard de Chardin was a tall and impressive figure with twirling moustaches, who spoke seldom but always to the point. His rare remarks were racy and unexpected, salted with humour and *bonhomie*. He had studied at the École des Chartes and devoted his life to exploring the archives of Montferrand—a work of immense local benefit—and to cultivating the various properties of his estate. Permanent Secretary of the Académie des Sciences, Belles-Lettres et Arts of Clermont-Ferrand, he had identified a letter of Jeanne d'Arc. He was at once an antiquarian, an ornithologist and a gentleman farmer. English periodicals—*The Field* among them—were conspicuous on his library table and he was an assiduous student of history. He read Dickens in translation, and the children read what he chose for them; moreover he personally supervised their Latin until they went to school. His study on the first floor was in every respect a *sanctum*; no one was allowed to enter it uninvited. Here he would sit writing by the hour with the quill pens which he insisted on making himself, and blotting the paper with *poudre d'or*.

His wife, Berthe, was a native of Picardy. A woman of exemplary piety to whom Pierre was later to confess that he owed '*le meilleur de moi-même*', she instilled in him a devotion to the Sacred Heart, which was to be the radiating centre of his own ardent spirituality. Its popular—and aesthetically repugnant—image hung in the salon at Sarcenat, reminding the boy that it was to this foyer of divine love that his mother had dedicated him at birth. Berthe Teilhard de Chardin was a self-effacing character. She rose early; walked every day to Mass before dawn so that she might be at home to breakfast with the family; gave much of her time to charity; was indifferent to the conventions of society even when she conformed to them; and generally

[1] 'Fiery their force and heavenly their home.'

preferred to sit on a hard chair. The *mulier fortis* of Ecclesiasticus could not have found a more serene or striking illustration.

The days passed to the rhythm of a supple and intelligent discipline. The children rose at seven-thirty; breakfasted with their German governess; lunched at eleven; and dined at six. If there were a party Emmanuel Teilhard de Chardin preceded the others into the dining room with the principal lady guest on his arm. At eight-thirty the household gathered for evening prayers. These were announced, not by a bell, but by the tramp of wooden clogs along the passage as the workmen on the estate came in to join the family. Emmanuel Teilhard de Chardin would rapidly run through the Our Father, the Hail Mary, the Creed, and perhaps the Litany of Our Lady before returning to his game of whist. On Sundays the children attended Mass in the neighbouring church at Orcines; the Teilhard-Chambon cousins regularly came up from Clermont for lunch; and after Vespers they would all play charades while the grown-ups took tea in the salon. There was also roller-skating on the terrace, in which they were encouraged by an English friend, Miss Beveridge. Was it she, perhaps, who introduced them to *The Swiss Family Robinson*?

The colder months of winter, from January to March, were spent at Clermont where the family shared an old eighteenth-century house, Fontfreyde, with their Chambon cousins. The outside spiral staircase to the left of it, with its intricately carved stone balustrade, suggested an earlier time before the Roi Soleil had reduced the feudal aristocracy of Auvergne. It was at Clermont that the deep friendship between Pierre and Marguerite Teillard-Chambon put down its early roots. Marguerite remembered him, not more than three or four years old, at a fancy dress party, and she remembered Fontfreyde:

> These old houses, with their cellar-like entrances, their huge staircases, cold and damp, and their sombre, lofty rooms, were a grim setting for our childhood. But they never stopped us from playing—the 'terrible quartet' of boys, Albéric, Pierre, Gabriel and Joseph, wild and noisy, the girls more sedate, Françoise, Bernadette, two Maries, two Marguerites. . . . We used to meet again, after Vespers in the Carmelite Church.[1]

In April they moved to the family house at Murol for the Easter holidays and stayed there till the end of May, returning in September

[1] Teilhard de Chardin Album, p. 15.

for a further visit. Murol, near Maringues, on the banks of the Allier, offered fishing in the spring and snipe in the autumn. The grassland of the park rolled away beyond a house more formal in style than Sarcenat. These migrations composed a pleasant, patriarchal, and heavily protected existence, in which evil, so far from being committed, was not even mentioned by name, and where ill was spoken of no one. The large family, with its visiting cohort of cousins, was in itself a sane and self-sufficient society, an element of strength in a France still recovering from the disaster of 1870 and not yet divided by the Dreyfus case and the consequent schism in national morale. These children of patrician ancestry and upbringing were hardly conscious of a world elsewhere. The alternations of play, study and prayer, sensibly regulated by parental control, both reflected and reinforced the false security of the nineteenth-century sunset. Here the family was the fortress and the Faith its most important possession, to be guarded and transmitted by *chevaliers sans reproche*.

At no time did Pierre Teilhard de Chardin react against his background. He continued to cherish the natural setting and familial atmosphere of Sarcenat. He remained very much a man of his *milieu*, although he looked—and how far he looked!—beyond it. His manners, his conduct and personal relationships, his pastoral tact—all reflected an inherited code not only of faith and morals, but of behaviour also. He did not indulge a vain nostalgia for a way of life that was rapidly passing, for his eyes were always on the future; but he did not depreciate it, simply because it seemed to be disappearing. Moreover, it had taught him from an early age the secret of living and working in society. Another man, aflame with ideas of a profound and percussive originality, and frustrated of their natural communication, might have been embittered, and through bitterness have lost the impetus of his thought. Pierre Teilhard de Chardin, though he had learnt the mystic's use of solitude, knew that the scientist's more communicable secrets were generally the result of communal effort; and he was never more happy than when he was working with others on the same matter of research. A large family is the best school of unselfishness and humility, and it does little to foster even the most excusable *amour-propre*. Pierre Teilhard de Chardin's confidence in his own vision of the world was matched by the lack of conceit with which he propounded it; just as the authority of his genius was matched by his submission to the authorities who did everything they could to inhibit its expansion. The story of his life is in great part the story of this tension; and he little guessed, in those tranquil summers at Sarcenat and Murol, how carefully he was being trained by circumstance, surroundings, and upbringing, for the struggle and the exploration that lay ahead.

Curiosity was already astir in him. On one occasion he played truant with his favourite sister, Marguerite-Marie, to the mountains near by, and when asked to explain his absence replied that he had been to see 'what there was inside the volcanoes'. Was it on one of these escapades that a local farmer remarked: 'I just met one of the little Teilhards—eight years old and not more than six feet tall'—for Pierre already promised to be as tall as his father? Auvergne has been described as 'the geologist's paradise', and it was this secretive soil which gave to the young Teilhard de Chardin his unquenchable thirst for the Absolute. Already, when he was only six or seven years old, '*le cœur de la matière*' was the axis of his interior life. He wanted to possess, in the abstract or the concrete, something precious, consistent and unchangeable, beside which everything else was no more than 'an ornament or an accessory'.[1] He compared it to 'a note of music, or a colour, or a particular taste, inpossible to confuse with any other passion of the soul—ncither the joy of knowledge, nor the joy of discovery, nor the joy of creation, nor the joy of love; not so much because it was different from these, as because it was of a higher order, and because they were all contained in it'.[2] He was, he tells us, a 'sensible, affectionate and even pious' boy, and devoted to the Infant Jesus; but his essential self was elsewhere.

Secretly, then, the 'little Teilhard' would withdraw into the contemplation of his '*dieu de fer*', until he was shocked to discover that iron was liable to rust—and that a lock of hair offered no resistance to the fire:

> I looked for equivalents elsewhere. Sometimes in a blue flame over the logs in the hearth—at once so material and so pure and so impossible to get hold of. More often in some stone more transparent or more brightly coloured; crystals of quartz and amethyst, and above all shining fragments of chalcedony which I was able to collect in my country of Auvergne. The cherished substance had to be resistant, unassailable and hard.[3]

[1] *Le Cœur de la Matière*, 1950.   [2] *ibid*.
[3] Interview with Marcel Brion, *Les Nouvelles Littéraires*, 11 January 1951.

Some of these stones, carefully labelled in the boy's minuscule handwriting—one suspects the quill pen at work—are still to be seen under a glass case at Sarcenat; azurites and aragonites, an agate from Villefranche, a garnierite from New Caledonia, and a fibrolite from the gravelly banks of the Allier. Teilhard assembled, in fact, a very disparate collection of idols—a plough-spanner; the hexagonal top of a little metal rod sticking up from the floor of the nursery; scraps of ammunition collected from a neighbouring field where the artillery were practising. From metals it was a natural step to the minerals from which they were made. Metals were manufactured and fragmentary, whereas minerals were 'planetary'—the very stuff of the evolving universe. Teilhard felt the need of contact with some 'universal root or matrix' of whatever was alive, and the consistency of minerals pointed him to a further element which was incorruptible because it was ubiquitous.

The animal and vegetable also had their place, though a less solid one, in this first decisive impact of the universe. Many years later, from the desert spaces of Mongolia, he would recall the red and yellow lilies, the scarlet polyanthus, the peonies and orchids of Sarcenat. But flowers and insects were 'scandalously inconsistent and destructible',[1] and butterflies even more so. He preferred beetles—the harder and hornier the better. In April 1892, however, the gentle rhythm of the nursery was interrupted, and Pierre was sent away to school at the Jesuit college of Notre Dame de Mongré at Villefranche-sur-Saône. The three-storeyed building had the dual grimness of an ecclesiastical and an educational barracks. Its two quadrangles were separated by a chapel, hideously ornate in style. Even the confessionals suggested that the sins of adolescence could not be absolved without a flourish; and on the walls between the fussy little pillars the Stations of the Cross told their story in a frieze of weak drawing and anaemic paint. Outside, the meadows of the park were dotted with clumps of conifers and chestnuts. Among the teachers was Henri Bremond, to whom we owe a perceptive glimpse of the young Teilhard de Chardin:

> Thirty years ago one of my classical pupils was a little fellow from Auvergne, very intelligent, first in every subject, but disconcertingly well-behaved. The most backward and thick-skulled mem-

[1] ibid.

bers of the class occasionally came alive; their eyes would light up when they were given something more thrilling to read or something more exciting to do. But he, never; and it was only long afterwards that I learnt the secret of his seeming indifference. Transporting his mind far away from us was another, a jealous and absorbing passion—*Stones*.[1]

Pierre was, in fact, an excellent pupil and in August 1897, after five years at the college, he was awarded seven prizes. Among them was the coveted Prix d'Honneur which he won for an essay on 'Reason and Good Sense'—faculties both of which were strong in him. He had shown an equal proficiency in science, Latin, Greek and German, and he returned to Sarcenat for the *grandes vacances* with five fat volumes of biography. The Jesuits of Mongré claimed to teach their pupils the sanctification of science by religion and the service of religion by science. Teilhard de Chardin would not have put it quite like that, but the formula was relatively advanced for its time. Although 'stones' had no place in the curriculum, one of the science masters, Père Describes, would escort parties of the boys on scientific expeditions into the Beaujolais, and Pierre naturally went with them. In general, however, the aim of the college was to produce soldiers rather than scientists or even administrators, with *Le gré de Dieu mon gré*[2] as its motto. It was run on the traditional Jesuit lines, down to the gaudily painted proscenium in the assembly hall where the figures of Racine and Corneille presided over such play-acting as was then allowed.

Teilhard won only a single prize for religious knowledge; a failure due, it seems, not to a tepid spirituality but to a certain contrariness where the letter of the catechism was in question.

They told us that God blessed Jesus. But how could he, if Jesus was already part of the godhead? And those goody-goody romances about the saints and the martyrs! Whatever normal child would want to spend an eternity in such boring company? *Quelle fantaisie!*

All round the galleries on the first floor of the college hung the imaginary portraits of Jesuit saints in various attitudes of rapture, and the likeness of St. Ignatius above the well of the central staircase might have been a discouragement to any tentative vocation. For the time being, however, Teilhard kept his contrariness to himself. He had

[1] *Le Charme d'Athènes.*   [2] 'God's will is my will.'

made his First Communion at Mongré, on the feast of the Ascension 1892, a few months after his entry into the college. He was later enrolled in the various sodalities where the Jesuits liked to group their pupils of the same age, and in 1896 he was elected secretary, and afterwards prefect, of the Congregation of the Immaculate Conception. We find him, on 8 December, visiting the old men who were being cared for by the Little Sisters of the Poor. He arrived with the other members of the congregation, preceded by a little harmonium—on wheels, one imagines—and distributed cakes, tobacco and liqueurs. They brought similar gifts to the Infirmary, where they sang various songs, secular and sacred, and finished up with an exhibition of fencing. Pierre had made his act of personal consecration to the Blessed Virgin on this same feast of the Immaculate Conception in 1893; and we shall see later how the naïve devotion of the adolescent would develop naturally into the mystical insight of the seer.

II

The Jesuit Fathers of Mongré gave Teilhard something more important than a formal education; they gave him a vocation to the Society of Jesus. Already, at seventeen, the desire for perfection in the moral and spiritual order was meeting his passion for the absolute in the mineral world. It was natural, in the circumstances, that he should have turned to the Jesuits. The long discipline of the Society was calculated to purify rather than to suppress the personality; to encourage a man to do better that which he was able to do best. He discussed the matter with Père Describes, who agreed that his vocation was probably genuine, and on 4 June 1897 he was writing to his parents with the assurance that they would put no obstacle in his way. For reasons of health, however, he did not enter the novitiate immediately on leaving college; instead he spent six months at Sarcenat and Clermont preparing for his *baccalauréat* in elementary mathematics. He passed this without difficulty before a local jury. His Sundays were devoted to the 'stones' which abounded in the neighbourhood. As he looked back on his boyhood seven years later, he could tell his father that those years 'were worth all the rest' and that he doubted 'whether it was possible to be happier on earth' than he had been during that time.[1] He knew what he was giving up, as well as what he hoped to gain.

The novitiate for the Lyon province of the Society was at Aix-en-Provence, in the Rue La Cépède, 'a calm and silent'[2] street. Today it is just as sombre but not so silent. The plaster flakes from the grim, grey walls and the niches between the Corinthian pilasters of the adjoining church are bare of statues. The pompous interior of the church is built in a monotonous yellow stone, and in Teilhard's day a statue of St. Louis, swathed in a cloak emblazoned with the fleur-de-lys, presided over the high altar—an appropriate patronage for novices who were exhorted to be '*distingués*'. It was not advice of which Teilhard stood in any need. Some of the rooms looked out on to a fountain court, embellished with urns and shaded by maple trees and a single yew. In one corner a vine climbed rather tentatively over an iron pergola. Teilhard arrived on 19 or 20 March 1899, and left at the end of September 1900. Here were laid the ascetic and spiritual foundations of his unique apostolate; there was neither time nor permission for 'stones'. His happy temperament enabled him to assimilate the training without scruples or servility; it is not easy to imagine the geologist of the Gobi desert taking his bath in a robe of blue serge and removing it under a linen tent! Such absurdities, however, were still prescribed for the neophyte; they went hand in hand with saccharine devotions and uncritical hagiography Teilhard was described as a

model novice, modest and apparently shy, but always ready to oblige others . . . simple and unassuming, anxious not to appear in any way different from others, gay and lively, and a great walker . . . A big fellow, very friendly and affable, with a ready smile, unobtrusive, well set up on his long legs . . . very much the 'gentleman'.[3]

Fortunately Teilhard had with him as fellow novices two men who became, and were always to remain, his closest friends in the Society. Pierre Charles, who developed some original ideas about original sin, established himself later as one of the most influential theologians at Louvain; and Auguste Valensin, the friend and confidant of Maurice Blondel, had few equals as a Dante scholar. Both gave a precious sup-

[1] *Lettres d'Égypte*:
[2] Interview with Marcel Brion, *Les Nouvelles Littéraires*, 11 January 1951.
[3] Quoted from several sources by L. Barjon in his unpublished biography.

port to Teilhard when others were shocked or scared by his ideas. We shall generally find one or other of them at the crossroads of crisis or decision. There was also a young English convert of precocious intellect and frail physique—Cyril Martindale—with whom Teilhard immediately made friends. On the clerical staff was Henri Bremond, Teilhard's old teacher from Notre Dame de Mongré. Bremond was already suspected of modernism. He was later to leave the Society and write his classic history of religious thought in France during the seventeenth century. Even the novices at Aix were disconcerted by his critical approach to questions which they had been taught were closed for ever.

Every religious institution in France was at this time a redoubt of orthodoxy and, almost necessarily, of political reaction. Militant atheism was not only in the air, but in the government. If Teilhard had pursued a military career, he would have known that his *dossier* at the Ministère de Guerre contained precise details of his religious observances; whether he went to Mass, whether he did so merely to accompany his wife, and whether he carried a missal in his hand. His subsequent development, with that of his more intimate friends in the Society, can be better appreciated if we see it in relation to these sharp political tensions.[1] In October 1900 he passed from the novitiate at Aix to the juniorate at Laval. This included Jesuit scholastics from the provinces of Paris and Lyon, and here Teilhard took his first vows on 25 March 1901.

> 'At last I'm a Jesuit, [he wrote to his parents] . . . if only you knew the joy I feel now that I have at last given myself completely and for ever to the Society, particularly at a time when it is being persecuted.'[2]

The first years of the juniorate are devoted to literary studies. Teilhard composed his Greek and Latin verses, and read Aeschylus in the original. He even wrote a pastiche of *The Frogs* of Aristophanes. But these humane studies were interrupted by the arrival of Emile Combes to power and the passing of the *lois laïques*, which compelled the Jesuits of France to pursue the training of their *cadres* in England or the Channel Islands. The insane anti-clerical fury was at its height, and

[1] For certain details of the Aix novitiate I am indebted to Father Philip Caraman's *C. C. Martindale* (1967).
[2] Teilhard de Chardin Album, p. 25.

the professors and pupils at Laval judged it more prudent to leave their headquarters in civilian costume. Top hats and motoring caps were among the motley gear that their families hastily despatched for their disguise. The juniorate was moved to Jersey where the Society had two adjoining houses—a secondary college, Bon Secours, whose uncompromising rectilinear aspect suggested a reformatory; and Maison St. Louis, whose bland façade recalled its original function as a seaside hotel. It was here that the scholastics in philosophy were installed. Teilhard turned his attention to philosophy, and found the pupils a good deal more inspiring than the teachers. Paul Doncœur and Victor Fontoynont, with Valensin and Charles, were among those chafing at the neat, scholastic syllogisms which were supposed to answer the questions of the twentieth century, as they had answered those of the thirteenth.

Compare a photograph of Teilhard and a photograph of Valensin, taken about this time,[1] and you see the difference between the two men. Valensin, with his thin face, sharp features, high forehead, and eyes inquisitive behind their spectacles, looks already the philosopher, and—inimitably—the Jesuit scholastic. One seems to have met him, all down the years, at Campion Hall.[2] With Teilhard the face is broader and the forehead rather lower, suggesting the soldier that he might have been as well as the scientist he became. In fact these early photographs of Teilhard show him as more serious, or at least more solemn, than he was afterwards to appear. The effect is not without significance, for he was suffering from a deep interior division. The normal difficulties of adolescence seem to have passed him by, but it was not easy to reconcile the detachment of the *Imitation* with an increasing attachment to the cosmos. The two absolutes were in conflict. Already, at Mongré, he had felt the strain, and he now wondered whether he should not abandon the second for the first. That he did not do so was due to the robust good sense of the 'spiritual father', Père Paul Troussard, who told him that the crucified Lord was awaiting the natural expansion of his being, no less than its sanctification. He was free, therefore—and, what was even more important, felt himself to be free—to pursue his geological researches on the island of Jersey. A note on its minerals, signed by himself and a fellow Junior,

[1] See Teilhard de Chardin Album.   [2] The Jesuit house of studies at Oxford.

Félix Pelletier, appeared in the annual *Bulletin of the Jersey Society* for 1904. At the same time he was studying elementary physics, in which neither the Quantum Theory, nor the atom, nor relativity had a place.

Other trials, not so close at hand, were a severe test of character. On 27 September 1902 his eldest brother Albéric, a naval officer, died at Sarcenat, and at about the same time his younger sister Marguerite-Marie—known in the family as Guigite—became permanently bed-ridden after an attack of pleurisy. Two years later his sister Louise died of meningitis at the age of twelve. In all these afflictions Teilhard counselled to his parents a resignation which neither he nor they can have found at all easy to command.

The next three years—1905 to 1908—were spent as reader in chemistry and physics at the Jesuit secondary college of the Holy Family in Cairo. It stood close to the railway station in a small garden, where the kites swarmed among the trees and robbed the nests of the jackdaws; and the open country of Matariya with its immense bamboos was within easy reach. Here, among the wild flowers, Teilhard noted a kind of *vanessa* with tawny petals which he remembered from the collection at Sarcenat. A photograph shows him, almost unrecognizable in a dark beard, with the Fathers—two of them Auvergnats like himself—and some of the students of the college. His teaching left the class in a state of bewildered fascination; they admired him without understanding a great deal of what he said. He seems to have been aware of this, for he writes:

> My dominant impression is that for so long as one is not teaching, one is hoarding an immense provision of truths only half understood. This means that one has to work a little to make them clearer, but the job is a salutary one, and it gives me a deep satisfaction to affirm that I am learning at the same time as I am teaching. For the matter of that, I don't find the classes in the least tiring; in fact I think that life at the college is restful.[1]

It was certainly regular with the annual examinations, occasional excursions into the desert on the greater feast days, the eight-day retreats in July, and the August holidays by the sea at Ramleh, a few miles from Alexandria. Nothing in his letters home, fascinating as they are, suggests the originality of genius or, still less, the stirrings of revolt. He is tireless and meticulous in his observation of natural phe-

[1] *Lettres d'Égypte.*

nomena; mentions his friends or superiors only in passing; and does not question or criticize his daily routine. There is no hint of introspection and we believe him when he declares himself to be 'perfectly happy and none the less attached to my family'; or again: 'I need not repeat how happy I am to have taken the road on which I find myself, nor how grateful I am to you for making my entrance upon it so easy.' The family would have been equally reassured by a letter from his superior: 'I am happy a thousandfold in trying to take your place with this dear Pierre, whose father it is my good fortune also to be.'[1] There is no hint, either, or any reaching out towards a larger synthesis of science and revealed truth. If Teilhard thought about these matters, he does not say so. His piety finds an unforced expression in devotion to the Blessed Virgin and the Sacred Heart. Although he is sometimes called upon for a sermon, he would rather teach than preach. The impression throughout is of a searching eye and sympathetic heart rather than a questing mind. But these appearances were deceptive. Behind the world of physics he felt the essential 'matter' of his childish dreams and now, in the spring of his vocation, he vowed that he would 'force the secret of its mysterious gravity'.[2]

But Teilhard's letters, for the greater part, are a dossier of natural history. In so far as they are addressed to his father, it is one naturalist talking to another. A tree on the Île de Boulak reminds him of a similar tree at Sarcenat—'l'arbre de Françoise', they used to call it; and when he goes into the desert, the dried-up river beds and precipitous ravines remind him of the illustrations to a book on the Holy Land which had been much thumbed in the library. A friend from the Jersey scholasticate, Bovier-Lapierre, joins him in his explorations; and he profits by the acquaintance of a French geologist, M. Fourtau, who is always breaking into Latin and helps him to fix the origin of such fossils as he finds on his expeditions. One of these is the fossilized vertebrae of a fish, 'large as a 5-franc piece'. The fish's teeth he sends to a M. Prieur of Paris, who was in touch with the Geological Society of France—one specimen had the honour to be christened *Teilhardi*— and a number of crystals are forwarded to Paris also. Teilhard is particularly happy in the friendship of an Egyptian naturalist, Ines Bey, who has a remarkable collection of shells, butterflies and stuffed

[1] *Lettres d'Égypte.*　　　[2] *Le Cœur de la Matière.*

birds. Europe seems very far away, although Teilhard is moved by the wreck of the *Hilda*, a steamer plying between Southampton and St. Malo, which he had often watched go by from the Jersey cliffs. This revived memories of a sea greener than the Mediterranean and of the seaweed clinging to the rocks.

On the feast of the Immaculate Conception he takes part in the annual procession to Matariya, where legend recorded that the Holy Family paused in their flight, and where now a hundred soldiers from an Irish regiment sang English hymns. At the New Year he spends six hours among the palms and casuarina trees at Ismailia, noting the dead hippocampuses, with the jellyfish and cuttlefish, on the shore. Sometimes he takes a group of students with him, trying to awaken their curiosity before a bed of oysters. There were still some fine tortoises along the Nile, with skunks, jerboas, tiger-beetles, fat lizards, and spiky rats. One of his pupils was Anastase Alfieri, afterwards Secretary-General of the Egyptian Entomological Society. Alfieri would carry Teilhard's bags, butterfly nets and water flasks; and in summer, when the school was closed, the two would go farther afield. Teilhard surmised that the water flowing down from the red mountain of Abbassieh would wash away the sand and reveal palaeontological specimens underneath. In the Suez desert he collected two species of very curious grasshoppers; and became acquainted with the viper of the Pyramids which he promptly preserved in alcohol. He brought fishes' teeth from Mount Mokattam, where the swifts flying in their dozens among the rocks were a fresh reminder of Sarcenat; and sea-urchins from Minieh in Upper Egypt. To the south of Minieh he was struck by the massive rectangular dovecotes, where the pigeons nested under a forest of pottery; and he explored the ancient quarries in the mountains between Cairo and Heluan. These reminded him of the grottoes at Saint-Paul-Trois-Châteaux where he had been on pilgrimage during his novitiate. Here, during the short Easter vacation, he discovers a Greek inscription, admirably preserved, to Alexander II and his family; and in the distance, on the further bank of the Nile, were a series of fifteen to twenty pyramids—evidently built from the same quarries, for there were still traces of the road along which the stones had been transported. To the north-west of Cairo he visited the ruins of On, and brought back a flint saw which he handed over to the curator of the Maspero Museum. A thistle with blue flowers, and leaves not much wider than a thorn, reminded him once again of the flower-beds at Sarcenat.

As yet Teilhard was only an amateur in research, but he became known to a number of specialists, entering into correspondence with a M. Pallary of Oran, who advised him on the collection of shells and classified the examples that Teilhard sent him. In 1908 he published a study on the *Éocène des Environs de Minieh*, and already he was pre-occupied with the Tertiary era of the earth's development. But what chiefly interested him in Egypt was its deposit of marine fossils. He brought back a respectable cargo of these from the Libyan desert, a little to the south of the Pyramids of Gizeh, dating from the time when the lower valley of the Nile was a fjord inundated by the sea. In the Fayum, at Kasa-el-Sagha, he discovered strange fossils, the bones of whales, and the monstrous skulls of the arsinoitherium. This was an eight days' expedition and Teilhard's account of it—*Huit Jours au Fayoum*—in *Relations d'Orient* (December 1907) was the first essay to be published entirely under his own name. He described the blue waters of Lake Moeris, with the fishermen beating the tench into their nets; the saffron cliffs of the desert looming overhead; the dwarf tamarisks with the snipe and herons startled into sudden flight; the ducks and coots skimming the surface in close formation and disappearing into the long reeds. Then the light would fail, and the waters appear milky in the rapid twilight, and the mountains darken to purple as the sun went down. Here, in the desert, was the confrontation of East and West; the cosmos naked under the eye of its Creator; the *milieu divin*; and sounding unmistakably, perhaps, for the first time, the irresistible missionary appeal. Teilhard had not only glimpsed the Orient; he had avidly imbibed it. He was not, as yet, much interested in its history; what held him captive was its light, its fauna, and its vegetation. He was now twenty-seven years old, and it was under this initial spell of the exotic that he felt the fermentation, still confused, of his '*amour passionné de l'Univers*'.

But the moment for answering the call was not yet. The world so resplendently opened out for him in all the purity of its slow, millennial evolution was now to be partially veiled during four years of intensive theological study. This mystical *visuel* would have to concentrate his vision on what could only be seen with the eyes of intelligence and faith.

CHAPTER II

CHANNEL CROSSINGS

THE French Jesuits had three houses in England, all within easy reach of one another. The tertianship[1] was established at Hales Place, just outside Canterbury; the novitiate at St. Leonards; and the scholasticate close by at Ore Place, on the summit of the hill above Hastings. This was a forbidding edifice in red brick, four storeys high, ugly and institutional in style, with a private house of gentler aspect adjoining it at one end. The place was set in spacious grounds, which excluded any disturbance of study or meditation. The windows of Teilhard's room looked westward on to the wooded expanse of the Sussex countryside, and he could still catch a corner of the sea when the ships, P & O liners and ordinary cargo boats, passed close in to the shore.

In his letters home[2], regular and vividly descriptive, Teilhard tells his parents everything likely to interest them; but they are not the things that principally interest his posterity. His days were filled with theology, and about theology he says practically nothing. In these years of the anti-modernist reaction theology was a dangerous subject. There are references to the taking of the anti-modernist oath enjoined by Pius X; and to the rather artificial *disputationes* in which he would defend, in Latin, six theses, two of which were vigorously counterattacked by a fellow-scholastic. The dialectical rite, hardly altered since the Middle Ages, went on for an hour in the morning and for an hour again in the evening. Apart from the usual courses in moral and dogmatic theology, the student was expected to have a nodding acquaintance with Hebrew; and in the refectory he could listen to an interminable history of the Council of Bâle, concluding that, all things considered—including Cardinal Merry del Val—one was fortunate to belong to the Church of the twentieth century.

[1] Jesuit priests spend the last year of their long training in devotional reading and exercises. This is called the tertianship.

[2] *Lettres d'Hastings et de Paris.*

It is often pleaded in Teilhard's excuse that he was not a professional theologian; that is to say, he did not devote, or intend to devote, the greater part of his time and thought to theology. At the same time it would be misleading to underrate the solidity of the formation he received at Ore Place. Even in these years of strain when George Tyrrell was dying, excommunicate, not so very far from Hastings, and Bremond risking his clerical skin to say a prayer at the graveside, it was still possible to say in the privacy of the classroom what could not be said in the publicity of print. Theology was honoured at Ore Place, not as a mechanical formula but as matter for continuous speculation and research. Among the professors were men of marked brilliance: notably Père de Genouillac who expounded the ideas of Durkheim in the application of Christianity to social science; and Père Léonce de Grandmaison, who left shortly after Teilhard's arrival to take over the direction of *Études*. Teilhard would refer to him as '*le divin Léonce*', and in fact he was never to find a stauncher friend in the Society. Equally important were his fellow-scholastics; Pierre Rousselot, a theologian of genius, whose thesis on *The Intellectualism of St. Thomas* won the plaudits of the Sorbonne, but whose later work was condemned by the Jesuit authorities in Rome; Valensin and Charles, his old friends from the Aix novitiate—it was Valensin, Teilhard used to say, who, more than anyone, taught him 'how to think'; Joseph Huby, whose *Christus, manuel de l'histoire des religions* became a classic in its kind; Guillaume de Jerphanion, a specialist in Byzantine art and Christian iconography; Jules Lebreton, afterwards famous for his *Origines du dogme de la Trinité*; Félix Pelletier, the companion of his scientific expeditions; Auguste Décisier, who became his Provincial and also his ally; and Victor Fontoynont, a fine Hellenist and an Auvergnat like Teilhard himself. It was a very remarkable group of young men, and of their influence there can be no question. Valensin must have introduced Teilhard to Newman and Blondel, for no book was more seminal to Teilhard's thinking than Newman's *Essay on the Development of Christian Doctrine*; and Rousselot certainly shared, if indeed he did not inspire, Teilhard's ideas about the consistence of the universe in Christ.

It would be a serious mistake, however, to suppose that these tutors and contemporaries, or that Teilhard himself, were tinged with Modernism. The tendency of Modernism is to diminish the transcendent stature of Christ: Teilhard's concern was to enlarge it to cosmic proportions. So far from inventing a Christ to fit his own ideas, Teilhard had already found him in St. Paul. It was 'He in whom all things consist';[1] 'He who fills all things';[2] 'the Christ who is all in all';[3] and 'has ascended high above all the heavens to fill all things with his presence'.[4] It was the Christus Pantocrator of Byzantium, and more particularly the Christ of the Sacred Heart, freed from its popular iconography. Where the Modernist tends to imprison Christ in history at the same time as he questions the historicity of the Gospels which give him to us, Teilhard adores him when he is transfigured on the mountain, rises from the tomb, or is lost in the clouds above the heads of the Apostles. Whatever certain neo-modernists may pretend to the contrary, the opposition could not be more clear.

Teilhard admits that he does not always find theology '*bien amusante*'. He refused to get excited over the hoary dispute with the Dominicans over grace and free will, and cherishes a few private doubts on the liquefaction of the blood of St. Januarius. Above all, though, he now views his scientific interests in a new perspective. 'Theology', he says, 'makes one think of many things, and I am beginning to see that there are so many other questions, less agreeable, perhaps, but more vital than the sciences, that I wonder whether I shall not leave science aside some day or other—unless I am told to stick to it—which is very possible.'[5] He did not suspect, as yet, that so far from leaving science aside, he would dramatically enlarge its horizons. Theology had the advantage of 'maturing many ideas', but these were still in an early process of formation. Life at Ore Place was 'undeniably austere'; and it would need the very different austerities and the more testing solitude of military service to bring Teilhard's originality to full and provocative expression.

We may assume, in any case, that his parents would have understood little of theology, even if he had tried to elucidate its problems. He wrote to them, instead, on subjects of mutual interest, and here the natural sciences were common ground. The wood owl that sang outside his window awakened tender memories of Sarcenat and he wrote of the robin, greedy and impatient, that came to eat out of his hand; of three storks flying in triangular formation; of the thousands of starlings winging their way out to sea; and of the bird-catchers on the

---

[1] Colossians 1.17.   [2] Colossians 2.10.   [3] Colossians 3.11.
[4] Ephesians 4.10.   [5] 23 April 1910.

cliffs trapping the migratory yellowhammers in their nets. The gardens of Ore Place were full of thrushes, and Teilhard learns with pleasure that a little grey owl with black spots, living off the mimosa trees in Egypt, has been officially christened *Emblemma Teilhardi*.The discovery of a heronry at Brede—where the cradle of Jonathan Swift was only of incidental interest—delights him and stimulates his powers of exact description:

> The herons were at their post, screaming like geese, and fussing around their young, who seemed almost big enough to fly. We could follow all their movements through our binoculars and more original than anything else was the way they crammed the young birds who sat up spreading their wings and stretching out their necks into which the parent birds plunged their beaks to an unexpected depth, with a movement like the piston of a machine.[1]

On the monthly holiday, or greater feast days, or during the short Christmas vacation, Teilhard was free to roam the countryside. He began by describing Hastings as the 'Cannes de l'Angleterre', and it may have merited the description rather more obviously in the first decade of the century than it does today. But then he discovered that Eastbourne was 'more elegant' and we find him at Winchelsea and Wadhurst, at Bodiam and Brightling, and eating snails soaked in whisky at the Battle Fair. Sometimes he went further afield, to Camber and Rye, Folkestone and Hythe, Selsey and Chichester. But his favourite haunt was Ashburnham Park, not far from Hastings. Teilhard was very much a man of *la vieille France*, and the patrician aspect of English life and the English countryside, threatened as these were by Mr. Lloyd George on a radical rampage, powerfully appealed to him.

It was in autumn, when they were shooting the first snipe at Murol, that the country exercised its most subtle charm. From his window at Ore Place he could see the russet tops of the birch trees, and on an afternoon walk he would accidentally send the pheasants scattering, with a flap of wings like thunder, from their preserve. At Ashburnham the great oaks and chestnuts stood in their November sadness and splendour, reflected in the series of small lakes which filled the valley. The fallow deer and Scottish cattle browsed in the pastures beyond, and the house itself, set in a forest of rhododendrons, seemed

[1] 23 May 1911.

very simple by contrast—the Sleeping Beauty might have slumbered there. Nothing, in fact, escaped Teilhard's microscopic eye, from the smallest insect to the six vipers on which he stumbled during an exploration of the cliffs; from the weevils and ermines to the rabbits caught in their traps; and the East Sussex Hunt in full cry, reminding him of the old drawings by Caran d'Ache which hung in the salon of his uncle Joseph and around which the conversation turned, inexhaustibly, during the winter evenings in Auvergne.

He was attentive to the flora as well as to the fauna of Sussex but, of course, his principal interest was geology. He had already learnt that the Weald was formed by deposits of the Secondary era left by the estuary of a great river and notable for the remains of saurians and iguanodons. It was not long before he was discovering their traces on the cliffs with the curator of the Hastings Museum, and picking up fossils, teeth, and fragments of tortoise-shells. More important was the tooth of a megalosaurus and several teeth of a small crocodile— rare in the Channel waters—which they sent to the British Museum. Teilhard was further encouraged by a letter from the museum confirming that the tooth of a mammifer he had sent to them appeared to be a new specimen. It was afterwards presented to the London Geological Society, and its discovery reported in flattering detail at one of their meetings. At the same time Teilhard's catalogue of the minerals on Jersey was shortly to appear in the *Annales de la Société Jersiaise* (1910), and we find him busy correcting the proofs which had arrived in a 'deplorable condition'. On 31 May 1909, he writes to his parents:

> ... I have made the acquaintance of a local geologist, Mr. Dawson, in amusing circumstances. Visiting a quarry near here, we were astonished to see the manager prick up his ears when we talked to him of fossils. He had just discovered a huge bone of the pelvis of an iguanodon, and had a telegram from Mr. Dawson announcing his arrival. I have learnt since that the iguanodon was found pretty well intact, bit by bit, and that the fragments are being packed in a case to be sent to the British Museum. Mr. Dawson turned up while we were still on the spot, and immediately came up to us with a happy air, saying: 'Geologist?' He lives near Newhaven, but he may be able to help us. At least we shall have someone we can inform about anything which is too big for us to manage ourselves.

This acquaintance was to have momentous and even embarrassing consequences, as we shall presently see.

Outside events made their occasional impact, and the odd visitor came to Ore Place. Father Bernard Vaughan lectured on his American travels—'his gestures and diction certainly have an extraordinary power'.[1] The first aeroplanes circle over the Channel, and Teilhard describes them as 'one of the finest things I ever saw in my life'.[2] The *Oceania* founders in the same channel just off the coast at Hastings, and the bodies of the drowned are laid out on tarpaulin sheets on the shore. Shackleton reaches the North Pole and the *Titanic* goes down in the North Atlantic. King Edward VII dies amid national mourning and King George V inherits a political crisis. At Hastings, as ever a Tory stronghold, Mr. Redmond is depicted on the posters dancing on the Union Jack with a bag of dollars in his hand, or as a nurse pushing a perambulator with Mr. Asquith helpless inside it, or as a harrier on the point of catching Asquith the hare, in company with the huge black hound of Socialism. Of more immediate concern to Teilhard was the Portuguese revolution which he hoped would give the Pope a greater liberty of manœuvre in those reactionary latitudes, since it appeared that the Portuguese clergy were 'in great need of reform'. Teilhard's natural optimism must have been rosy indeed, if he expected this hope to be shared by Pius X.

In the autumn of 1908 he was asked to write an article on the miracles at Lourdes for *Études*. This gave him the chance of a lightning visit to Paris, where he met Dr. Boissarie who was director of the medical bureau charged with the verification of the alleged cures. He also dined with his two younger brothers off '*bœuf nature*' in honour of Sarcenat; and it was probably a relief to be discussing snipe instead of Suarez or St. Thomas Aquinas. He spent the summer vacation of 1909 at Bon Secours, which the Jesuits made available to their priests and older scholastics while the boys from the secondary college were on holiday. Teilhard visited the Isle of Wight and Guernsey en route; went back to his favourite quarries at Rosnez, superbly situated on its tongue of land; and found the museum at St. Hélier notably enriched since the early days of his scholasticate. Returning by Weymouth, he had an expert eye for the Portland quarries, and passing quickly through London registered the silhouette of St. Paul's and a small boy,

[1] 1 February 1911.   [2] 17 July 1911.

supposedly from Eton, in his topper and short black jacket. In September 1910 he spent several days at the Jesuit scholasticate at Gemert in Holland, working in the geological laboratory. He was met, on arrival, by a reading of Pius X's condemnation of the Sillon.[1]

It will trouble a great many people, and many others, no doubt, will see in it a condemnation of social works. All the same it seems to me that Pius X could hardly have acted otherwise, or spoken better. I should be curious to know the impression made by it in France, and what is the attitude of the Sillonistes.

The young François Mauriac was among those who could have enlightened him, with a painful candour, on both points; Teilhard himself has not reached the stage of interior liberty when he would question, even privately, the wisdom of pontifical decisions.

On the way home, he stopped at Brussels and Louvain, and the journey had given him, both on his departure and his return, a further chance of spending a few hours in London. He saw the Japanese Exhibition and found one of his own geological discoveries under a glass case in the Natural History Museum. He dined at a Lyons and visited Westminster Cathedral, contrasting its expanses of bare brick with the rich ornamentation of two side chapels: 'The English have no regard for money'.[2] He walked through Hyde Park; wandered through the British Museum; and returned to an examination in moral theology. Now there remained only a single year of study before his ordination as a priest, and this was the recurring theme of his letters. 'When you make your vows, you have rather the impression of offering yourself; when you receive the grace of ordination, you should feel above all else that someone is taking hold of you.'[3] Meanwhile he received the minor orders of the diaconate and subdiaconate on 25 and 26 March 1911, the first of these carrying with it the obligation of reciting daily the Divine Office, and as the day of ordination approached, his parents sent him a chalice. But now a cruel bereavement came to overcloud, and at the same time to deepen, his initiation into the priesthood. His sister Françoise suddenly died from the smallpox in Shanghai. Teilhard's faith withstood this loss with the fortitude which never failed him in any of the very different trials which it would be called upon to undergo:

[1] A Christian Democratic movement, founded by Marc Sangnier.
[2] September 1910. [3] 19 March 1911.

How many times [he wrote] has she not spoken to me of her desire to go to God and to see Him as soon as possible . . . Our Lord is rewarding her before her time; and we have not even the right to regret the good she would have done if she had lived longer. It is a beautiful life which fulfils the designs of God. In Françoise you have found and given to God a saint; you could not dream of a finer future for your child.[1]

Nevertheless the stricken parents came over to Hastings, as arranged, and they knew by then what Françoise had written to her brother in the last letter he received from her:

Don't forget, and I want you to remember this most especially, to ask Our Lord at your first Mass to take me entirely to himself, and to keep me for China till my dying day.

Teilhard was ordained priest on 24 August 1911, by Monsignor Amigo, Bishop of Southwark, in the chapel at Ore Place. He said his first Mass the next morning, the feast of St. Louis, served by two of his brothers, Gabriel and Joseph; Victor and Gonzague were also present. Gabriel was noted for his piety, and Teilhard used teasingly to say that he was the true Jesuit of the family, whereas 'I am only a spiritual adventurer'.

The fourth and last year in theology was now diversified by the ministry of word and sacrament, for the priest-theologians were in demand beyond the enclave of Ore Place. We find Teilhard celebrating Mass at Ashford where the presbytery was embellished with a variety of cats, sardonically deformed, in china, plush, or other material. Even a matchbox represented two cats viewed from behind, a large one with a rough back and a little one with a smooth. The superscription read: 'Don't scratch me; scratch my mother.' Sir William Watson, a popular but now forgotten poet, lived near by in the seclusion of a park, and Teilhard was shown his house. It was not a very distinguished introduction to contemporary English verse. Shortly afterwards he was giving a retreat at Malvern where a community of French nuns were installed, and he seized the chance of visiting Oxford on his way back. The memory of Newman drew him to St. Mary's, and he was particularly impressed by the hall of Christ Church. Term had not yet begun; the Bodleian was closed; and the

---

[1] 7 June 1911.

streets were quiet except for an occasional horse omnibus or hansom cab.

During Holy Week (1911) his duties took him over to Belle, a scattered parish of large farms, near Boulogne, in the fat pasture land of the Wimereux valley, where the trout and otters were abundant and where, in the intervals of preaching, hearing confessions, and the prescribed liturgical practices, he was obliged to consume an immense quantity of buttered bread. He knew the coast from holidays with Albéric, and he revisited these old haunts with a cousin who escorted him back to the boat. Further ministrations took him to Bramber, and it was in the course of this visit that he first became involved in the story of 'Piltdown Man'. Charles Dawson had invited him to break his journey at Lewes, and here he breakfasted with Dawson and his wife in a house perched among the ruins of the castle. At ten o'clock Dawson and Teilhard set out for Uckfield, where they were joined by Professor (Sir Arthur) Woodward, head of the palaeontological department of the British Museum. Teilhard described him as 'a little man, with grizzled hair, very hale and hearty, but externally rather cold'.

We embarked in a motor-car, with the elements of a picnic, which took us three miles, mostly across Uckfield Park, and deposited us at the place where the hunt was on. This was a stretch of grass, 4 or 5 metres in width, beside a wooded glade leading to a farm. Under this grass there is a layer of pebbles, about 50 centimetres thick, which they are digging up, bit by bit, for road-mending. A man was there to shift the earth for us. Armed with spades and sieves, etc., we worked away for hours and eventually with success. Dawson unearthed another fragment of the famous human skull—he had already found three other pieces—and I myself laid hands on the fragment of an elephant's molar. This find considerably enhanced my reputation with Woodward, who jumped on the piece with the eagerness of a boy and I could see all the fire which his apparent coldness conceals. I had to leave before the others in order to catch my train. This first tooth of an elephant impressed me in the way another man is impressed by bringing down his first snipe.[1]

While he was at Bramber Teilhard visited the Parkminster Charter-

[1] 3 June 1912.

house, where he tasted the traditional Chartreuse and had a brief glimpse of a way of life as far removed as possible from the vocation he was himself to follow. He returned greatly impressed by 'the powerful affirmation of the supernatural which constitutes the life of these men, who neither work like the Trappists nor write books like the Benedictines'. After this there was time for a last walk over the Downs in the pouring rain before returning to Ore Place for his final examination in theology, and a visit from Dr. Woodward who pillaged his collection of fossils for the British Museum. In less than four weeks he would be with his family at Sarcenat.

II

Such, in brief outline, is the story of Teilhard's daily doings during his four years' residence at Ore Place; but it leaves out of account the more important question—what had been happening to his mind? The answer can be given in two words—Bergson[1] and evolution. The quest for fossils and the observation of natural phenomena had, step by step, convinced Teilhard that the world was in evolution, and that this evolution had a cosmic and spiritual significance; and now the flame of Bergson's *L'Évolution Créatrice* met the fire that was already consuming him, heart and mind. Quickly, the germs of a future synthesis began to bear their fruit, in which the triple cult of Matter, Life and Energy had suddenly acquired the 'organic dignity of a Cosmogenesis'. The full dimension of his discovery was not immediately apparent; only the magic word of 'evolution' echoed in his mind 'like a refrain, a taste, a promise and an appeal'.[2] It was inseparable, as he looked back forty years later on the Bergsonian revelation, from 'the extraordinary density and intensity with which the English landscape then appeared to me—especially at sunset—when the Sussex woods seemed to be laden with all the fossil life that I was exploring, from one quarry to another, in the soil of the Weald'.[3]

Édouard Le Roy—who will also have his place in the story—had written of Bergson's great and seminal work that

[1] For Bergson's influence on Teilhard see Raven, *Teilhard de Chardin: Scientist and Seer*, and much more extensively Madeleine Barthélemy-Madaule, *Bergson et Teilhard de Chardin*.

[2] *Le Cœur de la Matière*.   [3] *Le Cœur de la Matière*.

it has been prepared by the contemporary idea of evolution which it investigates and perfects, sifting it from its ore of materialism and turning it into genuine metaphysics. Is not this the philosophy suited to the century of history? Perhaps it indicates that a period has arrived in which mathematics, losing its rôle as the regulating science, is about to give place to biology?[1]

Le Roy expanded his analysis in two articles for the *Revue des Deux Mondes* (February 1912), and we may be sure that Teilhard would have read them. Later he reached his own understanding of Bergson, and difference from him, through his close friendship with Le Roy. Meanwhile *L'Évolution Créatrice* had not yet been placed on the Index, and was presumably available above the counter at Ore Place. Everything in Teilhard's education and upbringing had encouraged him to regard his 'divine matter' as no more than the servant, if it was not the adversary, of the spirit; and the spirit as no more than

a shadow which, on principle, I must venerate but for which (intellectually and emotionally speaking) I could feel no vital interest. Judge then of my feeling of inward liberation when I realized, from my first hesitant steps in an 'evolving' universe that the dualism which had imprisoned me up till then dissolved like a mist before the rising sun.[2]

Every Jesuit awaits 15 August with a certain anxiety because on that date he receives his assignment for the coming year. Teilhard was ordered to pursue his scientific researches at the Museum of Natural History in Paris from the beginning of October. In the meantime he spent a fortnight at Sarcenat, relieving the parish priest. It was four years since he had been there, and he left with mixed feelings:

It doesn't take long [he wrote] to get used to Sarcenat again, and yet my natural place is no longer there—which doesn't mean, as you know, that my affection for you is any the less. Seeing you all there, on the spot, was a real resumption of contact: to have prolonged my stay would not have been in the line of my life, and would have added nothing essential to the good and true results of seeing each other again. We have maintained and strengthened the family ties, and these have God's blessing.[3]

[1] Henri Bergson, *A New Philosophy*, p. 201.
[2] ibid.   [3] 23 August 1912.

The visit was naturally overclouded by the illness of Guigite, who alternated between partial recovery and painful relapse. As she was herself to write:

The particular form of my illness is to vanish only to reappear at the gallop.... There are three trials which bear fruit on condition that you fight them: temptation, scruples and illness. The good God uses illness to make us know our own personality. Get it into your head that illness is never sent to diminish us, but to increase our moral stature. It's for us to profit from it.[1]

For twenty-nine years, until her death in 1936, Guigite was to give proof of her faith and courage. Teilhard's presence at Sarcenat was as necessary as it was agreeable. The bracing sympathy he brought to his family in their trial is shown in a letter written shortly after he had left:

You must find strength in the thought that suffering accepted in the right spirit has the most valuable, the most lasting and the happiest results. Suffering assures us that we are associated with the work of Our Lord and united to him. We must believe this and console ourselves with the reflection that, in spite of appearances, the most difficult moments are when we are most fully and fruitfully alive. Besides, they will pass ... One day you will see that it was just as good that Guigite should be immobilized as it was that Albéric, Françoise, Louise and Mariette should be taken from you. It's hard; but God knows how hard.[2]

Teilhard's return to Paris coincided with the opening of the métro, and after registering this milestone of human progress he proceeded to the college of Antoing in Belgium where he was to work with Père Edmond Cugnien, professor of natural history. There was a quarry in the park, fairly rich in trilobites, and Teilhard was shown the place where Villèle had transformed a rabbit into an otter. Clearly there were no limits to *transformisme*. Cugnien took the ardent young geologist to Fontenoy, where fossils had lately been discovered, and to Mons with its layers of chalk rich in phosphate. In an abandoned coal pit they found the imprint of bracken, seals and natterjacks, returning loaded like donkeys with booty which included an enormous oyster that Cugnien—who already had three in his bag—was reluctant

[1] *L'énergie spirituelle de la souffrance* (1951).
[2] 22 September 1905.

to throw away. Teilhard left Antoing to take part in the Semaine Ethnologique at Louvain. Here more than a hundred participants, nearly all of them priests of various nationalities and belonging to different religious orders, had gathered to discuss the problems of the mission field. It was hard talking and listening with five sessions daily, and Teilhard welcomed its radical conclusions. He did not realize as yet that he was to be a kind of missionary himself, or that so much of his life would be spent in *pays de mission*.

He made his way back to Paris by easy stages. On September 5 he was at Charleroi, visiting the mines with a robust Belgian Jesuit, Père Schmitz, taking three hours to descend 900 metres and noticing a good number of fossilized plants. Later he was in the grottoes at Huccorgne on the way to Florennes, where the novices and younger scholastics of the province of Champagne were established in a picturesque château which had once belonged to the Dukes of Beaufort. From here he made two expeditions to the valley of the Meuse. In the section between Vireux and Haybes he could see the junction of the Lower Devonian and Pre-Cambrian soil, and at Deville the Pre-Cambrian slates were injected with porphyry. The schists were apparent down the whole length of the valley. A day spent at the Benedictine Abbey of Maredsous was also useful. The offices he attended in the church gave him an understanding of the 'sense and utility of monasticism'[1]—although Teilhard was generally indifferent to liturgical punctilio, had little ear for music, and used to say how glad he was to belong to an order which dispensed with the choral office. He also made the acquaintance of an eminent geologist, Dom Grégoire, who had assembled a unique collection of carboniferous sea urchins found in a neighbouring quarry. Teilhard paid a second visit to Maredsous before going down the river to Namur, and thence to Brussels and Enghien, where the Jesuits of two French provinces had their scholasticate of theology. The terrain offered the same geological characteristics which he had already noted in the Ardennes, the schists pierced, here and there, with fine layers of porphyry, thoroughly exploited. In the huge quarry of Quenast he saw the amphitheatre where 1,200 men produced the paving for many of the roads in northern Europe.

By 30 September he was installed in his new quarters on the fifth

[1] 17 September 1912.

floor of a house which formed an angle between the Rue du Vieux-Colombier and the Rue de Rennes. The windows of his room gave on to the Rue de Rennes, and beyond were the towers of St. Sulpice, just as they were represented in a picture hanging on the walls of his father's study. The entrance to the métro was immediately underneath, but in spite of the grinding of the trains and the noise of continual traffic in the street, he found it '*assez gai*' to be perched above so bustling a scene. 'I shall soon get used to it, supposing I have much work to do at home.'[1] In fact, his work lay elsewhere. The Institut de Paléontologie Humaine, which formed part of the Natural History Museum, had been founded by Prince Albert of Monaco, and it was under the direction of Marcellin Boule. Teilhard had knocked on the door of Boule's laboratory one afternoon in July. The professor was on the point of leaving for his summer holiday, but he received Teilhard and proposed that he should work with him. Boule was an Auvergnat like Teilhard himself, bearded and authoritarian, with a sharp tongue to match his keen intelligence. Indeed the two men represented the classic types of Auvergne; the one tall, thin and aristocratic, the other short, stout and plebeian. Boule was an inveterate anti-clerical, but Teilhard would hold his own with him when he had the experience and the prestige to do so. Such difference as there was between them was a difference of generation as much as outlook. Writing much later of Boule's fundamental work, *Les Hommes Fossiles*, Teilhard indicates an opposition between scientific theory and religious faith which he spent a lifetime trying to remove:

> What the author defends with a justifiable energy (perhaps with rather more energy than has now become necessary) is that the human species appeared on earth in obedience to the same fundamental laws as every other species. Hence its past and present structure. What he did not unfortunately see as clearly (the fault is perhaps the fault of his generation) is that this similarity in 'embryogenesis' does not prevent man—rather the contrary—from representing an *exception* in nature (an exception of eminence and emergence, and not of anomaly) without which everything on the Tree of Life is meaningless, even from a scientific point of view.[2]

Teilhard's spiritual duties took him to a crystal factory at Le

[1] 30 September 1912. [2] *Études*, vol. 252, pp. 127–8.

Bourget, where the owner had founded a home for orphaned boys between fourteen and eighteen and given them employment. Apart from these excursions, Teilhard's life followed an undeviating routine. After saying his Mass at 6 a.m. and breakfasting with the Jesuits at their house in the Rue du Regard, he plunged into the métro at 9.30, and except for luncheon in the Rue du Regard remained at the Museum until 5 p.m. He would generally walk back to the Vieux-Colombier before returning to the Rue du Regard for supper; in fact, a disproportionate amount of his time was spent in tramping the streets—and they were always the same streets. In a fortnight he did not once cross the river.

On Sundays, however, he would walk in the Bois de Boulogne, wishing it were the brushwood of Auvergne, and visit relations for luncheon or dinner—his uncle Georges whose apartment was '*un intérieur vraiment bien Teilhard*'; or his aunt Pauline at Montreuil, reminding him of how he used to bring frogs into his bedroom when he was staying with her at Vernière; or his uncle Teillard-Chambon, who had moved to Paris from Clermont-Ferrand. Here were the two paintings of partridges suspended by the feet which Teilhard had known ever since he was a boy, and the two cousins, Jeanne and Marguerite, to whom he was so attached. Marguerite—a young woman of exceptional intelligence, sensibility and charm—was in charge of a boarding school for girls, the Institut Notre-Dame-des-Champs, in the Rue Montparnasse. She was also a writer under the name of Claude Aragonnès. The friendship formed in the earlier days at Clermont-Ferrand was now cemented—and it is through his letters to Marguerite Teillard-Chambon that Teilhard most intimately reveals himself. She could meet his mind in a way that his parents could not, and their relationship, as it grew, had an emotional depth which must be recognized, though it should not be misunderstood. Already, during this first year in Paris, we find Teilhard lecturing on evolution to her young *pensionnaires* at the Institut Notre-Dame-des-Champs. Meanwhile he was learning the 'physiognomy of a jaw', and through his membership of the French Geological Society making a number of useful acquaintances—Louis Joubin, Professor at the Museum of Natural History, and Hugo Obermaier, an Austrian priest who was a specialist in the prehistoric archaeology of Spain. More significant still was Teilhard's introduction to the Abbé Henri Breuil, who has been called 'the Pope of Prehistory'. Their friendship ripened quickly over long conversations and leisurely strolls in the Jardin des Plantes, and before many months were over it was to bear important fruit. Breuil was the older by some years and very different in temperament and physique. Short, squat, and vivacious, he had the look of a mischievous squirrel, and a mind that came curtly to the point. He shared none of Teilhard's mystical preoccupations. When they had reached a certain equality of status, Teilhard was fond of teasing him.

Teilhard's researches led him to the laboratory of comparative anatomy, where everything that died in the Jardin des Plantes eventually found its way. 'Eventually' was here the *mot clef*, and when Teilhard winced a little he was warned that he had better wait until they received the corpse of a hippopotamus. There were also expeditions further afield; to Cormeilles-en-Parisis on the right bank of the Seine opposite the forest of St. Germain, where all the layers of soil in the neighbourhood of Paris could be traced in the quarries; and to Normandy where Teilhard's 'god of iron' lay buried deep in the mines at May, and the ammonite was encrusted in the clay on the beaches at Villers-sur-Mer. Nor did his priestly duties confine him to Paris. He was preaching a Lenten retreat for women at Gap, remaining there for Holy Week and Easter, and spending a few days at Sarcenat before returning to Paris.

In June 1913, he was invited to join a party of five on a visit to the grottoes at Puente Viesgo, close to Santander. He owed the invitation to Breuil who did not, however, at first accompany the expedition. The others included Obermaier and his Alsatian assistant; an Englishman, Burkitt, the son of a Cambridge professor; and an American specialist in the study of pre-Columbian civilizations. This was Teilhard's first experience of working with an international *équipe*. They lived in the semi-monastic quarters of a thermal establishment, and a photograph shows Teilhard standing among the wine bottles and napery of a picnic luncheon. In the vestibule of the grotto there were twelve layers of rock bearing the signs of human habitation, and all but three of these had already been cleared of their débris—the remains of horses, deer, rhinoceros, bear, lion and hyena, but not, unfortunately, of man. The grotto itself was 200 metres in length and hung with stalactites. Here were the prehistoric paintings of elephants, horses and deer, and the outline of human hands achieved by placing the left hand on the wall of rock and covering the rest of the surface with ochre so that the hands stood out in white on a red background. 'I can tell you', Teilhard wrote, 'that seeing these traces of a humanity earlier than any known civilization really gave us something to think about; it's wonderful to stand in front of it, alone, in an absolute silence that is broken only by the sound of water dripping from the stalactites.'[1] A two-hour drive from Puente Viesgo brought them to the cavorting bisons on the roof of the grotto at Altamira:

When one thinks that these paintings were done in the age of the reindeer,[2] at a time when no trace of Egyptian civilization was yet visible, one is simply astonished. But I confess that one is also a little thrown out of gear, and it requires an effort to situate these paintings in so remote a past, and to try to embrace all that they evoke. I must admit that I have not yet succeeded in doing so.[3]

At the end of June the Abbé Breuil joined the party. He showed them the grotto of Pintal on the coast to the west of Santander, and then went off with Teilhard in search of insects. At Puente they were still exploring the last layer when Teilhard was obliged to leave. He stopped at Lourdes on the way home; said Mass in the Basilica; and was admitted to the medical bureau, where a number of interesting 'improvements' were registered, and one doubtful cure. By the end of July he was at Canterbury. 'Here I have found the peace of a great park, two-thirds of it wooded with magnificent trees... rabbits are all over the place, also squirrels, thrushes, pigeons, and of course the robin redbreast.'[4] Beyond were the towers of the cathedral, and the ancient church of St. Martin—the oldest in the United Kingdom—and one of Stephenson's first locomotives, the *Invicta*, reposing beside the ramparts after making its last journey to Whitstable. It was cricket week, and Canterbury was gaily beflagged. Teilhard listened to the grave Anglican chants in the cathedral; admired the choristers in their violet cassocks and broad white collars; and noted the '*très gentleman*' canon who officiated. The weather was warm in this last August of a world at peace, and in the evening one could lie out under the trees.

From Canterbury Teilhard went on to spend three days at Lewes with Charles Dawson, who was still busy with 'Piltdown man'. Dr.

[1] 16 June 1913.   [2] i.e., Magdalenian Period.
[3] 16 June 1913.   [4] 6 August 1913.

Woodward joined them, but they discovered nothing new except the tiny fragment of what might have been a nose. Teilhard was already puzzled by the Piltdown remains; nevertheless he accompanied Dawson and Woodward to London, where these were being shown to a congress of medical anatomists. At a second meeting, which Teilhard did not attend, Woodward was severly criticized by Professor Keith who maintained—and Teilhard agreed with him—that the Piltdown skull should be reconstructed in a different way. 'In my opinion', Teilhard wrote, 'all these reconstructions . . . add nothing definite to the interest of the fragments. The important thing is to look for some more pieces.' His own part in the search was interrupted by an eight-day retreat at Ore Place, but early in September he was back at Uck-field with Dawson and Woodward. This time they were luckier; Teilhard found the canine tooth of what they all believed to be 'Pilt-down man'. This seemed to justify Woodward's reconstruction of the skull; it was the last digging of the season; and after a few moments of mutual excitement Teilhard returned 'light-heartedly' to Hastings. The following week he was staying with Woodward in London and invited to add his name to those of other geological celebrities on a piece of embroidered cloth. These rejoicings, as we shall see, were ironically premature; but when Teilhard looked back on them with amused embarrassment he did not forget the 'nice tea-parties' in the house of a Mrs. Kenward who lived near by. 'All these things seem to be so far away! And they were so sweet memories.'[1]

After a short visit to Ipswich and a fortnight at Bon Secours in the company of old friends, Teilhard returned to Paris and resumed his pastoral work at Le Bourget. It was no bar to his friendship with M. Paris, director of the factory, that Paris had a shoot in the plain near St. Denis, where the partridges were brought down by the dozen. There were visits to the archaeological museum at St. Germain-en-Laye where Breuil was classifying the weapons of the Magdalenian period and excursions to the valley of the Somme around Amiens, where a party of eminent geologists hoped to discover silex in the alluvial deposits. Obermaier was among them, and Count Henri Bégouën, whose son Max was soon to become one of Teilhard's closest friends.

For the Lent of 1914 Teilhard was attached to a parish in Lyon,

[1] Letter to Mrs. Kenward, 2 March 1954.

giving as many as ten sermons a week. He had no particular taste or talent for preaching, but at least he could purge the pulpit of insincerity. In the middle of July he left for the French Alps, to explore certain rock formations in the neighbourhood of Briançon and the first intimation he seems to have had of impending catastrophe were the train loads of reservists coming up to man the Italian frontier. General mobilization was ordered on 1 August, when Teilhard took the evening train to Paris from Grenoble, expecting to receive his summons within the next few days. Since he had not done his military service, there was no regiment for him automatically to rejoin, and on 9 August he was writing to his parents:

> There is no talk, as yet, of mobilizing the untrained auxiliaries to which I belong, unless we are sent to fetch in the harvest(!) Impossible to get into an ambulance service. . . . The great thing is to hold ourselves in readiness for a call which may never come. There are good reasons for this anomaly, but you'll agree that it's annoying to hang about doing nothing when, a fortnight ago, I was capable of spending 13 hours a day climbing the mountains, without fatigue.

Ten days later he was still in Paris, having failed to get appointed as a military chaplain, and he resumed his work at the Museum. The city was deserted and dead until the crisis of early September when the Germans were reported at Compiègne and the exodus of terrified refugees had its picturesque as well as its pathetic side. The wounded were now awaited in the hospitals and Teilhard envied one of his best friends who was a chaplain at the front, leading 'a life exposed, but as interesting as possible'. Meanwhile he was pleading with his family that his youngest brother Victor, who was only twenty-four hours under military age, should be allowed to join up. On 24 September he was himself called up—to begin his tertianship at Canterbury, '*en attendant*'. After making the Spiritual Exercises of St. Ignatius—a retreat of thirty days—he learnt that his brother Gonzague, aged only twenty, had been killed during the assault of a German trench. Of his death Teilhard wrote in much the same way that he had written of the death of Françoise:

> You could not dream of a more beautiful ideal for your sons than to see them devote themselves, with a Christian spirit, to what is undoubtedly one of the greatest tasks that History will record.

This was the France—military and Catholic—from which Teilhard was never, through all the migrations of a lifetime, to be spiritually uprooted. In November he was declared 'good for service' and a month later, attached to the 13th section of medical orderlies, he reported for duty at Clermont-Ferrand.

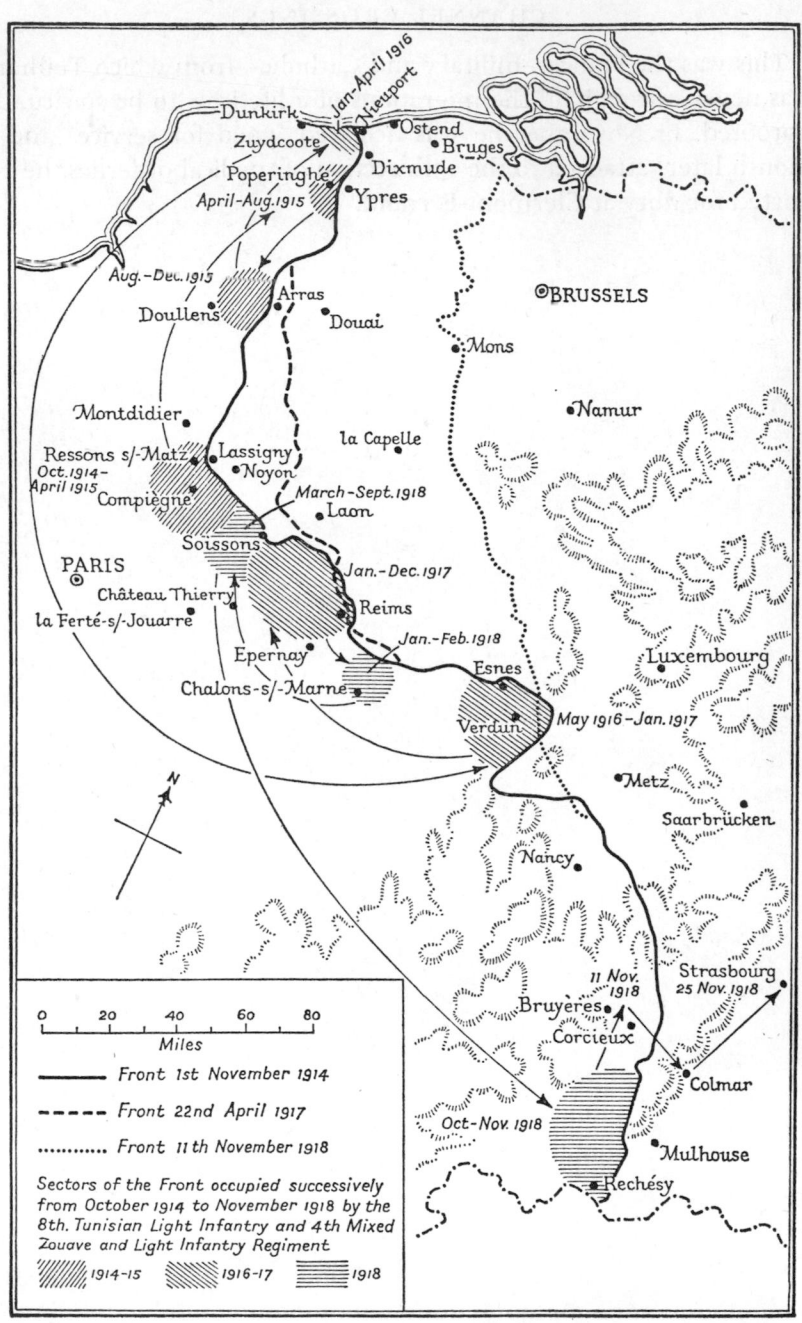

The Western Front, 1914–18

CHAPTER III

THE FIRST WORLD WAR

Teilhard was anxious only to reach the Front, already stabilized along the Aisne and the Somme in the precarious impasse of trench warfare. He arrived there on 20 January 1915, *brancardier*[1] of the second class in the 8th regiment of Tunisian sharpshooters. This was to become, later in the same year, the 4th regiment, mixed, of sharpshooters and Zouaves. Teilhard was the only priest in a unit where a good many Christians might need his spiritual as well as his medical care. The medical major, an Auvergnat like himself, described him as 'simple in manner and distinguished in appearance, very tall, with a clear expression in his eye'. He wore the *képi* and blue uniform of the French infantry in contrast to the khaki of the African troops, and as *brancardier* his business was in the front line. He would have felt just as priestly, he wrote, 'sitting behind a machine-gun as carrying a stretcher',[2] and if he were not to be a combatant, he would rather have been a chaplain. At Cuvilly he found himself ten kilometres from the Germans—and this was already too far. By the fifteenth of the month, however, the regiment had moved up to within four or five kilometres of the trenches at Ecouvillon. Since these ran through the forest, the presence of the enemy was felt rather than observed.

Teilhard wrote constantly to his cousin, Marguerite. Her vocation at the Institut Notre-Dame-des-Champs was in some respects a trying one, and Teilhard was always ready with advice. Their minds met on every level; she was the *anima* to his *animus*, and she also had her practical uses. Very soon he was asking her for two or three woolly waistcoats and a pair of braces. The contents of the parcel, when it arrived, were variously distributed; a woolly cap to the corporal and the woolly waistcoats to the sharpshooters in the trenches. The braces were simply lifted—we are not told by whom. Teilhard had at first

[1] Stretcher-bearer.   [3] Letter to Père Décisier, 23 December 1917.

57

been posted in a casemate, like the other *brancardiers*, but was afterwards moved to a more central position. This was less to his liking, for he felt that he should be seen as much as possible, all along the line. He had spent five days in the cellars of a farm, from which the enemy lines from Lassigny to Soissons were clearly visible. Only the bare walls were standing, with the skeletons of agricultural implements beside them; but there was compensation in the splendid panorama of undulating woodland. At night only an occasional shot in the far distance and the hooting of an owl disturbed a silence beneath which the hidden life of the war became mysteriously apparent.

In a mixed regiment of Africans and French Teilhard found it easy to make friends. The French were glad to converse with one of their own kind. He said Mass in the cellar of the Commandant's billet and dined with the officers. He noticed that the men needed books—novels or history—and games; and he asked his cousin to procure them. By the middle of May the regiment had moved up to Boesinghe, near Ypres, on the banks of the Yser, and here the German artillery gave them little respite. One of their best captains was gravely wounded, and in aiding him Teilhard experienced the power of his priesthood as he had never experienced it before. This was the true baptism of fire, with the air smelling of chloride and the shells decimating the tall poplars. Teilhard carried the Blessed Sacrament wherever he went, and celebrated Mass in a ruined inn, using the buffet as an altar. He could not help remarking how rarely, even under the imminent menace of death, the religious sense of the troops was awakened; and he was also struck by the extraordinary vulgarity which this atrophy engendered.

In July the regiment moved up to Zuydcoote for manœuvres among the sand-dunes of Dunkirk. To the north an ocean of ripening wheat stretched as far as the eye could reach, only broken by a farm in its little circle of trees or the steeple of a church. Out to sea the mines floated and the submarines glided between them. Here Teilhard was cheered by the company of a White Father, still a deacon, who served his Mass. The brigade was reviewed by Marshal Lyautey, and the regiment honoured by colours presented to it by President Poincaré in person. By the middle of August they were back in the front line on the Yser canal. To reach it one had to thread one's way through six hundred yards of communicating trenches and oozing mud, and an atmosphere fetid with the stench of corpses inadequately buried or not buried at all. Once arrived at the parapet, one was too close to the enemy to catch his shells, but one still had to play hide and seek with his bombs and bullets. There were intervals, however, of intense quiet when Teilhard could watch the sun setting over France before the artillery opened its implacable nocturne. On 29 August, no doubt as a result of the part he had played in the recent fighting, Teilhard, now a corporal, was mentioned in the Divisional Order. 'At his own request, he quitted his casualty post to serve in the front line trenches. He displayed the greatest self-abnegation and an absolute contempt for danger.' The Moroccan sharpshooters in the regiment used to say that he was protected by the *baraka*—a Moslem–Arabic word meaning 'spiritual structure', often applied to Gandhi—and the medical major wrote of him in the following terms:

Two features of his personality struck you immediately: courage and humility. He was the one I sent to the critical points of the battlefield, unless he went there willingly of his own accord; for both the head of the medical corps, who appreciated his worth, and myself gave him complete liberty of movement. He knew just what to say and to do in order to revive the *morale* of the troops at the right moment . . . When they addressed him, the men said 'Monsieur Teilhard', thus marking him out from the common run. The Moslems, who had an equal trust in him, spoke of him as the Sidi Marabout.

In the trenches—and this showed his simplicity— he lived like the rest of the troops, and so did the officers for the matter of that. But in the rear, or just behind the front line, he insisted on carrying his knapsack. Often I heard him refuse my offer to relieve him of it, and put it in a little car. 'Like the others' he replied without a moment's hesitation.[1]

One day in the summer of 1915 a corporal of the colonial infantry found Teilhard washing his linen in the pond of a farm near the Belgian frontier. Teilhard recognized him; 'Max Bégouën?', he enquired. 'That's my name', the corporal replied. 'I'm Teilhard.' 'Ah!', said Bégouën, 'you're the Piltdown man.' Bégouën was the son of Count Henri, who had discovered the 'bisons of clay' in a cave on his property in the Ariège. Max asked Teilhard how he managed to keep

[1] *Lettres d'un Voyageur*, French edition, pp. 257–8.

so calm in battle. 'If I'm killed', Teilhard answered with a smile, 'I shall just change my state, that's all.' There is also the testimony of Max's brother Jacques: 'I was wounded and saw in the cross-fire a stretcher-bearer rise up before me. He bandaged me and carried me to the first-aid post. I thought I had seen the appearance of a messenger of God.' This disposes of the idea that Teilhard was indifferent to suffering, because he could recognize its creative as well as its cathartic force. We have Max Bégouën's word for it that he was 'overcome when he found that anyone was suffering. All the capacities of heart and mind were set in motion to bring comfort and relief.'[1]

In the middle of September 1915 the regiment was moved to the south of Arras, where they spent a full fortnight in preparing for a new attack. At Ypres they had been hurled into the battle without time for thought; at Arras they could see it coming closer to them day by day. New trenches had been dug; all had been made ready for the quick evacuation of the wounded; and on the eve of the attack Teilhard made the round of the trenches to offer communion to those who wanted it, moved to the depths of his soul by the embrace of a man to whom he had just given the Blessed Sacrament. Meanwhile the shells volleyed overhead to demolish the trenches where the French hoped to be advancing when the bombardment had stopped. Teilhard realized that only those who went over the parapet to the assault with bayonet fixed and hand-grenade ready could fully experience both the burden and the grandeur of war, and he was chagrined not to be of their company. He had to watch his best friend in the regiment, Commandant Lefébre, lift his *képi* and shout 'Forward, my friends—for France!'—and then to see him fall twenty feet farther on, making the sign of the cross. Teilhard himself ran only the normal risk of being caught in a dug-out by a direct hit—a passive, and, as it were, accidental death; not the active death he would have wished for, if he were to die at all. Nor did he forget his brothers, Olivier and Gabriel, both fighting with the French army in Champagne. Although the September offensive had spared them there were severe losses among Teilhard's Jesuit friends. The finest minds of the Society were being sacrificed, one after another; and it was already four months since Rousselot had been reported missing in the Argonne.

For the regiment this engagement had been brief and bloody, and

[1] *La Table Ronde*, June 1955.

it was quickly withdrawn behind the lines, though still remaining in the mining district to the rear of Arras, a 'territory rich in brave hearts as well as in mercantile resources'.[1] A bomb killed six chickens in the grounds of the convent where Teilhard said his Mass, and he was able to enjoy the fattest of them for dinner. At Christmas he celebrated midnight Mass in the village church of Azincourt. This had been prettily decorated by the son and daughter of the château and Teilhard had taught some hymns to his military congregation. There was a modest *réveillon* afterwards, with apple tart made by one of the *poilus*. From January to April 1916 the regiment was again posted near Dunkirk.

The sea washes the endless monotony of the Belgian coast—the grey sea where the cunning mines float, washed back here and there by the tide, like enormous and evil shells. The stretches of calm water among the dunes, reflecting the pale sky, are full of a penetrating charm, enhanced, when the big guns and the trench-mortars stop firing, by the great silence of two armies watching one another. This is the setting of smiling poetry and generally relaxed strife in which I have been thinking and praying.

He went on to tell Victor Fontoynont of all that was going through his mind—thoughts that he was very soon to organize in a more systematic way. It was a long letter:

So that is what I glimpse and what I'm unpacking, still shapelessly, on to these pages, just as if I were chatting outside your door at Ore Place. I want to be able to love Christ passionately, and at the same time love the Universe a great deal. Is this a chimera or a blasphemy?[2]

There is record of a Mass celebrated by Teilhard in a rat-infested shelter so low that he was obliged to officiate kneeling. He had a congregation of five and the Mass was said for the intention of their families. As he was putting away the sacred vessels and vestments, a shell exploded near by. No one was hurt, and Teilhard observed that 'It was the will of Christ who is among us that none of us should be touched'—and gave them his benediction before rejoining his post at the casualty station.

[1] 15 March 1916.

[2] *ibid*. This important letter is partly reproduced in Henri de Lubac's *The Religion of Teilhard de Chardin*, pp. 241–5

But generally the Front was quiet. Teilhard was now quartered in the undamaged section of an attractive villa; his room had a heavy marble mantelpiece and massive table, and in the library there survived at least half of a Larousse dictionary. In the distance the Ostend lighthouse switched its lantern to right and left for the better reassurance of the submarines. The war struck him more nearly when a young and charming Jesuit of his acquaintance, a brigadier of artillery, had his legs crushed by a shell in an observation post where Teilhard had visited him only a few days before. Both his legs were amputated, but he had survived the operation with invincible good humour. On recovering from the anaesthetic, he had observed to a cousin, who was a naval officer: 'You realize, old boy, that I've lost my paws.' It was exactly what Teilhard would have said under the same circumstances; like many another man, Teilhard de Chardin could always be judged by his friends.

In June the brigade was moved up to a sector of the Front northwest of Verdun. 'For me', Teilhard wrote to his cousin, 'Verdun was prose'—and it was in a prose of which he was already a master that he described the burnt-out ravine of the Hauts-de-Meuse, and the smoking fortress. Nevertheless it was disappointing to be stationed so far from the *mêlée*, although even in the rear the network of telephone wires and tracks cut through the brushwood, indicated the utilities, if not the perils, of war. Farther southwards, on the outskirts of Bar-le-Duc, these were less in evidence, and Teilhard could stroll beside a little stream, and wanted only for congenial company. Returning to the Verdun sector in July, they once again saw nothing of the horror and the heroism. In his peaceable billet Teilhard was cheered by the arrival of an African priest, appointed as chaplain to the brigade. The two men, equally open-minded and untainted by ecclesiastical unction, found themselves in ready sympathy; and early in August a visit from Jean Boussac, an expert in palaeontology and a close friend, relieved the monotony of enforced repose. Boussac was killed later in the month; his view of the universe was more pessimistic than Teilhard's, but with him disappeared 'one of the pillars of my future'.[1] Teilhard's mind, as we shall presently see, was now moving quickly, and it was a cruel blow to have these fruitful conversations cut short. He would have remembered Boussac at the Mass celebrated for those

1 *The Making of a Mind*, p. 123.

fallen at Verdun, at which Nelly Martyl of the Opéra Comique sang with 'a very commendable modesty'.[1]

In the last days of October the regiment took part in the final offensive at Verdun. They captured the village of Douaumont, and the colonials seized the fort. The losses were few, but the little White Father was among them. Teilhard's battalion was in reserve, so that he did not see the actual assault; and it was only on the following morning that he was able to set foot on the conquered territory. He was once again depressed not to have been in the middle of the fighting. Dragging himself along like a snail through an ocean of mud, he wandered over ground where his friends had fallen earlier in the year and where now a whole population of the wounded and the lost, night-walkers of every sort, were huddled together in the shell-holes or the shattered dug-outs. Now and again the sharp voice of an officer rang out in command. All around Douaumont the slopes of a normally fertile countryside stretched out in naked desolation. The contrast between the battlefield and the relative peace of the reserve billets was so striking, and the passage from one to the other so sudden, that the landscape of Verdun already appeared to Teilhard, when he wrote of it, in the livid perspective of a dream.

For all that, he had his place in the story of Verdun. An army citation of 17 September 1916 declared him to have been

> a model of boldness, self-abnegation and self-control. From the 15th to the 19th August he directed the teams of stretcher-bearers on ground shaken by artillery and spattered by machine-guns. On the 18th August he went to within 20 yards of the enemy lines in search of an officer who had been killed, and brought him back to the trenches.

The story behind this citation is one of exemplary courage. Captain Courtiaux, in civilian life a professor at the lycée in Tunis, had been killed by a shell or machine-gun bullet. Although he was an unbeliever, Teilhard liked him well and proposed to the colonel that he should go alone, in place of a volunteer patrol, and bring back the body. The colonel reluctantly agreed. Courtiaux had fallen in front of a nest of machine-guns, and it was not until the early morning that Teilhard, who had left the French lines at 10 p.m., returned with the body on his back.

[1] *ibid.*

Now, in November, he was revived by the russet colours of the woods in autumn—always his favourite season; by the humid fragrance of the dead leaves; and by the rivers winding through the meadows. He was sharing the apartment of the *curé* at Ligny-en-Barrois, and even had a bed to sleep in. It was a repose earned by the attack on Louvemont which had been captured by the brigade. Here, again, the French losses had been light, and the war had never appeared more picturesque. On the following day Teilhard found himself in charge of a dozen prisoners, who had been set to work to evacuate the wounded. He managed to talk to them and found them anything but warlike. It was evident that without its artillery the German resistance would quickly crumble.

At the beginning of January 1917 the regiment was moved north to the neighbourhood of Soissons, and remained there for the rest of the year. Teilhard was detached from the battalion and relieved of many of his more specific military duties so that he could devote himself to spiritual ministrations. He was not altogether pleased at the change, for he missed the immediate solidarity with the troops. Meanwhile the Nivelle offensive to the north of Soissons at the end of March brought them the whiff, but not the substance, of victory; and in June further hopes were roused and disappointed by the epic of the Chemin des Dames. Teilhard described it in an article which appeared later in *Études*;[1] the clear night on the hilly ground where the fumes of poison gas still lingered among the poplars and the crickets continued their chirping after the last echoes of an explosion had rent the air. The windings of the Aisne stood out, here and there, like patches of milk in the early mist, and the crest of the Chemin des Dames was etched like the blade of a knife against the sunrise. On 20 June 1917 Teilhard was awarded the Médaille Militaire; his citation read as follows:

> Excellent non-commissioned officer. He has won confidence and respect by the elevation of his character. On the 20th May 1917 he went specially into a trench, under violent bombardment, to recover a wounded soldier.

In March 1918 the brigade was moved to comfortable quarters in the Forest of Compiègne, and from here it met the full brunt of Ludendorff's last offensive:

> It was both tragic and impressive to march against the stream of

[1] November 1917.

Pierre Teilhard de Chardin about 1884
Pastel at Sarcenat

A novice at Aix, 1899

fleeing troops towards an enemy who seemed to be advancing like an irresistible wave. In fact we were thrown ahead, with no allied forces in front of us. I really think that, if we hadn't been there, the Boches would have been in Compiègne a week ago. On Good Friday we attacked, in order to hold our ground. On the Saturday the enemy counterattacked strongly, but we stood firm. For us, those two days were the only serious ones. After Easter the storm passed northwards—for the time being. My regiment was quickly relieved, without disproportionate losses. By an odd coincidence I'm in almost exactly the same corner of the Oise from which I left for Ypres on 10 April 1915. It's a pretty country, now that spring is here. But the ruins! Once again I've seen villages collapse that were inhabited four days ago. We were living in cellars crammed with apples and cider barrels. The cattle were wandering about the fields, and we were trampling on the green corn.[1]

By July the allied counteroffensive was in full swing, and Teilhard was in the first wave of the assault, not far from Villers-Cotterets. It was the country of the Marne, except that now the troops, famished for victory, could see every night, lumbering up under cover of the woods to their support, a mysterious procession of tanks. They seemed, when they went in to the attack, like ships navigating the huge *plateaux* of the Soissonnais. Only too often they were bombarded to a halt, stranded in an envelope of thick smoke. Overhead the aeroplanes passed in waves, until they, too, would expire in flame. Teilhard described the scene as implacable, and yet strangely inanimate. It betrayed nothing of human fear or ferocity; only the material shock of two material forces locked in a final struggle to survive.

The brigade had the Americans for neighbours. Teilhard admired their courage—an admiration which was universally shared—and only criticized their rashness. During the night of 21 to 22 August he lived through his most dramatic experience of the war. Running through the wheat fields of no-man's-land, he lost touch with the main body of stretcher-bearers, only to discover two of them beside a couple of wounded men who had been lying in the same spot for forty-eight hours. The Germans were raining shells on the place, and raking it with machine-gun fire. It was unthinkable to leave the men

[1] Letter to Paul Jodot, 8 April 1918.

where they were and almost impossible to carry them away. At last they shouldered them and brought them to the shelter of a wrecked tank. Fortunately, at that moment, the Allied artillery put up a barrage and the aeroplanes dropped their bombs. The next morning Teilhard brought up two complete teams of stretcher-bearers and completed the rescue. He had the sensation, now, of living in another world, although there, in front of him, was the wooded crest of the hills where he had walked in autumn. But the values and proportions of everything were changed; they had assumed the dimensions of catastrophe, of a passage from life on earth to a life beyond.

In May his brother, Olivier, had been killed, and in August his brother Victor was awarded the Croix de Guerre in the field. In the following month Teilhard's regiment was moved to Alsace. Here the landscape reminded him a little of Auvergne, and memories of childhood came up to meet him when he recalled how many of their governesses had come from these valleys of the Vosges. Even the presbytery of the village had once been a Jesuit house at the time when the Jesuits were combating the Lutherans in those parts, and Teilhard felt himself doubly at home. He preferred the bushy forests of the Vosges to the classic glades of Compiègne, and from their summits he could see the ridges of the Jura to the south and the Black Forest to the east. The armistice halted the brigade at Docelles just as it was about to move forward to the capture of Metz, and by 18 November Teilhard was writing to his cousin from the reconquered territory of Alsace at Illhäusern. It was the moment that all France had been waiting for since 1870. Alsace was on the extreme limit of the country but, psychologically speaking, it was at the centre of its nervous system. The frontier post pulled up in the premature offensive of 1914 and planted above Paul Déroulède's grave at La Celle St. Cloud would no longer be an ironic memorial.

All along the valley of Kaisersberg, from which the regiment emerged into the plain, the villages were decorated with flags—flaunted in the face of the retreating enemy—and the troops entered them under triumphal arches. Teilhard was in Strasbourg when Pétain made his ceremonial entry on 26 November. Although the brigade was in the rear of the procession, the crowds had not tired of shouting its delirious welcome as it passed. Through the outer circle of forts, trenches and redoubts; past the pointed gables of the old houses, where the souls of France and Germany seem to meet in a mutual *Gemütlichkeit*; past the ranks of Alsatian women, hundreds of them, in the coloured skirts and wide headgear of the local costume; and on to the cathedral where—the parade now over—the *poilus* were gathered, gazing in noisy but respectful curiosity at the ingenious clock. Here, at the striking of every hour, the Twelve Apostles circulated for the delight of the children and tourists; and had done so for generations under Bourbon, Bonapartist or Hohenzollern rule. Teilhard, for his part, was struck afresh by the concentration of prayer which gave to the great cathedral—to any great cathedral—its air of majesty and quiet. The austerity of the nave; the exact geometry of the vaulting; the undisguised emotion of the Pietà, for all its garnishing of jewels and drapery and gold—here was 'the vital synthesis and religious integration' of which he had read in a recent article, and which the scholarship of Émile Mâle had so acutely analysed. Outside, a band of Strasburgers were methodically closing a German *brasserie*, and among those watching the proceeding from the *parvis* of the cathedral was an old friend of Teilhard's from Ore Place—Père Décisier—chaplain to the 18th regiment of *chasseurs*. They fell into each other's arms and exchanged memories and ideas for hours on end. The enthusiasm of the Alsatian clergy; the excellence of the Grand Séminaire at Strasbourg; the anaemia and externalism of religious life in France—these were themes of peace and the moment was ripe for their discussion. Teilhard would still have to wait a few months before he was demobilized, but the war was over and his eyes were fixed, as ever, *en avant*.

II

Such was the active part played by Pierre Teilhard de Chardin in the First World War, and its distinction needs no emphasis. But only a very few people realized at the time that the war was the matrix of his whole thinking about the nature of man and the universe. 'These thirty months', he had told Victor Fontoynont, 'have been like a long retreat. I have become at the same time very mystical and very realistic'.[1] And many years later he was writing to his medical major:
No doubt my ideas were there from the beginning, like 'genes',

[1] 27 July 1917.

but it was only in the atmosphere of the Front that I really began to be aware of them, in the 4th Mixed Regiment of Zouaves-Tirailleurs, when we were together.[1]

Teilhard's patriotism was sure but unassertive; never does a word of hatred for the enemy escape him. Although he was so closely involved in the conflict, he viewed it, as it were, at one remove. 'What will come out of this frightful struggle?', he asks; and then defines it as 'the crisis and desperately slow evolution of a European renewal'. He also believed, with an optimism which has hardly been justified, that the war would unite the nations of the earth in a way that nothing else could have united them. The hope was encouraged by a performance given by the Théâtre aux Armées under the chestnut-trees in the village of Nant-le-Grand. Here were soldiers from France, Sénégal, Martinique, Somaliland, Annam and Tunisia, all applauding the same things at the same time, but each group preserved its own customs and *cuisine* although all were members of the same regiment. This solidarity Teilhard had experienced for himself whenever he moved up into the battle zone. Then it seemed natural—though not agreeable—to see others die and to die oneself. One became the impersonal element of an immense, impersonal activity.

Neither the politics nor the grand strategy of the war seem to have interested him very much. But he was impressed by the Allied reply to Wilson's Fourteen Points; if the Germans produced a theory to fit their practice, they would be forced to a Nietzschean profession of faith, which would clearly reveal the war as a conflict between two moralities. This was a troubling prospect—and who would arbitrate between the two ideals? The United States, or History, or the Pope? Like many others, Teilhard was disturbed by the reticence of Benedict XV, and he hoped that the Allied statement would make a favourable impression in Rome. As the war approached its end, Wilson's idealism and serenity encouraged Teilhard in his belief that Christianity could not afford to dispense with the salt of the earth, even if it were mined on Presbyterian soil. Wilson had cleverly not given the impression of refusing peace, and Teilhard did not believe that the average French soldier was so drunk with victory that he would bear a grudge against those who would prevent him marching to Berlin. Later, it is true, Teilhard's belief in Wilson's sagacity was somewhat modified. For the

[1] 11 September 1951.

rest, whenever he was in the rear, he never ceased to experience a nostalgia for the front line, perceiving in it the crest of a wave that was washing humanity forward to an unpredictable destiny. It was the extreme limit of action and sensation; a maelstrom of energy, lucidity and freedom hardly to be discovered in ordinary life; a *milieu* where the individual soul was living in communion with the quasi-collective soul of mankind. This was a painful elevation, to be sure; but it was an elevation none the less. Teilhard was not seduced by the shibboleths of a sentimental democracy—a word that was coming fast into fashion. The only true democracy was one that favoured the maximum accession to an *élite*.

For Teilhard the years of war were a continuous and fruitful oscillation between solidarity and solitude. He had much time for reading. Marguerite Teillard-Chambon sent him *Le Correspondant*, *La Revue des Deux Mondes*, and even the *Daily Mail*. The *Action Française* had no difficulty in reaching the officers' mess, and the officers would not be reluctant to assist its circulation. Teilhard admired Ernest Psichari's *Le Voyage du Centurion*. Psichari was the grandson of Renan, and his discovery of the faith in the Moroccan desert, and through the discipline of arms, found an echo in Teilhard's own experience. Psichari was destined for the Dominican novitiate when the war broke out, and if he had not been killed Teilhard would have relished his acquaintance. An anthology of verse picked up in the trenches revived his interest in poetry. He was disturbed by the softness of Musset's ideas which a metrical harmony could not conceal; Ronsard, and particularly Vigny, were more to his taste. Vigny's *Grandeur et Misère de la Vie Militaire* had an immediate and moving resonance, although Teilhard found his style too pompous and studied. But nothing moved him so much as Péguy's verses from *Ève*: 'Heureux ceux qui sont morts . . .' He was surprised to discover Péguy marching in the same direction as himself; Péguy's anxiety to defend and proclaim the 'earthly cradle' of Christ was in tune with Teilhard's deepest preoccupations. Very different was d'Annunzio's *Le Feu* (*Il Fuoco*), whose *brio* he could not help admiring, but whose emotional and melodramatic excesses he deplored. The same ferocious naturalism was in Verhaeren's *Les Forces Tumultueuses*; here, nevertheless, were certain pagan aspirations whose validity could not in justice be denied. Teilhard enjoyed Léon Daudet's *Salons et Saisons* not only for its verve, but for the glimpse it gave him of the literary and artistic coteries, and of the joy of working hand in hand with people who shared the same interests. It was a joy that he would experience to the full during the years ahead; and he would go far to realize the ideal inspired by a reading of these rather superficial memoirs—to spend half the year with a group of fellow-workers, and half in the solitude of private research. He was also lent the *Chartreuse de Parme* by a fervent Stendhalien of the regiment; but he did not think its austerity of style and psychological observation warranted the 'fetichism' which coloured so much commentary on Stendhal. One would not have expected Teilhard to include among his favourite authors a man who admitted that he did everything possible '*pour être sec*'. Dryness was not a Teilhardian characteristic.

No, his apprehension was poetic, although he did not set out to be a poet, and he thought that the classical forms of poetry were not always adequate for the expression of poetic truth. It was not easy to enshrine a new idea in a metrical frame which had been manufactured in advance. He believed that every poem should discover its appropriate rhythm. It should have its own themes and harmonies, even its own typography. It should be as personal as a piece of music. A prefabricated metre was all very well, but it belonged to the infancy of poetry. Whatever one may think of these ideas, they go far to explain the form that much of Teilhard's writing was eventually to take—a kind of poetic rhapsody.

If he found the reiterative rhythms of Péguy more bracing than the pessimism of *Les Fleurs du Mal*, it was Dante he loved beyond anyone else, because in Dante mysticism and poetry were allied. It is possible that here Teilhard allowed to mysticism a larger sense than a professional theologian would have conceded. People will always debate whether Teilhard himself was a mystic or merely a mystical writer, and even whether his mysticism was of the natural or supernatural kind. He would certainly have agreed that the true mystic was the man who looked at the pennies on the pavement as hard as he looked at the stars in the sky; and what he prized in Dante was his firm anchorage in reality. Dante's love for Beatrice was the sovereign example of a universal feeling inspired by an individual person. It was also very much to Teilhard's point that this person was a woman. The other writer standing, as it were, midway between the sacred and the secular—though on a very inferior level—was Robert Hugh Benson.

Teilhard had come across some extracts from *The Lord of the World* in the *Revue Hebdomadaire,* and he was charmed by Benson's description of the pantheist *mystique* and the conceivable unification of the human *monade.* But he saw now—what had not been so clear to him when he read the book at Ore Place in 1910—that there was a world of difference between his own cosmic vision and the pantheism described, and condemned, by Benson. Teilhard refused altogether to admit that an enthusiasm for the 'spirit of the world' must necessarily be the property of anti-Christ. The earth could be loved—and should be loved—because God had created it. The defeatist Catholicism in Benson's novel was unacceptable to Teilhard not because it was persecuted, but because it was bloodless—equally against nature as above it.

Teilhard read as the spirit took him; one does not see him setting aside so many hours a day for what is called 'spiritual reading', even when this was possible. All worthwhile reading was spiritual reading. But it cannot be too strongly insisted that the foundation of his thought and his apologetic was St. Paul. He did not inquire whether St. Paul had in fact written the Epistle to the Hebrews—such questions were still dangerous even in the less coercive pontificate of Benedict XV; it was enough that a very Pauline pen had written, '*Hebraeus sum? Et ego.*' In due course Teilhard was to better his master's instruction and put '*Homo sum; plus ego*' as an epigraph to *Le Milieu Divin.* And another text from the same Epistle, '*fides substantia sperandarum rerum*'—'the substantial faith in things to be hoped for'—suggested that faith was the element which stabilized and divinized the future. St. Paul and St. John were both the guarantors of a certain Christian pantheism, in which all energy was maintained and soldered together to be assumed into the humanity of Christ, and moulded afresh in a personal, transcendent unity. St. Paul spoke of the world as often as he spoke of the individual; he met Teilhard at each end of his meditation.

Ardently as Teilhard loved his friends, and easily as he moved in society, he had a natural taste for solitude; and it was for that reason, among others, that his enforced translation to a *milieu* where he was compelled to keep his thoughts to himself was so valuable. He was captivated by Newman's *Apologia,* and would even translate the 'I' of Newman's 'He and I' into the universe centred in the self, so that the destiny of the whole world was played out in each individual soul. Did he perhaps foresee in the intellectual martyrdom of Newman a pre-figuring of the obstacles which the originality of his own thought would encounter? It was the vitality of Newman that appealed to him; the invitation to reconcile the love of God with the love of life in all its natural forms. When Newman wrote that it was more important to resist fundamental deviations of thought than to make a few conversions, or to waste one's time over inter-confessional quarrels; that the intellectual task of the Church was to sift the positive dogmatic developments realized by the whole body of the faithful; and that those who wanted some particular truth to prevail before the time was ripe for it risked ending up as heretics—as Teilhard came upon these and similar perceptions, he felt as if he had long been familiar with them, so intimately did they correspond with the way his own mind was working.

From the world of books he looked out, untiringly, on the world of nature. Here the pantheism to which he was prone was refuted by his dissatisfaction with a universe which had not yet reached its term. The terrestrial, however captivating, was superficial; and when one dug down deep enough one came up against the hard rock, which was only another name for death. Death was all around him and he saw it as the condition of change, not as the cessation of life. The more one changed the more one died—dying to one life to be reborn in another. Death was not suppressed by trust in God, but it was at least made tolerable; and the greater one's faith as death took hold of one, the greater one's chance of reaching a higher level of existence. Death had too often been treated as a theme for gloomy or ascetic meditation, as 'a vaporous theological entity'; it should be seen as a vigorous, though transient, reality in a world which was a continuous Becoming. Nature was the basis of a pyramid at the summit of which stood a Person upon whom all its energies converged; and its appearances were for Teilhard an object not of contemplation but of research. This is not to say that he was insensitive to their beauty, which he described with precision and power; but for him the aesthetic ecstasy was only a half-way house, conditioning the mind to greater things. Art and poetry, like nature herself, might lead to nothing more than an enervating pantheism, essentially pagan in character. Their true purpose was to dispose the soul to a larger ambition, to increase its sensitivity to the music of the cosmos and the spheres. The Shakespearian conception of 'great creating Nature' meets Teilhard's thought exactly of an active rather than a passive power.

And then he looked from the world of nature to the world of men. First of all, to his own sanctification. There were very few things, he wrote, which urged him so imperatively to this as the feeling that the cosmos itself needed to be purified, and that matter and spirit were engaged in a common struggle for unification. Teilhard's optimism was neither insensitive nor unqualified. He remarked how God constantly permitted the removal of those instruments best fitted to procure his glory, even when they were engaged in the holiest tasks. And to the eternal, tormenting question—why had not God created a more perfect world if it had been in his power to do so? Teilhard replied, in effect, that 'more perfect' begged the question. Every possible universe had its special beauty, by virtue of which it was more perfect than all the others. Another universe, with less evil apparent in it, would seem to us 'better' because our reasoning was effeminate. Would our ideal universe be likely to nourish the kind of sanctity which flowered in the shadow of the Cross? He had seen what happened to the French peasantry when an anti-clerical legislation persuaded it that the Cross was an obstacle to progress. A kind of spiritual decomposition set in, once the religious instinct had been removed.

For all that, Teilhard was not entirely censorious when he surveyed the modern world. Those who believed that there was nothing beyond the present life seemed to have a direct and concrete pity for their fellow beings, and a disinterested zeal in working for their betterment. On the other hand belief in God involved the risk of a formal charity and a spiritual egoism. The remedy was a conviction that God is only attained at the price of human effort, and that one's neighbour must be loved for himself and not for the reward that one's charity may earn. Teilhard was not a natural ecclesiastic. One day in the depths of the citadel of Verdun—perhaps at Douaumont after its recapture by the regiment—he was drinking a *bock* with a young lieutenant who confessed his adherence to a 'religion of the spirit'. He believed in Christ and read the Gospels, but he would have nothing of ritual or dogma. Teilhard pointed out to him the contradictions of this attitude; if there were no dogma and no authority to certify it, why should one prefer the Christ of Catholicism to the Christ of Renan or Harnack? The only logical choice was between an integral

Catholicism and an agnostic liberalism. The young man, however, was not convinced; and Teilhard, while he preached the necessity of ritual and visible institutions, could not help feeling—and not for the first time—the attraction of a religion purely of the heart and the intentions. But then he remembered Isocrates who had killed the spirit of Athens by wishing to separate it from the letter of its political organism. He also remembered Maurras and the positivists of the *Action Française*—men far removed from his own mentality—who insisted that the spirit of freedom in the Church was indissolubly linked to its corporate body, however vulgar and objectionable the appearances and even the actions of that body might be.

Teilhard, more easily than most men, could penetrate appearances. It must be allowed that no form of Catholic piety is more repellent in its visual aspect than devotion to the Sacred Heart. Yet this was at the very centre of Teilhard's spiritual life—more than the Crib and more, even, than the Crucifix. It was, for him, the fountain of energy and love. He would complain, to be sure, of its sentimental presentation— but only to remind himself that a love which was open to all was for that reason open to popular excess. It was the same with the Rosary, which he saw for what it was—a prolongation and an echo down the ages of the angelic salutation. No doubt, for the majority of Catholics, it responded to an instinctive love for the Blessed Virgin, and its recitation was a prayer of interested petition. But it could easily be transformed into a prayer of sympathy, so that the heart of the Virgin became a kind of mirror in which the entire structure of dogma was reflected; and its sequence of Mysteries found their parallel in human joy and suffering. Nevertheless Teilhard's spirituality remained, even in its Marian developments, essentially '*Christique*'—to employ a word which echoes as a refrain all through his writings. Everything must end where it had begun—in the *foyer* of the Sacred Heart, whose image greeted him in the salon every time he returned to Sarcenat.

Such, in brief outline, were the workings of his mind as he opened it in a stream of letters to his cousin. 'You were given me for the war', he told her, comparing their friendship to 'a note of music which gives a tone to our whole life'.

CHAPTER IV

EARLY WRITINGS[1]

WRITING TO HIS COUSIN was not enough; Teilhard wanted to set his ideas in circulation. Between the outbreak of war and the end of 1918 he composed thirteen essays which contain, in germ, the future development of his thought. He described them as his 'intellectual honeymoon'.

> To tear away the mask of atheism from these new currents of thought and expose them as Christian—that is my great hope, and I need not tell you that it urges me on as a vocation.[2]

In Teilhard's guidance of his cousin's pen we can detect some of the principles which guided his own. He advised her to avoid the ugly consonance and the repetitive word; to eschew the ambiguous objective or pronoun; and to create a synthesis, not merely a connection, between one paragraph or passage and the next. This was particularly important when the argument was interrupted by quotations. For himself, he realized from the start that his writings would have to pass the ecclesiastical censorship, and that he would always have the Jesuit censors in Rome, not to mention the inquisitors of the Holy Office, looking over his shoulder. It will be as well to point out here that Teilhard did not object to the principle of the censorship, mortified as he often was by the practice of the censors. Naturally, in matters of the soul where an interior acquiescence was required, constraint must be delicately exercised; and in matters of the intellect authority could forbid expression, but it could not impose conviction. Nevertheless Teilhard admitted that the preventive measures of the Index, revolting and often absurd as they might appear, were among the legitimate rights of a Church which claimed to be in possession of the truth.

[1] All the writings discussed in this chapter, and in the first section of Chapter V, are included in *Écrits du Temps de la Guerre*

[2] Letter to Victor Fontoynont, 22 July 1916.

Humanity was not yet ripe to walk unassisted by anything but its own reason, and the mass of men still needed—and would need for a long time—to be led on the leash.

From the moment he put pen to paper, he was correct and dutiful with his superiors. Modernism was still in the air, although, with the accession of Benedict XV, Merry del Val was in retirement and Monsignor Benigni's Gestapo had been dissolved. But Teilhard had ideas about the immanence of God in the universe which caused the more conventionally orthodox to shake their heads. It was not surprising, therefore, that when he came to take his solemn vows at Sainte Foy-lès-Lyon in May 1918, Père Chanteur, the Lyon provincial, nervous of his pantheist leanings, should have been opposed to his doing so. Fortunately, another Jesuit priest of recognized spiritual discernment, Père Vulliez-Serment, vouched for his solidity. It is never quite impossible for a Jesuit to leave the Society, but the solemn vows represent a final stage of mature and mutual commitment. Teilhard was in no doubt what they meant. He was to take a vow of poverty; yet he had never more clearly realized how money could be used for the glory of God. He was to take a vow of chastity; yet he knew how man and woman in union could assist each other in the supernatural life. He was to take a vow of obedience; yet he had never understood better the liberty of the service of God. All this he confided to a friend, who asked him whether he had been altogether at ease in so engaging himself. He replied that he had never had a moment's anxiety. Probably only his superiors, and his friends in the Society, realized to what an extent Teilhard de Chardin was Ignatian.

It was in this frame of mind, at once determined and docile, that he started to put his ideas into literary form. From Nieuport, early in 1916, he told his cousin that he had certain things to say about the magical appeal of Nature, its reality and significance; and of the fulfilment that Christianity could bring to pantheist aspirations, if these were properly understood. He prayed to be kept 'equally humble and bold', for he admitted that his ideas were 'far from being clear' and needed to be 'strongly controlled by those who are very saintly and very human'. His meditation resulted in *La Vie Cosmique*, written, as he admitted, out of sheer exuberance and the necessity of living, to express his passionate vision of the universe. The essay was a prayer rather than an argument; Teilhard described it as his '*testament d'intellectuel'*. In Christ was resumed the 'implacable grandeur of the world'; He was union and multitude, spirit and matter, the personal and the infinity, the part and the whole. He was sweetness and intimacy and power. Life on earth only continued because the cosmic Christ was still in the act of formation; he was the natural as well as the supernatural consummation of all created activity; and for that reason evolution was 'holy'. The sole business of the world was the physical incorporation of the faithful in Christ, and this work proceeded with 'the rigour and harmony of a natural evolution'. But it was the transcendent *fiat* of the Incarnation which made it possible. Teilhard compared the action of grace to the sap rising from the same trunk into many branches; to the blood circulating in all the veins under the impulsion of the same heart; to the nervous control of the limbs by the same head. And the head and heart and trunk were all the identical Christ.

In a note adjoined to his MS Teilhard made an important distinction between two conceptions of Christian asceticism. According to the one, suffering was above all 'a punishment and an expiation'. The fruit of original sin, its efficacy was sacrificial; it was a way of reparation. According to the other, suffering was the consequence and the price of a work still in process of development. It was the sign of a continual effort, and its efficacy lay in this. Physical and moral evil were the result of what was coming to be; everything in evolution had to endure its travail and commit its faults. The Cross—Teilhard went on boldly to assert—was an evolutionary no less than an expiatory symbol. The two points of view coincided if one admitted that the natural consequence of original sin was to make mankind work 'with the sweat of his brow', but Teilhard recognized the sharp difference of emphasis, and thought it only loyal that he should point it out. Nevertheless in doing so he exposed his failure to see that 'the only guarantee of evolution's success was Christ's conquest of man's capacity for disunion and hatred on the personal level';[1] and at the same time he exposed a flank of which his adversaries were quick to take advantage.

In September of the same year (1916) Teilhard turned from his personal testament to the task which he saw confronting him. The Church was still under the spell of a pessimism which the Syllabus of

[1] Christopher Mooney, s.j., *Teilhard de Chardin and the Mystery of Christ.*

Pius IX had disastrously confirmed, whatever historical reasons might be pleaded in its excuse. The protest of the Reformation, the paganism of the Renaissance, the scepticism of the Enlightenment, and the raucous clamour of political and industrial democracy had reduced the magisterium to panic. It confused the world which Christ had redeemed with the world he had condemned. To save his soul the Christian would do better to avoid the contamination of secular concerns. Against this emasculated pietism Teilhard set his face. He saw the 'intensive socialization' of a world in the throes of transforming itself as a movement of the Absolute rejoining the forces of renewal and inviting their response. The very idea of evolution was meaningless unless it posited a term—and for Teilhard, secure in the option of faith, this could only be the transfiguring image of Christ. To synthesize the truths of revelation with the just, and inevitable, advance of knowledge—this was the task he assigned himself; and he described his acceptance of it as a 'conversion'.

He began to elaborate his ideas in *La Maîtrise du Monde et le Règne de Dieu*. Christ was 'the principle of unity who saves a culpable creation in process of returning to dust'; critics of Teilhard should here note the admission of culpability. The evolution of matter was a scientific truth so clear as to need no further demonstration, but now mind itself was evolving. Less evident was his contention that history, in spite of its accidental convulsions which were all around him as he wrote, was infallible in its phases and fortunate in its results. 'After each new crisis Humanity must yield to the evidence that it has progressed, that it has changed to its own advantage. For Life, and Life alone, knows what is good for its children.' Here was the Teilhardian optimism which would survive all the shocks that the twentieth century had in store for it. Léon Bloy, in a dictum that Teilhard was very fond of quoting, had said much the same thing; '*tout ce qui arrive est adorable*' —although he often wrote as if everything that happened were detestable. In Teilhard's view the conquests of humanity were irreversible; it would make its mistakes, but it was incapable of permanent regression; and it was here that revelation proposed an apex to the ascending pyramid of man's endeavour. The Church, the divinely appointed guardian of revelation, would be failing in its duty if it did not encourage 'the sacred duty of research'. Some Christians might be called to a life of perfect chastity and contemplative immobility, but this was an exceptional vocation. By far the greater number, 'even when they were dedicated to the counsels of evangelical perfection', must regard 'the sacred task of nourishing natural life . . . among the most pressing and efficacious factors of sanctity'. The critics of Catholicism should have no further excuse to say of Rome that she was afraid 'of anything that moved and of anyone who thought'.

There followed, later in the same year (1916), *Le Christ dans la Matière: Trois Histoires comme Benson*. These stories, although their narrative content is very slight, were inspired by a reading of Robert Hugh Benson, and they expressed ideas which Benson might have developed. Teilhard gives himself the alibi of a friend with whom he imagines himself in conversation. The friend has died at Verdun and Teilhard recalls an evening when he had spoken of his vision of Christ, of how the universe had come to assume for him the lineaments of the divine figure. Pausing one day before a conventional image of the Sacred Heart, he had wondered how an artist could represent the humanity of Jesus without giving it a beauty too individual and exclusive. Gradually the contours of the picture—the folds of the robe, the radiance of the head—dissolved without quite disappearing, so that on the surface of separation between Christ and the world the limits of either were indistinguishable. The vibration extended to the limits of the universe itself, but when the objects included in it were examined one by one they still preserved their individual character. They were transformed, but they were not lost; leading the gaze of the beholder back to the source of their illumination which was the face of Christ himself. This was compared to the changing lights of certain stars or the passing of a bubble over certain colours, so that every imaginable beauty seemed to be reflected in them. And within the face it was the eyes that held the spectator captive—now with a tender reminiscence of his own mother; now with a woman's passionate and imperious purity; now with a man's strength, courage and refinement, at once submissive and sublime. But the ultimate expression of the eyes was beyond description or analysis; the speaker could not say whether it translated an excess of joy or suffering. He had seen the same expression, since, in the look of a dying soldier.

In the second story Teilhard, or his *alter ego* interlocutor, watches the expansion of the Host in the monstrance till it becomes incandescent, consuming and transforming all the energies of love in the universe. The white patch of consecrated bread then contracts slowly, leaving behind it 'certain refractory elements' in outer darkness. The third story, *La Custode*, is even more directly autobiographical. Teilhard takes the reader back to the time when his regiment was in the line near Verdun, and he was carrying the Blessed Sacrament on his own person. How was it possible, he asks, that the springs of life and the richness of the world should be so close to him and yet defy his penetration? Even at the moment of communion he feels that they are still not truly a part of him. All his powers of recollection are in vain; the centre of what he holds attracts him but eludes his grasp. But at last, and in proportion as his efforts are redoubled, the Host takes on the form of a brother who needs his love or consolation, the memory of some joy or suffering, the thought of some work to be accomplished. The entire universe is reconstituted in the particle of bread and borrows its appearances. Teilhard then understands the nature of the obstacle which bars him from a perfect union with the object of his love and his pursuit—namely 'the whole substance and surface of the years which remain for him to live and to divinize'. Teilhard goes on to admit that he had always had 'a naturally pantheistic soul', and that he had found these native aspirations hard to reconcile with his faith. In a note, added later to the story, he was careful to distinguish between the classical pantheism which insisted that God 'became' everything, and the Pauline doctrine of God 'being everything in everybody' by the differentiating activity of love. This view was of course perfectly orthodox. And so he looked forward to a day when the 'vast décor' of the universe might wither or collapse—looked forward to the imminent possibility of his own death—without any diminution of joy because 'the substantial Reality would remain intact'. The rays of energy would retire upon their source and he would still embrace them.

> This is why even war does not disconcert me. In a few days' time we shall be thrown into battle for the recapture of Douaumont: a grandiose, almost a fantastic exploit which will mark and symbolize a definitive advance of the world in the liberation of souls. And I tell you this: I shall go into this engagement in a religious spirit, with all my soul, borne on by a single great impetus in which I am unable to distinguish where human emotions end and adoration begins.

Père Auguste Valensin, s.j.,
Teilhard's lifelong friend
and correspondent, aged 70

Professor George Barbour
in New York, 1934

Teilhard in 1918

And if I am destined not to return from those heights I would like my body to remain there, moulded into the clay of the fortifications, like a living cement thrown by God into the stonework of the New City.

The 'Benson' stories were written in the presbytery at Nant-le-Grand on 14 October 1916 'before the affair of Douaumont'. They stand on the border-line between mystical experience and the expression of a mystical idea. Each is closely linked to Teilhard's own vocation; like his *alter ego*, he had contemplated the image of the Sacred Heart and adored the Host exposed in the monstrance or carried secretly beneath his uniform. Only a few months before, Maurice Blondel had written to Valensin of the Eucharist as the 'Catholic remedy for pantheism', because it affirmed 'the absolute and distinct reality of God and the creature, as well as their intimate union', thus correcting at the same time as it fortified the movement of Teilhard's thought. These stories are the effect of a mystical imagination working on the stuff of actual experience, and also upon real intuitions which the author was able to clothe in impressive literary form. He sent the MS to de Grandmaison in the hope that it might be published in *Études*. De Grandmaison replied in a letter which Teilhard regarded as both 'generous and just'. Quite apart from any debatable ideas the stories might contain, their tone would have disconcerted 'the placid and sensible readers of the review'.

In 1917 followed *La Lutte contre la Multitude*. Here Teilhard broached the problem of the one and the many—a question that was to haunt him for many years to come as the socialization of human life made such rapid, and often such disconcerting, progress. The philosophical importance of the essay seemed to him 'obviously very limited',[1] but it brought him to a precious definition of the 'pure in heart'. For Teilhard, purity of heart simply consisted in loving God above everything else and in seeing his presence everywhere in a world that was waiting to be conquered and perfected by him. Thus individual objects lost their superficial multiplicity. The natural privilege of the pure soul was to move at the heart of an immense and superior unity. Where the carnal sinner was dispersed in his passions, the saint escaped from their complexity and made himself to that extent immaterial. For him, everything was God and God was everything, and Jesus was

[1] Letter to Marguerite Teillard-Chambon, 24 March 1917.

'God and everything combined'. The specification of purity was to unify the interior powers of the soul in the activity of a single passion. Overcoming the multiple and distracting appeal of objects, the pure soul steeped its unity in 'the ardours of the divine simplicity'. For Teilhard de Chardin purity of soul was only another name for singleness of mind. And where purity operated in solitude, charity operated in society. This was the chief work of human life; and it was by this that we should be justified or condemned.

Le Milieu Mystique—most important perhaps of Teilhard's earlier essays because it prefigured *Le Milieu Divin*—was composed at Beaulieu-les-Fontaines in the Forest of Compiègne. It was finished on 13 August 1917 and was at once sent to his sister Marguerite-Marie. He intended also to submit it to a Jesuit Father at Lyon in whom he had 'absolute confidence'—no doubt Père Vulliez-Serment, who was master of novices. In summing up, Teilhard disclaimed any intention of describing the mystical life in itself; he wished only to disentangle its 'natural and cosmic roots'. Just as there was a single matter created to support the additions of consciousness, so there was a single, fundamental idea and aspiration at the base of every variety of mysticism— the innate love of the human person extended to the whole universe. This was liable to many deviations. It might evaporate into an empty poetizing or degenerate into a pagan pantheism. Nevertheless it was here, and here alone, that mysticism had its primitive beginnings. Once again Teilhard's passionate quest for unity is troubled by the multitude of created beings; he shares the mystic's obstinate passion for 'the stable, the unchanging and the absolute'; but then he perceives that 'the Real is not only transparent but solid'. The world is 'full' and its fullness is the fullness of the Absolute. In loving an object he discovers that the opacity of that object, and the barrier of separation between itself and him, are dissolved into a unifying transparency by the intensity of his own attachment. In and through his perception of another, he has come to possess everything in himself.

The creative activity of God does not knead us, as the potter kneads his clay; it is more like a vivifying fire, and it is through living that we surrender ourselves to its possession. This surrender is in fact an incessant task of self-correction and self-development, in which the soul can have no rest until every least discordance has ceased between its own vibration and the *milieu divin*. The mystic must be obedient to the

slightest imperatives of temporal duty and the most delicate prompt-
ings of supernatural grace. He must open his heart, develop his mind,
purify his affections, and intensify his visible activity. He must create,
if he wishes to be more fully created; and in becoming a more perfect
instrument in himself, he will identify himself with the creative in-
strumentality of God. As the thought takes him, Teilhard passes from
analysis to reflection and from reflection to prayer. For a moment a
cloud of pessimism overshadows him; nature is a bungler and progress a fraud; all that we see and hear is inert and gross; and only in
the wheatfields of the catalyzing Spirit is there a harvest of energy
and good will. And so he dreams of a common centre where the live-
liest energies and sharpest sensibilities of the cosmos will put down
their roots. This is the *milieu mystique*; this is the *milieu divin*. But the
source is personal; and it is to a person that Teilhard directs his prayer,
and a person who answers it:

This is I to carry, fructify and pacify your work. Above all, though,
I am here to relieve you of it and to bring it to completion. You
have struggled enough for the divinization of the world. It is for
me to force the gates of the Spirit. Let me come by.

These are the accents of prophecy, although translation can only
faintly recapture them. In the years to come Teilhard will pursue his
researches with a scrupulous fidelity to fact; but already, as the
scientist prepares to sharpen his tools, the seer has made his 'stones' to
speak.

The boldness of Teilhard's thought, and his patient integrity in
propounding it, may lead one to forget or to undervalue his humility.
De Grandmaison had warned him that the censors might find this
'scientific-cosmic philosophy' a shade too revolutionary for their
taste. So Teilhard puts his trust in purity and prayer 'suspended like
an impassable light between the universe and God', and in the
Blessed Virgin who is their synonym. With a premonition of exile and
frustration, he gives thanks for the disappointments that may 'dash
the cup' from his lips and the chains that may force him to go where
he has no wish to go; for the inexorable flight of time; and for death
which has its terrors for the mystic, as for another, but which also
crowns his beatitude. Christ is the supreme consistency, and Teilhard
invokes him neither as light nor as matter, but as fire—the ardent
centre of an ardent universe. There is here a pregnant suggestion of

mystical experience when Teilhard speaks of 'the intuition of the first encounter'—which had been an intuition of fire. It was thus that God had appeared to Moses in the burning bush, and we should be rash to see in his answer to Teilhard's prayer no more than a figment, however carefully wrought, of literary imagination.

II

In a letter to his cousin (8 October 1917) Teilhard declared his intention of writing the outline of a philosophical synthesis under the title of *L'Union Créatrice*. It was not intended for publication, but rather as a clarification of ideas which he would have eventually to defend before his ecclesiastical censors. The idea that the act of creation was essentially an act of union brought him at once into apparent conflict with the Catholic dogma of creation *ex nihilo*. Teilhard's denial—or apparent denial—of this doctrine has always been among the more serious charges brought against him by his theological opponents. What he was attempting here was to transpose a theory which seemed to him evident from his observation of the physical world on to the metaphysical plane. He was fully aware of the difficulty and finally, realizing that metaphysics were not his *forte*, he abandoned the attempt, although the question continued to preoccupy him. For the moment, he was dissatisfied with the 'limpid' explanations of scholastic orthodoxy, and sought to remedy them by a theory of creation which would take more account of scientifically ascertained phenomena:

> It is infinitely more worth while to present, for the time being, a mixture of truth and error, than to mutilate reality by trying prematurely to separate the wheat from the tares. I have followed this Gospel principle without hesitation, since it is the principle of all research and all scientific progress.

Or, as he wrote to Père Fontoynont, 'Under control of the *Ecclesia docens*, it is necessary to organize and develop the *Ecclesia quaerens*'.[1]

Admitting the certainty of evolution, he saw that the movement of evolution towards mind was a movement in the direction of the Absolute, and that the shape of the world could only be explained if the genesis of mind were understood. What differentiated man from the animal creation was a spiritual substance which united the organic

[1] 26 July 1917.

components of his being, and survived their dissolution. Another name for this was the power of reflection; as Pascal had said, man was a 'thinking reed'. Teilhard attributed some kind of 'soul' to the animals, but this 'soul' was perishable. Between the animal 'soul' and the human 'soul' the passage was crucial; as Teilhard put it, one section of the cone had become the summit. Here there was an important distinction between the Bergsonian and the Teilhardian view of evolution. Where the Bergson of *L'Évolution Créatrice* had seen the cosmos as a divergent radiation from a central point, Teilhard's '*union créatrice*' was a convergence upon that centre of a 'sphere infinitely distended'. But who created the sphere? To posit its existence challenged the doctrine of creation *ex nihilo*.

Teilhard was well aware of the difficulties raised by his conception of a 'positive nothingness' on which the '*union créatrice*' was at work. It seemed to contradict the doctrine of gratuitous creation; it smelt of Manichaean heresy. But it seemed to him more satisfying than 'merely verbal explanations'. Here a more rigorous metaphysician would reply that the notion of 'positive nothingness' was in itself a 'purely verbal explanation'. Teilhard evaded but did not overcome the difficulty by asking why 'the necessary existence of an absolute unity should not involve as a secondary consequence, *ad extra*, like an antithesis or a shadow, the appearance, at the antipodes of being, of infinite multiplicity. I do not think that this diminishes our respect either for the Worker or for his Work.'

Teilhard envisaged the work of creation in two phases. The first, quasi-organic, resulted in the appearance of pure multiplicity—which was the antagonistic effect of the divine unity; the second was the quasi-organic unification of the multiple—in other words, creation as generally understood. From this he went on to consider the relation of quantity to quality, and again the image of the pyramid served his turn. Just as the height of a pyramid depended on the breadth of its base, and the angle of its summit was proportionately sharper, so the created being was more spiritual in proportion to the multiplicity of elements concentrated in itself. In the same way the sheer immensity of the cosmos, so far from being a useless expenditure of space, was 'an organic condition of our thinking faculties'; and the immensity of time was 'a function of the immensity of space'. The apparently unending sequence of the centuries was as necessary to the simplicity of the soul as the profusion of the stars. The infinite abyss into which Pascal had gazed with terror only confirmed Teilhard in the security of his belief. Quality was 'the daughter of quantity', and essentially superior to it. There was no virtue in numbers; true power lay in their reduction. The 'multitude' had pre-existed in the 'positive nothingness', and the work of creation had been to unify them. 'A real multiplication ... which increased the *absolute* number of existing beings would be a return to plurality and division', and the perfection of the universe would be correspondingly diminished.

In *La Vie Cosmique* Teilhard had envisaged human beings as connected one with another by the forces of matter, but now he saw the vital passage from the merely sentient to the reflective as the effect not of matter but of mind. 'It is the soul—not, strictly speaking, the body—which holds the monads together.' This had important moral consequences, since it determined the significance of sexual love and explained its aberrations. The purpose of love was union, but it was only too clear that the purest affection could degenerate into the grossest forms of physical congress. Experience condemned a method of union which led both to the 'disappointment and irritation of desire, and then to its impotent and disgusted satiety'. The more two people sought to be united on a lower plane, the further they were torn apart. Their true *rapprochement* could only be found in a love which tended to their mutual spiritualization, a love less concerned with their mutual possession than with their convergence towards the same centre of divine unity. Human love, to be sure, could no more dispense with its material basis than the soul could dispense with the body, but the contact which it sought would be the closer and the more specific in proportion to its spirituality. This brought Teilhard to define the complementary rôles of chastity and charity:

> Chastity, in its warfare with the disintegrating forces of being, maintains and promotes, in their state of laborious coherence, the elements of spirit. *It unifies the monad in itself.* Charity, on the other hand, prevents the confinement of human energies in a selfish folding-back upon themselves. It loosens them, opens them out, and places them at the service of other people. ... *It unifies the monads one with another.*

The unity of the individual was only a step towards the union of the whole universe with Christ, and in this sense it was no more than provisional. The creative synthesis would exact its sacrifice of harmful or irrelevant attachments; segregation was the corollary to aggregation; moral effort was inevitably painful; and death was the accompaniment of change, for the better or the worse. But while for some it was a death *ad mortem*—a definitive decomposition—for others it was a recomposition leading to a higher life. By elevating humanity to the life of grace, the Incarnation had released a dynamism in the physical world which would restore everything to Jesus. In him was the 'Plenitude of the Universe'—the fulfilment of creation in unity—the accomplishment of the '*union créatrice*'. Like the ancient philosophies, this was more than 'a logical system satisfying to the mind'; it was a 'unique way of living and understanding all things'.

Teilhard discussed these ideas in correspondence with Valensin and Charles. He found Charles too scholastic; here the possibilities of creation seemed to correspond to 'a group of abstract characters, reconcilable one with another, without taking any account of the physical conditions under which they could be realized . . . this seems to me to belong to the world of geometry, not of reality'. Beside the 'intellectual' possibilities, the physical possibilities had also to be considered. In other words, a being could not exist 'outside certain laws of development, and certain associations with a multiple. By virtue of the laws of physical possibility, God has not only to *choose* the ends of his action among a group of entities coherent among themselves and in themselves; he is also obliged to set in motion the development of a whole universe in order to produce a being—an individual—he has determined to create.' Teilhard did not imagine the multiple as having

the consistency of a *co-eternal antagonist*, but the consistency of an essential and primordial stage (in the work of creation). At the very origin of the creative act, there was not a substantial base (of stuff or matter), but there was a gate, a channel, a necessary entry . . . and this already reduces considerably, as it seems to me, the rather childish and arbitrary way in which scholasticism conceives the creative act.

Teilhard did not formally deny the notion of creation *ex nihilo*; he only questioned its 'historical and experimental application'. It was merely—for want of a better word—a way of expressing the total dependence of the universe on God.[1]

---

[1] Letter to Valensin, 19 November 1917.

La Nostalgie du Front resumed Teilhard's feelings about the war very much as he had expressed them in letters to Marguerite Teillard-Chambon. It was at once retrospective and prophetic. He looked back to the journeys he had taken as a child, and to those he dreamt of taking in the future. The devastated ridge of a hill in front of him was easily translated into some desert plateau of the Orient. The waters of the Aisne dissolved into the waters of the Nile and whispered their tropical appeal. What was it, this 'enigmatic and importunate self', that so loved the line of battle? It was the 'self of adventure and discovery that was always longing to go to the extreme limits of the world, in quest of visions new and rare, and to announce what is ahead'. Teilhard could not have resumed his vocation more exactly.

So far from dreading his first advance to the trenches, he was not only curious as to what the experience would bring him but envious of those already inured to it. Whenever his regiment was withdrawn from the front line he could not understand why those who worked in the rear—the ambulance drivers, chauffeurs, and radio technicians —were not as curious and envious as he. He proposed the paradox— and proposed it without fear of contradiction—that to go up into the line was to go forward into peace. This sensation of peace was in fact a sensation of liberty. One night in particular he called to mind. Among the poplar trees, not far ahead, there still lingered the deadly aroma of poison gas; a bomb exploded in the wood; but the crickets continued to chirp, and Teilhard could wander at will, picking up a stray apple, and sleeping in the first shell hole that took his fancy. He had not forgotten the interests and anxieties which normally beset him, but he saw them in a new light and a more distant perspective. He was their master; and he described the sensation as one of 'inexplicable lightheartedness'.

But these were only the negative aspects of a more positive and creative liberty. The material and spiritual forces that the war had unleashed were an appeal to life, even though they were often a vocation to death—they engaged the last ounce of human energies. This freedom was a liberation of powers usually dormant for want of space for their expansion. As he wrote his essay in the rear, Teilhard felt that he had travelled an immense distance: 'I feel as if I had lost a Soul, a Soul greater than my own that inhabits the front line, and I feel that I have left it there.' He had left it in the plain of Yperlé, or on the calcined slopes of Souville. 'All the enchantments of the East, all the spiritual warmth of Paris, are not worth the mud of Douaumont.' This great humanist was the most human, but in a sense the least humanitarian, of men. Perceiving in the engines of war a concrete, though still crude, expression of the *élan vital*—the need to attack and to conquer— Teilhard was feeling his way towards his prophecy of twenty years later:

> May the moment come when the man in the street will under-stand that there is less poetry in a cannon than in a powerful in-strument designed to split the atom. That will be the decisive hour for mankind, when the spirit of discovery will absorb all the living force contained in the spirit of war.[1]

The hour, when it came, was decisive enough in all conscience; but even Teilhard seemed not to suspect that in this matter the Spirit of Discovery and the Spirit of War would be at one.

Only in the last paragraph of *La Nostalgie du Front* did he adventure on to a quasi-mystical terrain—and this paragraph was suppressed by the editor of *Études*. It seemed to Teilhard, as he took a last look backward at the crest of the Chemin des Dames, that the 'sacred line . . . assumed the form of something superior and very noble, which I was conscious of taking shape under my eyes but which only a spirit finer than my own could have mastered and understood. I felt, at that moment and in face of this Thing in process of formation, like an animal whose soul awakes to perceive groups of connected realities but cannot grasp the link which will explain their meaning.' The impression came to him 'in a flash of uncompleted intuition', and once again we are on the border-line between imagination and mystical insight. Did Teilhard really see something, or did he vividly imagine what he might have seen? In any case, what he saw or imagined that he saw was wholly consonant with his vision of a world that was reshaping itself by ordeal of battle.

In January 1918 Teilhard composed *L'Âme du Monde*. Here the title begged the rather big question as to how far one could speak, with any precision, about 'the soul of the world'. In Teilhard's later writings the phrase disappears, but in 1918 he was struck by the religious character of so many secular aspirations; the best minds of his time seemed to find Christianity too selfish for their altruism. Charity was

[1] *L'Énergie Humaine* (1937).

not dead in them, but it looked elsewhere for its source and its sanction. It was seeking a 'reality more pure, more human, more elevated—an "Anti-Christ" whom it could passionately love'. This 'schism in charity' was a fact with which the Church would have to reckon, and the sum of these aspirations, closely linked as they were one with another, was what Teilhard meant when he wrote—inexactly—of the 'soul of the world'. The poets and the mystics had understood and expressed it; and science in discovering the inexhaustible energies of matter had revealed the unsuspected powers of a universe of which man was a part—a universe which, like man himself, had been created and redeemed and was awaiting its consummation in Christ. Teilhard appealed to the basic principles of revelation to show that 'Christ and the Soul of the World are not two opposed and independent realities, nor are they adequately to be distinguished *in natura rerum*, but that the one is the milieu in which we are transformed into the Other'. Teilhard was again looking forward to the elaboration of his theory in *Le Milieu Divin*, and to his conception of the *noosphère*—a conception less open to theological objection than 'the soul of the world'. Teilhard often gave the impression of carrying his handsome head in clouds higher than a normal eye could reach; but in fact he had his feet so firmly fixed in the contemporary situation that he was always ready to open his flank if he could meet what he considered a contemporary need:

> We have been taking pains to construct and to adorn a universe of theology and piety, and in our absorption with this work of esoteric arrangement we have failed to notice how quickly we have lost our attraction for the mass of human beings, because we seemed to be building our city in the clouds.

Teilhard de Chardin had his eye fixed so constantly on the point Omega of an unimaginable future that he could afford the accusation of bringing Christianity down to earth. In a sense that was where Christianity belonged.

Only a month later he completed *La Grande Monade*—described as a '*fantaisie sérieuse—au clair de lune*'. Watching the moon rise above trenches and its light filter across the coils of barbed wire, he saluted it as a 'symbolic star' prefiguring a new earth more conscious of itself and more unified—which was even now coming to birth in the trenches in front of him. For it was in the struggle against itself that humanity was achieving its solidarity; this was the law of secular strife and progress. But the moon was also the symbol of loneliness and death; it came to resemble the whitened skull which was the object of the ascetic's contemplation. Humanity would grow and multiply, but as its powers expanded it would find itself 'bound to a corpse'. The stiff crust of the moon's unchanging outline was a mocking reminder of the prison-house in which all human effort was confined. 'The only true death, the only good death', Teilhard wrote, was 'a paroxysm of life'; and it could only be achieved 'by a desperate effort of the living towards a greater purity, a greater dispossession of self, and a greater reaching out beyond the zone of its confinement. Happy is the world which comes to an end in ecstasy!' But for all that, our isolation was only partial. There was an outer circle, so to speak, which embraced everything and imprisoned nothing. This was the centre and the sphere of divinity incarnate in Christ who, in the words of St. Gregory the Great 'remains within everything and beyond everything, and below everything'. The complementary doctrines of immanence and transcendence had never received a more classic definition.

Teilhard's next essay has a particular biographical interest. He entitled it *L'Éternel Féminin*, and it is the only one of these early writings to carry a dedication as distinct from an epigraph. The connection is plain between the *Béatrix* of the dedication and the Beatrice of the Divine Comedy—a figure in whom Teilhard's vision of *le féminin* is made luminously clear; and the emotional resonance of the essay—or poem, for that is what it really is—will hardly escape the sensitive ear. It is woman who speaks in the person of eternal Wisdom, taking her text from the Book of Proverbs: *'ab initio creata sum'*.[1] She is also the *Ewig-Weibliche* of Goethe's *Faust*; the 'charm' introduced into the world to assist its grouping, and the 'ideal suspended above it' to encourage its ascent. She is always a few steps ahead of it, and 'the appropriate form of its beatitude'. She is the cause of violence in man who thinks he has found in her a companion, only to discover that in touching her he has touched the secret forces of life. Here are the 'innumerable smiles' that Aeschylus had seen rippling on the waves of the sea; and in her is the attraction of a 'universal presence'. But her knowledge is the knowledge of good and evil, and from the moment that man mistakes her for his 'personal universe' and attempts to en-

---

[1] 'I was created from the beginning.'

circle her in a world sufficient to itself, she escapes his grasp. She is the key that opens the way to the future, and it is man's besetting temptation to use her as a key to close the door upon the present. In proportion as he seeks her for his pleasure, the further he will stray from her reality. For a long time he was in two minds whether to fear or to adore her—for she was at once 'his force and his weakness, his hope and his ordeal'; and perhaps the desire which she inspired in him would have corrupted her beyond repair if Christ had not come for their redemption.

Teilhard was not frightened by the Pauline counsel that it was 'better to marry than to burn, and best not to marry at all', because he saw in the Christian ideal of virginity a principle of fecundity, not impoverishment. Here was the supreme crystallization of feminine power, the most radiant manifestation of its charm—'Christ has left men all his jewels'. The Blessed Virgin was both woman and mother; the Eternal Feminine remade; she was 'the incorruptible beauty of the times to come', the Bride of Christ, the Church which he had founded. Both the thought and style of *L'Éternel Féminin* are very reminiscent of Claudel, who more than once celebrated the mystical unity of the Church and the Blessed Virgin. As in Claudel, the eloquence breaks in irregular waves of rhapsody under the stress of emotion mastered by mind.

Even the friends to whom Teilhard had sent his writings were disconcerted, in varying degrees, by his ideas; and it was to explain these ideas more precisely to himself and to facilitate their correction by others that he set about the composition of *Mon Univers*. He looked back to his childhood and the 'stones' he had collected at Sarcenat. He was still only happy in the possession, or the contemplation, of consistent and unchanging things. His passion for natural phenomena was less scientific than religious, and in comparison with the universe and its limitless potentialities, the agitations of humanity seemed of very small account. Human activity was completely satisfying only when it went hand in hand with the movement of the cosmos towards its own perfection:

> All the problem, all the interest and charm of my interior life, have consisted, and still consist, in the joining together, or more exactly, the coincidence, within myself of the influences coming to me from the one Centre and the other (God and the World).

So it was that God came to appear as a prolongation, an expansion, of the attributes—'grandeur, intimacy, unity'—which had exercised their attraction upon Teilhard when he saw them reflected in the universe; and a Christ who was not in some sense coextensive with the universe would seem smaller than reality. In that case, 'the God of our faith would appear less great and less dominant than the universe of our experience'. If, however, the natural and the supernatural spheres of being were conceived not as independent or antagonistic but as linked, hierarchically, one to the other, then the natural could be sublimated by the supernatural without prejudice to its proper, though limited, autonomy. Teilhard imagined the concurrence of grace and natural human effort 'each playing its essential part, in the development of a spirit (or mind) which would continue to take shape in its natural substance at the same time that God was raising it to the order of the supernatural'. The world, thus conceived, would no longer be a mere terrain of activity; it would be 'a *work* asking for accomplishment'.

Teilhard was careful to protect himself from the accusation of hedonism. 'Every aspiration towards the beautiful and the good' must be captured for God, but it also followed that there was no progress either on the natural or the supernatural plane without hard work and renunciation, and that all natural development was subordinate to the rule of God. It also followed that the centre of gravity of human effort would gradually shift towards spiritual occupations, in the degree to which certain lower forms of activity were left behind, their usefulness exhausted. Teilhard was sensitive to the criticism which his theory of '*union créatrice*' had encountered, and he did not pretend to meet all its difficulties. He was trying to elaborate a 'philosophy of union', to discover by what law everything was transformed *in ipso et per ipsum*. This was classical doctrine. The Pseudo-Dionysus had spoken of God as 'incomprehensible and inaccessible, yet at the same time intimate and close'; and for St. Bernard he belonged 'both to himself and to everything'. The theory of '*union créatrice*' resolved— or so it seemed to Teilhard—the conflict between monist and pluralist tendencies in minds which felt a *real* need to understand the world, for the unity of the world was achieved by the individualization of the men and women who lived in it. The same theory resolved the tension between matter and spirit; and Teilhard recognized in the capture by the soul of those material attributes which most attracted him 'one of the recent, and substantial, advances in my thought'.

So much for philosophy; but Teilhard was more adept in the ways of mysticism than philosophy, and here the theory of '*union créatrice*' appealed to him because it brought the whole movement of the world into an act of communion. For him, the best philosophy would always be the philosophy which allowed him most effectively to 'feel' the presence of Christ 'necessarily and everywhere'. He was less concerned to find a metaphysical solution to the mystery of the universe than to discover 'an historical and practical shape for the developments of Creation'; and the '*union créatrice*' seemed to him the '*apparent* and empirical law governing the sanctification and perfecting of creatures'. The spectre of Christian dualism continued to haunt him. How should one reconcile a 'renunciation of the world and the attachment to the earth indispensable to human effort'? How should the soul escape being caught in a trap between the claims of two absolutes—'the absolute of experience and the absolute of revelation'? Moreover the tendency towards pantheism was so widespread and so tenacious that it must surely contain a core of truth susceptible of baptism. Teilhard maintained that whatever might appear 'forced or risky or peculiar' in his writings was derived from the most authentic articles of Christian belief provided one 'took the trouble to see these doctrines as a whole', not merely in a formula of words but in 'a coherent *reality*'. He recognized that, both in theory and practice, one ran the danger 'of eclipsing or materializing God in one's aggrandizement of the universe'; and of 'utilizing the resources and natural affections of life for the purpose of a pagan profit and pleasure'. But these were dangers which Catholic good sense and Christian prudence might avoid, and Teilhard de Chardin was not lacking in either.

III

Le Prêtre, written shortly before he took his solemn vows, summed up the whole sense of his priesthood, and his vocation to a world which believed it could dispense with Christ. He would be the first to take cognizance of the world's travail and aspirations; the first to suffer, to sympathize and to search; the first to sacrifice himself, in becoming 'more broadly human and more nobly of this earth than any servant of the world'. Meditating once more upon his vows, he resolved to recover in the very act of renunciation 'whatever of heavenly flame might be contained in the triple concupiscence; to sanctify in chastity, poverty, and obedience the power residing in love and gold and independence'. Here the last word is significant. Teilhard did not understand by obedience the abandonment of liberty, but rather its exercise in a special relationship with others. The *nuance* will become important as the obligations of obedience are subjected to strain.

The elements of the Eucharist recalled him to the delights of labour, and their transubstantiation to the pains of death—to the 'life which increases man so that he may be capable of sanctification, and the death which diminishes him in order that he may be sanctified'. This was the mystery and the meaning of the chalice—that the blood of Jesus should be mingled with the suffering of the world. It is true that Teilhard felt the travail of the cosmos in the deepest fibres of his being, and to that extent was the apostle of an activist spirituality, but his activity was passive to the guidance of grace. 'It is you that work upon me, Lord; you that change me into yourself.' This invasion of divinity, ever more dense, more close and more ubiquitous, was the '*Fiat, Fiat*' of Teilhard de Chardin's sacerdotal prayer—a prayer directly inspired by the stress under which it was written. 'Thank you, my God, for making me a priest—*for the War!*'

One of his favourite texts for meditation—there are many references to it in his notes for retreat—was the passage in which Peter is invited by Christ to come to him across the waters of the lake; 'Why do you hesitate, O man of little faith?' In his next essay—*La Foi qui opère*—Teilhard examined the character of his own belief in contrast, or in complement, to the varieties of secular belief that he saw around him. Man, in his earthly condition, was suspended above an abyss; necessity and contingence yawned on either side of him, and he must find a cure for his giddiness. If he looked ahead, instead of round and about, death was at the end of his perspective. Teilhard knew, better than many, what he was talking about. 'Those who have never had a narrow escape from death have an incomplete notion of what lies in front of them.' The aim of the scientist, with no faith in anything but his own knowledge and the instruments of his discovery, was to shape the future by these means alone; and he dismissed as visionaries those who believed that the future could be affected by the will and the action of the human psyche. Against this 'scientism' Teilhard opposed the doctrine of *audaces fortuna juvat*—'fortune favours the bold'—a counsel which the common sense of mankind had long ago deduced from its experience and used in answer to a mechanical determinism. The mistake of the naturalist was to seek a transformation of the 'experimental universe' alone, and to imagine that this could be effected by only human agency. Teilhard did not neglect such recent phenomena as faith healing and Christian Science, but these rested upon a 'purely nominal supernaturalism' in which Christ was not the end but the means. As the instruments of a definitive salvation, they were quite inadequate to their task.

In resting firmly on the promise of Christ that 'whatever you ask shall be granted you', Teilhard understood these words in the sense that 'the providential government of the universe visible to each individual soul is ordained to a heavenly, not a temporal, fulfilment. Even when we are exercising all our faculties of belief, Fortune will not necessarily turn out in the way *we want* but in the way *it must*'. Faith did not normally break any particular determinism or deflect events from their natural course, but it could—under the impetus of prayer—force them into a new combination. Christianity did not necessarily succeed on the level of 'natural human success, but on the level of supernatural sanctification'. God was at once the agent and the source of Christian belief and the *milieu*—the context—in which it was exercised. But Teilhard was careful to distinguish it from the 'idle Lutheran abandonment', since it used science for the verification of knowledge and fortified itself with all the dynamism of the will. It was as 'industrious as if the whole future depended on its calculated prevision'; and it justified the popular adage that 'heaven helps those who help themselves'. The Christian must believe so boldly in the virtue of death that life would spring from its shadow. This was what it meant to go confidently forward with Peter when Christ stretched out his hand across the water.

After the celebration of the armistice in November 1918 Teilhard was given a room in the Grand Séminaire at Strasbourg. Here he spent the greater part of his time, except for sleeping and meals; and it was here, in the last three weeks of December, that he composed the *Forma Christi*. Each morning, before settling down to work, he meditated in the cathedral close by, discerning in the interplay of column and vaulting, and in the radiance of glass, a current of life, both practical and mystical, which was analogous to the synthesis he was trying to construct in his own mind. He was concerned, once again, to counteract the tendencies of a Christianity 'too extrinsic and particularist', a dogmatic structure which seemed to have no attachment to the universe. It was not surprising that men in close touch with concrete reality found the Christian revelation 'cold and infantile' if they were only shown its 'scholastic and disciplinary aspects'. This led Teilhard to consider the 'dual respiration' of Christian asceticism, its active and passive functioning. After an initial period of retreat—Teilhard may well have been thinking of his own Ignatian formation—the converted soul was bound to 'plunge into the midst of things, and let itself be carried away by the life-enhancing passion for research, discovery and creation'. But this would gradually inspire the taste—not merely impose the necessity—for renunciation. First of all because the effort demanded by the natural evolution of the world was both 'mortifying and disinterested'; secondly because the desire for attachment to a totality 'vaster and ever vaster' accustomed the soul to relinquish its hold on the petty and the particular; thirdly because 'the insurmountable limits of life in the body would make it long for the liberation of death'. By this triple education the soul would no sooner arrive at the heart of things than it would feel the urge to escape from them. It was at this point, and working upon this natural aptitude for growth and self-abandonment, that Christ—so to speak—took the place of the aspiring soul. It was a moment painful for the lower nature of man conscious of his diminishing powers; but for the man of faith, it was a moment of delight. One 'had to have loved the world a great deal to feel the need of getting beyond it', and it was for want of this love that religion had become anaemic. In preaching renunciation for the wrong reasons, it had lost the power to practise it for the right ones.

These two components of the interior life—spiritual growth and natural diminution in Christ—were not mutually exclusive. They might be alternating or simultaneous, directed towards a 'mobile and supple equilibrium'. The action of Christ in his 'information' of the universe was at once a cosmic and a personal possession, restricted only by the recalcitrance of human liberties. Finally Teilhard broached the article of Christian faith most difficult to imagine, if not to believe—the resurrection of the body. He saw this as a 'cosmic rather than individual phenomenon', and for this reason its apparition was plausibly postponed until the end of time. But here and now, 'thanks to an immense sum of infinitesimal efforts, and the accumulated effect of good desires and good communions, an indestructible world is in course of construction by our souls and bodies, under the shelter of Christ incarnate'. In so far as the universe of monads was moulded in the '*forma Christi*', it would assume, in its eventual perfection, the shape and substance of his body as well as his soul.

No doubt these early essays of Teilhard are repetitive and to some degree imprecise. Each is carefully organized, but in their sum they are redundant, and their effect is occasionally rhapsodic. To read them is to be reminded of music where now one theme, and now another, is taken up and developed, and where the same theme constantly recurs. They belong to the order of poetry and meditation, less exactly to the order of analysis. Naturally Teilhard's ideas are debatable—'as if one could write anything entirely undebatable without repeating what has been said already'.[1] His explanations of original sin or the creative act are not unquestionably orthodox; nor, in the view of many, are they satisfying to the mind. But it is through debate—often very heated and prolonged—that orthodoxy arrives at its conclusions; and as the debate goes on, Teilhard's views on creation and culpability are already being taken into serious account. It remains to add that only one of these essays was published in the author's lifetime. Claude Cuénot has compared Teilhard to Gerard Manley Hopkins; in this respect, as in some others, the comparison is just.

[1] Letter to Bruno de Solages, 26 May 1950.

CHAPTER V

COMING TO GRIPS

TEILHARD was lodged in the village of Honheim, on the outskirts of Strasbourg, and well looked after by Sisters of the Congregation of Ribeauvillé. He slept under an eiderdown and was nourished on cakes and kirsch. Both Clemenceau and Poincaré paid triumphal visits to the liberated city, but Teilhard was soon beginning to talk about 'the disappointments of the peace'. Early in February 1919 he was moved to Goldscheuer on the eastern bank of the Rhine. Ducks, pheasants and hares swarmed in the marshes, and the Black Forest was only twenty kilometres away. Here he had abundant leisure to read and write, and was now at work on three new essays. The first of these[1] was not designed for publication. It was a memorandum for his superiors, and in it he expressed, rather more brutally, the ideas he had already sketched out in *La Maîtrise du Monde et le Règne de Dieu*. With the authority of experience, if not of years, behind him he pleaded that if St. Ignatius were right in reminding the Christian of his duty to 'feel with Mother Church', it was equally the duty of Mother Church 'to feel with mankind'. It was ridiculous for the clergy to spend their time in the 'beatification of a Servant of God', in the propagation of special devotions, and on the minutiae of funeral rites, when they should be preaching and practising 'the Gospel of human effort'. The present business of the Church was to meet the reproach that it produced 'souls interested in their own selfish advantage, uninterested in the common task; and therefore uninteresting' to those inspired by a new morality—which accorded a primacy of 'justice over charity, and labour over detachment', and held that it was better to develop the human faculties than to mortify them. The Christian and the human ideals no longer coincided; this was the 'great schism' which now threatened the Church. Teilhard asked for priests who

[1] *Note pour servir à l'évangelisation des temps nouveaux.*

99

would devote themselves to science or sociology as a part of their vocation, and who would not be afraid to let their fellow-workers see that they too experienced 'the richness and the anguish of doubt'.

He may have described his text as a memorandum, but it reads more like a manifesto. Those who converted, or perverted, mankind —he announced in an epigraph—were those 'in whom the soul of their time burned most intensely'. He observed in his contemporaries 'a *natural* religious impulse' very strongly at work, but these men and women could only be reached 'through their own ideal and by seeking in common with them the God that we already possess but who is present among us as if we didn't recognize him'. The God awaited by the twentieth century must be a deity 'as *vast* and mysterious' as the cosmos itself; as 'immediate as life' itself; and as 'linked *to our own effort* as humanity' itself. It was not too late, in this January of 1919, for Teilhard to quote Woodrow Wilson for his purpose: 'I have the feeling that the time has come for people to forget their local attachments and to unite in a grand enterprise in which free men will be united for good and all.' The current notions of asceticism must be enlarged— without in the least diminishing the doctrine of the Cross—to include all the dynamism of which man was capable; for charity and chastity, rightly understood, were both forms of human activity and love. Nowhere does Teilhard show himself more in advance of his time than in this brief and ardent essay; this is how men were thinking—and even daring to speak and write—in the liberated Paris of 1944.

The title of the second essay—*Terre Promise*—was quasi-ironical because it was already clear that the victorious Allies were not entering upon a promised land; financial chicanery and political horse-dealing were making a mockery of so much effort and sacrifice. Nevertheless Teilhard clung to his experience of the *union sacrée* which had shown how men could reach a level of higher spirituality when their individual faculties were exalted in collective action. It was a momentary resurgence, no doubt; but it held out the hope that an ephemeral effort called forth by the war and mobilized against evil might open the way to a lasting effort in the promotion of good. So far Teilhard was reasoning like any other disappointed spectator of affairs, resisting the temptation of an easy cynicism. When he reasoned as a Christian, he argued that if Christ had come to earth in the time of Moses or Abraham, it was unlikely that anyone would have understood him at all. Even now they understood him imperfectly, for want of that extra degree of moral sensibility which would complete their humanity and make them naturally responsive to the divine appeal. Teilhard, for his part, would go forward into the future stronger in his double faith as a Christian and a man: for, in spite of everything, he had stood 'on the mountain and caught a glimpse of the Promised Land'.

L'Élément Universel, composed about the same time, was also not intended for publication. It was the most concentrated exposition he had as yet made of his doctrine. As he worked on it, he remembered how his sister Françoise had emphasized the reality of God, and the importance of this reality in her own life of service and self-effacement. Perhaps, he now thought, they had been more like each other than he had ever realized—with this difference that the realities of earthly life must inevitably occupy a larger place in his life than they had in hers. He measured the distance he had travelled since *La Vie Cosmique*; admitted that his preoccupations were the same; but felt that they were now better organized and digested. He began by criticizing the pantheist solution, which was a doctrine of absolute immanence. Everything was identical with God. But this was, rationally speaking, unthinkable because it presupposed the alliance of 'two contradictory properties, necessity and contingence'. Nor did it satisfy, in practice, the aspirations of a 'cosmic conscience' which felt the need to give itself to something else—since there could be no such submission where each part was equal to the others in dignity, and where the whole was no more than an aggregate of these parate parts drawn together by the force of some internal attraction. Nor could there be any question of union, since union presupposed the unification of distinct entities.

Teilhard then outlined the three stages by which he himself had resolved the problem of going to God with 'the total sincerity and plenitude of an irremediably cosmic soul'. First he had recognized the 'immediate and tangible reality of a divine will' animating the universe, and also the reality of something in the universe itself between himself and God, other than 'a perpetual and universal contact in action and abandonment'. Secondly—and here he relied upon dogma as well as instinct—he came to recognize the creative action of God in everything that moved or existed. St. Ignatius had developed similar ideas in his *Meditatio ad amorem*. But there still remained between the soul and God 'a hiatus, a gap, a coldness—the distance separating the necessary being' from the being that shared its life. The soul was conscious of its juxtaposition to God, not of its union with him. It was only after writing *Le Milieu Mystique* that Teilhard discovered his missing term which he called 'the cosmic influence of Christ'. This was the 'universal element', and this was what St. Paul had meant by the pleroma; for Christ was not only the head of the body—which was the Church—but the head of all creation. Here was the corrective to Teilhard's ambiguous conception of 'the soul of the world'; the vivifying action of Christ had taken its place. And here were reconciled the opposing tendencies of human thought and effort, since it was through assisting the world to its fulfilment that one came to Christ. In searching for a definition Teilhard fell back, with unconscious irony, on a word which would eventually become the watchword of his adversaries and was already a synonym for the rearguard actions of Catholic thought—*intégrisme*.

As he looked for the right point at which to direct his personal effort, he was encouraged by de Grandmaison's approbation of *Terre Promise* where the belief in Progress—with its capital letter—had a more generous deal than it normally received from Catholic writers of that time. We shall only understand Teilhard's difficult relation to Catholic authority if we take into account the difference, temperamental as well as theological, between those who think it more important that man is fallen and those who think it more important that he is redeemed. It is a difference of emphasis, not of doctrine. Teilhard questioned no article of Catholic belief, but he placed these beliefs in such a new and personal perspective that their official custodians were alarmed. Possessing his soul in patience, he was cheered by a letter from Charles, who was a better theologian than Teilhard and was beginning to exert a powerful influence at Louvain. Teilhard would henceforward rely upon his judgment as well as on his moral support.

A letter from his superior towards the end of February 1919 suggested that he should move to Paris as soon as possible and devote himself to geology, even if he were not teaching at the Institut Catholique. He was demobilized on 10 March, and was soon back at his old quarters in the Rue du Vieux-Colombier, already dreaming of composing a 'hymn' to the 'spiritual power of matter'. On this Good Friday of 1919 he went to hear the singing at St.-Germain-l'Auxerrois, and afterwards made the Stations of the Cross there; and on the following day he finished *Les Noms de la Matière*, a short introduction to the Hymn which was already taking shape in his mind. Everything was looking a little different from Paris, particularly in the direction of Versailles, where President Wilson's *gaffes* were stacking the cards heavily against optimism. In conversation with his Jesuit colleagues, Teilhard sometimes found it difficult to hold his own.

Teilhard reviewed matter under several different aspects. It was that which made a being capable of union with other beings, and Teilhard described this as 'formal' to distinguish it from 'concrete' matter where the potentiality of union did not yet exist. 'Universal' matter was the sum total of elements destined for eventual unification, as distinct from 'total matter' where the elements of the world were allied to the sum total of the links converging on to mind (or spirit). Teilhard then considered matter as 'relative', or inferior, to mind. Here the vegetable was regarded as 'relatively material' in comparison with the animal, and man was 'relatively spiritual'. For every sentient being the important 'matter' was whatever thing—less unified than itself—dominated and surrounded it. In human nature matter was either 'live' and therefore capable of spiritualization and union, or 'dead' and therefore an agent of disintegration. This led Teilhard to some interesting reflections on the doctrine of original sin, which bring us very close to Newman's 'aboriginal calamity':

> The spectacle of this evil and painful plurality, abandoned like so much rubbish by the world, easily explains the idea—so persistent in the human race—that the original multiplicity of the cosmos is the evidence of some pre-cosmic fall 'as a result of which a Spirit crumbled away'. In the light of this hypothesis the laborious *evolution* we experience would be the expiatory phase following on a culpable *involution*. There is surely a profound . . . analogy between these beliefs—and they are often bizarre—and the dogma of original sin. . . . From the Christian point of view the tendency to pluralism, mixed in the manner of a temptation with all our struggles towards unification, represents in effect a real *decline*, an evil *crease*, the *memory* of some former state. And this positive tendency to retrogression is complicated by the equally positive part played by the powers of darkness.

Distinct from matter 'live' and 'dead', or decomposing, there was the matter—which Teilhard defined as 'new' or 'secondary'—resulting, not from sin or retrogression, but from the 'normal and progressive play of spiritual activity'. Something independent of us came to birth in the course of our activity, something stronger than ourselves, and we should do wrong to cry out against it. We were the 'slaves of our own liberty'. 'Interior automatisms' or 'external situations' were the conditions of progress and the better organization of human beings; they were the 'skeleton' around which the spiritual organism of the world would take its shape. But they were only transitory.

> From the midst of matter not yet spiritualized, and from the depth of spirit in the way of continual materialization, the aspiration of mankind has never varied: 'Who will deliver me from the body of this death?'

How would this liberation take place? The 'live' matter would free itself from the accidents of pluralism, and the 'dead' matter would be segregated in the fullness of time—the 'irreducible wastage of the universal salvific operation'. Here was Teilhard's vision of the Last Judgment which he acknowledged to be a 'fearful mystery'. As for the contingent matter—the tissue of habits and circumstances which have formed the envelope of our earthly life—we shall shed these like a chrysalis, but enough of them will remain even in our separated souls to form the matter of an eventual resurrection. These souls will still feel the necessity of union but they can only unite in a way which 'integrally reflects their own history'; and so long as their attachment to matter remains broken this union is impossible. Was it not conceivable that in activating their need for union, God would 'reconstitute in an identical cosmos this dust of floating monads according to the particular texture of each'? Having achieved this solidarity one with another in accordance with the law of their origin and their existence on earth, they would have resumed possession of a body and a universe that was theirs. Here, within the limits of orthodoxy but reaching far beyond any orthodox formulation, was Teilhard's vision of the resurrection of the flesh. It was not for nothing, as we shall see, that he prayed to be 'delivered from the body of this death' on Easter Sunday—and that the wish was granted him.

II

The month of August 1919 was spent agreeably at Bon Secours with Charles and Valensin for companions. Valensin was deep in the study of pantheism. He admitted that the universe formed a natural whole, and only subsisted in dependence upon Christ. But for Valensin the question was primarily intellectual; he was concerned to build a philosophy where Teilhard was concerned to venerate a presence. Their thought was to that extent complementary. Valensin was influenced by the philosophy of Maurice Blondel, and although he could not always follow Blondel in his views on the consistence of the universe in Christ, he told Teilhard that their late, and sadly lamented, friend Père Rousselot had not shared his hesitations. In theological circles Rousselot was already a name to conjure with.

Blondel lived at Aix-en-Provence, and since the Jesuits had their novitiate at Aix it was natural that any young novice philosophically inclined should have fallen, however indirectly, under his influence. As a result of his friendship with Valensin, Teilhard asked his friend to show Blondel some of the essays he had written during and immediately after the war. Their minds were in many ways akin. It was fifteen years since Blondel had written of Christ as the *vinculum perfectionis*.[1] 'Nothing will stop the effort of mankind to integrate Christ in a cosmology; otherwise Jesus would not be the Word', and it was thirty years since he had written to Victor Delbos: 'Christ grows in proportion to the growth of humanity'. Blondel was in agreement with Teilhard's *maximal* Christology. The alternatives, he wrote to Valensin, were 'retrogression towards a destructive symbolism, or advance towards . . . an integral realism which would reconcile the Christian metaphysic with the mysticism experienced by the saints, and even by the faithful'. But he laid his finger on Teilhard's temptation 'to represent the universal function of Christ in too naturalist and physical a way'. We should not 'build a principle of explanation on what our scientific mentality or our anthropomorphic images suggest to us'; nor should we suppose that 'the natural order has a divine stability as such, that Christ plays the same physical rôle that pantheism or monism attribute to the vague and diffused deity with whom they are satisfied'. A 'purely physical supernaturalism' was a contradiction in terms.[2]

Blondel put Teilhard on his guard against 'symbols, images, and

[1] 'Bond of perfection.'
[2] For this exchange of views see *Blondel et Teilhard de Chardin*, with commentary by Henri de Lubac, s.j., Bibliothèque Archives de Philosophie, Vol. XXIV, Cahier I.

specious representations' of an ineffable reality. The true prophet was the opposite of the visionary; he was 'the man who discovers in the darkness of contemplation the infinite richness of mystery'. Scientific and sensible realities were chiefly important for 'the moral decisions, and even the sacrifices', of which they were the occasion and the object. Teilhard, he thought, did not seem to realize that we must enter into communion with Christ 'in his concrete and singular humanity' before trying to find him in the sum total of things. Hence the need for 'testing and abnegation and dispossession'.

Although in one sense there is continuity in the order of the universe, in another there is a measureless gulf between this and the old man and the old nature. Both must be turned upside down before the new heaven and the new earth can be brought into being. . . . Symbols only enshrine an infinitesimal fraction of the truth.

Teilhard replied, through Valensin, that Blondel had only seen his more 'naturalist' essays. He distinguished between three forms of communion—with the earth; with God; and with God through the medium of the earth. Nevertheless, he was grateful for Blondel's correction and was in agreement that Christ must be loved 'like a world, or rather like *the* world; that is to say as the physical centre imposed on whatever part of creation had the right to survival'. He also agreed that '*fundamentally* the consummation of the world can only come about through death'. Where he disagreed was on the mode of renunciation. The drastic counsels of St. John of the Cross were not possible for ordinary people. Moreover our mystical life owed much to 'Plato, Leibniz, Pascal and Newton'; and charity might go to waste 'in a world which had been turned into a monastery'. We must reach out beyond the world and everything in it, and at the same time devote all our energies to its development—and we must do this 'not by rupture but by transformation. The supernatural plenitude of Christ rests upon the natural plenitude of the world'. We had no right to confine ourselves to the exercise of asceticism; the desire for withdrawal might well be the illusion of idleness. 'How to be as Christian as anyone and yet more human than anyone else'—that was the challenge, as Teilhard had expressed it to Fontoynont in the middle of the war. And as for the 'symbols' against which Blondel had warned him, our only road to God was through 'the laborious definition of images, concepts, and *things*'. The constructions of the human mind were none the less essential because they were provisional. For Teilhard Christ was '*something* of a demi-urge—incarnate for no other reason than to hold us in place, and therefore obliged to sustain the natural strata of the world'. Here the scholastic definition of 'a reasonable soul occupying the place of substantial and inferior forms' gave point to Teilhard's argument. In fact, his difference with Blondel was one of emphasis; where Blondel laid his stress upon transcendence, Teilhard put his accent on the physical.

Blondel answered—again through Valensin—that Teilhard oversimplified the doctrine of St. John of the Cross. The mystics had been remarkable 'for their large-heartedness, their practical sense, their clear-sighted prudence, and their effective action'. But for all that, the world could never be 'divinized' without 'the spiritual ferment of the mystical immolation'. Teilhard, he objected, was presenting the immanence of the supernatural 'in a way too physically imaginative', as if the supernatural were only a constitutive element: 'It is not by the fullness of things that we shall reach a salutary void: it is in the void that we shall discover the fullness.' This was classical doctrine, and Teilhard admitted that it was probably more orthodox than his own. Nevertheless he contended that if we had to wait for our mystical union with Christ before taking in hand our earthly tasks we should never begin at all. Concentration in Christ and ex-centration to secular tasks were 'simultaneous movements'. Or, in other words, 'possession of everything in Our Lord' was the final aim; 'pursuit of Our Lord through everything' was the provisional aim. If the 'void' was conceived as the attraction of God, this could only be 'hollowed out', so to speak, from a 'pre-existent fullness'; and the fullness did something more than leave its imprint—it was in some sense assimilated. In life, if not in logic, the notions of fullness and emptiness were not contradictory; the fullness was often the initial form of the void. 'The fruit must be ripe before it bursts open'. But Teilhard recognized that the 'complex and empirical attitude of the Church' contained 'infinitely more of truth than all our simplifying philosophies. The practice of the saints, even when it was difficult to justify in reason', was 'the imposed reality and the concrete truth'.

This very important exchange of views was in essence the confrontation of two temperaments, the one cast in the Thomist, the other in the Augustinian, mould—although we understand Teilhard more clearly if we see him as a follower of Duns Scotus rather than the Angelic Doctor. He was one for whom Christ would have become incarnate, even if mankind had never fallen from grace, in order to conduct it in triumph to a supernatural destiny. The exchange, no doubt, led Teilhard to define his ideas more carefully, and Blondel was to remember it nearly thirty years later. Jules Lachélier had expressed his longing to reconcile Darwin and the Bible, and Blondel commented: 'How Lachélier would have been comforted by the palaeontological science and serene faith of Père Teilhard de Chardin!'[1] Already, in 1919, Blondel could admit that he shared 'the ideas and sentiments of Père Teilhard de Chardin in face of the Christological problem'.[2] And in March 1920 the two met for the first time.

Teilhard was on a visit to Aix, where he had not been since the days of his novitiate. He discussed philosophy with Valensin, and wrote to his cousin

from a large room full of sunshine, paved with little hexagonal red bricks, and in front of me three little dwarf irises which I brought back yesterday from the white and sweet-smelling slopes where I had gone to rediscover what I was like as a novice nineteen years old . . . I find it almost impossible to put myself back into all that I was then, and it almost seems a stranger that I meet in the most familiar corners of the house and countryside. And yet I know that in some obscure way I had then everything that I feel I have today.

I had a long interview with Blondel in his study—a spacious hall, rather dark, with numerous books, and a lot of original detail, and a veritable mass of plants and flowers at the corner of his desk. I talked with him alone—Père Valensin had left us almost at once—for about an hour and a half. I think we understood each other very well—almost too well, because there were none of those fruitful disagreements which set one thinking further. In short I found a man extremely sympathetic, just as I had found him in his letters. We are thinking on exactly the same lines about the need to broaden Christ to the dimensions of an immense new

[1] 26 December 1947.
[2] In a letter, 15 December 1919, quoted by Mooney in *Teilhard de Chardin and the Mystery of Christ*.

datum of which the conservative theologians seem to have no idea.[1]

Teilhard admitted, nevertheless, that he would always be something of a 'philistine for the professional philosophers'. He was still preoccupied with things as much as theories, and during this holiday on Jersey he found a fruitful field of observation in the flowers and fishes of the island.

Thus we find him rummaging among the rocks at low tide and returning with strange and multiform creatures to be studied and dissected at leisure. At other times he worked on his 'Hymn'. This was an allegory in semi-poetic form, inspired by the history of Elias. The whirlwind in which Elias is caught up was the 'matter' which liberated all those who knew how to capture its spiritual power. These, again, were pages for himself and his friends. Nevertheless, they have an extraordinary incandescence and their personal resonance is clear; 'nothing is precious except that part of you which is in other people, and that part of others which is in you. Up there, on high, everything is all one'; 'purity does not lie in a separation from the universe, but in a deeper penetration of it—in a chaste contact with that which is "the same in all things"'; he had pity for those who are 'frightened of their own century, and can only love a single country'. When Elias came down to earth,

> a profound renewal had been wrought in him so that henceforward he could only be Man on another plane . . . he would be a stranger. . . . Even for his brothers in God, better men than himself, he could not help speaking an incomprehensible language, because it had been the Lord's decision that he should go by the way of the fire. Even for those he loved best, his affection would be a burden, for they would not escape the feeling that he was looking for something beyond them.

The essay concluded with the *Hymn*, properly so called. Its completion happily coincided with the feast of the Transfiguration (6 August) which was the feast that Teilhard loved beyond all others. He called down a blessing upon the 'matter' that was at once so rough and so strong, so dangerous and so impenetrable, and yet so mortal at the same time; matter that was the 'sap of the soul, the hand of God, and the flesh of Christ'; matter that reigned 'on the serene summits where the saints imagined they could escape from it', but where it

[1] 28 March 1920.

was 'so mobile and so transparent' that it was no longer distinguishable from spirit. One can easily imagine how these rhapsodies would have disconcerted a censor's eye and Teilhard had reason not to look beyond a private circulation.

Bon Secours closed its doors at the end of the first week in August, and the Jesuits who wished to remain on the island moved over to Maison Saint-Louis. This stood at the head of a little ravine, on the southern shore, leading down to the bay of St. Hélier. The garden was shady with cedars and eucalyptus. Beyond, the reefs of red granite broke the surface of a sea almost mediterranean in its gentle azure. In the near vicinity were a number of Carmels—expelled, like the Jesuits, from France—and it was in one or other of these that Teilhard celebrated his daily Mass. One night he was taken out fishing by an islander of his acquaintance and came back laden with plaice and cuttlefish destined not for the frying-pan but the microscope. An interesting cave had been discovered on the island with some remains of Neanderthal man. The excavations had been undertaken by a certain Dr. Marett, an Oxford professor and friend of Breuil and Boule. Teilhard visited the cave and made the acquaintance of the professor, who was a native of the island. He inhabited an old manor where the souvenirs, patiently accumulated and tastefully displayed, revealed a Jersey that Teilhard hardly knew existed—a Jersey petrified, as it were, in its own past. Teilhard was not insensitive to the charm of such things, and he was sad to see them menaced by social change. A similar nostalgia had been revived in him by a reading of Fromentin's *Dominique*. 'But the future', he wrote to his cousin, 'is more beautiful than all the pasts'; ardently, and now recuperated from the strain of soldiering, he prepared to meet it.

III

On his return to Paris Teilhard resumed the studies which had been interrupted by the war. He was preparing his licentiate in natural sciences at the Sorbonne in company with Pierre Lamare, a geologist from Bordeaux, who became a close friend. He passed from geology to botany and zoology, but seems to have wearied a little of his humdrum academic exercise. More interesting were his sessions at the museum with Boule; Alfred Lacroix, the professor of mineralogy;

and Paul Rivet, who was later to found the Musée de l'Homme. Teilhard was eager for personal contacts, and Rivet remembered the first occasion on which he expounded his plan to Boule. Teilhard was present at the interview, but so violent was Boule's opposition to the project that Rivet paid no attention to the young priest. Scarcely had he returned to his laboratory, however, than Teilhard knocked at the door. He wanted to express his enthusiastic agreement with Rivet; they talked together for a long time; and when Teilhard left they were already fast friends. On another occasion Maurice Barrès was visiting the museum. He asked Boule what effect all these discoveries would have on contemporary religious belief. Boule pointed to Teilhard in a gesture of reassurance.

One night during this same autumn of 1919 Teilhard was dining with Max Bégouën in an apartment behind the church of St. Augustin. They left at 9 p.m. and walked to the métro at the Madeleine. It was cold and rainy. Teilhard began expounding his ideas in reply to Bégouën's sceptical pessimism, admitting that he himself had known his hours of doubt and trouble during the war. They turned back from the métro, walking up and down the stretch of pavement between St. Augustin and the Madeleine and by the time midnight had struck the mists had cleared for Bégouën. 'That evening I was born to life—staggering like Lazarus as he came out of the tomb when the Lord called out to him: "Come forth!"'[1] Bégouën's subsequent career was in Morocco and French Guinea, and his path crossed only rarely with Teilhard's, but he and his wife remained among Teilhard's dearest friends. 'There are few minds I know of so fine, so intelligent and so clear.'[2] Bégouën, for his part, would always remember Teilhard's exhortation to be like a new-born babe in face of life, waking up to the discovery of the world, and to be always *en marche*. 'When God takes me, I pray that he may take me *en marche*.' As we shall see, the prayer was granted.

From Easter 1920 Teilhard set about preparing his doctoral thesis on the mammifers of the Lower Eocene in France, and the layers of soil in which they were found. He had studied the microfauna of Cernay assembled in the museum by Victor Lemoine, and also went to work on the spot with spade and pickaxe. The foundations of his

[1] *La Table Ronde*, June 1955.
[2] Letter to Madame Haardt, 28 December 1934.

thesis had already been laid in the trenches near Rheims, and it was to the hill of Berru, seven kilometres from Rheims, that he now returned. Here he spent seven or eight hours a day of hard manual labour, dressed in a workman's blouse and blue trousers, indistinguishable from any other peasant of Champagne. For this work he was awarded the Prix Viquesnel by the Geological Society of France. It was an important beginning and Boule paid his tribute to

> a penetrating observation, an association—as precious as it is rare —of the taste for analysis with the power of synthesis, and a great independence of mind. M. Teilhard may well have realized, when he communicated the results of his researches to the museum, that it was in the ancient depths of the Quercy caves or in the sands of Cernay that one had to look for the key to a serious knowledge of the distant origins of the human type.

In the same year Teilhard composed his *Note sur le Progrès* in which he argued that 'without biological evolution which produced the brain, there would be no sanctified souls; similarly, without the evolution of collective thought which alone can realize on earth the fullness of human consciousness, could there be a consummated Christ?' Here the activist in Teilhard was at work. 'Essentially progress is a force and the most dangerous of forces. . . . Progress is directed towards fostering in the human will reflective action and fully human choice.' *Science et Christ* followed in 1921. 'Far be it from me', he wrote, 'to think of deducing Christian dogmas from a mere inspection of those qualities which, according to the light of reason, characterize the structure of the world. . . . Science alone cannot discover Christ, but Christ fulfils the desires which spring up in our hearts from the teachings of science.'

In March Teilhard was at Chelles, and he spent Whitsun near Laon, visiting the old battlefields—Ribécourt and the Bois de Laigne. In June we find him at Épernay, and in September at Niaux with the Abbé Breuil and Dorothy Garrod, herself an excellent prehistorian and later professor at Cambridge. She was also a convert to Catholicism, and Teilhard did much to remove such doubts and scruples as still troubled her. His thesis was admitted with 'a very honourable mention' on 5 July 1922 by a jury that was not niggard of its praise, and before an unusually large audience. Teilhard's transformist theories were already adumbrated; and in this respect he was prepared to go further than Boule. Both found themselves in fruitless controversy with Louis Vialleton, an anatomist of great authority who was unable, nevertheless, to look beyond his special discipline.

The contacts multiplied. In August Teilhard attended an international congress at Brussels, where he made the acquaintance of Wong Wen-Hao, co-director of the Geological Service of China—the prologue to a long partnership. Teilhard's article on the structure of the island of Jersey had appeared in 1920 and attracted the attention of the English geologist, Henry Plymen. But more decisive was his friendship with the Abbé Gaudefroy, who occupied the chair of geology at the Institut Catholique. Gaudefroy had been introduced to Teilhard by the Abbé Breuil, who left the two men together on the top storey of 13 Rue du Vieux-Colombier. The interview started badly. Gaudefroy began by saying that he distrusted the Jesuits because they were a secret society; that nobody was allowed to know their rules; and that their mail was opened by their superiors. Teilhard burst out laughing, opened a drawer, and took out the Exercises of St. Ignatius. 'There you are', he said, 'those are my rules. I haven't any others.' This breaking of the ice did more than cement a friendship; it led to a division of the chair, with Gaudefroy teaching mineralogy which was his special subject, and Teilhard teaching geology. He had four students of whom three became professors at the Sorbonne, but the work was not altogether congenial. Teilhard would rather have concentrated on his own research at Beirut or Shanghai, where the French Jesuits had universities; or at Trinchinopoly where they had an important mission. He gave his courses from 1920 to 1923, and the Rector of the Institut, Monseigneur (later Cardinal) Baudrillart, did all he could to keep him there.

Already, however, there were rumblings of the approaching storm. Valensin, Charles and Huby had all suffered from the censure passed at the instigation of Merry del Val—now once more in power as Secretary of the Holy Office—on certain doctrines of Rousselot who was not alive to defend them. Teilhard's association with these men was well known, and when a senior Jesuit colleague remarked that it was time the Society stopped sending their young men to Louvain, he took this as an indirect warning to himself. Nevertheless he continued to thank Providence for putting Valensin and Charles in his path:

Time and obedience will clarify more explicitly what is immortal and essentially Christian in the censured ideas. I know that, for my part, I live on them and that without them I should not know how to nourish my thought or maintain my faith. Many people think as I do.

What he saw—and with good reason—was a declaration of war by one mentality upon another. On the one hand was the spirit of separatism and intellectual artifice; on the other were those who believed in organic unity in every domain. It was the struggle in which Teilhard would be engaged to the end of his life. He felt already the force of his own influence, and foresaw its possible consequence. At the Institut Catholique he would no nothing imprudent:

I hope never to do anything against the Church outside of which I can see no current having any chance of success. . . . I shall remain absolutely myself, because the farther I go the more I love and respect nothing but the truth—and also because the worst that could happen to me would be to be sent off to one of those distant shores where I should ask nothing better than to work and research.

The exile, when it came, was not accepted quite so easily; meanwhile Teilhard realized that it was virtually impossible for him to be true to himself without causing alarm. He could not present a theory of miracle which quarrelled with his deepest convictions, and he knew that his views on evolution were distasteful to authority. The only solution then was 'always to love the Church, the true Church, beyond the one that speaks to us and the one that we meet—and serve it by forcing its hand'.

He saw the Jesuit Visitor from Rome, who appeared struck by the spiritual damage of the censorship, and returned to make the authorities understand that one could not manipulate people's ideas as one promoted or degraded their status. In the meantime Charles and Huby (another friend from Ore Place) were resolved to hold on to their chairs at Louvain for as long as they were allowed to; and Teilhard willingly conceded 'that everything is not to be said immediately and indiscriminately to every member of a class in theology'.[1]

To understand the extent of Teilhard's influence in these post-war years, and the way his mind was working, we must try to reconstruct the rapid mental telegraphy which connected Paris (Teilhard), Lyon

[1] Letters to Valensin, 4 July and 11 August 1920.

(Valensin) and Louvain (Charles). Where Teilhard was the scientist and mystic, Valensin was the philosopher and Charles the theologian. They did not see each other very often but, religiously speaking, they had grown up together, each bringing a valuable corrective to the other's thought. And there were others, less close to Teilhard, against whose minds he nevertheless liked to rub his own. Maurice de la Taille set him thinking about contemplation—impossible, Teilhard concluded, 'without putting oil in one's lamp and a laborious effort of recollection'. Joseph Maréchal, an eminent philosopher, also from Louvain, agreed with Teilhard's biological views on evolution, but thought that Thomism, properly understood, taught the unification of the world without other factors intervening between the divine act, and hesitated to see in tradition the lineaments of Teilhard's—and Rousselot's—universal Christ. Teilhard insisted in reply that a unified face of the created universe should correspond with the unifying action of God. 'It would be very useful for me to put myself more *en règle* with scholasticism—especially since, as things stand in the Church at present, the Aristotelian way is the only way to get an idea in circulation.'[1]

All around him, about this time and later, men were returning to the Church through St. Thomas; and here the influence of Maritain counted for a great deal. Teilhard looked a little askance at these 'literary' conversions—Henri Ghéon, Jacques Rivière, Max Jacob, Jacques Copeau—because he did not think they went to the heart of the problem. Nevertheless, they proved the value of a system; and although Teilhard believed 'absolutely in no system', he admitted that unless you systematized you could not get at the truth. He had been powerfully struck by an article on astronomy in the *Revue des Deux Mondes*:

> Such incredible dimensions imply, of necessity, incomparably more 'spirit' in the world than we are accustomed to imagine. There is nothing to scandalize us in the thought that the spiritual immensities are destined for organization around the same Christ. But all the same, we must in this case set no limits to the enlargement of Christ—we must carry him, I mean, to the very organic centre of everything. And this is urgent.

But it was not understood by the Thomist theologians who regarded

[1] Letter to Valensin, 1 January 1920.

all such speculations as 'curiosities'. . . . 'Don't you think this attitude lamentable?'[1]

The life of the Church—like civilian life in general—was now returning to normal, and Teilhard felt 'the wind of reaction', and what he described as 'conservative beatitude', in every direction. It was a rather rough transition from the atmosphere of liberty in which he had conceived and written the *écrits de guerre*. And so, in March 1921, we find him anticipating the trial that was to face him five years later, and showing quite clearly how he would meet it:

> It would be impossible for me to seek loyally a way outside the Church. I'm like a man who sees a light shining through the mist . . . impossible to reach our Lord otherwise than by going forward through the mist—that is to say, than by belonging more and more closely to the Church. But impossible also not to wish that I could see its face more clearly.

He warned Catholics, or intending converts, that 'the greater the body, and the more we are led by it to a higher form of spiritual life, the more heavily, on occasion, it must weigh upon us and make us suffer'. In the same letter to Valensin he referred to the 'serene dogmatism of the young'; if that were true, 'so much the worse for the young; they're only children. Their successors will return to our point of view—more virile and more sincere—supposing this fine calm . . . lasts for a generation.' In the meantime they were trying 'to put the sea in a nutshell'.[2]

It was through Gaudefroy that he came to know the Lazarist priest, the Abbé Portal, who had a great influence on the young intellectuals at the École Normale Supérieure and the École Polytechnique, and was afterwards to figure importantly in the Malines Conversations. At the invitation of Portal, Teilhard gave regular conferences to the students, treating the Incarnation 'in its physical and evolutionary economy. I can see how that "goes down".'[3] For Teilhard, evolution was a method of thinking that no scientist could any longer escape. 'I don't know a *single* scientist who is not evolutionist.'[4] He quoted the four professors at the Sorbonne, and all respectable authorities in

[1] Letter to Valensin, 28 February 1920.
[2] Letter to Valensin, 16 March 1921.
[3] Letter to Valensin, 17 March 1922.
[4] Letter to Valensin, 5 January 1923.

London, Louvain, Berlin, Munich and the United States. Even Louis Vialleton, with whom Teilhard had been in correspondence, declared himself to be a 'convinced evolutionist'—although 'anti-transformist' in the strict sense of the word. Vialleton was a devout Catholic, and one has only to read Hilaire Belloc's controversy with H. G. Wells to see how readily he was enlisted against evolutionary theory. Teilhard had letters from him which proved how specious this opposition could be. 'His philosophic luminary appears to be Bergson'.[1] And so it was one thing for Teilhard to write to his cousin, or to test the reaction of men like Valensin or Charles; it was a different matter to communicate effectively with minds younger than his own, which had been subjected to an arduous scientific discipline:

> He uncovered the weakness and timidity of our beliefs, our intellectual cowardice, our persevering—though unconscious—quest for security—in fine, the puerility of our faith, and the cunning—even though hidden—duplicity of our spiritual life. His presence was a real viaticum.[2]

Another precious contact was with Édouard Le Roy, the eminent professor at the Collège de France—and in some ways this was the most fruitful of all. Punctually, at 8.30 p.m., on Wednesday evenings Teilhard would call at Le Roy's apartment in the Rue Cassette, and it was not long before the two men were thinking and speaking with a single mind. 'We have so often discussed these views together, he and I', Le Roy was to write, 'that we have come to assemble them in the same order and to translate them in practically the same formulas. From now on we shall not be able to distinguish between our respective contributions.' This friendship ran like a fertilizing stream all through Teilhard's life. Indeed it is difficult to overestimate, or accurately to distinguish, what each man owed to the other. Teilhard might well have met Bergson through Le Roy, for Bergson also had a chair at the Collège de France, but there is no evidence that he did so. It was partly, however, through these long Wednesday conversations that Teilhard assimilated, and gradually corrected, Bergson's ideas. Here were three men of supreme intelligence thinking along similar lines and setting out from much the same premises. Madame Barthélemy-Madaule, in her magisterial thesis,[3] has shown where they differed;

[1] *ibid.*, end of January 1923.　　[2] Marcel Légaut, quoted by Cuénot, p. 110.
[3] *Bergson et Teilhard de Chardin.*

and one may suggest that the difference was due, in some degree, to their respective characters and situations. Bergson was a Jew, with the spiritual antennae and intellectual sensibility of his race. Le Roy was a Catholic, obedient to the letter of ecclesiastical discipline; when his four chief books were placed on the Index in 1931, he submitted without protest. Both these men were philosophers in the professional understanding of the term. Teilhard was a practical geologist and very much of a practising priest. His thought, although it sprang from action, was equally directed to it. He did not claim to belong to the philosophical fraternity, and not many philosophers would have admitted him to it. Nevertheless Madame Barthélemy-Madaule warns us against excluding him too easily:

> The way is open to the discovery of new perspectives, and given Teilhard's creative gifts, we must wait to see whether his philosophy may not prove to have a justification unrecognized up till now. To refer Teilhard to former systems is not the way to know whether he can be allowed a place in the succession of philosophers. We must experience within ourselves the possibility of a philosophical reflection at the heart of his vision (and not only on its surface as material for thought, since it is well known that the philosopher can philosophize about any material) but in the motive forces of his vision, in the very act of his thought; for if there are no models or precedents for this in philosophy, there are criteria which are not so much formal as suggestive of an attitude of mind. ...
>
> One thing is certain. Although Teilhard turned his back on former systems, we cannot align him with any contemporary point of view; he was a stranger to them all. Some estranged him by their orientation towards a purely interior subjectivism, by their misunderstanding of the cosmic and evolutionary factors ... ; from those who did take account of nature and evolution (the Marxists) he was estranged by their whole materialism and exclusion of transcendence; he was interested by the action[1] and 'panchristism' of Blondel, but the dissimilarity of their points of view is well known. Le Roy, who was in agreement with Teilhard on so many things, differed from him over metaphysics which, in

---

[1] *Action* was the title of one of Maurice Blondel's most important works. For the relationship of Teilhard to Blondel, see pp. 105–8.

the case of Le Roy, Teilhard regarded as idealist; Bergson, whose evolutionary and spiritual outlook ought to have brought them together (as in fact it did), was at the opposite pole of the synthesis which Teilhard was attempting. Teilhard found elements of reflection and enrichment in each of these philosophers, but he could not adjust his position to any of theirs. Furthermore, he was deeply aware of the solidarity between his vision, and the science he directly practised, and the religion he lived as a priest. He was not a philosopher in the simplest and most literal sense of the word. He was a scientist and he was a priest. He was unwilling to usurp a title in which so much was previously implicit. Does this mean that his vision is not philosophical?

Madame Barthélemy-Madaule replies to the question by presenting Teilhard as a 'mediator between the scientific moment and the moment of total expansion reached in the mystical vision, which originates in intuition and the mystical life'. The philosophy of Teilhard was

> preparing to emerge by way of phenomenological reflection, just as we shall be able to read in the total development of phenomena at the end of time their ontological meaning. And it is only in the degree to which phenomenology is incomplete and philosophy provisional that the two approaches are justified. Bergson said that a science perfectly completed would be equivalent to an intuition of Being, and Teilhard . . . puts forward the image of a pole where everything comes together. If everything comes together, there must be a relationship between the two approaches. Phenomenology is the image of ontology in time, just as evolution is the image of creation in time. . . . The moment had come to achieve this transfigured science of which Bergson had an occasional presentiment. For Teilhard phenomenology is the living spirit of science on the march, and constitutes the prolegomena to a philosophy.

Teilhard's dialogue with Le Roy was the conversation of a lifetime, and their association became closer as Teilhard's ideas matured; but for Teilhard, that introduction at the meeting of young Normaliens and Polytechniciens was a milestone as important as the first meeting with Valensin in the novitiate at Aix-en-Provence:

> I loved him like a father, and owed him a very great debt. It was

not exactly that I owed any particular idea to him, but that, particularly between 1920 and 1930, he gave me confidence, enlarged my mind (and my feeling of loyalty to the Church), and also served (at the Collège de France) as a spokesman for my ideas, then taking shape, on 'hominisation' and the 'noosphere'. I believe, so far as one can ever tell, that the word 'noosphere' was my invention; but it was he who launched it. . . . There are men who should be recognized as saints for our times, Christians whose faith has impelled them to humanize themselves in every way and to the highest degree.[1]

It should surprise no one that the author of *Le Féminin* should have formed a close friendship with the authoress of the *Psychologie du Féminisme*. Léontine Zanta was an Alsatian by birth, the daughter of a professor in the humanities. She had sat at the feet of Bergson, passed her licentiate in philosophy with brilliant honours, and then taught in an institute of higher studies, the Mutualité Maintenon. Meanwhile she was preparing her thesis on *La renaissance du stoïcisme au XVIe siècle*, and on 19 May 1914 she became the first woman in France to be admitted to a doctorate in philosophy. During the war she taught philosophy at the Lycée Buffon; was elected president of the Mutualité Maintenon; and was soon playing a leading part in the development of French feminism. She was an ardent partisan of the causes in which she believed, but no fanatic. 'I sit at my desk', she wrote, 'trying to stiffen my soul against the misfortunes of the times, and reading once again the noble and melancholy thoughts of Marcus Aurelius.'[2]

It was through Marguerite Teillhard-Chambon, who had been her pupil, that Teilhard made her acquaintance—an acquaintance that ripened under the stimulus of a mutual sympathy. She was by some years the elder, with a serene beauty reminiscent of a 'Renaissance princess', and 'the graceful attitudes and charm of expression which defy the portraitist'.[3] Teilhard remembered her 'always with a smile'. She lived in the Avenue de Madrid, where a portrait of Erasmus and a reproduction of Raphael's *Dispute of the Blessed Sacrament* looked down upon the distinguished humanists who frequented her apartment—

[1] Cuénot, p. 59.
[2] *Lettres à Léontine Zanta*, introduction by Robert Garric.
[3] *ibid.*

Bergson and Père Sertillanges, Paul Bourget and Maurice Barrès. Here Teilhard met his old master, Henri Bremond, who had now left the Society, and the Abbé Mugnier who had been active in the conversion of Huysmans. Bremond was as tall as Teilhard himself, but Mugnier was like a tremendous flame shooting from a tiny candle. When they were all three of them there together Léontine Zanta would sometimes whisper to a visitor coming to the house for the first time that the tall young Jesuit who spoke so little was really the man to watch. On summer evenings the company would like to linger on the balcony which overlooked the Bois de Boulogne and watch the sun go down over the valley of the Seine.

On 21 May 1921, at the request of his old regiment, Teilhard was appointed a Chevalier of the Légion d'Honneur. The citation ran as follows:

> An outstanding stretcher-bearer, who during four years of active service, was in every battle and engagement the regiment took part in, applying to remain in the ranks in order that he might be with the men, whose dangers and hardships he constantly shared.

Teilhard had not forgotten them; Damène who now kept a kiosk of flowers on the boulevard; Grizard with his wife and son, happy among his miniatures; Pazzio and Desruels. There were occasional reunions, reviving '*la nostalgie du Front*'. But the Parisian honeymoon did not last for long. On 13 August 1922 Teilhard received a letter from Père Emile Licent inviting him to join him in central China. Licent was a Jesuit of the province of Lille who was ambitious to found a centre of Christian and scientific studies in the basin of the Yellow River and to create a museum-laboratory for his geological and botanical collections. He had lived in China since 1914, learnt something of the language, and travelled widely about the country. Teilhard did not know him personally, but Licent had sent a number of fossils to Boule who had handed them over to Teilhard. The two men naturally entered into correspondence, and already in July 1921 Licent was pressing Teilhard to join him. By the end of the year Teilhard had yielded to his persuasions. The Museum of Science in Paris, assisted by the Ministère de l'Instruction Publique, the Académie des Sciences, and the Institut de Paléontologie Humaine, would defray the expenses of the expedition, and Licent would be in charge of it.

The unique discoveries would go to the museum, and the duplicates to the museum of Hoang-ho Pai-ho. In February 1923, therefore, Teilhard sent off a brief telegram announcing that he would come out for a year and asking when he should arrive. An even briefer answer merely contained the words 'Arrive May 15'. The die was cast.

CHAPTER VI

THE MASS ON THE WORLD[1]

'THE WORLD HAS NO INTEREST FOR ME', Teilhard wrote in this same year, 'unless I look forward, but when my eyes are on the future it is full of excitement.' It was in this mood that he sailed from Marseilles on 6 April 1923, and in *Letters from a Traveller* we get a vivid sequence of his impressions as he proceeded to a destination which also a destiny. As the ship had glided down the Gulf of Suez, with the granitic mass of Mount Sinai on one side and the Egyptian shore on the other, his earlier exploration of the desert resounded in his memory like an overture to the voyage on which he was now embarked:

How I would love [he told his cousin] to have scrambled ashore and tested those rocky slopes. But not only with my geologist's hammer. I would love to have learned if I too could hear the voice of the Burning Bush. Has not perhaps the moment passed when God speaks in the desert?

When they put in at Colombo, Teilhard remembered the country of *Kim*, and the words of the Lama that the world is 'a great and terrible thing'. It was indeed; but the more anxiously Teilhard's thought revolved around its surface and explored its depths, the further he felt himself to be from the heart of the problem. Faith must penetrate appearances, and although these were for him transparent, for others—like his friend the ship's doctor—they were opaque. Was it better to be or not to be? If the answer were in the affirmative, then it was 'difficult to stop short of God'. A negative answer was hardly in Teilhard's temperament to give; but every day brought him further proof that his mission was to a world paralysed by negation. The believer said 'no' to evolution; the scientist said 'no' to faith. Teilhard was not alone in saying 'yes' to both, but he said it more triumphantly.

---

[1] All the quotations in this chapter, except where otherwise indicated, are from *Letters from a Traveller*.

Disembarking at Shanghai, he proceeded to Tientsin by train, through a country infested by bandits. Daylight, and two armed soldiers in each coach, were no more than a token defence against these, should they have mounted an attack. Tientsin had the status of a 'treaty port' where the Chinese had granted extra-territorial rights to foreigners. They lived in districts which were called 'concessions'. In one of these Licent had established his Musée Hoang-ho-Pai-ho— named after the Yellow and White Rivers. It occupied a wing of the École des Hautes Études in Race Course Road, which was in fact a junior college for business students run by the Jesuit province of Champagne. Licent came from the north of France, and his cold eye looked out at Teilhard from a strong physique. He kept the inquisitive at a distance, mounting guard like a Cerberus over his collection. Entomology was his *forte*, but he was more skilful in catching his butterflies than in classifying them. He was touchy and quick-tempered, ingenious and hard-working. Where Licent was content to work along his own lines, Teilhard was drawn to others engaged in similar research—particularly to the Chinese scientists whose collaboration was essential in a country already wakening to national consciousness. Nor did Licent take kindly to Teilhard's suggestion that his museum would be all the better for a 'new look'. He lacked altogether Teilhard's power of synthesis, and was a stranger to his mystical intuitions; but he knew the country and the language, and was an invaluable guide in the expeditions which they undertook together. Such intellectual life as there was in China centred in Pekin, and early in June Teilhard paid a brief visit to the capital. Here he made contact with the Geological Survey, and found the young student Wong, whom he last had seen in Brussels, wearing what may well have been a blue suit, now thoroughly repatriated in a blue robe. The geologists—many of them Americans or Swedes—were holding a meeting and Teilhard spoke to them, in English, about Licent's collection. He stayed at the house of the Lazarist Fathers, which had been besieged by the Boxers in 1900.

Teilhard and Licent presently set out from Tientsin by train with their twelve packing-cases, two hampers, camp beds, saddles and servants. The first day brought them to Kalgan and the second to Koci-Hoa-Tcheng. The basaltic plateau was very reminiscent of Auvergne, except that the fields were dotted with irises instead of gentians. At

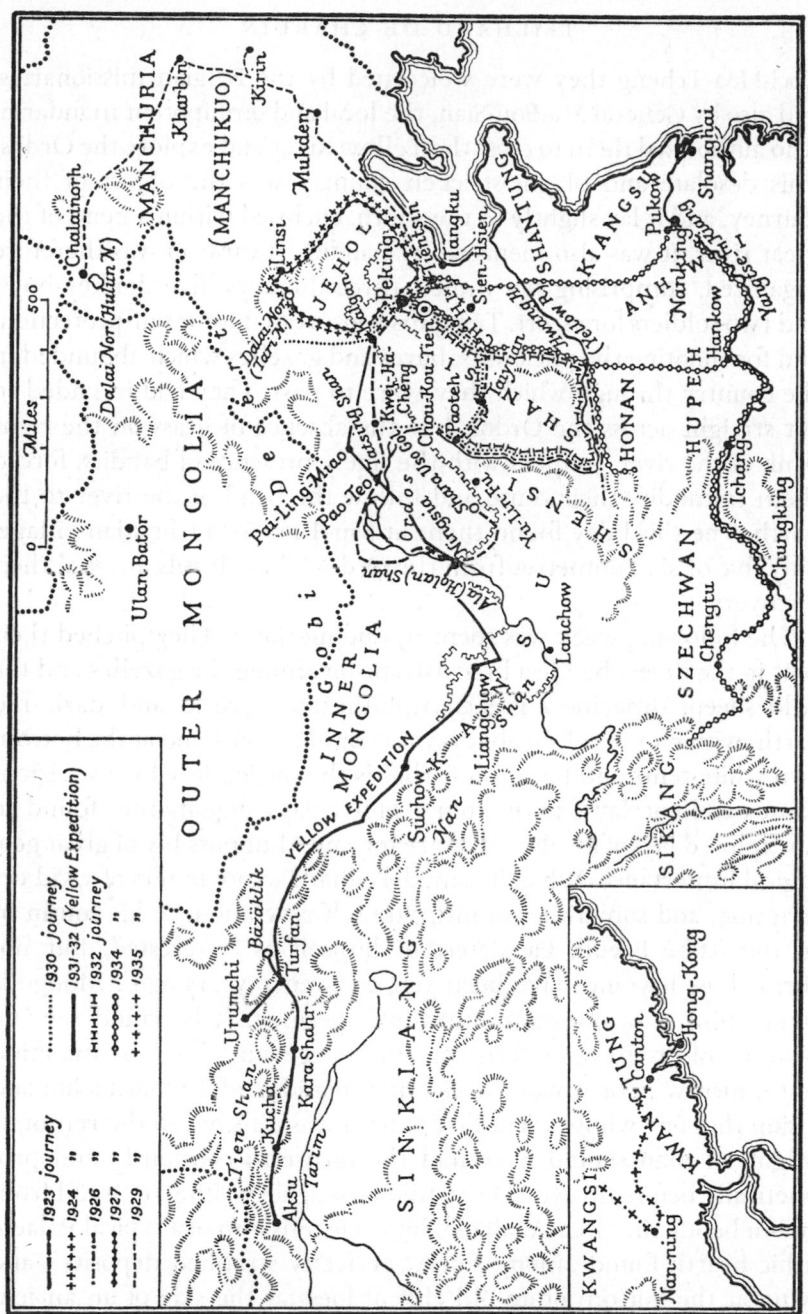

Teilhard's journeys in China

Koci-Hoa-Tcheng they were welcomed by the Belgian missionaries, and also by General Ma-Fou-Sian, the local and omnipotent mandarin, who authorized them to cross the Yellow River and explore the Ordos. This desolate and plague-stricken country was the object of their journey, and it lay slightly to the south, enclosed within a bend of the great river. It was also menaced by bandits. A caravan was therefore organized, comprising ten mules, three donkeys, five donkey-boys, and two soldiers for escort. Ten guns were available for self-protection, and for shooting the pheasants, hares and gazelles which abounded in the country through which they were to pass. They had intended to cut straight across the Ordos, but the absence of grass on the right bank of the river, coupled with the likely presence of bandits, forced them to modify their route and follow the bend of the river to the north. The third day found them at San-Tao-Ho, a Christian village, only five or six kilometres from the Ordos where fossils awaited their discovery.

The following week was spent in finding them. They pitched their tent in the desert beside a brackish spring among the gazelles and the wild sheep. 'Imagine a great amphitheatre of rocks and dark red earth, with clumps of shrubs every six or nine feet—and at the bottom two white tents and ten mules; that is the setting in which we spent some excellent days.' In the course of five days' digging they found an unexplored bed of fossils, not of great beauty but possibly of great geological importance. When it rained Teilhard wrote letters of vivid description, and sometimes of intimate self-revelation, to his cousin or to the Abbé Breuil. He describes himself as 'interested, but not thrilled, as I would have been ten or twenty years ago'. Mongolia struck him as 'a museum of antique specimens'; he could see 'no promise of progress, no ferment, no "burgeoning" for the mankind of tomorrow'. For it was the essential paradox of Teilhard's life and vision that one whose scientific research was directed to the remotest origins of man should have had the future so constantly and prophetically before his eyes. On 25 July he is again writing to Breuil from an inn beside the Great Wall of China. He tells him of a typical Palaeolithic hearth found among some 'perfectly stratified deposits', and lying at the bottom of an old cliff of loess at the side of an ancient watercourse. The loess was still inhabited, and Teilhard marks on a rough plan the place by the water where man must originally have had his dwelling, perhaps in a cave hollowed out of the cliff and now submerged. Teilhard believed this to be the first discovery of the kind to be made in China, or anywhere in the Far East. He was quick to send an account of it to Marcellin Boule. 19 August found them camped on the banks of the Shara-Osso-Gol, at the bottom of a deep canyon in a dried-up river bed, beside a Mongol 'house' scooped out of an abutting promontory. The Mongol and his family were friendly, and helped them with their digging. Already they had fifteen packing-cases crammed with the fragments of carcasses—rhinoceros, gazelle, bison, deer, horses, wild asses and wolves. But what interested Teilhard were the traces of primitive mankind. He was jumping to no rash conclusions, but man had certainly been there. Three months earlier no Palaeolithic localities *in situ* were known in China; now they had evidence of two.

In a subsequent letter to Breuil Teilhard lets slip a phrase which explains why he has fallen under the suspicion of scientists and theologians alike. He speaks of 'mystical science', or 'the science of Christ running through all things', as 'the only science that really matters'. No doubt, the phrase is inexact. Teilhard is working, and thinking, on the borderland between two spheres of knowledge. While he is digging and classifying, he allows himself to become 'caught up in the game'. But then he pauses to reflect, and his present occupation— vital though it is, in so far as it forms part of the 'total gesture' of his life—seems to him of no final importance. What really concerns him, in the leisure of his tent when the sun has gone down on the limitless landscape of Mongolia, is the new writing on which he is now at work. He calls this 'my Mass upon things', and goes on to reveal, in words that the reader will find only lightly transposed in *La Messe sur le Monde*, the heart of his inspiration:

It seems to me that in a sense the true substance to be consecrated each day is the world's development during that day—the bread symbolizing appropriately what creation succeeds in producing, the wine (blood) what creation causes to be lost in exhaustion and suffering in the course of its effort.

II

La Messe sur le Monde is likely to rank with the later and longer *Milieu Divin*, among the spiritual classics of the twentieth century. In the controlled splendour of its style; in its antiphonal blending of prayer and praise; and in the fearless adventure of its thought, this short essay of thirty-six pages takes one straight to the axis of Teilhard's cosmic vision. Even those who realize that no limits can be set to ecclesiastical timidity will be astonished that so ardent a profession of faith could have remained unpublished during the author's lifetime. Teilhard wrote it because he had no means of celebrating Mass in the desert of Ordos, and it seems to have been composed on the feast of the Transfiguration. The idea had been at work in him for some time. Already in *Le Prêtre* (1917) he had spoken of a 'real, even though attenuated, divinization' of the universe brought about by the descent of Christ into the eucharistic elements. In this same year of 1923 he had interpreted the priest's 'This is my Body' as reaching beyond the morsel of bread over which they were spoken. 'They bring to birth the whole mystical body. The action of the priest extends beyond the transubstantiated host to the cosmos itself. The whole of matter is subject, slowly and irresistibly, to the great consecration.'

There was nothing in the least unorthodox about all this, as many competent theologians have been quick to point out; but it would have been news to the inquisitors of the Holy Office who have never been on quite these terms with the cosmos. In 1922 Teilhard had written boldly to Valensin: 'I have the right to speak like St. Paul', and it was upon certain Pauline texts that he took his stand. It would hardly be an exaggeration to say that the Christ of the Gospels was too limited for the worship that Teilhard was prepared to give. 'And so, for a long time, even though I believed, I strayed, not knowing what it was I loved.' What conquered him and held him captive—the mainspring of his very personal apostolate—was the resurrected Christ visible in the world of appearances, and manifesting a power which the Resurrection had certified. In the same way, what attracted him to the Sacred Heart was its symbolic power and its superhuman appeal—the discovery 'in you of an element even more determinate, more circumscribed, than your humanity as a whole'. The Sacred Heart—not, let us repeat, in its usual representation—was for Teilhard a means of devotional escape from whatever was 'too narrow, too precise, and too limited' in the traditional image of Christ. Here was the furnace of love at the very centre of the divine being, and it became so intensely the subject of Teilhard's meditation that the form surrounding it seemed to lose its contours until they were indistinguishable from a world aflame. Here was the cosmic Christ 'whose forehead is of the whiteness of snow, whose eyes are of fire, and whose feet are brighter than molten gold'. The Christ and the cosmos were at one.

What is the average agnostic of today—or the average Christian for the matter of that—to make of *La Messe sur le Monde*? Is he to see in it no more than a rhetorical illuminism, the *souffle* of the poet rather than the seer? The sceptic or the cynic will always see it so. Teilhard's faith is a datum without which he cannot be understood, let alone accepted. Faith is a theological virtue, like hope—and no one could accuse Teilhard of wanting in hope. But what of charity—not the natural charity of the philanthropist, but the supernatural charity of the believer? Teilhard defines it not as the 'sterile fear of doing wrong, but a vigorous determination that all of us together shall break open the gates of life', just as the true purity was not 'a debilitating separation from all created reality, but an impulse carrying one through all forms of created beauty'. There is a sense in which Teilhard always brings you down to earth, and another sense in which he always lifts you up from it. What is this but the Pauline 'consistence' of all things in Christ? Even though he is not speaking here with a theological exactitude, what is there to disconcert the believer who does not shrink from the implications of this faith? And for those who do not believe, Teilhard does not shrink, in his turn, from the word which, in 1923, still seemed to justify a secular optimism; the word in which his science and his spirituality found a common anchorage; the word which was still a terror to the theologians—the talismanic word of evolution.

III

On 9 September Teilhard was writing to Breuil that 'mysticism remains the great science and the great art, the only power capable of synthesizing the riches accumulated by other forms of human activity'; and three days later he was crossing the Great Wall—here reduced to a series of towers at intervals of 500 yards—on their way back to Pekin. The autumn was Teilhard's favourite season; his mind went back to the high plateaux of Auvergne, and cool evenings in the Egyptian desert, and the sea wind blowing through the beech-trees on the Sussex Downs. As they floated down the Hoang-ho in their heavy barge, covering rapidly by water the distance they had laboriously traversed by mule, Teilhard asked himself what exactly he had gained by the journey. If he had hoped that travel was the road to truth, this was an illusion he had lost even before he had left Europe behind him. Space was 'a veil without seam which we can go over indefinitely without ever finding the least aperture through which to glimpse the higher spheres of existence'. In the present, as in the past, there was 'nothing really new to be found'. The only true knowledge lay in building up the future as life gradually brought it into being, and what he had hoped to find in Asia were the 'new currents of thought and mysticism . . . which were preparing to rejuvenate and fertilize our European world'. But here, too, he had been disappointed. Such thought as he had met was remarkable only for its absence, its senility, or its infantilism. There had been no opportunity to meet the rare solitaries who contemplated 'the cosmic circles and the eternal re-birth of Buddha'. Teilhard remained 'a pilgrim of the future on my way back from a journey made entirely in the past'—with the spiral horn of an antelope, now to be seen in the Museum of Natural History in Paris, as a witness of his wanderings.

Asia was asleep—or seemed to be—and Teilhard did not as yet sus-pect the strength and violence of its awakening. As he watched the sun go down from the battlements of Belgacoum, he remembered the victorious passage of Genghis Khan and then his eyes fell on the eroded soil 'struggling to keep the invading sands at bay'. Everything had apparently been lost; but here Teilhard's invincible optimism came to his support. So long as a few wise men had the secret of life in their keeping—their own life, not a life imposed upon them—creative energy might one day return to this ravaged landscape. In the mean-time Europe must carry the torch which had been handed on to it. Disappointed as Teilhard was to have found nothing in his travels but the traces of a vanished world—and yet these had been the immediate object of his journey—he believed that 'the wake left behind by man-kind's forward march reveals its movement just as clearly as the spray thrown up elsewhere by the spray. . . . If we want to understand the Far East, we must not look at it at dawn, nor at high noon; we must look at it at dusk when the sun, bearing the spoils of Asia with it in its glory, rises in triumph over the skies of Europe.'

Neither now, nor later, did Teilhard attempt to learn Chinese, and he was already hankering for the intellectual stimulus that Paris alone could give. As it was, he spent many weeks in Licent's museum at Tientsin, classifying their findings and preparing a report for a geological congress at Pekin. He went up there fairly often, and found people working and thinking on lines similar to his own. He particularly admired the Americans, and made friends with Dr. Granger who had led the great American expedition into the Gobi desert. It was here, too, that he first met George Barbour, a Scotsman, who was to be a devoted friend and fellow-worker in the years to come. Barbour visited him afterwards in Tientsin, where the two men discussed some freshwater shells which had been brought up from the bottom of a well. With the Chinese Teilhard was always inclined to be ingenuous, taking them at their word when they had no right to be so taken. He was impressed by Dr. Ting, head of the Geological services, who confirmed his belief that, for the time being, the Chinese did not think for themselves. Their philosophical traditions had been broken, and they were still under Western influences. Not only did they react against an inadequate tradition of their own, but they were by nature agnostic and pragmatical. Ting was an exception in this respect. With him, the quest for religious certainty was like 'a long-term scientific research'. He saw the problem in its true perspective.

In February 1924 Teilhard and Licent travelled on foot or by mule, to the borders of the Tchele and the Honan, a distance of 700 miles from Pekin. Escorted by a young missionary, Teilhard visited a number of Christian settlements and was able to judge for himself the difficulties of the missionary task. These devoted men were swamped in a mass of primitive human beings, good enough in their way, but inquisitive, importunate and tactless. The missionary was hard put to it to call his life his own. 'Relations between Chinese, and still more between Chinese and Europeans, are predominantly a matter of convention . . . and this makes you feel that the whole atmosphere is woolly—you can't get hold of anything.' The indigenous population lived in miserable conditions, eating nothing but cereal pastes and boiled millet, with an occasional dish of rice or corn.

The travellers assembled their caravan at Song-chen-tsoci-ze—Nôtre Dame des Pins—which was the episcopal residence of the Vicar-General for eastern Mongolia. From here they proceeded by stages to the Mongolian plateau, visiting the mandarins of the district who provided them with an escort of ten soldiers, and avoiding the bandits who were anyway disposed to leave missionaries alone. The caravan consisted of six carts drawn by Mongolian oxen—roughly built vehicles which could go pretty well anywhere. By 25 June they were encamped among the dunes between Kalgan and the Dalai-Nôr, having come upon a chain of Quaternary volcanoes, looking as fresh as the peaks of the Puys-de-Dôme. Teilhard had the impression that no one had pointed them out before. In Kalgan he was joined by Barbour, and the two men set out along the caravan route to the Mongolian plateau, with a Chinese student, a cook, and a muleteer. But they found no traces of the Early Stone Age Man whose implements Teilhard and Licent had discovered on their earlier exploration of the Ordos. These had been obliterated by the dust, whipped up into sand-dunes by the prevailing winds. They still prevailed and when Teilhard rejoined Licent, the sturdy Jesuit—who was nothing if not *débrouillard*—had much ado to fix the tent. The results of the expedition were inconclusive, although Teilhard advanced some radical theories with which Barbour was unable to concur but against which he could raise no certain evidence to the contrary. 'Even the fossils sent to Seward at the British Museum', he told his wife, 'are better than anything we could find today after an hour spent hunting at the same spot.'[1] All Teilhard could do—standing on the summit of a hill—was to offer the world of Mongolia to Christ in a place which had never heard his name. Later, as they came down to Kalgan, he was to see from a far greater height: 'spread out before us, in a scenic design that was completely new to our eyes, . . . China—the "great diamond" as the ancient Mongols called her, fascinated by the Promised Land from which the Great Wall shut them out.'

On 10 September Teilhard was at Shanghai kneeling at the grave of his sister who had given her life for China. Was he, too, to spend his life in the same cause? The question haunted him as he embarked for Europe three days later, and it was not long before he received an answer to it.

[1] George Barbour, *In the Field with Teilhard de Chardin*, p. 29.

CHAPTER VII

THE CRISIS OF OBEDIENCE

TEILHARD now resumed his teaching at the Institut Catholique and his researches at the museum. To reach the door of Boule's laboratory you had to climb the principal staircase, with its ramp of life-size chrysanthemums in bronze—a relic of nineteenth-century *art nouveau*; cross the upper hall; and traverse a gallery where a plaster Diplodocus and various other skeletons loomed at you in the uncertain light. The entrance to the laboratory was marked in black letters on a glass plate. Inside, Boule was at work, pipe in hand, and Teilhard was supervising the studies of two young scientists who were preparing their doctorate. There was little money for books; the galleries were unheated; and the specimens cracked under the cold. Teilhard, whom Hastings had inured to English habits, was grateful for the cups of tea surreptitiously brewed for him in the basement. The bones of hippopotami and rhinoceros which he had sent back from China were brought up in successive loads from below, and Boule was heard grumbling that 'the Father's bones will soon land us in the street'. Boule was no pedant and would have nothing of the Latin nomenclature commonly in use. 'Don't you think, Professor,' a student would ask, 'that this might be a *Felis catus silvestris*?' 'I suppose you mean a cat?' came the abrupt reply.[1]

Teilhard worked in a room at the foot of a short flight of stairs immediately below Boule. One of the windows looked out on to the Place Valhubert and the other on to the severe avenues of clipped plane-trees in the Jardin des Plantes. He sat behind a table of varnished oak with a larger and longer table on his right. The room was lined with shelves of shallow drawers, and the specimens were brought in from the *atelier de préparation* next door. Among the frequent visitors was the Communist intellectual, Vaillant-Couturier, whose

[1] Ida Treat in *La Table Ronde*, 1955.

wife also worked in the laboratory. Max Bégouën has described him as a 'large-hearted and deeply cultivated man, vibrant with artistic sensibility'. He and Teilhard had many conversations. 'What will you do with your unlimited and universal leisure when you have attained it?', Teilhard would ask, and to this Vaillant-Couturier had no reply. 'I know', Teilhard would mischievously rejoin, 'we will both dig a huge hole and then sit and contemplate it together.'

The museum wanted to annex Teilhard completely, but he preferred to keep his independence. His influence among the Social Union of Catholic Engineers and the Catholic students of the École Normale Supérieure was increasing. He was now openly evolutionist, and had not scrupled to publish his views in *Études* (1921) and the *Revue de Philosophie* (1923). The second of these essays makes ironical reading today because Teilhard, like nearly everyone else, still believed in the authenticity of Piltdown Man—although he was not able to explain him. If the Piltdown jaw really belonged to the skull discovered with it, there must have existed in the Quaternary a man with large canines and a long, oblique symphysis. Now these characteristics were specifically simian, and Teilhard held that there was a clear break between the line of hominids and that of the larger apes. Humanity appeared at the end of a process leading towards a shorter face and larger brain; 'already very old, fully developed, and almost at its extreme zoological expansion'. The evidence of his tools indicated that 'a crowd of people has lived on the earth that we occupy, of whom we can say absolutely nothing except that they had intelligence'. Piltdown Man, like the other groups of primates, stood in no known succession; but Teilhard believed that he 'admirably resumes Life's previous effort'.

Teilhard compared the primates to the branches of a conifer, all the elements of which are uniformly covered with overlapping leaves or scales. We must:

> momentarily follow then abandon each scale, one after another— one must jump from leaf to leaf—so that the path followed, whilst still keeping to the direction of the branch, is broken into a number of divergent sections. An obvious continuity, but hidden beneath a cloak of discontinuities.[1]

All we could do was to register 'the geometrical distribution of living creatures through time'. Teilhard did believe that 'the leaves which

[1] *La Paléontologie et l'Apparition de l'Homme* (The Appearance of Man; ch. 3).

serially envelop the zoological tree of the primates would hold directly together'. Unity of structure proved the existence of a material link in the chain, but even if the missing link were found history would not be able to explain it. Things were nowhere more incomprehensible than at their origin. Neanderthal and Piltdown Man did not follow each other in a morphological sequence; still less did they lead in direct succession to contemporary man. They should be seen, rather, as an 'envelope' between the anthropomorphic apes and the 'most central grouping of humanity today'. Nothing now remained of Chellean or Neanderthaloid humanity, and Palaeolithic man had disappeared before men appeared analogous to bushmen or eskimoes. Against these arguments no one could attribute to Teilhard the belief that men were descended from monkeys, even if, at some moment, remotely prehistoric, God had given them a soul. As we shall see, these views outlined at the beginning of his career were amply confirmed at the end of it.

In December 1924 we find him lecturing to one of Portal's groups on Gide's *Nourritures Terrestres*. The students were gathered round a very long table, covered with a green cloth, while Teilhard spoke, with his eyes half closed, as if he were speaking to himself. Gide's eulogy of the visible world did not frighten him in the least. Without any pretension to baptize the author against his will, Teilhard recognized in Gide's ecstatic prose 'the life-giving springs at which a Christian soul could drink'.[1] The same witness, re-reading *Les Nourritures Terrestres* after a serious illness, remembered something of Teilhard's 'mystical interpretation', and it was due in part to this 'enthusiastic theology' that he did not 'go to pieces' as a result of his physical suffering.[2]

Teilhard gave four lectures on evolution during the winter months of 1925; and at the same time developed his theory of the noosphere—a kind of cosmic envelope created by the reflection of the mind. The word was his own invention—it had come to him during the war—but the word and the idea were both adopted later by Le Roy and the Russian geologist Verdatsky, who was in Paris at the time. At the beginning of Lent, Teilhard preached a retreat in which he took for his theme ideas which were later to find magisterial expression in *Le Milieu Divin*. Human activity was seen as 'the most immediate

[1] Gabriel Germain, quoted by Cuénot, pp. 59–60.   [2] *ibid.*

realization of God's will, the extension of his most central designs for the world'.[1] But on 13 November 1924 Teilhard's own activity was brought abruptly to a halt when he received a letter from his Provincial, Père Costa de Beauregard, urgently summoning him to Lyon. Two years previously he had been invited by a Jesuit colleague, himself a professor of dogmatic theology, to write a paper indicating three different ways in which the doctrine of original sin might be represented for those who were left unsatisfied by its official formulations. It has been said that in face of original sin the theologians of today are in much the same situation as the pre-Nicaean Fathers before the problem of the Trinity; and that while 'the genius of Augustine clearly discerned the existence of original sin in humanity, neither he nor anyone coming after him has succeeded in explaining it in a satisfactory way'.[2] Teilhard had made it clear that his approaches to the subject were only tentative and 'certainly not viable in themselves'. He was doing no more than attempting to explain a doctrine which he did not deny. Mysteriously, however, his paper found its way to Rome; many believe that it was stolen from his desk at the Institut Catholique by a student anxious to prove his own orthodoxy.

We do not know what the fatal article contained. Dorothy Garrod was among those who had consulted Teilhard on the subject, and he may well have sketched out on paper the answer he had given her in conversation, and which he had discussed in correspondence with Valensin—that original sin was a kind of necessary flaw in the universe. The story of the Fall was a short way of describing the eternal infidelities of mankind, and we now had to put Adam into the plural because science showed us a humanity 'plunging into the animal kingdom by a large bundle of its roots'.[3] All we do know is that the article came to the eyes of Cardinal Merry del Val, who was alert to the suspicion of heresy as a foxhound is alert to the scent. He made sharp representations to the General of the Jesuits, Father Ledochowski, who had already been warned from other sources. Ledochowski was no more qualified than Merry del Val to appreciate the difficulties apparent to Teilhard, as they were to so many others, and Teilhard was asked to promise that he would neither say nor write anything

[1] Jacques Perret, quoted by Cuénot, p. 60.
[2] *Études*, October 1966, Père Rouquette, s.j., and Père Arruste, s.j.
[3] Letter to Valensin, 14 May 1922.

'against the traditional position of the Church on the matter of original sin'.

The demand was at once, he complained, 'too vague and too absolute'. He felt in conscience bound to reserve to himself the right of research among his professional colleagues—for this was a natural right, not susceptible of abrogation; and also the right to aid those who were themselves in intellectual trouble—for this was his priestly duty. He hoped to commute the formula proposed to some such terms as these: 'I undertake not to spread around, or to proselytize on behalf of, the explanations contained in my note.' New censors were called in, and in spite of all the efforts in his favour made by Monseigneur Baudrillart, Rector of the Institut Catholique, and by his own immediate superiors, Rome was implacable. He was finally requested to subscribe to six propositions, of which only the fourth caused him real difficulty. Should he sign this with an explicit or implicit reservation? By nature he tended to be explicit. In any case, on the advice of his friends—and not without considerable reluctance—he signed it.

Teilhard had always expressed himself with candour, originality, and occasionally with imprudence. He would reply to the questions of a young student or seminarian as he would have replied to a member of the Pontifical Academy of Sciences. The sense of human equality was strong in him; all men were enveloped in the same mystery and the task of penetration was a common one. A professor from the Institut Catholique recorded how, ten years later, he accompanied Teilhard to the seminary for deacons in the archdiocese of Paris. Teilhard gave a lecture of unimpeachable orthodoxy on the subject of human origins, but in the course of the discussion which followed the question of original sin was raised. Instead of distinguishing between a fact *of* history like the Battle of Waterloo and a fact *in* history like the human tendency to sin, Teilhard improvised a number of unconsidered replies. Original sin was not very easy to conceive; everyone must imagine it as best he can. With each answer Teilhard glided on to ground more and more slippery, until his friend—on the pretext that it was getting late—led him gently to the door.[1]

But Teilhard was not alone in jibbing against the Roman fetters. His closest friends in the Society were not always in agreement with

[1] '*L'Obéissance du Père Teilhard de Chardin.*' (*L'homme devant Dieu: Mélanges offerts au Père Henri de Lubac.*)

him, but they all desired a renewal of Catholic thought to meet the opportunity of the hour, and they all fretted under a similar frustration. It was to Valensin that Teilhard now wrote in his agony of mind:

> Dear friend, help me a little. I have behaved properly; but what I feel inside is something like a death agony or a storm. I think I see that if I went off on my own or kicked over the traces in one way or another (and humanly speaking it would be so simple and 'easy') I should be unfaithful to my belief that everything that happens is animated by our Lord; and to my belief in his worth, which is greater than all the elements that make up this world of ours. Furthermore I should compromise the religious value of my ideas. People would think I was straying from the Church; I should be accused of pride. I must show by my example that if my ideas appear in the light of an innovation, they make me as faithful as anyone else to the attitude in which I was formerly seen. That's how it seems to me—but even there, the shadows fall.[1]

For once, it was difficult for Teilhard to believe, with Léon Bloy, that 'everything that happens is adorable'.

The memory of the Modernist witch-hunt was too recent for Teilhard's Jesuit superiors—sympathetic as many of them were, and notably his own Provincial—to run unnecessary risks. It was ten years since Bergson had been put on the Index, and *Études* had taken the measure of a persecution which was still counting its victims. 'What is extraordinary, and what throws us into confusion, is the extent of the denunciations. Out of all that has been attempted during the past twenty years to defend religion in our country, nothing and nobody has been spared.'[2] They judged it better, therefore, in Teilhard's own interest as well as in their own, that he should confine himself to scientific research. His thoughts were his own affair, and what he said in his unguarded moments would travel less easily from Pekin than it did from Paris. Let him write on scientific matters as much as he liked—the Society was only too proud to have a star performer in its ranks—but he must keep his theological speculations to himself. He was accordingly compelled to withdraw from the Institut Catholique, although Monseigneur Baudrillart kept his name on its books as a 'professor on leave'; and preparations were put in hand for his return to China at Easter 1926.

[1] 16 May 1925.   [2] 5 January 1914.

In April 1925 he was in England with Breuil and Dorothy Garrod exploring the coralline crag near Ipswich, where J. Reid Moir had discovered flint blades which Breuil considered to be Solutrean; and in July he made his retreat with Valensin at St. Étienne. Previously he had seen his Provincial in Lyon—'most affectionate and full of trust in me'—and there was a meeting with other friends in the Society; Valensin's brother, and professors from Hastings and Toulouse. They were all in agreement about what Teilhard should do—as well as about what had been done to him. Such doubts as he may have had were resolved by this solidarity:

> When I thought of the comfort I drew from the appreciation of all these minds, which were really reliable and devoted to the Church, I realized what enormous damage and scandal would have been caused by any act of indiscipline on my part . . . nothing spiritual or divine can come to a Christian, or to one who has taken religious vows, except through the Church or his Order.[1]

After a fortnight at Sarlat in the Dordogne Teilhard had recovered 'an inward calm, without changing an iota of my views'; and on 22 August he was writing to Valensin as any man might have written to a friend about the pleasures of a good holiday:

> I have installed myself here in the quiet of an old country house with an agreeable, though limited, view of the hills—very green, and a nursery of truffles—and a small heap of pointed roofs, covered with yellow stone tiles. . . . I discovered silence and tranquillity (in spite of the numerous bugs) in the clean room of the Spiritual Father (Père Dissard) who has had the good taste to collect, in addition to cast-off clothes for the poor, a plentiful collection of novels, decent or not so decent. I have been dipping into Balzac or Daudet, and some other delicacies as well, to interrupt the editing of some geological work—the elements of which I brought with me here.
>
> More really and explicitly than before the crisis, and not 'by way of convention', I believe in the Church as the 'mediator' between God and the world, and I love it. . . . But I don't yet see the reforms which are desirable, and the bark which falls away, and also the bark which we must still jealously respect because it's *still* green (and *still* has life in it), but which will fall away tomorrow as

[1] Letter to Le Roy, 16 August 1925.

surely as the layers that one sees going brown along the trunk of the plane-trees.

After spending a few days with Boule in the grottoes of Les Eyzies, Teilhard returned to Paris where Baudrillart relied on him to continue his courses until the end of the year. In September there was a meeting with Charles—'still overflowing with vitality'—and Charles brought a few crumbs of theological comfort. He had found everywhere in the immediately post-Tridentine theology an absence of consensus, and in consequence a wide latitude of courageous thinking. As for the future, however dark it might appear, Charles advised his friend 'to drown it in a brighter light', but as the time of his departure drew near, Teilhard could not tell whether it was 'a light or a shadow that rose up so quickly' from his last three months in the Paris that he loved. He had continued to see Le Roy; their Wednesday evenings were 'among the best spiritual exercises of the week. I always come away from them better, and refreshed. He also continued to address a number of Catholic groups; but a report of this reached diocesan headquarters and an inquiry was set on foot, of which Marguerite Teillard-Chambon had to bear the brunt. It was small wonder, therefore, that in re-affirming his fidelity to the Church, Teilhard should have confessed his estrangement from its representatives:

In a kind of way I *no longer have confidence* in the exterior manifestations of the Church. I believe that through it the divine influence will continue to reach me, but I no longer have much belief in the immediate and tangible value of official directions and decisions. Some people feel happy in the visible Church; but for my own part I think I shall be happy to die in order to be free of it—and to find our Lord outside of it.

It had already been rumoured that Teilhard had been sent on his first visit to China because of his ideas. Now he had to conquer the most insidious temptation of all—was he using the excuse of fidelity to camouflage a want of courage? Even if he were not, would not the Gentiles accuse him of intellectual cowardice? Sometimes he felt like 'a pair of scissors being whirled about in a great wind'.[1] He knew that his roots were in Paris and that, if these were cut off, he would lose the greater part of his strength. Could he be sure that he would not desert?

[1] Letter to Valensin, 10 January 1926.

Yes [he wrote to Valensin], I believe that I shall communicate
with this little chalice—and do so *with a deep joy*—but at least I
shall be in no doubt that what I drink is the blood of Christ.

and yet again:

I shall swallow the obstacle in the act of my obedience.

II

There were few passengers on board the *Angkor* when Teilhard
sailed into exile at Easter 1926. The Orient had lost its first intoxicating
appeal, and looking out to sea he was now 'bored to tears'.[1] It was not,
however, in Teilhard's nature to be bored for long. He was interested
by a Russian naval officer whose ship had been torpedoed by the
Emden, near Penang; and one morning, as he was saying his breviary
on the second-class deck, he was observed by a young Catalan, Henry
de Monfreid, who was on his way to Ethiopia. Teilhard was dressed *en
clergyman*, and Monfreid was struck by

his long face, forceful and finely drawn; the features, emphasized
by premature lines, looked as though carved out of some tough
wood. There was a lively twinkle in his eye; humour, too, but no
hint of irony; forbearing and kind.

Teilhard looked up as Monfreid passed; their eyes met; and they fell
into conversation. It was the first of many talks. 'His words went
straight to your soul', Monfreid was to write afterwards, 'with the
persuasive force of an apostle.'[2] Monfreid and his wife disembarked at
Djibouti, hoping that one day Teilhard would join them in Ethiopia.
Teilhard, on his side, was impressed by their 'humanity and independence of mind'.[3]

On arrival in Tientsin, he spent a few days cataloguing the fossils
that Licent had collected in his absence, and then proceeded to Pekin.
A lecture by Professor Parker of Harvard reminded him of the gulf
separating the world of thought and scholarship in which he was now
increasingly to move from the theological idiom with which he was
familiar. The one was as real as the other, but they were mutually incomprehensible; and Teilhard now wondered if he were capable of
'so using the first language as to make it fairly express what the other

[1] *Letters from a Traveller*, p. 124.   [2] *La Table Ronde*, June 1955.
[3] Letter to Le Roy, 15 May 1926.

contains but puts into words that most people can no longer understand'.[1] This ambition was Teilhard's wrestle with the angel, and all
the criticism directed against his formulations from one side or the
other is merely evidence that in such a struggle there must be defeats
as well as victories. What matters is that the struggle went on.

Meanwhile the political chaos of the country was as plain as its
spiritual apathy. There was no central government, with the Chinese
Bolshevists only a few miles from Pekin and the nationalist troops in
peaceful occupation of the capital, and a Russian armoured train actually in the station. Teilhard and Licent had planned an expedition to
Shensi in the loop of the Yellow River, and from there to Lanchow in
Kansu, within striking distance of Chinese Tibet. Travelling through
the most ancient parts of the Chinese empire, and its former capitals
at Laoyang and Sian Fu, they reached Tangyuan; but were halted
900 miles further on where they found their way barred by the ragged
army of soldiers, bandits and peasants who were challenging the central authority. It was a *drôle de guerre* and exceedingly picturesque, but
it put paid to palaeontology. There was nothing for it but to traipse
home along the track of a projected motor-road through the villages
with their dilapidated pagodas and belligerent Buddhas until, on
26 August, they were back in Tientsin.

After a short trip to Sang-Kan-ho—a two days' journey to the west
of Pekin—where the two Jesuits were investigating some fossil-bearing
deposits discovered on their previous expedition, Teilhard settled
down at Tientsin to work on two essays of capital importance. The first
contained his views on transformism as these had developed over the
past few years. He had written it on the voyage out and was now typ-
ing it. He had been struck by a phrase of Paul Morand: *nothing but the
earth*. This was true in more senses than one. Nothing less than the
whole earth had been required for the emergence of man, but once
he had emerged he was conscious of his restriction. He was reaching
for a way out; the planet of his expansion had become the prison in
which he was confined. Teilhard was attempting to 'express the psychology—the mixed feelings of hope, disappointment, expectation—
of the man who sees himself no longer as a Frenchman or a Chinaman
but as a *terrestriel*'.[2] Concurrently he had also decided to write the
essay which was to contain the essence of his spiritual doctrine: a doc-

[1] Letter to Breuil   [2] *Letters from a Traveller*, p. 133.

trine, he told Le Roy, 'which you know as well as I do and knew before me', which had owed much to the conversations in the Rue de Cassette:

> I mean to put down as simply as possible (he wrote to another friend) the sort of ascetical and mystical doctrine that I have been living and preaching so long. I call it *Le Milieu Divin*, but I am being careful to include nothing esoteric and the minimum of esoteric philosophy. . . . I really mean to try to 'get across' and to have the book read. I think that if I could manage to get it printed, it would do good in two ways: it would spread ideas which I believe might open new frontiers for many minds, and at the same time my efforts might be rewarded by some sort of approval from the Church. I have settled down to my little book. I want to write it slowly, quietly—living it and meditating on it like a prayer.[1]

There was pathos as well as promise in these expectations. *Le Milieu Divin* did indeed open new frontiers for many minds, but it was not published in the lifetime of its author. It has influenced Christian spirituality by the force of its own persuasion and in face of criticism not always ill-intentioned or ill-informed. For those who are not equipped to estimate Teilhard's philosophy of evolution, or his contribution to palaeontological research, *Le Milieu Divin* will stand upon the summit of his work. It is complementary to *The Phenomenon of Man*. Neither can be properly understood without the other; their meanings converge.

It was five years since he had told Victor Fontoynont of the desire 'to systematize *my own* interior life', and in one sense the teaching of *Le Milieu Divin* is systematic; but the system is built upon personal experience. It is Teilhard's way to God. Nor is the teaching so new as all that. Teilhard is out to prove that the 'most traditional Christianity—Baptism, the Cross and the Eucharist—can be translated in such a way that what is best in contemporary aspirations can find a place in it'. It is difficult to accuse the author of a flat disbelief in original sin after reading *Le Milieu Divin*; the doctrine is specifically affirmed in four places. All he wishes to do—'without the slightest concession to "nature"'—is to 'reconcile . . . the love of God and the healthy love of

---

[1] 8 November 1926; quoted in *Bergson and Teilhard de Chardin*, M. Barthélemy-Madaule.

the world' and to 'nourish the one by the other'. Development and detachment must go hand in hand. Man is body and spirit—both real and both good—and the two, separated only by death, will be rejoined by resurrection. The development of each individual soul reflects, in microcosm, the growth of the universe; and the spiritual efforts of individual men and women will transform the world of matter into 'the new earth or the Heavenly Jerusalem'.

Christ the King is the 'great sun' of our interior life, and so long as we keep our faces turned to it, no secular activity is unfit for divinization. Artists, manual workers and scientists can safely discover in a passionate dedication to their work the open way to 'the supreme completion' of their human being. God is attained 'inexhaustibly, in the totality of our actions'; he awaits us in what another master of the spiritual life had called 'the sacrament of the present moment'.[1] As ever, Teilhard is alert to the objection of modern atheists that men are made inhuman by Christianity, and all the first part of his essay is devoted to prove that the Christian, if he rightly understands his vocation, is neither a malingerer in the ranks nor a fifth columnist outside them. Nevertheless for Teilhard, with his eyes fixed on the Mount of Transfiguration, this was only the first part of the journey; further ahead there could be no escaping 'the dominating arms of the Cross'. Human activity, with its mastery of inertia and its necessary fatigue, was in itself a form of detachment from facility. The navigator trimming his sails to the landward breeze was forced to put to sea. The Christian, like Jacob wrestling with the angel, must end by adoring his antagonist—and adoration is the *mot clef* of *Le Milieu Divin*. In the 'forces of growth' which sustain his effort and in the 'forces of diminution' which inhibit it—'seductive, expressionless or hostile'— he must learn to recognize the divine regard. He possesses nothing that has not been given him; and he submits equally to life and to death.

Death was more than 'the sum of all our diminutions'; it was a physical evil in so far as it was 'the organic result of the material plurality in which we are immersed'; and a moral evil in so far as this plurality was 'engendered by the wrong use of our freedom in the society where we are placed'. But in the conquest of death by resurrection Christ has abolished its sting so that nothing need kill any

[1] Père de Caussade, s.j.

Marguerite Teillard-Chambon, Teilhard's cousin (Claude Aragonnès)

Teilhard and companions after a visit to the Grotte des Trois Frères, 28 August 1928. *Front row (left to right)*, Comte Bégouën, Abbé Breuil, local guide. *Second row*, Max Bégouën, an architect from the Beaux Arts, Lancelot C. Sheppard. *Standing*, Kevin Clark O.P., F.G.S.

more and everything is susceptible to the will of God. Death is an evil thing and we must fight against it; in that fight we shall be defeated; but our defeat will be transfigured. We are like soldiers who fall in a battle which is the prelude to peace. Even if we seem to fall as individuals, the world, in which we shall live again, will triumph through our deaths. Here Teilhard relies upon the classical texts: Augustine's *'felix culpa'*[1] and St. Paul's *'omnia convertuntur in bonum'*[2] and Christ's *'necessarium est ut scandala eveniant'*[3]; in a fallen world which is getting on its feet again shocks and scandals, moral as well as physical, are unavoidable. Not even the perfection of God himself availed against the 'nature of things'; and a world presumed to be in the way of perfecting itself was, by the nature of things, partially disordered. 'A world with no trace or threat of evil would be a world which had reached its consummation.'

'It is not enough', exclaimed Teilhard in a celebrated phrase, 'that I should die in communion; teach me to communicate in dying.' The Christian's resignation to the will of God, so often condemned as an opiate, was an active resignation; it had no other sense than orthodox spirituality allowed. A true renunciation must 'transcend everything that the world contained and at the same time aid its development with a passionate conviction'. The Christian must cherish not only the 'fullness' of life but its 'emptiness', for it was here especially that Christ would transform into himself the personality that we have been trying to develop for him. The combinations of effort and detachment were as various as the vocations of mankind—there was room in the Church for an Aquinas and a Vincent de Paul beside a John of the Cross. Sometimes it was 'the constructive human effort' which took pride of place; at other times it was 'the mystical annihilation'.

This led Teilhard to a more detailed consideration of Christian asceticism. He allowed, and indeed exacted, a place for penance; the lesser must be sacrificed to the greater; but man had no right 'to diminish himself for the sake of diminution'. He compared the Church to a strong tree with its roots spreading under the earth and its leaves exposed to the sun. The supernatural came to the support of nature only at the price of apparent annihilation, and the ultimate sacrifice of

[1] O happy fault.
[2] Everything is converted into good.
[3] It is necessary that scandals shall come.

individual progress to 'renunciation in God' was explained and justified by the Cross. Teilhard's name and doctrine are so commonly, and
on occasion so exclusively, associated with the Risen Christ that people
imagine him as somehow by-passing Calvary on his way to the Empty
Tomb. Nothing could be farther from the truth. But what he saw in
the crucifix was less the aspect of suffering, human and divine, than
the sublimation of the law of life. 'The royal road of the Cross is no
more nor less than the road of human endeavour, supernaturally
righted and prolonged.'

Finally, he did not shrink from the doctrine of eternal punishment.
The aggregation of souls and consummation of matter composing the
tissue of the '*terre nouvelle*' was also a segregating process. Matter
which had not overcome its multiplicity would be rejected, and men
might be rejected with it. Hell was not only *below*; we had the word of
Christ himself that its darkness was also *beyond*. Teilhard clung to his
right to believe that it was eternally uninhabited. But the Christian
choice presupposed the Christian risk; and Hell, however we conceived it, might be considered 'a structural element of the universe'.
It added

> an accent, a gravity, a contrast, a depth, which would not exist
> without it. The peak can only be measured from the abyss which
> it crowns. The fires of Hell and the fires of Heaven are not two
> different forces, but contrary manifestations of the same energy.

Looking back on *Le Milieu Divin*, Teilhard considered it 'better
balanced perhaps than anything I have ever written'[1]—'a mouthful
of bread, more or less well baked, thrown to the mass of Christians
perishing of cold and hunger in a dehumanized Church'.[2] It was not
simply an epistle to the unbelievers. Completed in March 1927, Teilhard immediately sent it to Charles at Louvain. The Jesuits of Louvain
wanted it for their collection *Museum Lessianum*, and many reports on
it were favourable. In September 1928 Charles expressed himself
strongly in favour of publication, although there were still a number
of points that he asked Teilhard to clear up. A year later he announced
that the essay would be printed immediately. Teilhard, in a letter to
Valensin, remained sceptical; but in February 1931 he wrote again
from New York. 'Before leaving, I saw Charles who handed me the

[1] Letter to Madame Haardt, Easter 1938.
[2] Letter to P. Décisier, 6 February 1948.

last revision of *Le Milieu Divin*. They want a few alterations which I shall try to make in the course of the year; if that is done, they'll accept it.' But the Jesuits at Louvain were too optimistic. At Christmas 1932 Teilhard received the reports of the two censors officially appointed to approve the book. Both were extremely favourable; one of them asked for a greater precision in the passage on the significance of the Cross—a request that Teilhard could easily satisfy—and another thought that not enough room had been left for grace and the supernatural.

What I wanted to present [Teilhard wrote in reply] was neither a complete treatise on the interior life, nor a work of theology or even of catechetics. I was simply analysing a spiritual development in the domain of experimental psychology, for a soul caught in a modest current of the 'illuminative' way. (That is why, let it be said in passing, there is so little *explicit* treatment of sin, because sin is at the reverse end of the point of view in question.) . . . For example, when I speak of effort I use the word in its popular, current and human sense, without denying in the least (and I'll state this here and there) that its primary source is in God. Enthusiastic as I am for the value of human effort, I think that, both by conviction and intellectual bent, I stand at the antipodes of Pelagianism.[1]

Reporting the encouragements of Louvain to Valensin, Teilhard is forced to add: 'A pity that everything is held up through intervention from Rome.' What had happened? An unrevised copy of the MS had been mysteriously 'seized'[2] and was under examination. Typed or roneoed copies of the definitive version were nevertheless widely distributed, and Teilhard was cheered by the approval of his fellow Jesuits in France, even by those of an older generation who might be supposed to take less kindly to his ideas. When *Le Milieu Divin* was published by *Les Éditions du Seuil* in 1957, two years after Teilhard's death, it still lacked an *imprimatur*. But by that time *imprimaturs* did not greatly matter.

III

In December 1926 Teilhard took part in a Pan-Pacific Congress in Pekin. With the Australians, New Zealanders, Americans and French,

[1] Letter to P. Lévie, 2 March 1932.   [2] *ibid.*, 23 October 1932.

the cocktail parties and the rose-scented wine, and the congenial conversations, life in Pekin was not very different from life in Paris. Towards the end of the month Teilhard accompanied his old friend Alfred Lacroix, permanent Secretary of the Académie des Sciences, on an expedition to Kalgan. A photograph of Lacroix suggests a King Lear in modern dress, and when he was in the field he must have recalled Turgenev's 'Lear of the Steppes'. Teilhard thought him 'one of the three or four finest examples of a man of science' that he knew. The director of the Chinese Geological Survey went with them. It was a fifteen-hour journey in broken-down railway carriages and icy weather. They reached the edge of the Gobi desert—familiar territory, but with three geologists for company Teilhard felt as if he were seeing it for the first time. He was generally unimpressed by such examples of *chinoiserie* as came his way:

> Anything large the Chinese have made (palaces, gates, walls) is built of mud, and their only work in durable materials (jade, bronze, porcelain) is no more than pretty trifles. The most massive and intricately carved statues are revolting anatomically. The awful grinning lions that stand at the entrance to palaces have a terrifying number of teeth, and they all have a little bell round their necks.[1]

What he most admired, he told Léontine Zanta,[2] was 'the geometry of the walls, the curve of the roofs, the multiple stages of the towers, the poetry of the old trees weighed down with crows, the desolate profile of the mountains'. And there were certain jade ornaments, dating from 2000 B.C., where the lines had the purity of Egyptian jewels. The reader may blink at Teilhard's insensibility to the beauty of Chinese porcelain, but he was too concerned with the turbulence of the present to pay much attention to the tranquillities of the past. He anticipated the victory of the Cantonese influence over Pekin, hoping that when the south met the north its Bolshevik ardour might cool. He believed that such a victory might be 'the first step in the reorganization of China'. The country had 'three revolutions on its hands ... political, social and intellectual'. It was 'a very grave crisis'[3] and one year would not see the end of it. In fact the internal

[1] *Letters from a Traveller*, p. 136.
[2] 10 January 1927.
[3] *ibid.*

dissensions among the Cantonese forces and the raid on the Russian legation at Pekin had played into the hands of what was already being spoken of as 'Chinese Fascism'. Eighteen students had been executed at Tientsin, and Teilhard hoped that the 'conservative reaction would not be too brutal and prolonged'.[1] His sympathies remained 'obscurely' with the Cantonese; he trusted, perhaps naïvely, that their humanitarian instincts would prevail over their xenophobia. He still believed that a frank co-operation between East and West was possible, for Teilhard stifled in any grouping narrower than humanity itself: 'man, and nothing but man, and nothing less than man' must be 'the framework of our ambitions and our organizations'. The Communist failure in the Far East—which Teilhard admitted was deserved—had been a failure of international action motivated by hatred, and it should be the signal for an international effort based on sympathy and mutual aid. 'What distresses me is to see Communism opposed by Fascism, which is the brutal and retrograde negation of what the many *good* elements of the Communist awakening have obscurely wished and felt for.'[2]

Here Catholicism appeared anything but catholic, and Teilhard, still smarting from the impotence of exile, opened his mind very freely to Léontine Zanta, as he had opened it to his cousin—in similar terms—ten years before:

Really one sometimes has the impression that our little churches are hiding the earth from us. . . . They want to identify Christian orthodoxy with an '*intégrisme*'—that is to say with a respect for the slightest workings of a microcosm constructed centuries ago. In reality, the true Christian ideal is '*intégralisme*'—by which I mean the extension of Christian directives to all the resources of the world. '*Intégralisme*' or '*intégrisme*', dogma as an axis or dogma as a cage—the fight has been going on in the Church for more than a century. '*Intégrisme*' is simple and convenient, for faithful and authorities alike. But it implicitly excludes from the kingdom of God, or implicitly denies, the enormous potentialities which are everywhere in movement around us, in society and morals, philosophy and science, etc. That is why I have definitely declared war on it—though I don't quite know how I shall manage to wage

[1] Letter to Léontine Zanta, 7 May 1927.
[2] *ibid.*

this war now that my possibilities of external action are more and more restricted.[1]

He was writing at the same time to Père d'Ouince:

Believe me, once you have penetrated to the very axis of the Christian outlook, the theological, disciplinary and ceremonial excrescences count for little more than the musical theories when you are listening to music. There really is a Christian note which makes the whole world vibrate—like a huge gong—in the divine Christ.[2]

In the first disappointment of exile Teilhard had even doubted his vocation, just as he had lost his taste for the prehistoric past. Now his doubts were dispelled, and the vision of the past was rediscovered in his vision of the future.

In February 1927 he was invited by the Carnegie Foundation to supervise the work on vertebrate and human fossils in China, but he continued to represent the Paris museum. Boule was reluctant to see his energies divided in this way and stopped the subsidies from the museum, but Teilhard, working with an international *équipe*, was impatient with his master's separatist chauvinism. He describes, for contrast, a meeting which was the 'prelude to many partings . . . the table was strewn with apple-blossom, a sign both of spring and its storms; we each spoke in turn of friendship, of collaboration, of our hopes for small or great things'.[3]

In May he undertook a further expedition of ten weeks in the direction of the Dalai-Nôr, where the geology of a rocky mountain chain, intersected by several valleys, awaited careful exploration. The country had been allowed to go to ruin by the Chinese settlers; the storms carried torrents of stones and earth through the cracks opened up in ground denuded of its trees. This was a misfortune for the animals and the plants, but it was a boon for the geologist. In contrast to the desolation of the Dalai-Nôr were the woods and pastures of Weichang—a basaltic plateau reminiscent of Haute-Auvergne—with roebuck and blackcock in the woods and gazelle in the open country. It was 'a botanical paradise' with its 'carpet of red and yellow lilies, scarlet primulas, white-striped rue, wide single peonies, lady's slipper

[1] *ibid.*
[2] 1926.
[3] *Letters from a Traveller*, p. 138.

orchids with flowers as big as walnuts, and masses of iris'.[1] Here Teilhard spent some time under canvas before returning to Tientsin, where an abundant mail awaited him. It included permission to return, temporarily, to France, and on 27 August 1927 he embarked.

[1] *ibid.*, p. 142.

SINANTHROPOS[1]

ON RETURNING HOME Teilhard spent several days with his cousin Marguerite and her sister Alice at Le Chambon in the Cantal. This was a grey stone house, near Laveissière, with the Allagnon—still a mountain stream—running beside the paddock. The bookshelves in the salon were dark with old leather bindings—thick legal tomes, a *Buffon de la Jeunesse* with delightful illustrations, and three volumes of *Clarissa Harlowe* in translation. The country was chiselled to Teilhard's taste, and the three friends, joined by Léontine Zanta, explored it indefatigably by car.

At the end of September we find him with Breuil in the eastern Pyrenees for two days of discussion and research. Max Bégouën, detained in Paris on business, had lent them his house, Les Espas. It looked on to the bare serrated crest of the Spanish frontier, with wooded limestone hills in the foreground, honeycombed with caves. It was here that Count Bégouën, the father of Max, with Breuil hot upon the scent, had discovered the *bisons d'argile*—prehistoric drawings of fantastic animals, tall as a man, strong as a bull and feline as a leopard. Stalactites hung from the roof of what Breuil described as the 'nuptial hall', and the approaches to it were engraved with horses, reindeer, and little bears. A strange personage with a horse's tail and wearing the antlers of a reindeer also formed part of the cortège. All this was nothing if not phenomenal, and it may well have spurred Teilhard to the first tentative pages of *Le Phénomène Humain*[2]—a short essay to be distinguished from the later and much longer work which bore the same title.

[1] For a detailed account of the finding of *Sinanthropos* the reader should refer to Dr. George Barbour's *In the Field with Teilhard de Chardin*. I have drawn largely on this in the pages which follow, even where the source is not explicitly indicated.
[2] *The Vision of the Past*, ch. II.

He defined the *'phénomène humain'* as 'the extraordinary power to think'; to a distant observer the earth would appear 'luminous with thought'. And so he was led to an eloquent description of the noosphere:

> The phenomenon of man represents at the very least a general transformation of the earth by the establishment on its surface of a new envelope—the thinking envelope. More vibrant and a better conductor, in a sense, than any metal; more mobile than any liquid; more expansive than any gas; more assimilative and more sensitive than all organic matter. And what gives this metamorphosis its full grandeur is that it did not take place as a chance accident, but in the form of a crisis, prepared in essence from the beginning, by the very play of the general evolution of the world. (Clearly inspired by the Creator.)

In tracing the ascent of man from the anthropomorphic apes to the first makers of tools, from *homo sapiens*—black, white or yellow—to Neolithic man who had taken possession of the earth, and so to our present stage of unification and industrialization, Teilhard saw humanity 'supported by a giddy scaffolding of improbabilities to which each new progress adds a new platform'; and he contrasted 'on the one side great numbers swallowing up unity; on the other unity born of great numbers'. Mankind was the 'spearhead' of evolution whose flight could not be arrested and whose worst danger was 'not some external catastrophe or famine or plague—but rather that spiritual sickness—the most terrible because the most directly anti-human of all scourges—the loss of appetite for living'. If anyone charged Teilhard with being hypnotized by his own synthesis, he would reply by asking:

> Who can say at what point a seductive harmony is not the nascent charm and precursory sign of the strictest truth?

He sent these pages to Louvain for 'revision'—not without some fears that people unfamiliar with his ideas would find them 'a little crazy'.[1] He hoped that they might appear in *Scientia*. Meanwhile his article on Édouard Le Roy—*La Pensée dans la Science*—had just appeared in *La vie catholique en France et à l'étranger*[2] under the pseudonym of Max Bégouën. To such desperate shifts was he now driven.

[1] Letter to Léontine Zanta, 28 September 1928.
[2] No. 203.

Teilhard lodged in Paris at the Jesuit house in the Rue du Regard. He saw a good deal of Le Roy with whom he was in close agreement, only wishing that he would express his ideas at shorter length and in a more nervous prose. Le Roy had just published two important works: *L'exigence idéaliste et le fait d'évolution* and *Les origines humaines et l'évolution de l'intelligence*. Teilhard would always criticize Le Roy's idealism, but the mind of each had so fertilized the other than Le Roy could write:

> We have discussed the views presented here so often and in such detail that we have come to arrange them in the same order, to express them in almost the same words, and to find it difficult to determine the limits of each one's contribution.[1]

Teilhard also made a number of new acquaintances—notably Paul Valéry whom he met with Boule at the museum. 'I am a post-hominian', the great poet observed as he examined various skulls, and indeed no one would have taken him for anything else. They had several subsequent meetings, and one would give much to know what they talked about. The resurrection of the body, perhaps? Valéry once said that this was the essential Christian dogma—the only one capable of interesting a man—and that beside it all the others were of little importance. Teilhard sat for his portrait to Edmée de la Rochefoucauld; here there was a portrait of Valéry on the wall of the studio and a picture—painting or photograph—of the Chinese coast. But China must have seemed already remote for Teilhard as he lunched with Leprince-Ringuet and Maurice de Broglie; argued for evolution with Vialleton; or slipped up to Louvain where Charles would tell him what chances (if any) there might be for *Le Phénomène Humain*.

Charles, no doubt, was cautiously encouraging; and so was Maréchal who was charged with the revision of the essay:

> As in his other works the author supposes admissible a certain continuity of evolution from matter to Man. This can be understood in a perfectly orthodox way and even fits easily into the Aristotelian theories of causality. . . . Maintaining that the spiritual soul is *only* created '*in corpore*', and *only* operates in conjunction with matter, the Thomist philosophers admit by that very fact a 'noosphere' linked to the rest of the material world by necessary correlations. So there is, in their eyes, a 'natural science'

[1] See Cuénot, p. 58.

not only of the human body but of the whole man. This natural determinism of Man in his entirety does not exclude spontaneity, even in its highest expression which is the liberty of action.

Teilhard hastened to send this revision to Valensin; and Maréchal's reconciliation of Teilhard with a school of philosophy with which he is not normally associated, and from whose classical formulations he seemed to be disengaging himself, has been confirmed by a later Jesuit theologian, Jean Daniélou. Père Daniélou does not minimize Teilhard's distaste for, and divergence from, the categories of scholastic philosophy. Teilhard wished to 'start from zero' ... from the point at which science had reached in his lifetime. It was a time when 'nuclear physics had revolutionized the conception of matter, had shown that matter and energy were reversible, and that in consequence matter might be considered as a field for the forces of energy'. It was a time when 'biological evolution had revealed itself as the most plausible explanation for an ensemble of data' which it made intelligible. Teilhard spoke the language of this science; a language very different from that of traditional scholasticism.

In what then did the philosophical significance of Teilhard consist? He made the language of science universal and extended it to the whole of existence. He transposed scientific categories into metaphysical categories. The 'general laws of life—complexification, evolution, personalization, socialization—are verified at every level. They allow one to grasp the totality of things, to establish liaisons. And metaphysics are precisely that—for there are no metaphysics without analogy.' In the same way the Aristotelian and Thomist philosophy had started out with physical and biological analysis, and it was in the prolongation of this analysis that the metaphysical realities were analogically conceived. Teilhard had rediscovered the basic attitude of the traditional philosophy of the Church, but he had stripped it of a language consonant with a science now out of date, and had invented a new language which expressed the science of today:

This operation, however, was only possible because Teilhard was the heir of scholastic philosophy, the essential elements of which he had preserved. This saved him from materialism and pantheism and evolutionism alike. This is how the categories of personality, creation and God come to be the constituent factors of his thought. But he only retained the fundamental categories of scholasticism, interpreting these in accordance with the scientific data of his time.[1]

Teilhard resumed his talks with the students from the École Normale. The death of the Abbé Portal had thrown them into some confusion, and Teilhard restored their harmony, attending their dinners to which Normalien alumni and students from elsewhere were invited, and giving them a three-day retreat at Gentilly. Here he pursued the theme of *Le Milieu Divin* and even allowed the students to carry off a copy of the manuscript of his *conférence*. Étienne Borne was among those who never forgot this retreat. Hesitating between the poetic mythology of Alain and an authentic supernaturalism, he learned from Teilhard 'the overwhelming reality of the Christian fact'.[2] In August 1928 Teilhard took part in one of Maurice Vaussard's 'intellectual retreats' at Juilly. It was here that the young Bruno de Solages came to interview him on the subject of evolution. The meeting was to have important consequences. Teilhard sent his interviewer a copy of *Le Fondement et le Fond de l'évolution*, and the Abbé was so impressed by this that he became, in later years, one of Teilhard's staunchest allies. The courage of Bruno de Solages was proved during the French Resistance, as a result of which he spent some time in a Nazi concentration camp. Later, as Rector of the Institut Catholique at Toulouse and a domestic prelate to the Pope, he was able to add a powerful voice to those who were pleading Teilhard's cause at Rome.

Among Teilhard's younger Jesuit colleagues working in the same field was Pierre Leroy, with whom he formed an enduring friendship. Leroy was studying for his degree at Nancy, and had been chosen by his superiors to join Licent at the Tientsin Museum. He met Teilhard in Boule's laboratory:

His simple and natural greeting immediately put me at my ease. He offered me a chair, while he sat casually on the edge of the table. His eyes, filled with intelligence and kindly understanding, his features, finely drawn and weathered by the winds of sea and desert, the glamour that surrounded his name, all made a deep impression on me.[3]

[1] 'Signification de Teilhard de Chardin', *Études*, February 1962.
[2] See Cuénot, p. 88.
[3] *Letters from a Traveller*, Introduction.

So the months passed until 7 November 1928, when Teilhard embarked once again for the Far East. He was under the same instructions as before—to remain in China for a limited but indefinite period. The exact duration of his stay would depend upon political events as well as upon the fossils he collected and sent home. The voyage gave him, besides, the chance of accepting an invitation from Henri de Monfreid to spend a couple of months in Ethiopia and French Somaliland on his way out. He was accompanied by his geologist friend, Pierre Lamare, with whom he shared a cabin from Marseilles. Monfreid had advised travelling light in order not to frighten the natives, and it was thus equipped—with a metal canteen for cooking in the field—that the two men, disembarking at Djibouti, proceeded to Obock, where de Monfreid had one of his many establishments. His wife and two children were with him, and they welcomed the travellers with feudal hospitality—for de Monfreid defied the local authorities with a quasi-feudal *insouciance,* roaming the country and the coast very much as he pleased.

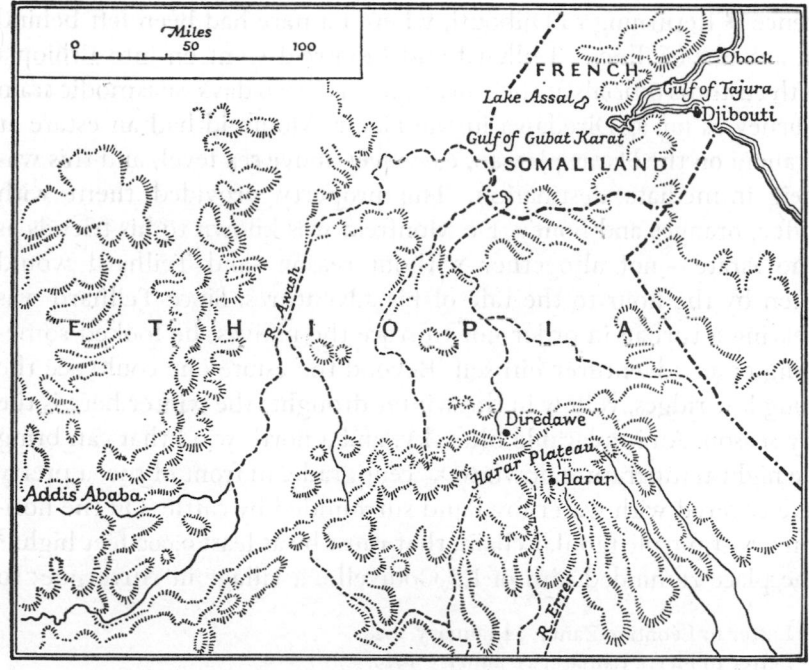

Eastern Ethiopia and French Somaliland

Imagine a big old house situated between a sea of blue or phosphorescent green, which comes beating up against our walls, and an immense desert plain, golden in colour and fringed to the westward by high, purple mountain peaks. Then put twenty straw-mattresses around the house and imagine them arranged in such a way that they remind you—apart from some tents formerly fixed up by Madame de Monfreid—of a fisherman's hut or the deck of a ship.[1]

Such was the setting, and here they spent a few days rising with the sun, and the mewing of cats for an alarm-clock. Teilhard was particularly anxious to penetrate the Mabla Massif, and he had found a mule to carry his light equipment and two Danakils for guides. De Monfreid was as popular with the natives as he was distrusted by the authorities, and in the event he was only able to escort Teilhard as far as the foothills. The plateau of Obock seemed to be composed of two marine transgressions superimposed on a coralline foundation, and among the gravel of the Mabla there was evidence of a pebble industry, considerably developed. The Mabla itself was a 'huge volcanic intumescence'.[2] Returning to Djibouti, where Lamare had been left behind on account of illness, Teilhard and Monfreid went on into Ethiopia with customs officials at their heels. It was a two days' spasmodic train journey as far as Diredawa in the Harar. Monfreid had an estate at Aranoui on the Harar plateau, 6,000 feet above sea level, and this was their immediate destination. The property provided them with coffee, oranges and honey. De Monfreid was known to his friends as 'the Pirate'—not altogether without reason—and Teilhard would listen by the hour to the tale of his adventures. Since Teilhard was wearing a turban in order not to scare the natives, he looked something of an adventurer himself. Beyond the estate one could see the 'long low ridges, yellow in the winter drought: the winter here is the dry season. An implacable blue sky, and a north wind that can bring the night temperature down to 5° centigrade. In front of me, a pretty lake covered with water fowl and surrounded by cattle. On the horizon a vast purple tabular chain, that must be at least 9,000 feet high.'[3] The place reminded him of La Godivelle, a village in Auvergne; so

[1] Letter to Léontine Zanta, 24 January 1928.
[2] Letter to Pierre Lamare, 21 January 1929.
[3] *Letters from a Traveller*, p. 147.

many places reminded Teilhard of Auvergne. On Christmas Day he celebrated Mass in the Capuchin chapel at Harar, with the skin of a zebra for altar-cloth. The Capuchin Fathers, like so many Capuchins all the world over, seemed 'lost behind their beards'.[1] The travellers stayed a month in the valley of the Errer, south of Harar, and Teilhard wrote to Le Roy of

> the typical African bush, with its innumerable, thinly scattered mimosas, its huge euphorbia shaped like cactuses, and spreading out like candelabra, its antelopes, its multi-coloured birds, and its ant-heaps . . . and our friends the apes, perched up high, and the baboons that come down from the trees. They go about in large groups, and when you meet them they make off at top speed . . . and the toucans and the humming-birds and the cardinal sparrows, the most common of all the creatures. They're not at all timid here, because no one addresses a word to them. The *people* are magnificent copper animals. Even in the cultivated plain they trot around in Indian file, generally armed with a long lance and a broad knife. The more sedentary types live like pure Neolithic men, with agricultural implements of the Stone Age. These people will either disappear or mix with other races. The Abyssinians who lord it over all these tribes seem to me pretentious and half-civilized, spoilt perhaps by their residual and undeveloped Christianity, inferior to the Chinese.[2]

These impressions do much to explain why, a few years later, Teilhard thought there might be room for a civilizing mission in Ethiopia, whatever specious reasons might be given for it and however questionable the methods it employed.

In the same district Teilhard discovered a grotto, difficult of access, with frescoes which were later to attract the attention of Breuil; and it was again upon Teilhard's indications that he was led to examine the red ploughed-up earth covering the lower terraces of the Errer and, higher up, the mounds of grass—evidence of chalky springs—which emerged, like huge ant-heaps, from the granite slopes. Teilhard was particularly anxious to see the Fantale volcano, two-thirds of the way on from Diredawa to Addis Ababa. Fortunately the railway ran close to it, since it was dangerous to wander more than half a mile from the stations and there was a total absence of water. To have climbed the

[1] *ibid.*, p. 148.   [2] 30 December 1928.

volcano would have required a minor expedition, but Teilhard sent to Lacroix such observations as he was able to make from the lower ground:

It rises up (600 metres!) in the middle of a perfectly flat plain, covered with a layer of light green igneous breccia, overlaid with black obsidian, which has the curious property of forming blisters scattered over the plain (over a hundred of them, I'm sure), like huge mole-hills. Each blister is hollow, and the roof is covered with lava stalactites, showing that the bubble was formed while the lava was flowing and not as a result of recent eruptions (in the vicinity).[1]

On their return he made some interesting geological discoveries on the coralline plateau behind Obock; a number of tools were found, fashioned, it seemed, by men living in a similar topographical situation.

Before re-embarking for China Teilhard cruised along the coast with de Monfreid. The two men had become intimate friends, and de Monfreid was to write many years later of

two weeks spent on the barren coast of the Red Sea, sleeping under the stars on the deck of my sailing boat, with only savage Danakils for company—their souls no different from the souls of their cave-dwelling ancestors. That strange gulf of Gubet Karat, where a fantastic landscape out of the book of Genesis rears its innumerable craters in a décor of lava and slag. All this chaos is fixed in black basalt. The blood-coloured rhyolites seem to be still moving and palpitating—the overheated air coming up from its furnace below gives one the illusion of a mirage.

Teilhard and I came upon a beach of black sand, and crossing the layers of slag rising up like monsters from the apocalypse, we found ourselves on the threshold of the plain of death—a depression 200 metres below the level of the sea. Here Lake Assal stretches out, cut off from the gulf by the earthquakes which had opened up the Red Sea and were no doubt responsible for the tidal wave known to legend as the Flood.

Not a bird or an insect in the crushing silence of these solitudes. We listened to the mysterious rumour of life whispering in our ears, as if life itself, lost and hopeless in this dead world, were de-

[1] 14 December 1928; Teilhard de Chardin Album, p. 85.

La Croisière Jaune: Bäzäklik, on the edge of the Gobi desert

Crater Lake, Oregon, 1933. Teilhard playing with a chipmunk

fending the precarious and vital milieu outside of which it would cease to exist.

At night, lying on the deck of my boat, Teilhard and I would meditate on the infinity of the stars. And so, far removed from human vanities—and remote, also, from the ephemeral décor of nature that marks the seasons, in a setting where nothing evolves any more, the words of this sublime man made clear and understandable to me the ineluctable eternity of the human soul. I measured its immensity and grasped its divine essence; and while we gazed into the depth of the sky, our minds were carried out to the limits of those spheres where worlds gravitate in space. During this silent reverie, in which two men were able to understand and communicate with each other, I understood why Teilhard could look indulgently at his fellow men when they excite themselves to no purpose, and very often against all reason. How many unfortunate people, discouraged, embittered and revolted by the blind hostility of the mob, by injustice and want of understanding —how many of these disinherited men and women, perverted and brought near to destruction by a contempt for themselves, have been comforted and saved by this man with the clear regard who knew how to bring dead consciences to life, just as Jesus of Nazareth brought Lazarus back from the dead.[1]

No more impressive tribute has been paid to the charismatic personality of Pierre Teilhard de Chardin, and no more striking portrait of him exists. Nevertheless, travelling with so controversial a character as de Monfreid had its disadvantages. Alfred Lacroix had been obliged to guarantee the respectability of Teilhard and Lamare to the French Government, and de Monfreid heartily reciprocated the ministerial distrust of his activities. He had nothing but contempt for French colonial policy, or for the Governor of Somaliland before whose palace soldiers had recently downed their arms. Teilhard was not, of course, embroiled in these disturbances, although he looked back on French Somaliland as 'an uninhabitable pool of frogs'. He remained, however, warmly attached to de Monfreid and particularly to his wife. Here was

one of the few friendships I have known which are a pure force—

[1] *La Table Ronde*, June 1955.

which dispose and encourage one for action, I mean, without ever weakening one with complaints and regrets.[1]

With Lamare Teilhard had more in common than geology. Lamare was well acquainted with the Moslem world and was attracted by it: Instinctively [Teilhard had written to him] I share your preference for a Christ who would be 'simply the Word'. But a Christ, without historical personification, would not be capable (either in fact or reason) of emerging from metaphysical abstractions or hypotheses. The 'success' of the Christ of Christianity is due to the association of his birth (which gives him the value of a *fact* or concrete *element* in the world) and his resurrection (which lets us grant him superhuman and, as it were, cosmic attributes). . . . The Modernists wanted to reduce Christ to a Mahomet, and this would mean the collapse of the whole physical edifice of the universe in Christ. Personally I feel myself at the antipodes of Modernism. . . .Christ must be endowed with certain physical properties—'theandric' as theology puts it—radically different from those of a simple prophet—who is a vehicle of truth without being in the least a centre which organizes the universe. Christ must always be far greater than our greatest conceptions of the world, but for two or three centuries we have allowed him to appear hardly equal to them, or even smaller. That is why Christianity is so anaemic at the present moment.[2]

II

After despatching five cases of fossils to Lacroix, Teilhard embarked at Djibouti at the beginning of February 1929. He was the only ecclesiastic on board, and the weather was perfect. He made friends with a French banker and his wife, and read Malraux's *Les Conquérants*. Events were moving fast in the direction that Malraux had imagined. The seat of government had been shifted to Nanking, and Pekin—'the Northern Capital'—had become Peiping—'the city of the northern plain'. On arrival in Tientsin Teilhard found Licent obsessively preoccupied with the prestige of his museum—threatened, as he supposed, by the scientific group in the capital who clearly had a higher

[1] Letter to Pierre Lamare, 1 January 1930.
[2] 23 April and 26 December 1929.

regard for Teilhard than for himself—and more concerned, as always, with the label he could attach to a fossil than with the evidence of prehistoric life which it appeared to suggest. In the meantime Teilhard's old friend from Brussels, Dr. Wong Wen-hao, now director of the National Geological Survey, had asked a fellow-seismologist, Father Ernest Gherzi, s.j., for the name of a geologist to serve as advisor to the Survey. Gherzi had worked with Teilhard in the old days of their scholasticate, both at Hastings and on Jersey, and it was on his recommendation that Teilhard was invited to fill the post. When he accepted the invitation, Licent virtually closed the museum to him.

Teilhard liked what he called the 'cynical serenity' of Pekin; moreover, as we have seen, he had many friends there. Among the Chinese specialists on the Geological Survey were Dr. V. K. Ting, Dr. Wong Wen-hao, Dr. C. C. Young, Mr. Pei Wen-chung, Professor J. S. Lee, and Mr. Eddie Bien; among the others—and both were to be of great importance to Teilhard—were Dr. Davidson Black of Toronto and Dr. Amadeus W. Grabau of New York. The personalities of these men were sharply distinctive, and they all played a part in the development of Teilhard's scientific thought. He was associated with them all in the discovery and identification of what came to be known as Sinanthropos, or 'Pekin man'.

The story began in 1918 when Dr. Gunar Andersson, a Swedish prospector, was invited out to China as adviser on mining to the Pekin Government. He was at work on a small coalfield near Chi-Ku-Shan, forty miles from Pekin, when he discovered a rich cache of fossils in a pocket of limestone rock, of the Ordovician age. He was struck by the 'modern' look of the fossilized animals, and returned two years later with an American and a Swedish expert. They found a second pocket, even richer than the first, in a quarry just above the village of Chou-Kou-Tien in the same neighbourhood. Some chips of white vein-quartz—which is not usually found in limestone caves—led them to suspect that hereabouts lay the origins of primitive man, if only they could find him. Amongst the material sent back to Uppsala were two teeth of seemingly human character. Controversy between the experts immediately broke out, but Andersson proclaimed his discovery on 22 October 1926 on the occasion of the Swedish Crown Prince's visit to Pekin. Teilhard himself—increasingly convinced that the teeth were of human origin—gave his views at the official luncheon.

Meanwhile Davidson Black, who was then Professor of Anatomy and Neurology at the Pekin Union Medical College, obtained the support of the Rockefeller Foundation for the setting up of a Cenozoic Research Laboratory to be administered jointly by the P.U.M.C. and the Geological Survey. For two years excavation at Chou-Kou-Tien went on under the direction of Dr. Birger Bohlin from Uppsala. At the end of his first year's digging Bohlin discovered a well-preserved left lower molar, which he was quite sure had belonged to a human being. As a result of this, and further explorations, the Cenozoic Research Laboratory was inaugurated in April 1929 with Davidson Black as Honorary Director, Dr. C. C. Young as Assistant Director and Palaeontologist, Teilhard de Chardin as adviser and collaborator, Pei Wen-chung in charge of the field work at Chou-Kou-Tien, and Bien as assistant. The laboratory occupied the science wing of the medical school building which had once belonged to the London Missionary Society. It was known as Lockhart Hall.

Within a month of his return to China, Teilhard was examining the fossils from Chou-Kou-Tien in the newly-opened laboratory, and at the end of April he set out, with his camp bed and a few provisions, to examine the excavations on the spot. Without suspecting the sensational discovery which was presently in store, he was fairly satisfied with what he found. In the meantime, however, he was obliged to accompany Licent to Manchuria. A train journey of thirty-six hours, followed by two days in a cart, brought them to a Christian hospital mission. The country was hideous and barren, and the population primitive in the extreme. Teilhard was interested to observe, with more precision than had hitherto been attained, the stratification of the land and to establish its connection with similar Chinese territories. What he saw enabled him to take a good step forward in his theories about the geology of the Quaternary era in the Far East. From the banks of the Sungari he left with a Russian engineer—'a pleasant and majestic ex-baron from the Baltic'—for the Mongolian plateau. It was a long journey by the Trans-Siberian railway and when he reached the Dalai-Nôr he reflected that he could be in Paris within nine days. Nothing had changed since his visit in 1924. He compared notes with some Russian geologists; gave a lecture; and was back in Tientsin on 10 June.

But not for long. He was now committed to a journey into the Shansi and Shensi—the first he was to undertake on behalf of the Geological Survey. Accompanied by a young Chinese assistant, three boys and six mules, he left on 6 July 1929. The advantages of an official Chinese as companion were soon apparent. The work was more enjoyable and the cooking notably improved. Also, a welcome from the local authorities was never in doubt. They followed the great loop of the Yellow River from Shensi in the east to Shansi in the west; and a fortnight's excursion to the north of Pao-Teo brought new evidence for determining the geology of the Yellow River. Teilhard thought this went back to Palaeolithic times, and he was able to extend his 1923 findings by several hundred miles. They went up into Mongol country as far as Chungar where the 'king' of the place received them royally in a fortified farmhouse 'crowded with lamas and standing in the middle of the sand'. Proceeding from one inn to another, they sat down to the same ceremonial meals at the same unearthly hours, and were treated with the same kindness wherever they went. Only the flies were hostile.

Teilhard was back in his office at Pekin by the beginning of October. The winter was approaching earlier than usual, and Pei who was digging at the foot of the escarpment at Chou-Kou-Tien was warned to suspend operations at the end of the month. He obtained permission, however, to continue for a week or two longer. Various teeth and fragments of bone had by now been discovered from four different levels on the vertical face of the excavation, but nothing fresh had been turned up during November. On 2 December, therefore, Pei dismissed his workers and went up to the site to measure the exact dimensions of the hole he had been digging. George Barbour, who had visited the place not long before, describes what followed:

Probing with a yardstick in the sand under a limestone overhang, he suddenly exposed the smooth dome of a skull, embedded in cave travertine. Loosening the block with a hammer and chisel, Pei saw at once that the top of the cranium was larger than that of any ape so far unearthed. He carried it back to his room with care. A battery of candles from the village store had given just enough light for a time exposure of the find *in situ*. He got another photograph of his prize wrapped in burlap soaked with flour paste, and balanced above three braziers so that it could dry out during the night. By dawn it was ready for the trip to Pekin, without fear of shedding fragments on the road. Pei wrapped the treasure in his soiled linen, bargained with a rickshaw puller, and set out for the city, the precious bundle between his feet hidden by the long skirt of his . . . Chinese scholar's gown . . . Pei covered the thirty-five miles safely and delivered his trophy to Davidson Black at the P.U.M.C. well before dusk.[1]

Black worked on the skull with dental instruments, detaching it from the matrix in which it was embedded, and re-assembling the headbones until its original shape had been delicately reconstructed. He carried out these operations at night, rarely leaving the laboratory until 3 a.m., having locked up the skull in a safe. It was photographed at various stages of its reconstruction; prints were despatched to three selected scientists in different parts of the world; and plaster replicas were made, and similarly distributed. A duplicate of each type was sent to the British Museum. It was at this point that Teilhard, readily at hand, justified the prescience of Davidson Black in appointing him to the Cenozoic Laboratory. Black was perfectly certain that the skull was a human skull, but Teilhard could help him to establish the geological era in which the caves had been inhabited. This was made easier when the stone tools in the lowest part of the diggings came to light. Human habitation was already indicated by charred bones, cracked nuts, and the broken shells of ostrich eggs; but, as Barbour explains, the 'study of the associated mammal fossils—Teilhard's particular *forte*—did promise a time index of the relative antiquity. It could give the percentage of vertebrates which had evolved to modern type, as compared with the number of genera or species now extinct. . . . Over sixty distinct animal types had been found in the breccia and gravel layers filling the cavern.' Some of these 'were related to forms Teilhard had found in deposits of like age in Europe, Egypt and elsewhere'.[2]

It has been loosely stated that Teilhard 'discovered' Sinanthropos. This is, of course, untrue, as he was always the first to emphasize. But he naturally, as the only Frenchman on the spot, did a great deal to publish and explain the findings in French scientific circles. As excavation progressed, the hominid fossils went to Black while everything else was examined by Teilhard and Young at the Lockhart Hall

[1] *In the Field with Teilhard de Chardin*, p. 52.   [2] *ibid.*, p. 54.

laboratory. So while credit for the actual discovery and its immediate identification must be given to others, Teilhard's association with it was of the utmost value.

The excavations continued for eight months every year, with up to a hundred workmen employed on the site, until the Japanese occupation of the country temporarily brought them to a standstill. Blasting was used to clear the ground, and an upper cave was discovered with evidence of much later human habitation. It showed a rich industry in quartz, but Teilhard sharply disagreed with Breuil that it proved the existence of a second man. This was an idea which belonged, if not to pure fantasy, then at least to prehistoric fiction. Breuil, on his side, recognized that Teilhard had 'a wonderful geologist's eye in the field' and was 'an admirable palaeontologist', but thought he 'lacked experience of prehistoric techniques, where the evidence of industry partially escaped him'.[1] Teilhard recorded and analysed the progress made in two articles which appeared in the *Revue des Questions Scientifiques* (20 July 1930 and vol. xxiv [1934]). Three years later he was able to summarize his conclusions for *Études* (5 July 1937); and he returned to the problem—for the experts were divided over many aspects of the discovery—in a long essay, *The Question of Fossil Man*, which was published in Pekin in September 1943.[2]

By 1936 the Sinanthropos site, 100 metres long with an average of 30 metres in breadth, and more than 50 metres deep, had revealed an enormous mass of deposits. The fossils, mostly of species long extinct, were the remains of animals that lived in the cave—tigers, panthers and bears—and of their weaker prey—ostrich, horse, rhinoceros, wild sheep, bison and deer. Teilhard agreed that these deposits belonged to the early Quaternary era—roughly, that is to say, one hundred thousand years ago. During the ten years of excavation five almost complete skulls, three of them adult; important fragments of three others; a dozen more or less complete jaws; and a great number of isolated teeth, had been unearthed. They represented, in all, about thirty individuals. Neither the anatomy of these specimens, nor the composition of the fauna associated with them, altered significantly with the depth of the deposits. Virtually no part of a skeleton was found beside the skulls, and to whatever depth you penetrated into

[1] *La Table Ronde*, June 1955.
[2] All these articles are reproduced in *The Appearance of Man*, chapters 4, 7 and 8.

the site there was the same 'abundance of ashes, calcined and broken bones, and stones rather roughly but visibly shaped'.

There was no doubt that Sinanthropos was hominian; this was proved by his cranial capacity, which varied between 900 and 1,200 cubic centimetres. Nothing indicated a degenerate type, but his 'cranial architecture' was so distant from that of modern man that the question arose—was he intelligent? Here the palaeontologists disagreed. Boule was among those who held that the cave had certainly been inhabited by an intelligent being, but he doubted whether this man was Sinanthropos. He believed that the skulls had been brought to the cave as trophies by someone else. Nothing showed that Sinanthropos, with his primitive cranial characteristics, was capable of the activity attributed to him. To this objection Teilhard could offer no certain proof:

> To remark that no bone remains of this hypothetical man he postulates have yet been found at Chou-Kou-Tien is not an entirely satisfactory answer; plenty of prehistoric sites are known in Europe that have never yielded the least fragment of their ancient inhabitants among the quantities of ash and flints of their deposits. Theoretically, the thing might very well occur at Chou-Kou-Tien.

Nevertheless he thought it safer—in default of positive evidence to the contrary—to assume that Sinanthropos was a 'being in whom the fire of thought was already alight and had no doubt been so for a long time—as already *Homo faber*, walking upright and using his hands as we do', and 'in shape exactly intermediate between Pithecanthropos and Neanderthal Man'.[1] If this view were accepted, Sinanthropos represented an ancient human group of the lower Quaternary era localized in South-East Asia, and his existence certainly confirmed evolutionary views on the origins of the human race. It did not, however—and Teilhard stated this with emphasis—'threaten (quite the opposite) a spiritual conception of humanity'.

III

Teilhard was now living with the Lazarist Fathers. On his weekly visits to the headquarters of the Geological Survey he invariably

[1] Letter to Pierre Lamare, 1 January 1930.

lunched with Dr. Grabau, and among his more precious acquaintances was George Barbour who had been appointed Visiting Physiographer to the Rockefeller Foundation. His job was to link 'the recognizable stages in the development of the North China landscape with the conditions under which the cave (at Chou-Kou-Tien) came into existence'. This was the beginning of a close collaboration and warm friendship between the two men. While Pei was still digging at Chou-Kou-Tien in November, Teilhard and Barbour, with another companion went up into the Chaitang Basin of the Western Hills. Barbour gives a vivid and exact portrait of Teilhard in the field. He

exchanged his clerical garb for a khaki drill suit of military cut with four large tunic pockets. A folding penknife, hand lens, marching compass, and loose money went into his trouser pockets. The padlock key of his kit-box was on a loop of string in his watch pocket. Banknotes and his passport went in an inside breast pocket, because the left upper pocket always carried his breviary, while the right one held matches and a crushed packet of Job or Gauloise cigarettes. The right side pocket held his small shiny black notebook with graph paper. The contents of the left pocket were apt to vary with the occasion—a folded map, a piece of string, a chip of lava, a fossil wrapped in newspaper, or even an unfinished square of chocolate wrapped in silver paper.[1]

Where Barbour used coloured crayons to distinguish the various formations of rock or soil, Teilhard carried these differences in his head. He was armed with a hammer and chisel; dispensed with rucksack or water-bottle; and only used an army haversack if he were searching for fossils or lunching out of doors. His kit-box was a relic of the First World War. It contained maps, papers, clothing to suit the climate, and a thin black cassock. The notes or sketches he made in the field were in rough contrast to the drawings he made in the laboratory, which were often more precise than a photograph. But he regretted his incapacity to make relief diagrams of the land formations he was studying.

When we arrived for the night and had found a spot for our folding camp cots, the cook would start a fire, and then forage for noodles, eggs, an occasional chicken, 'turnips which tasted like pears'. Our wooden supply box—which came home loaded with

[1] ibid., p. 33.

rocks and fossils—furnished the extras: sugar, coffee, condensed milk, confiture, marmalade, tinned fruit, chocolate, candles, matches and insect lotion. By the time we had washed up and changed shirts, water was boiling for a cup of tea. Teilhard would then hunt for his brown felt pantoufles with the red stripes, light a cigarette, and relax.... After supper he would light another cigarette, and I would take out my pipe. Then, completing our field notes for the day, we would compare conclusions while they were fresh in our minds, and lay plans for the morrow.[1]

As night fell and the camp fire burned low, the French Jesuit would talk to the Scots Presbyterian of the ideas which he was putting down, indefatigably, in his essays and letters. The challenge of Marxist materialism, the inertia of the Church, the poverty of the peasants among whom they had made their bivouac—the conversation was at once a meditation and a mutual enquiry, and it continued until the smoke of Teilhard's last Gauloise had evaporated into the thin air. As his thought deepened and his very competent English failed to respond to it, he would slide into his native tongue; but even Teilhard's French was not always adequate to the complexity of his ideas—and then fatigue would overtake him, and unless his breviary detained him, he would turn in for the night.

Two more expeditions followed. In January 1930 he escorted Barbour to Shansi; an easy journey, now, along the new motor road. Barbour confirmed Teilhard's views on his previous findings; and they were back in Pekin in time for an American party to celebrate Washington's birthday. The evening ended—as evenings with Teilhard had a way of ending—with a discussion on the meaning of life; on this occasion with the Swedish explorer, Sven Hedin to whom he seemed more like a big brother, intimidating no one and keeping no one at a distance. In May he was setting out for Mongolia with a group of Chinese geologists, and furnished with a silver cigarette lighter which Barbour had given him to reduce his consumption of matches. But Barbour had forgotten that the rapid evaporation in the Mongolian climate would place a considerable strain on the fuel tanks. Teilhard abandoned the lighter in the Gobi desert—'somewhere', he explained, 'near latitude 45 north and longitude 105 east of Paris'[2]. In Mongolia he saw 'the lowest strata of humanity' spreading awk-

[1] *ibid.*, p. 37.   [2] Letter to Pierre Lamare, 22 October 1930.

wardly over the monotonous steppes. Later in the year he set out once more from Pekin, this time with American colleagues, under the direction of Dr. Andrews, who presented him with a thick fur coat and sheepskin sleeping bag. Teilhard described Andrews as 'a wonderful man, full of real-life stories of hunting from the Yunan to Siberia'. If meat was in short supply, he would go off in his car and return 'with a couple of gazelles on the running-boards'. Whipped by gales and sustained each morning by 'hearty breakfasts', they went up into the Gobi where there was 'nothing in sight but a few yourts beside the streams', and their only companions were 'the wolves, eagles and gazelles'.[1] But they found some genuine mastodon deposits. Teilhard's objective was to link the geologies of China and Mongolia, and he returned to Pekin early in August well satisfied with the evidence that would enable him to do so.

IV

This active and enjoyable existence concealed sombre preoccupations of which Teilhard would hardly have spoken to his scientific friends, unless he lifted the veil with George Barbour round the camp fire. The four years that followed his return to China in 1926 were undoubtedly the most critical of his whole life. If he had been going to leave the Society he would have left it then, at a time when his feelings —desires, revolts and passions—ran high. 'I don't think I was ever really tempted to free myself', he told Valensin; nevertheless he continued to feel a 'deep and native opposition' to the contemporary forms and idiom of Catholicism. He 'literally stifled' in the world of ecclesiastical documents and official actions. Catholicism had ceased to be catholic; it had allowed itself to shrink to the dimensions of a system and a sect. Moving, as he did, among the Gentiles, Teilhard saw a vast number of truths and attitudes for which orthodoxy should find a place. 'Irreducibly', he wrote, 'I am hyper-Catholic.'[2]

His dissatisfaction with existing forms extended to the Society. On the one hand he saw that Christ—as necessary to him as the air he breathed—would 'evaporate . . . without a traditional and historic revelation'; and yet it was precisely those things which he saw to be irreplaceable in the Church and the Society that were farthest removed from the picture both of them presented today:

[1] *Letters from a Traveller*, pp. 165–6.   [2] 29 June 1926.

How I should love [he exclaimed] to meet the St. Ignatius or the St. Francis that our present age needs so badly! To follow a man of God along a new road, in freedom, urged forward by the fullness of the religious sap of *his own* time. What a dream that would be! I often ask God to let me be the ashes from which this great expansion will spring, and which our generation has missed.[1]

The prayer was in some respect a prophecy, although Teilhard was not to see its fulfilment. He would have been content to spend eighteen months alternately in China and Paris; and he would have liked to go to Rome in order to make them understand that his influence in circles closed to missionaries depended on his being known to be 'someone' in his own country. On his periodic returns Baudrillart advised him to resume his activities at the Institut Catholique, unless he were expressly forbidden to do so; and Baudrillart even went to Rome himself on his behalf—uselessly, as it turned out. In April 1927 one of Teilhard's well-disposed intermediaries from Lyon wrote to remind him that 'the Society is not an order of pioneers'. Teilhard energetically disagreed, but assured his friend that he had not the slightest intention of leaving it. Indeed he was only too anxious to 'soften' his ideas and bring them into line with what was regarded as orthodoxy.

When he was in Paris during the winter of 1928 he found some of his old friends converted to Communism, but their fervour dismayed him. Seen from outside, there was too much to hate in a movement which profited from the French tendency to a naïve extremism. The same tendency had been at work in the *Action Française*, but although Teilhard had no sympathy with its ideas, he questioned—as did many others—the method of its suppression:

One can't change one's ideas as one changes one's clothes. Perhaps Rome did not realize that in a too over-simplified, 'political' intervention it was striking at the springs of faith in souls which had established in themselves (happily or less happily) the link between what is Christian and what is human.[2]

There were already rumours that Édouard Le Roy's latest books would be placed on the Index. A Jesuit, of conservative stamp, had actually asked Teilhard whether Le Roy was a Christian. For his own

[1] Letter to Valensin, 31 December 1926.
[2] *ibid.*, 14 February 1928.

part, Teilhard was resolved to defend himself to the last inch on what he considered 'extra-theological' ground. Meanwhile, in Tientsin, there were difficulties with Licent. Teilhard's heart, and the greater part of his time, were with the Geological Survey in Pekin; but he was unwilling to sacrifice Licent, for 'reasons of friendship and gratitude and decency and care for the interests of the Jesuit Mission; Licent is really a "clerical"; and I—well, you know what I am'. Relations got better, and then worse. Teilhard was not really interested in the museum:

> But the Mission at Tientsin (to which I'm sincerely devoted) and Licent (to whom I owe a great deal and whom I basically admire and like) have put too much money and pains into it for me not to wish to support it in all sincerity.[1]

Teilhard's good intentions could not prevail, however, against an incompatibility of temperament. Licent had a good heart and was an exemplary religious; nevertheless, in December 1929, he said things to Teilhard 'to which, in the world, one replies with a blow'. This uneasy situation—continually being patched up 'till the next time'—reminded Teilhard of an unhappy marriage. There was 'something implacable and uncontrollable' about it, 'like the growth of an organ'[2]; and it is the only case on record where Teilhard failed to get on with a fellow-worker.

It was not altogether without misgiving that Teilhard had accepted the invitation of the Geological Survey. He knew that his religious superiors in Europe thought he was in the habit of acting too independently, and he only hoped that his successful collaboration with the Chinese would allay their fears. The transfer of the Rector of Tientsin, to whom he was immediately responsible, and who was entirely on his side, was a further cause for apprehension. He trusted him to smooth over any difficulties which might arise with his successor before he left. On 15 April 1929 he was writing to Léontine Zanta:

> This winter I have been through a rather acute crisis of anti-ecclesiasticism, if not of anti-Christianity. And now this upset has given way to a broader and more peaceful state of mind. Since my only rule, both in judgment and in practice, tends more and more to become 'Believe in the spirit', it would be very unjust to regard the Church as the one place where the spirit is not to be

[1] ibid., 29 November 1929.   [2] ibid., 30 December 1929.

found. I begin to think that most of our weaknesses are due to the fact that our 'belief' is too narrow, and that we don't believe through to the end. To stop believing a second too soon, or not to believe enough, is sufficient to ruin the whole structure of what we are building.

Teilhard was still dreaming of some permanent work that would keep him in Paris, but everything depended on his official contacts with Rome. Here he doubted, and with good reason, whether his 'virginity' would ever be restored:

I underline 'official' because, at a deeper and interior level, I don't think you need have any anxiety on my account. I seem recently to have 'emerged' definitively and morally from my Order, in the sense that I now have the impression of surmounting and judging it (without any trace of vain superiority, I think; but simply because, in some way or other, I have grown up). But at the same time, though for very different reasons than I had when I was a young man, I find myself deeply and cordially attached to the Order, as though it were the natural point of my insertion in the Universe. And except in the case—which is very unlikely—of my being driven into a corner where I should be faced with intellectual disloyalty, I have decided to remain faithful to it, at any cost. This means that, thanks to God and my friends, I hope to have passed the turning point of last year, which was certainly a critical juncture in my intellectual and emotional life, without a break.[1]

It was a 'rather dangerous cape'[2] that he had rounded, these last years, but now he had come into harbour. Four months later he was writing to Pierre Lamare with the same serenity:

It may be a question of age, or the hardening produced by a good many avatars, or the result of certain pretty fundamental 'mystical' tendencies in my own make-up, but I have been feeling for the past six months as if I had reached a sort of zone of serenity where the great universe seems to me more and more majestic and exciting, and matters of strictly personal advantage or annoyance have ceased to exist for me at all.[3]

Teilhard went down to Tientsin early in February 1930 to write a

[1] Letter to Léontine Zanta, 23 August 1929.
[2] Letter to Valensin, 29 November 1929. [3] 1 January 1930

further twenty pages of *Le Phénomène Humain*. Here the news reached him of the death of Louis Vialleton, the last considerable opponent of the evolutionary theory upon which all Teilhard's phenomenology was based. It was a strange coincidence. 'A good heart', Teilhard commented, 'in spite of a mind inclined to stop too short. What is he thinking now?'[1] Later, his correspondent sent him news of Bergson which moved him deeply. 'I pray for this admirable man, whom I venerate as a kind of saint.'[2] Bergson had written that 'the intellect feels at home as long as it is left among inert objects, more especially solids'; his mind and Teilhard's moved on a similar terrain, and the time would come when he would arrive at Teilhard's conclusion that 'the world is a great and terrible thing... nothing we are able to touch is the real consistency we are searching for'. It was the moment of the baptism of desire. All this was a sharp recall to what Teilhard described as 'the substantial spiritual excitement of Paris',[3] for there was 'no other battlefield of ideas'.[4] Leave from his superiors being now obtained, he prepared, in the autumn of 1930, to return to it.

[1] Letter to Léontine Zanta 7 February 1930.
[2] *ibid.*, 3 April 1930.
[3] *ibid.*, 7 February 1930.
[4] Letter to Pierre Lamare, 1 January 1930.

CHAPTER IX

THE CROISIÈRE JAUNE

ON 10 September 1930 Teilhard boarded the Trans-Siberian express. On the two weeks' journey to Paris he had time, and to spare, to consider an offer which had been made him a year earlier. The Citroën company were organizing an expedition into Central Asia which became known as the *Croisière Jaune*. Teilhard was to be attached to this as geologist. The Citroën representative in Pekin was a certain Lieutenant Victor Point of the French Navy, who proposed that Teilhard should spend the spring of 1931 in visiting the western part of China by car—a Citroën, needless to say—as part of the caravan travelling from Pekin to join the expedition. The *Croisière* would then take him on to Hanoi. Teilhard had initial doubts as to whether he should accept the offer, but his Provincial gave him the necessary permission and he decided to go.

After a visit to Sarcenat, where he found his father in rapidly declining health, he dined in Paris with Henry Field, the grandson of Marshall Field, the Chicago millionaire and founder of the Chicago Field Museum. The young Field was a friend of Breuil and the brothers Bégouën, both of whom were present at the meeting.

Invitations to lecture for the Osborn Research Club in New York and for Columbia University persuaded Teilhard to return to China by way of the United States. Paul Claudel was then the French Ambassador in Washington and happened to be staying in New York when Teilhard was there. Claudel, a very acute man of business as well as a distinguished diplomat, was naturally interested in the Citroën expedition, and he invited Teilhard to his hotel. Teilhard found him 'charming and friendly', but the two men—equally sensitive to the majesty of the cosmos—were really talking at cross purposes. Claudel, liberated by conversion from determinism, could not see the adversaries whom Teilhard was straining every nerve to turn into allies. He was less hostile to evolution than indifferent to it. The intellectual crisis of twentieth-century man seemed to him an anachronism. It was not quite true to say of Claudel that he was 'the pure poet for whom everything is a question of aesthetics', for whom the planets 'danced for his delight'.[1] Claudel had a powerful intelligence and deep spiritual intuitions. But where Teilhard would always go as far as he could to meet the unbeliever, Claudel stood stock still and waited for the unbeliever to come to him, although, when he came, the rough arms were there to welcome him. Anyone reading the *Cinq Grandes Odes* or *Connaissance de l'Est*, and *Le Milieu Divin* in quick succession might imagine that the poet-diplomat and the palaeontologist-priest—both intimately acquainted with the Far East—would have had much in common. So indeed they had—but a profound difference in temperament divided them; and the meeting on the thirtieth storey of a New York hotel had no sequel.

Teilhard took New York in his stride, spending most of his time in the Museum of Natural History, of which his friend Osborn was a director, and where two luncheons were given in his honour. He then proceeded to Chicago where Henry Field met him again and showed him the Field Museum, and on to San Francisco by the Santa Fe route. He summed up his first impressions of America to Breuil; many a traveller visiting the country under academic auspices has felt the same:

> Yes, I liked America: doubtless, of course, because I was made a fuss of ... but still more because everyone engaged in research gave me the impression of freshness and keenness without an eye on a chair or some other academic advantage. I should only have to turn up in New York, or Chicago, or San Francisco, this very moment, and I'd immediately find work or an appointment.[2]

French intellectuals were still writing about America from behind a Chinese wall of cultural complacency; Teilhard, who knew something about the actual Chinese wall, had no patience with such chauvinism. On this point, at least, he was at one with Paul Claudel.

At the same time he was writing in his latest essay—*L'esprit de la terre*—that 'the day of "nations" is over'. Work on this occupied him for the twelve days' voyage on the *President Garfield* from San Fran-

---

[1] *Letters from a Traveller*, p. 168.
[2] ibid., p. 170.

cisco to Kobe. It had been in his mind since 1926 when he wrote to Gaudefroy:

> I'm thinking about a sort of 'Book of the Earth', where I should be speaking not as a Frenchman, nor as any part of any compartment whatever, but as man—or just as a terrestrial being. I should like to express the confidence, the ambitions, the plenitude, and also the disappointments, the anxieties, the sort of vertigo of someone who is aware of the destinies and interests of the whole earth, and of all humanity.

For Teilhard the earth was spirit rather than matter; or, more exactly, spirit informing matter—and this was life. In the light of evolution a special place should be found in the physics of the universe for the forces of conscience and spontaneity. Either life—and its consummation in thought—was an illusion; or else it was the centre of everything. Such was 'the true scientific situation'. The duel was between life and entropy. Were they the two sides of a single reality, held in perpetual balance? Or was one of them 'naturally more primitive and durable than the other'? Life, in Teilhard's conclusion, would no longer be livable at all unless it felt itself to be 'at least partially irreversible, and thus superior to the opposite attractions of entropy'. Man, in the natural order, was no more than the culminating point of this cosmic evolution. He was no longer a 'spark accidentally fallen on the earth from somewhere else'. 'The birth of Spirit' was 'the thread of Ariadne' to guide us in our understanding of the universe; 'and the hand which passes it to us' was 'the loyal recognition of the Phenomenon of Man'.

Teilhard next examined the origin of moral obligation. Duty was nothing else but the 'reflection of the universe in the atom'. The choice lay between an unfettered individualism and a forward movement in which the individual was transcended. Teilhard recognized that the assertion of individuality was one half of the joy of life, although the other—and better—half was its transcendence in something greater than oneself. Individuals and nations were naturally inclined 'to plant their tents on the first summit they had conquered', and there was 'no lack of systems to give a colour to this selfish lethargy', or of specious arguments to justify the 'unique value of the present moment'. But this way of looking at the world—to which artists and writers were especially prone—was 'rudimentary and childish'; it would not stand up to a serious analysis of the structure of things. . . . Unless man's belief in humanity was stronger than his belief in himself, he would be left with no alternative but despair.'

It may be objected here that Teilhard had little understanding of the aesthetic adventure, for there was no way in which man transcended himself more completely. If his vocation were to 'build the earth'—a favourite Teilhardian formula—a great work of art was a noble, and a necessary, part of its construction. And when Teilhard maintained that the universe advanced through the affinities of disinterested love, it is reasonable to find an analogy and a complement to this in the workings of the creative imagination. That artists are often egoists in their private lives is beside the point. Teilhard admitted the natural tendency of men to fall apart from one another, and he himself, although he was sociable, was not in the least gregarious. But then he looked back on the periods in his own life—periods of research or of struggle—when he had been 'caught up by the breath of affection or comradeship; on the moments of peril or enthusiasm when suddenly, in a flash, you realize the wonders of a common soul. These pale or brief illuminations give you some idea of what tremendous power of joy and action lies dormant beneath the waters of humanity.' And this victory of union—this 'huge intoxication of brotherhood and friendship'—was above all things a summons 'to *attack*'. The military metaphor was very characteristic, for 'the spirit of warfare' would be absorbed in the *élan* of research; and this in turn would have the ardour of a religious impulse.

So Teilhard was unable, after all, to keep God out of the argument. As the '*esprit de la terre*' became master of itself, it would discover 'the vital need for adoration'; and 'God, as the result of a universal evolution, would emerge in the consciousness of men, greater and more necessary than ever'. Religion could easily become an opium, and Teilhard would have agreed with Marx that in practice it was often little else. But its 'true function was to sustain and stimulate the progress of life'. If the 'universal energy was an energy of thought', we were forced to recognize in it 'a transcendent form of personality'; and so there reappeared 'no longer sentimental or instinctive, but closely linked to contemporary views of evolution . . . the traditional conceptions of a God exerting an intellectual influence on immortal monads, distinct from himself'. The attraction of the many by the

One had at first been a purely vital attraction; but since the appearance of man it had awakened a 'reflective liberty' and consequently a religious belief:

Religion which is not a strictly personal crisis, or option, or intuition, but represents the prolonged explanation of the being of God through the collective experience of humanity taken as a whole—God reflecting himself personally on the organized sum of thinking monads to guarantee a certain outcome, and to fix precise laws, for their hesitant activities—God bent over the mirror of the earth—a mirror now become intelligent—in order to imprint upon it the initial gleams of his beauty.

II

The boat put in at Honolulu—'an interlude of almost nostalgic charm'—and Teilhard spent forty-eight hours in Japan. The temples of polished wood, buried in their dark envelope of trees, left him appreciative but unmoved. He was relieved to be back in Pekin with its dust, its blue sky, its apple-blossom, its rickshaws, its dilapidation, and the continual cry of the pigeons passing overhead, with a whistle in their tails.[1]

Preparations for the *Croisière Jaune* were now going forward. This had two objectives: first to demonstrate the mobility and adaptability of the Citroën tracked vehicles, and secondly to reopen for economic and political exchanges the route traversed in former times by the silk merchants across the central Asian depression. One party, led by Georges-Marie Haardt, was to travel through Persia and western India as far as the Pamir massif. Haardt had already proved his competence by leading the *Croisière Noire* from the Sahara to Madagascar. The second party was led by Victor Point and was to start from Pekin, crossing the Central Asian deserts and entering Sinkiang which had hitherto been closed to foreigners. It was to link up with Haardt at Kashgar, and then the two parties would return together by a different route to Pekin.

Teilhard, who was attached to the second party, was to join the caravan at Kalgan. He and Point were to travel there by train. The

[1] Letter to Pierre Lamare, 25 April 1941.

expedition got off to a belated start, since the rubber tyres of the Citroën caterpillars burned under the tropical heat when they were only ninety miles from Pekin. Spare tracks had to be sent from Paris and Teilhard, chafing at the delay, was left kicking his heels in the capital, feeling that the 'human objective' of the expedition was hardly worth its pains. The days of foreign expeditions seemed already numbered; perhaps the *Croisière Jaune* would be the last of them. As always Teilhard was in two minds about China—just as China was in two minds about itself. 'I like enormously certain Chinese, but I cannot escape the conviction that the standard of the race as a whole is below the human average.'[1]

He went down to Tientsin for Holy Week, and on Easter Sunday morning ran into Père Leroy who had just returned from the Shantung peninsula. It was the pleasantest thing that could possibly have happened on Easter Sunday. He took Leroy back with him to Pekin; showed him the Chou-Kou-Tien deposits; and then early in May left with two supply trucks to join the main column of ten heavy vehicles, due to resume its journey to Kalgan. It started on 10 May. Teilhard travelled with two fellow Auvergnats—Fernand Chauvet, a mechanic; and André Reymond, a young naturalist fresh from the Sorbonne. By 22 May, when Teilhard was writing from Pai-ling-miao, north of the Yellow River, they had covered 500 miles:

> Pai-ling-miao is an important junction of tracks that run to all the chief centres in China—long files of camels carrying opium disguised as inoffensive loads of hides; it's an organized trade between the Chinese Governors, the Mongol princes and the bandit chiefs. The place itself consists of a fine lamasery, red, white and gold, and two Chinese inns, the whole set in a granite gorge on the banks of a crystal-clear stream; a few stunted elms in the ravines and some enchanting apricot trees covered with pink blossom; and a swarm of lamas in their long red robes.[2]

By 16 June they had reached Suchow where the Gobi desert—750 miles of sandstorms, wild sheep and solitude—merges with the foot of the Celestial Mountains. It had been hard going. At times the vehicles ran into a sandbank, and Teilhard's large hand, outspread 'like an open flower', was seen disengaging them from behind. At other times, as he ran with the vigour of a man half his age in search of

[1] *Letter to Pierre Lamare*, 25 April 1941   [2] *Letters from a Traveller*, p. 178.

a stone which had caught his attention, he seemed 'like a flag vibrating in the Asian sky'.[1] On 25 May they were camping beside a lamasery and a small duck pond. The lamas were forbidden to shoot the ducks, so they asked a member of the party to shoot one instead. They were anxious to witness an assassination for which they could not be held responsible. A duck was duly shot and hung suspended above the heads of Teilhard and his companions as they sat talking in the cool, dry evening air. The conversation turned on the existence of God, and one of the party expressed his doubts. Teilhard replied in the same casual tone 'as if he were demonstrating a theorem'. 'God is a choice; a very simple choice; the choice between a Yes and a No, between the sign + and the sign —. None of us can avoid making this choice, and it is extremely difficult to make the wrong one.'[2]

The going was not always peaceful. On 28 June the caravan stumbled upon the battle of Khami, a particularly bloody incident of the Civil War. Georges Le Fèvre, the historian of the expedition, described how

The road was blocked with the corpses of men and animals. Terrified children were hiding under overturned carts. A woman was weeping and wailing by the side of a dying man, her husband. A Chinese soldier had emptied the pockets of one of his dead comrades and was hastily pulling off his shoes. Tethered animals were stumbling against their ropes. Some of them had shaken off their loads, which were lying on the ground. Tugging madly at their halters, they were tearing their nostrils, with piercing screams. The ground was littered with empty cartridge cases and ammunition pouches. . . . Delastre[3] had already set up his little aid-post, and, with Père Teilhard, who volunteered to help, was immediately surrounded by some thirty casualties. The badly wounded were brought to him, but for these nothing could be done. They had lost too much blood. The lead bullets the Shantu use inflict terrible wounds, and death is generally from haemorrhage.[4]

On 7 July Teilhard was writing from the Turfan deep, 600 feet below sea level, where the Tarim flowed through a forest of wild poplars to lose itself in the basin of the Lop-Nôr. Here were mosques and minarets; the muezzin summoning to prayer; men 'dignified, grave

[1] André Reymond in *Cahiers Pierre Teilhard de Chardin*, vol. 2.
[2] *ibid.*
[3] Doctor to the expedition.   [4] Teilhard de Chardin Album, p. 103.

and bearded; and women like gypsies with their long plaits falling over their long, gaudy dresses'.[1] Teilhard was 'in the heart of one of the most mysterious and sacred of geological regions',[2] and he was establishing by slow degrees its relation to eastern China. The contours of the mountainous country to the west told him that he had passed from 'the monotony of Mongolia to the monumental formations of Upper Asia',[3] and Kashgar—750 miles ahead of them—no longer seemed like the El Dorado of an explorer's dream.

At this point, however, difficulties began. Turkestan was forbidden territory to Europeans, and the mediation of the Chinese was necessary to secure their passage. The Nanking party demanded that control of the expedition should be divided: Teilhard, acting through a Russian interpreter, handled the tricky negotiations, and signed the agreement reached on 20 June. Warnings, however, reached them of fighting to the west, and they were held up for a month at Urumchi, the capital of Chinese Turkestan. It was cooler here than at Turfan, and 'the people's faces, the types of crop, the look of the flowers and trees'[4] carried a foretaste of Europe. But the hostility of Nanking to any European expeditions in China seemed an obstacle to further progress, although the party could not turn back until Haardt, approaching Kashgar from the west, had given the order to do so. Since they were forbidden the use of radio, they could do nothing but wait. Teilhard wandered in the pinewoods along 'a carpet of geraniums, aconite and arnica';[5] wrote the first draft of a memorandum on his researches; and meditated an essay—never, so far as one knows, to be completed—on *La Prière dans la durée*. More easily than the other twenty-nine members of the frustrated caravan—twenty of them Frenchmen like himself—he was able to fall back on *prière*; but they all knew the meaning of *durée*. Other subjects were also running in his mind—*l'Univers personnel* and *la Conversion du monde*—and these projects were eventually brought to fruition. Meanwhile, although they were able to send letters through India or Russia, they could not receive any. The Governor of Urumchi was politely hostile; the glorious autumn days dragged on with their reminiscence of Auvergne; and the only relief for Teilhard was the intellectual companionship of Victor Point, Charles Brull the engineer, André Reymond, and the doctor.

[1] *Letters from a Traveller*, p. 180.
[2] *ibid.*   [3] *ibid.*, p. 179.   [4] *ibid.*, p. 182.   [5] *ibid.*, p. 183.

At last permission was obtained for four tracked vehicles to continue the journey until they joined up with Haardt. Teilhard was among those selected to leave. It was a 700-mile trek along the southern slope of the Tien-shan, and it was expected to take them a fortnight. No motorized vehicle had ever traversed the route, but the Citroën caterpillars took the marshes, rivers, and rocky passes in their stride. Hearing that Haardt had already left Kashgar, the party halted at Aksu four days short of their destination; but they had crossed the greater part of Sinkiang. The mountains rose to 21,000 feet; willows, tamarisk and poplars were the only vegetation; Afghans, Persians and Hindus mingled in the villages; and Teilhard reflected that he was just half-way between Paris and Pekin. He was writing 'in a very pretty garden belonging to a big Aksu trader, under a pergola from which hung mighty bunches of grapes, with peach and apple-trees to one side, weighed down with fruit; the sky an unchanging blue, with just a trace of cloud; the heat of summer's last days'.[1] *La Prière dans la durée* was almost finished in his head; and no doubt it was this contemplation of *durée* that gave him so sharp an awareness 'of being now on the downward slope of life'.[2]

Haardt, with the rest of the party from Pamir, duly arrived in Aksu, and Le Fèvre described how Teilhard met them:

A golden dust rises from the horses' hooves on a road spangled with blue shadows and bordered by a stream. By the stream, a fisherman in overalls, sleeves rolled up, drops his rod, waves his arms and runs up: 'So you're all here at last! We've had a pretty long wait for you, you know.' 'Father! My good friend, my dear friend!' Greetings and embraces: we all dismount and lead our horses by the bridle.[3]

To André Sauvage it seemed as if Teilhard were 'capable of walking on the waters',[4] and we owe to the same witness a striking description of how he appeared to others in these middle years of his life:

A man of unequalled style; of a self-effacing and irresistible distinction. His voice, his diction which had the tone of a harpsichord, his smile which never quite turned to laughter, impressed themselves on anyone who was in the least attentive. Total lack of

---

[1] *Letters from a Traveller*, p. 186.   [2] *ibid.*
[3] '*La Croisière Jaune*', quoted in Teilhard de Chardin Album, p. 107.
[4] André Sauvage in *Cahiers Pierre Teilhard de Chardin*, vol. 2.

ecclesiasticism. As simple in his gestures as in his manners, but with the simplicity of a stele. Anxious to welcome, but like a rock of marble. You felt that even if you were as tall as he, you were still infinitely far removed from the storehouse of his thoughts which were never inflated. As a rule you stopped dead before that rough-hewn face that Greco had prefigured, and you fell back on the ordinary chit-chat of the expedition.[1]

Teilhard returned with the reunited caravan to Urumchi where the Governor was now the soul of affability. Teilhard shared a comfortable and well-heated room with Hackin, director of the Guimet Museum and Commandant Pecqueur. Parties enlivened the winter evenings, with Russians, Danes and a singular Mongolian lady, known as 'Princess Palta'—'Parisian to her finger-tips with whom some members of the Expedition had danced in Paris and Pekin'.[2] Teilhard now talked with her about the existence of God. Sven Hedin's geologist, Norin, was also in Urumchi, and Teilhard spent long hours with him 'building up the geology of Central Asia',[3] on the evidence of their mutual research.

The route homewards lay through the dead cities of the Gobi desert where the January cold threatened to freeze the radiators and compelled them to keep going for twenty out of the twenty-four hours a day. Le Fèvre described how the enforced immobility reduced the passengers to a strange insensibility. They

> sat there inert, dozing in snatches, while the red-eyed mechanics struggled on, with hardly a couple of hours sleep a night, crouched over the wheel. Twice a day, however, we stopped for a meal in the open. Speed was essential or the boiling hot soup ladled into mess-tins would be ice before we could drink it. We took it greedily, standing up; and at night, silent, muffled in furs that made any movement impossible, and without knowing who was who, we stood in a group round the mess-vehicle, outlandish dummies with shadows distorted by the glare of the headlamps.[4]

For all these rigours and discomforts, Teilhard was quick to spot the prehistoric tools littering the ground:

> His sharp eyes picked out the smallest palaeolith whose red stood

[1] ibid. [2] *Letters from a Traveller*, p. 187.
[3] ibid. [4] *La Croisère Jaune*, pp. 292–3.

out against the grey bareness of the wind-swept ground. He would stop his vehicle, get down, and pick up one stone after another: traces not of a centre of Palaeolithic culture, but of the southern limit of a vastly ancient human wave that set out from Siberia.[1]

The small party to which Teilhard was attached visited the Pleistocene terraces and caves at Bäzäklik; and nearby an ancient Greco-Buddhistic city lay half-buried in the sand. In his report on the expedition Teilhard was to write:

At the end of the Pliocene, immense and widespread erosion spread out sheets of gravel around the rocky massifs of the mountain chains, while clouds of lighter sediments were continually carried towards China by the winds. This began the massive process of denudation. Then, during the Quaternary, the hollows were still filled with great Nors of whitish, sterile mud, while the last dusty deposits of loess, swept up by the glacial winds, fell like snow on the mountains of Shansi, Shensi and Kansu. The desert was established once and for all.

Out of it, not far from the banks of the Yellow River, there reared up the gigantic pinnacle of rock known as 'the anvil of Genghis Khan'. It might have stood for all that 'vision of the past which—like a mirage that rises, shimmers and becomes ever more substantial, sharper and clearer—is seen by a geologist crossing the Gobi'.[2]

The caterpillars crawled along at ten kilometres an hour, and when the passengers complained, a mechanic would reply, 'What are you making a fuss about? The army-kitchens don't do more than four.' Once again the conversation turned on the existence of God. 'God', said Teilhard with his habitual detachment, 'is a note of music'—and his hand traced a spiral in the air.[3] For all his courtesy and charm he preserved an essential solitude, and André Sauvage found him an evasive subject for the cinema. At Bäzäklik, where the others were inspecting the mural paintings in the grottoes, Teilhard was busy with his hammer fifty metres above, breaking the stones. This was the only occasion when the photographer, hidden in a hollow of sand, was able to catch him at work.

[1] *ibid.*, p. 189.
[2] Teilhard de Chardin Album, p. 111.
[3] André Sauvage in *Cahiers Pierre Teilhard de Chardin*, vol. 2.

A skirmish with bandits, in which no one was hurt, ended with Oriental politeness. Three of the brigands invited the leaders of the convoy to 'take a cup of tea with the General and accept his card'—which was signed 'General of the Independent Horse'. Haardt thought it very independent indeed to have fired on a convoy flying the French flag; and Teilhard had reason to consider the bandits of the south 'intellectual, refined, and people of great style'.[1] New Year was spent with the German Fathers of the Divine Word near Liangchow. At Haardt's request Teilhard said Mass for the members of the expedition, and in a letter to his wife Haardt described 'all these men in their travelling kit recollected before God'—none of them practising Catholics; and went on to say: 'Père Teilhard is a prince of the Church, but he has the expeditionary spirit as fully as any man can have it.'

A member of the party, Audouin-Dubreuil, kept a copy of Teilhard's address. Whatever Teilhard's sermons may have been like, the *Croisière Jaune* had never heard them, and when, during a tedious delay at Urumchi, someone began to imitate a preacher, the genial parody pointed in his direction. 'Oh no!', he objected, 'that's a Dominican!'—evidently relishing the riposte; and then he went on to speak of the saints, stripping them of all *bondieuserie*. Now, on this bitter New Year's Day, he offered his Mass in order that

success may crown our enterprises, joy dwell in our hearts and all around us, and what sorrow cannot be spared us be transfigured into a finer joy, the joy of knowing that we have occupied each his own station in the universe and that, in that station, we have done as we ought.[2]

Once they were back in Pao-Teo Teilhard was tempted to take the train to Pekin, but there were still sixty miles of country to investigate and he preferred to stay with the expedition to the end. He would not have it said that he had joined it in order to enjoy himself. Moreover the enjoyment had been relative. The months spent with the *Croisière Jaune* had been among the hardest, but also the most rewarding, of his career. Many opportunities had been missed; others he had been unable to follow up. The personnel of the expedition was too mixed for Teilhard to have time, or occasion, for the quiet recollection on which his peace of mind and the progress of his ideas depended. Normally he

[1] Letter to Pierre Lamare, 25 April 1931.
[2] Teilhard de Chardin Album, p. 115.

spent an hour a day in meditation. This was possible when he was with Barbour and Licent; it was quite impracticable with the *Croisière Jaune*. But he was compensated by 'the treasures of friendship' which he found among his companions. On the staff of the expedition, with no account taken of the mechanics, there were seven men, brought up as Christians, who had abandoned the faith. In spite of their obvious desire for a religion, they had 'real difficulty in looking beyond immediate and individual perspectives'. Scepticism and pessimism were counteracting 'an unconcealed longing to hope and believe'.[1] Teilhard was comforted to discover, later, that Le Fèvre and several others had read *L'Esprit de la Terre* and been much impressed by it.

The results of the expedition could not compare with those achieved by Sven Hedin's rival party. But it was much, as Teilhard wrote in his appendix to *La Croisière Jaune*, that they had been able to

establish the intimate connection between the geology of the Gobi and that of Sinkiang, and so distinguish and follow out more clearly, under secondary modifications, various basic features of the internal structure and external appearance of the great continent.[2]

For himself it was a rich reward 'to have now seen with my own eyes the vast zone that lies between Kashgar and Tsitsikar'. His knowledge of Asia was nearly doubled, and 'for that, ten months of life, even at the age of fifty'[3] was not too much to pay.

The festivities which greeted the return of the expedition to Pekin were clouded by the sudden death of Haardt in Hong Kong. Teilhard had been captivated by his 'generosity and warmth of heart',[4] and was sad not to have been there to ease his passing. A further grief was the death of Emmanuel Teilhard de Chardin on 11 February 1932. Teilhard owed his father much; not only tastes acquired and ambitions realized, but a 'certain fundamental balance on which everything else was built'. At about the same time he learnt that four of Édouard Le Roy's books had been placed on the Index. In three-quarters, or more, of these Teilhard could see no objection whatever. In making his retraction Le Roy did not pretend to understand the meaning of the censure; he submitted merely to demonstrate his willingness to obey authority. Cardinal Verdier—the new Archbishop

[1] Letter to Valensin, 13 March 1932. [2] *Letters from a Traveller*, p. 193.
[3] *ibid.*, p. 190. [4] *ibid.*

of Paris, in whom Teilhard and his friends had great confidence—had done all he could to avert the blow, but—not for the first time—Paris was powerless to affect the decisions of Rome.

It was in a sombre mood, therefore, that Teilhard went up into Shansi Province in July. He was travelling once more by mule, sleeping in filthy inns, and plagued by flies. He had undertaken the journey from a sense of duty, but he hoped that it would be the last of its kind. New vistas were opening out as he peered along the 'downward path'. An official photograph taken for the *Croisière Jaune* shows a more anxious Teilhard than earlier, or later, likenesses. His curiosity was alert as ever, but the satisfactions of curiosity were not an end in themselves. Scientific knowledge exacted its proper discipline, for which Teilhard had a scrupulous respect; but knowledge was a sterile acquisition unless it was a means to love. The rhapsodic idiom in which Teilhard more than occasionally wrote, and which has disconcerted the professional scientist and the professional theologian alike, was the lyricism of a lover for whom words are necessarily insufficient. And we understand nothing of his life unless we see it as a love affair; nothing of his research unless we see it as an apostolate as well as an apologia. 'I see very well what he thinks', objected Étienne Gilson, 'but what does he *know*?'[1] Teilhard's thought and Teilhard's knowledge were not to be so neatly divided.

[1] *Seminarium*, vol. 4.

CHAPTER X

UP THE YANGTZE[1]

TEILHARD returned to France in September 1932. He was still raw with embittered sympathy for Le Roy and now, in October, came the death of Abbé Laberthonnière,[2] 'in a crisis of melancholy, and without a *sou*'. An article in *La Croix* had kicked him when he was already as down as an independent thinker could be in those difficult times:

From now on [Teilhard wrote to Valensin] the sole aim of my life —and more so than ever—will be to work to break the circle in which, by a bitter irony, the 'children of light' have imprisoned the spirit. We are dying for lack of anyone who knows how to die for the truth. . . . So one can no longer even speak of things which are only distantly relevant to religion, and Christians are beginning to find this situation quite normal. Soon we shall ask for nothing better than the régime that the Gospel came to break 2,000 years ago.[3]

Teilhard was back in Pekin by the end of March 1933. The threat of Japanese invasion overhung a city outwardly quiet. The collections from the Imperial Museum had been sent off to the concessions in Shanghai; and much of the material from the Geological Survey had been transferred to the Rockefeller Foundation. Teilhard was forced to watch his 'furniture and drawers being carried by coolies through the city'.[4] The Chinese themselves were leaving Pekin *en masse*, but then an agreement with the Japanese was patched up, and the packing-cases were returned to the Survey. Profiting from this *détente*

[1] For much of the material in this chapter I am again indebted to Dr. George Barbour's *In the Field with Teilhard de Chardin*.

[2] Lucien Laberthonnière (1860–1932): Oratorian, priest, accused of Modernism. Several of his books were put on the Index and further publications forbidden He submitted, but continued to write works published posthumously.

[3] 20 October 1932.

[4] *Letters from a Traveller*, p. 198.

Teilhard went up to Shams with an American friend, setting up their headquarters at a Protestant industrial school south of Taynan. He visited a mountain of particular beauty with temples clinging to the summit, and found the forests of silver-barked firs so well preserved that he felt 'transported straight into the scene of a Chinese painting'.[1]

Such euphoria was no more than momentary relief from anxious preoccupations. In May he had word of the latest *diktat* from Rome, forbidding him to accept any official situation that might be offered him in Paris. It was annoying, as he wrote to Père de Bonneville, his Provincial at Lyon, 'that they don't try to see in Rome what is constructive and conservative in my effort'. There had been fresh delations. 'Whatever my accusers may think, the outside world is not deceived; people may not think me much of an ecclesiastic, but no one has ever doubted I was a believer.'[2] Marguerite Teillard-Chambon had herself written to Father Ledochowski telling him—no doubt politely—that he did not know how to handle her cousin. Nevertheless Teilhard continued to pour out his ideas on paper, although he realized that nine-tenths of his work would never see the light of publication. 'I resign myself to the activity of a microbe.'[3]

In the same year, as he was waiting for the *Croisière Jaune* to start, he had composed *La Route de l'Ouest* in which he claimed for Christianity a superiority over eastern religions precisely because it offered a safeguard against pantheism. The one led to the 'paroxysm of what is most incommunicable in each element'; the other to the 'dissolution of the individual in a diffused immensity'. In *Christologie et Évolution* (1931) he was arguing that 'original sin (under its present form) opposes at every point the expansion of our religion on the natural level'—a statement that would have been castor oil to the censors. In pursuing the argument Teilhard allowed himself an admission which must have been as painful to make as it is painful—and also pathetic—to read. 'Once I was made to deny this major premiss by a theological censor, without any further explanation. Today I still cannot avoid recognition of its truth.'

This throws a valuable light on what the paper stolen from the Institut Catholique may have contained. Teilhard saw evil as a 'natural

[1] *ibid.*, p. 199.
[2] *Letters to Léontine Zanta*, Introduction.
[3] Letter to Pierre Lamare, 1 July 1934.

feature in the structure of the world'. The creative act was opposed to the *néant* in the same way as unity was opposed to multiplicity; creation was the 'passage from a state of initial dispersion to one of final harmony'. Evil was the 'enemy', necessarily raised up by God when he decided on creation. In the Christology to which Teilhard looked forward the idea of sin would be assimilated to the idea of progress; not in the sense that progress was necessarily sinful, but that sin inevitably accompanied it. God was not omnipotent to the point of cancelling what had already happened. Creation was 'an adventure, a risk, a battle' in which he was 'totally engaged'; hence the grandeur of the Cross. Jesus was not only he who bears the sins of the world, and in whom moral evil was mysteriously compensated by suffering. The Cross was also 'the symbol and the gesture of progress'. Redemption was more than expiation; it was victory as well. Just as the Greek Fathers—always closer to Teilhard's thought than the more juridical westerners—had seen baptism as immersion in the fire of a 'purifying struggle', and not only in the waters of cleansing from original sin, so Teilhard refused any longer to see the shadows cast by the Cross; he only saw the ardours and endurances which it represented. It was an active, not a passive, emblem. 'We have had too much talk of sheep; I want to see the lions come out.'

What he objected to was the classical representation of the Fall; its localization at an unidentified point in time, and in a place and circumstances which made nonsense of evolution. These he regarded as pure 'verbal affirmation' and a yoke around the neck of contemporary man. It was one reason why 'the best unbelievers that I know would feel that they were lapsing from their moral ideals if they allowed themselves to be converted. They have told me so themselves.' And so he came to sketch out a new, and subtly transformed, spirituality in which adoration would consist in devotion to the creative act; charity in devotion to the general advancement of mankind; chastity in the sublimation rather than the suppression of the flesh; detachment in the very intensity of one's attachment to beauty and truth; resignation only in the last convulsions of one's struggle with the angel; communion with God through communion with the world. A missionary—widely regarded as a saint—had observed to Teilhard: 'History shows that no religion has lasted more than two thousand years. After that, they all die. Christianity will soon be two thousand years old.'

Teilhard was never tempted to believe that Christianity would die, but he took note of its second millennium. It must grow up, and radically change its appearance, while remaining fundamentally the same. Yet from all the dramatis personae of his cosmogenesis there is one significant absentee. Where, one cannot help asking, is the Devil? The sinister activities of the *multiple* were not easy to explain without him. Teilhard had no difficulty in believing in the good angels. They belonged to a higher plane of the universe which had already emerged into God. Their evolution was ended. But essentially they remained elements of our own world and exercised an influence upon it. More spiritual than ourselves, they were still intimately bound to the universe of matter. So much for the good angels; but was Teilhard too optimistic—or too innocent— to believe in the bad? Not quite; we must continue to act as if hell and its demons existed, but they belonged to a lower order of reality. The ideas expressed in this essay seemed to him 'a little bold', and later in the year he was writing to Valensin: 'All I ask for is to be given advice.' When Valensin gave advice, Teilhard generally took it: and in this case his friend had no criticism to offer.

On 27 June 1933 Teilhard sailed for America with Davidson Black to deliver a paper in Washington at the eighteenth International Geological Congress. In New York he met a number of friends from Paris; to one of them, who expressed his delight at seeing him again, Teilhard replied, 'I feel the same way, but for an entirely different reason—now I *know* the world is round.' After the Washington Congress—where he also handed over the MS of his essay on Fossil Man in China—he joined *Excursion C-2*, crossing the country in two Pullmans and a baggage car. George Barbour, who was with the party, describes how these were

> coupled to a succession of trains during the nights, and left on sidings during the day while we were out in the field. The nerve centre of the party was the famous Princeton University car which had been rebuilt as a mobile office and conference room, fitted with map table, blackboard, projection screen, and storage facilities for equipment, rock samples, and geological paraphernalia. The third unit of our caravanserai on wheels was a standard Pullman sleeping-car with sections of double-deck berths and a

single drawing-room, the latter normally reserved for married couples.[1]

A photograph shows Teilhard bent over a chipmunk beside Crater Lake, Oregon; but he left the party at Eugene, Oregon, and with a couple of students drove down the Redwood Highway to the University of California at Berkeley. Later he followed the coastal range to the outskirts of Santa Barbara and explored the Mariposa-Yosemite valleys—each time in company with other geologists. He was struck by 'the fundamental tectonic analogies between the Mesozoic and Tertiary chains of California and those of China and Sinkiang. The Pacific acts like an immense Tarim basin.'[2] The light and contours of the natural settings; the forests of sequoias; the sunbaked mountains with their sparse vegetation of ilex and laurel, cactus and yucca; the expansive informality of American life—all continued to fascinate him. After a month in California he felt 'really at home',[3] and he wrote to Barbour of the need for 'bridging the Pacific'.[4]

By 11 November he was back in Pekin where the new discoveries at Chou-Kou-Tien awaited his interpretation. But a cruel blow was now in store for him. Davidson Black had been suffering for some time from heart trouble. On 15 March, however, he returned to the laboratory at five o'clock in the afternoon, saying that he 'felt fine and was anxious to get back to work' on the specimens from Chou-Kou-Tien. It was observed that he walked slowly, and he was presently found sitting at his desk, anxious whether his plans for the Cenozoic Research Laboratory could go forward. He wished to extend its reconnaissance into Central Asia, for he was still convinced that the origins of the human race were to be found in the heart of the Eurasian continent. Shortly after his last visitor had left he was discovered dead on the floor. Teilhard broke the news in a letter to Breuil:

His heart had been giving trouble for some time, and five weeks ago we had a warning of what might happen. We were hoping that he was pulling round, but then the end came suddenly. Black was feeling better (or seemed to be); he had just been talking briskly with some friends and was full of plans, as usual. A

---

[1] *In the Field with Teilhard de Chardin*, p. 61.
[2] Letter to George Barbour, 6 September 1933; *ibid.*, p. 63.
[3] *Letters from a Traveller*, p. 200.
[4] *In the Field with Teilhard de Chardin*, p. 62.

moment later he was found dead, by this table, in this Lab you know so well, between the Sinanthropos and the skull from the Upper Cave.

The loss put Teilhard's faith to a severe trial; in the same letter he goes on:

But what an absurd thing life is, looked at superficially; so absurd that you feel yourself forced back on a stubborn, desperate faith in the reality and survival of the spirit. Otherwise—were there no such thing as the spirit, I mean—we should have to be idiots not to call off the whole human effort.[1]

Some critics have gone so far as to assert that Teilhard had lost his faith in personal immortality. To such calumny these lines are a sufficient answer. Nevertheless the death of Davidson Black was 'like a shadow continually overhanging me'. Teilhard had' loved him almost more than a brother',[2] and he was not comforted by 'the stifling atmosphere of agnostic condolences'. He concluded a letter to the Bégouëns with a resolution wholly in keeping with his character:

I swore to myself, on the body of my dead friend, to fight more vigorously than ever to give hope to man's work and inquiry.[3]

II

The appointment of a successor to Black at the head of the Cenozoic Laboratory would depend on the Rockefeller Foundation. Of possible candidates V. K. Ting had accepted the directorship of the Academia Sinica in Nanking, and J. S. Lee, head of the Nanking Geological Institute, had taken up a professorship in the National University at Pekin. Wong Wen-hao, director of the Geological Survey, was immobilized and still unconscious from a fractured skull. Under these circumstances Dr. Roger Green, Field Director of the China Foundation of the Rockefeller Board, appointed Teilhard as Acting Director of the Cenozoic Laboratory until a permanent successor to Black could be found.

Meanwhile George Barbour was on his way from Honolulu with a letter from Black, received in New York, outlining the plans which he

[1] *Letters from a Traveller*, pp. 201–2.
[2] Letter to Pierre Lamare, 1 July 1934.
[3] *Letters from a Traveller*, p. 202.

hoped that Barbour and Teilhard, with others, would carry out during the summer on behalf of the Cenozoic Laboratory. These included a journey up the Yangtze river in the hope of discovering whether the Lushan Range had undergone glaciation. Barbour had already visited the lower reaches of the river in 1931, and made his report upon them; but the country was unfamiliar ground to Teilhard, who only knew it from the train. J. S. Lee was to accompany them on the first part of their trip up the river and while they were waiting for him to come down from Pekin, they explored the flats of the Yangtze delta—a labyrinth of dykes and canals where the water buffalo and shallow river boats contrasted with the camels and rickshaws of the landbound cities to the north. Later they went up into the hills south-east of Nanking:

> At the end of the bus line, we left the low ground, and for half a dozen miles rode in bamboo chairs slung on poles carried shoulder high by bearers who shuffled along at a jog trot, their step timed to the bounce of the springy poles. They travelled at better than four miles an hour, with only the briefest of halts every twenty minutes. An extra runner trotted along nearby, ready at a shout to slip under the poles and take the strain to the same rhythm, replacing a fore or aft bearer, without missing a step or dropping a passenger. Teilhard pointed out that once you got over your fear that you were going to land in a paddy field, or be thrown out at each heave, you could relax at ease and fall asleep to the soothing swing of the chair.[1]

Lee not having yet arrived from Pekin, Teilhard decided to start without him. But Lee had persuaded Erik Norin, just returned from Chinese Tibet, to join the party; Young came with the necessary passports; and they started up the river—a party of four—on the *Kiang-An* (River Peace) on 11 April 1934. The navigable stretch of the Yangtze may be divided into three sections: from the estuary at Shanghai to the junction with the Han at Hankow; from Hankow to Ichang at the entrance to the gorges; and from there to Chungking, the last considerable port below Pingshan. Nanking is situated about 200 miles up the river from Shanghai. The river valley runs south-west for 300 miles and then turns slightly north-west as far as Hankow. Onwards from there its course is pretty well due west. The main purpose of the ex-

[1] *In the Field with Teilhard de Chardin*, p. 72.

pedition was 'to learn what we could about the stages through which the landscape of Central China had reached its present relief and thus be able to compare its evolution with that of North China; second, to visit all accessible places from which fossils of recent geological age were known to have come. Together the two undertakings should help to confirm our ideas as to Pekin Man's antiquity, and throw light on his geographic and climatic environment.'[1]

Lee eventually joined them at Kiu-kiang, roughly three-quarters of the distance to Hankow, at the point where the river turns northwards. Here they chartered a bus which took them into the high country of Wan Fou Shan to the south. They stopped at the Fairy Glen Hotel at Kuling (3,500 feet) which was owned by a Scot, and the moorland scenery must have reminded Barbour of Scotland. From a peak 3,800 feet high they could look down on Poyang Lake and the Yangtze winding away in the distance. The streams trickled over the boulders down the saddle-back valleys, and Lee's theories about the glacial origin of the country seemed to be confirmed. The others, however, were not quite convinced, for the ice had not left its 'usual earmarks' on the landscape.

Lee and his assistant Yu returned to Nanking, while the rest of the party continued up-river to Hankow. Here an incident occurred which demonstrated to the full Teilhard's trust in human nature. They had been recommended to a hotel under German management commonly known as Teh-Kuo (Land of Virtue). With every anticipation of *Gemütlichkeit* they scanned the quayside for its representative; were puzzled by a tout of sinister aspect waving a card with the words 'Teh-Kuo Fantien'; and disturbed when they saw Young—who spoke fluent Chinese—concluding some kind of bargain with him. The man led them, in a procession of rickshaws, into the sordid heart of the city, finally pulling up before a shady establishment, called the Oriental Hotel—'Teh-Kuo Fantien'—on the edge of the red light district. Barbour describes what they found inside:

> All our material had been pounced upon and carried upstairs to a large room at the far end of the corridor, with whitewash flaking off the walls and obviously not cleaned for a generation. It was furnished with one rattan settee, three broken chairs, and a couple of red tables, and lit by a single fly-specked bulb with a

[1] *ibid.*, p. 84.

dangling strip of fly-paper attached. Husks of chewed water-melon seeds had been swept into corners; the doors would not latch, and there were no sanitary arrangements. Each time any of us left the room, painted ladies appeared at the doors of cubicles down the corridor.[1]

The irony of the situation was underlined by the fact that Teilhard was known to the Chinese as 'Teh'. He went so far as to admit that Young 'might perhaps have made a mistake', but he would not hear of clearing out since this would involve a loss of face for Young in a country where face meant everything. So they piled their luggage against the door to ensure that any importunate entry during the night could not fail to waken them, and concealed what valuables they had in their sleeping bags. In the morning Teilhard regretted that he was 'at the mercy of circumstance', but insisted that Young had made 'an honest mistake'—as no doubt he had.

Further progress was impossible because Norin would only be free for another week, and Young—on whom the material arrangements had hitherto depended—was anxious to return to Pekin. No trace of glaciation was found in the hill country north of Hankow, and the party caught the train back to Pekin. Their conclusions on the geo-logical problem of Lushan differed from Lee's, but they worded their report as tactfully as possible. On 13 May, however, Teilhard, with Barbour and Young, caught the night express to Hankow where they put up at the authentic 'Teh-Kuo', and then continued their west-ward journey aboard the *Changsha*. The river meandered through a monotonous landscape until they reached Ichang. Here it cut its way through the gorges into the mountain belt. For the 1,000 miles from Ichang to the sea it had fallen less than one-and-a-half inches per mile; for the 360 miles to Chungking its gradient was more than a foot. The boat anchored for the night off Wushan, and the party rowed ashore. Teilhard was curious to examine a clump of tung-trees, which pro-duced the oil for varnish.

They arrived at Chungking on 29 May. Teilhard was anxious to go northwards by road to Chengtu, where Georges Béchamp, Director of the French Medical Mission and an old friend, wished to see him; Barbour was just as eager to reach the centre of the Red Basin. This was fully in accordance with Black's intentions, but the Chinese mem-

[1] *In the Field with Teilhard de Chardin*, pp. 79–88.

bers of the Cenozoic Laboratory considered the trip unnecessary and expensive, although Barbour had offered to put up the money for it. Teilhard decided to override their objections and set off with Barbour on the morning of 4 June. Young, pedantically obedient to orders, remained behind. It was 280 miles of hard going in a rickety car which enabled them to make geological sense of the coloured sandstone. They were both guests of Béchamp in Chengtu, and in the evening heard music and talks from Paris 'as clearly as though it came from the next room'.[1] A member of the science faculty at West China Union University guided their car the next day to Kuanshien, forty miles to the north-west. Here, on the borders of Tibet and at the extreme limit of civilization, the Min river flowed down from the foothills of the Chinese Alps, and just outside the city gates they

met mules and yaks on their way down from the mountains. My camera caught Teilhard in his pith helmet and khaki uniform walking down the main street, looking at the knives and trinkets laid out in the market to catch the eye of the swarthy men from the hills.[2]

Szechwan seemed to Teilhard 'a China more Chinese than the north. The pagodas are more brilliant and more mannered, hats are wider and more pointed, the whole countryside more like the China we know in books'.[3] On the Sunday he said Mass for the hospital staff of French and Belgian sisters.

They sailed homewards from Chungking and disembarked at Wanhsien, rather more than 200 miles downstream. Teilhard took Young with him to the Catholic Mission where they were miserably lodged and received with ill-disguised suspicion. Young's Mandarin dialect was barely intelligible in Szechwan, and Teilhard was a scarcely credible Jesuit. Teilhard was eager to examine a limestone ridge at the head of the tributary stream which came into the Yangtze at Wanhsien. This was said to be the source of the 'dragon bones' everywhere for sale along the river from Hankow. Teilhard and Barbour concluded that they had lain 'in caverns or solution cavities dissolved in limestone much more ancient than the animals they once belonged to—as has been the case with the Chou-Kou-Tien trove'.[4] They went on to

[1] *Letters from a Traveller*, p. 204.
[2] *In the Field with Teilhard de Chardin*, p. 94.
[3] *Letters from a Traveller*, p. 204.
[4] *In the Field with Teilhard de Chardin*, p. 96.

Yen-Ching-Kou where the water from wells dating from the Ming Dynasty (c. A.D. 1600) still tasted salt, and where the local farmers dug for fossils in the deep pockets of bedrock. On this occasion they brought up the broken jaw of a *Stegodon*, or Pliocene elephant, with an uneven tooth still in its socket. Teilhard's identification of this proved that the pitfall from which it had been extracted agreed with the conclusions they had already formed about the geology of the district.

On their return to Wanhsien they found a much more hospitable welcome at the Mission. The local priest had telegraphed to Chengtu and confirmed the *bona fides* of Teilhard and Young, who caught a boat the next morning to Ichang. Barbour joined them, travelling by plane, and overtaking them on foot a mile downstream.

The question at issue was the precise date of the warping of the earth's crust which had transformed the landscape by pushing up the highlands, while permitting the sagging of the basins and depressions drained by the great river.[1]

On June 18 they were back in Pekin. Teilhard wrote: 'I have learnt and understood a great deal: mountains whose peaks look down on great lakes and icefields; pinewoods, pagodas, bamboos, hills covered with azaleas in flower. The green vegetation and the colours give a fresh look to the austerity of northern China.'[2] But enjoyable as the journey had been, its aftermath was not agreeable. Motivated, it seemed, by jealousy of Teilhard, Young had been sending back reports criticizing the trip to Chengtu. Barbour pointed out to Ting, Acting Director of the Geological Survey, that Teilhard was not a salaried Survey employee; that the funds behind the expedition were Rockefeller money; that Black had wished them to push on into Szechwan; and that although the Cenozoic Laboratory was a unit of the Survey the management of its affairs had been in the hands of Black and that Teilhard was now responsible for them. The idea that Teilhard as acting director, once in the field, could not alter a plan without telegraphing for permission was ridiculous. The four days in Szechwan had cost the Survey nothing, since Barbour had paid for them. 'It shows', he concluded in a letter home, 'that they want to pull the whole Cenozoic structure back into their own hands and absorb the funds by finding an excuse to discredit Teilhard before the

---

[1] *ibid.*, p. 97.   [2] *Letters from a Traveller*, p. 203.

new director is appointed. . . . Without Davidson Black to support him, Teilhard's life will be no easy one in the months ahead. In fact, I marvel at his having met some of these smiling faces without disillusion. . . .'[1]

All but one item of Black's programme for the Laboratory team had by now been carried out. The province of Honan, with the Tsinling Range dividing north from central China, had been reduced to anarchy by the bandits and was unsafe of access. Teilhard described it as a 'wasp's nest'[2] where even the Chinese geologists were afraid to venture. Recently, however, Chiang Kai-shek had restored a semblance of order, and Teilhard decided to see how far he could get towards the sources of the Han river in the hills south of Tientshui. He left Pekin with Barbour on 17 July. Eddie Bien was an agreeable replacement of Young, and an efficient cook-technician completed the party. They reached Loyang two days later; assembled a caravan; and continued their journey into the hills with an escort of three armed guards—themselves converted bandits. In one sense, at least, their progress was spectacular:

Outside one country town, a play was in progress on the stage in front of a temple as we approached. The audience, a hundred strong, deserted *en masse* and tore down the slope, like the herd at Gadara, to watch us pass on the road below—even the players stopped till we had passed. At another point, a pitiful little procession, marching around a temple enclosure with banners and branches, beating gongs and praying for rain, seemed to feel their efforts were not in vain—at least they had our show to talk about for the week—and after all it did rain before nightfall.[3]

Teilhard was quick to compare this countryside with the Shansi, which he and Barbour had explored together, wondering whether the loess might not be an older deposit than the layers he had seen in the north—perhaps of the Samnenian era. At Yiying they were forced to wait three-quarters of an hour outside the city walls until the captain of the guard was called out of bed and came to examine their papers. As compensation for this annoyance the city magistrate entertained them to supper at 11.30 p.m., after which they sat on discussing

[1] *In the Field with Teilhard de Chardin*, p. 100.
[2] Letter to Pierre Lamare, 29 September 1934.
[3] *In the Field with Teilhard de Chardin*, p. 103.

Darwinism into the small hours and slept in the courtyard under the stars.

Such courtesy was *de rigueur*, but it involved inconvenient delays. At Lushih, on the Lo-ho river, Teilhard was sitting patiently on the steps of the Yamen watching three soldiers unloading a restive mule. One of the soldiers called out in Chinese that the beast had an ugly temper, but Teilhard could not have understood what he was saying, even if he had been listening. In fact he was discussing a quotation from Li T'ai-Po to the effect that 'It is as hard to travel in Szechwan as to climb to heaven.' Teilhard certainly did not think the ascent to heaven an easy one—and then the mule struck out with its hind leg and caught him on the temple:

The blow broke a blood vessel, and within a few seconds he had a blood blister the size of a pigeon's egg over the temporal artery. It took less than five minutes of Bien's diplomacy to commandeer a nearby room in the outer court, unpack, and set up a camp cot. Ice does not exist in a Honan village in July, and the medical orderly of the post had no supplies of any kind except a little ether. Throughout the night, I kept Teilhard's temple cool with constantly changed compresses. I read to him the office of the day from the breviary he had been using in the cart earlier in the afternoon, and waited in fear for the dawn while the candle burned down. Through all of this Teilhard's only concern was for '*ces pauvres gens*' who had prepared a meal with such care, and had no guests to eat it.[1]

Two days later he was fit to travel. The cart and driver were paid off and the party continued over the pass on foot, putting their baggage on the mules. Barbour's movie camera caught Teilhard bathing in a mountain stream; and when Teilhard saw the film many years later, he observed: 'Do you not think that if the head of my Order in Rome saw me like that in the middle of the river, he would consider me prematurely unfrocked?'[2] Teilhard could now see for himself what a real barrier was formed by the Tsinling range. It was 'an axial band of Palaeozoic granite, bordered to the north and south by thick formations of the Tertiary fissured in the course of a pre-Pliocene elevation of the chain'.[3] The deposits containing the *Hipparion* fauna

[1] *In the Field with Teilhard de Chardin*, p. 105.   [2] *ibid.*
[3] Letter to Pierre Lamare, 29 September 1934.

seemed only to be found in the north. The millet and corn, which were the staple crop north of the Tsinling, were replaced by paddy fields and sugar-cane when you had gone a little way down its southern slope. The graves were dug in the terraces of the river beds instead of being marked in the rock. Each village lived on its particular produce —lithographic limestone, leather for whiplashes, the slate for marbles and chessmen. As the trail widened out, the party met a train of camels westward bound, and Teilhard was taken for a ride in a sail-driven wheelbarrow. The water buffaloes were competing with the mules as beasts of burden; and the tobacco fields bordered the road as the party came to the end of its journey. They reached the railway at Hsuchung after twenty-four days on foot, and from there caught the train to Pekin. Teilhard's hopes for the expedition had been more than fulfilled.

He was also encouraged by a letter from Père Maréchal to whom he had sent a short paper on 'the place of man in nature'; published the previous year in the *Revue des étudiants de Pékin*. 'There is no one', Maréchal wrote, 'who has such a grasp as you have of all the material bearing on the problem of evolution, theological, philosophical and scientific.'[1] Equally encouraging had been the appearance, in 1933, of *Dieu ou Rien* by the great Dominican theologian, A. D. Sertillanges. Here certain ideas, and even expressions, of Teilhard were in circulation. Teilhard—unlike so many Jesuits—had no prejudice against Dominicans. 'Their humane and Christian influence', he wrote to Madame Haardt, 'is large-minded and progressive. It is an Order that has breadth, tradition and breeding.'[2] In a letter to Sertillanges, whom he did not know, Teilhard showed how far he was from depreciating St. Thomas Aquinas, whatever he may have thought of his modern interpreters:

> With your voice so measured and so authoritative, you are at last beginning to make people hear the word that I have long dreamt of hearing resound, frankly, in the Church.

Teilhard and Sertillanges looked to very similar horizons which our Christ should be able to envelop and illuminate—'*neque longitudo, neque latitudo, neque profundum*'. I imagine that St. Thomas would recognize himself in the happy audacity with

[1] *Letters from a Traveller*, p. 206.
[2] 3 March 1936.

which you see them extending, every day, a little more before our eyes.[1]

The idea had been mooted that Teilhard should go to Rome for 'conversations', but he did not see how he could make his peace with intellectual honesty, and his Provincial discouraged the project. Further charges had been brought against him—notably, and most absurdly, arising from a purely technical article on an anthropological subject. This had not been followed up, but Teilhard knew that his *dossier* at the Holy Office was a heavy one, and there were many 'floating mines'[2] in the waters he was navigating. Surely, he asked, it should be to the Church's interest to make use of his acknowledged reputation, even if it were not justified? But Teilhard de Chardin was in his grave before the Church—or an important section of it—was to see the matter in the same light.

[1] 4 February 1934.
[2] *Letters to Léontine Zanta.*

CHAPTER XI

INDIAN INTERLUDE[1]

TEILHARD spent the autumn of 1934 sifting and interpreting the material from Chou-Kou-Tien. Barbour had returned to London, but Breuil had arrived in Pekin for a second examination of the Sinanthropos findings. In January 1935 Teilhard left with Wong and Pei for the provinces of Kwangtung and Kwangsi, the southernmost limits of the country. At the end of the month he was writing from Kweilin, where the Kwei Kiang ran 'through a maze of fantastic rocks' and the 'forest of high pillars or needles of limestone (about 80 or 90 metres high)' formed 'a most extraordinary landscape' almost entirely naked of trees. It was a 'country of oranges, mandarines and pomelos',[2] and the weather was cold. In the caves which they explored 'implements of the Mesolithic type were found in an accumulation of consolidated ash and freshwater shells', and also traces of *Stegodon* and orang. These deposits seemed to be the 'exact equivalent of the Sinanthropos beds in northern China and of the Pithecanthropos beds in Java'—a supposition which was confirmed in 1955 when teeth of Gigantopithecus and *Stegodon* were discovered in Kwangsi; and again in 1958 when two mandibles of Gigantopithecus, 'close in appearance to the human', were found in the same province.[3]

Meanwhile Breuil was still in Pekin and early in May he and Teilhard left for Paris by the Trans-Siberian railway. Teilhard stopped at the Jesuit house in the Rue de Grenelle, and seemed to be greatly consoled by this renewal of contact with the Society. It must always be

---

[1] For a detailed account of Teilhard's visit to India the reader is referred to Helmut de Terra's *Memories of Teilhard de Chardin*, pp. 22–69. All the quotations in the middle section of this chapter are taken from this, except where otherwise stated.

[2] Cuénot.

[3] For Teilhard's summary of his findings, see Cuénot, p. 187.

remembered that the Jesuits, at any rate in France, were his most powerful protectors. They may not have won his battles, but at least they waged them. He himself used to say that he regarded the Society as his mother; and on another occasion he compared it—not without irony perhaps—to a '*grande dame*'; and Teilhard was nothing if not a *grand seigneur*. In this relationship with his Order breeding counted for a good deal. Breuil, viewing it from the outside, summed it up as a 'double miracle'. Teilhard himself was a miracle; but only the miracle of the Jesuits—'in other words St. Ignatius'—had made it possible. In what did the second miracle consist?

In a complete submission of the religious and at the same time a complete liberty of soul, of internal sincerity and of sincerity towards his superior. In the respect of this liberty by the superior who recognizes and protects its legitimacy, at the same time as he controls it. This control—even when its exercise is humanly speaking debatable—has a double advantage. First it obliges the religious, through criticism, to perfect his means of expression in order that the mass of people shall more easily assimilate it; and secondly it protects him against censure. Teilhard was a Jesuit from the bottom of his loyal heart, obedient up to the extreme limit of his strength and still keeping intact the fidelity to his own thought and his right as a priest to make it known to those who needed it. Hence the simplicity with which he snatched at every means of evasion not expressly forbidden—such as the brochures which he had duplicated on the invitation of his friends, and which he submitted to the examination of his equals and his Jesuit colleagues, always ready to take account of an opinion which he had asked for. Teilhard *willed* to remain a Jesuit, and the Jesuits kept him as they found him. In this way he gained in depth and fullness, and also gained protection against the threats which any precursor has to face. This protection would have been unavailing if Teilhard had not been an exemplary and constantly submissive religious. An ordinary, isolated priest, undefended by the flag of a powerful collectivity, would have lacked this corporative protection and control—a control which was deepening as well as embarrassing in its effect. A kind of heroism was required for Teilhard to combine a perfect and sincere obedience with a complete liberty of thought purified by trial and contradiction.

A comparison with Luther suggested itself. The German princes had exploited Luther's justified revolt against ecclesiastical abuses, and had thus divided the Church. The reaction against neo-paganism had 'retarded by many centuries the necessary adaptation to the rediscovery of Greek thought, and in particular to the newly born experimental science'. This had resulted in the 'apparent antinomy between science and faith' to which Teilhard had given his courageous answer.[1]

So it was not only among the *avant-garde* of the Society—an *avant-garde* that rarely loses touch with the main body—that Teilhard found his friends. The young Bruno de Solages was now a monsignor and Rector of the Institut Catholique in Toulouse; behind him, as archbishop, was the indomitable Saliège, afterwards to be the cardinal of the French Resistance. Bruno de Solages had asked Teilhard for an essay to explain why and how he believed. Teilhard readily acceded to the request:

You are one of those friends and faithful counsellors without whom my life would go I know not whither . . . I am all too often reduced to soliloquize, as impressions take me, without feeling the spur or the attraction of a concrete end in view.[2]

He had sketched out the essay in September 1934 under the title of *Comment Je Crois*. In tracing his progress of belief Teilhard stressed that faith was not a matter of temperament, since it was through the most incommunicably personal part of ourselves that we touched the universal. All faith was born of faith in something else. The sceptic (he might have argued) could not believe in his own reasoning unless he believed in his own existence, and he could not believe in his own existence unless he believed in his own mind. To believe was to 'operate a synthesis whose . . . origin is impossible to seize. . . . If, as a result of some interior reversal, I came to lose successively my faith in Christ, my faith in a personal God, my faith in the spirit, I think that I should continue to believe, invincibly, in the world.' The world, for Teilhard, constituted a whole, made up not of 'things' but of 'elements'. Most people were by nature either monists or pluralists, but pluralists were really monists 'who don't know it'. If man were the key to an understanding of the earth, as Teilhard believed, why

[1] *Cahiers Pierre Teilhard de Chardin*, vol. 2.
[2] 7 January 1934.

should not the earth be the key to an understanding of the world? Evolution rescued, at the same time, man and matter; and if spirit came to birth through the functioning of matter, why not construct a physics based on spirit instead of the other way about? The whole, in Teilhard's vision, was not 'the sea where the grain of salt is dissolved, nor the fire which consumes the straw. It is a *centre*. For the human *monade* to lose itself in the universe is to be raised to a greater height of personality. What was at first a confused intuition of universal unity has become the awareness of a presence—an awareness reasoned and defined.'

Once again, Teilhard affirmed and analysed his belief in personal immortality:

My visible actions and influence count for very little beside my secret self. My real treasure is, *par excellence*, that part of my being which the centre, where all the sublimated wealth of the universe converges, cannot allow to escape. The reality, which is the culminating point of the universe, can only develop in partnership with ourselves by keeping us within the supreme personality: we cannot help finding ourselves personally immortal.

The whole of this essay is of great biographical interest. Teilhard looked at the religions which had gained, and still solicited, the adherence of mankind almost as if he had not yet made his choice between them. For the Orient, matter was 'a dead weight and an illusion'; for the Occident it was 'charged with sublime possibilities', and the modern world was 'eager religiously to legitimize its conquests'. The religion of the Hindu gave Teilhard the impression of 'an abyss in which you throw yourself to catch the reflection of the sun'; with the humanitarian pantheists of today he seemed 'to stifle under too low a sky'. To be absolutely candid with himself, and with others, Teilhard admitted that—at least at the beginning—he had found it difficult to reconcile his 'sense of the earth' with the Jesus of the Gospels. How came it then that expectations, which the pantheisms neither of East nor West were able to satisfy, had been fulfilled in Christ? The answer was given by the Incarnation which he described as 'a synthesis between Christ and the universe'.

In no other kind of cosmos, and in no other place, has any being—no matter how divine—been able to exercise the function of universal animation and consolidation which Christian dogma attributes to Jesus. In discovering a summit to the world, evolution makes Christ possible—just as Christ, in giving a meaning to the world, makes evolution possible.

I shall only become the other by remaining absolutely myself. I shall only reach the spirit by liberating the ultimate forces of matter. The total Christ is only consummated and only attainable at the end of universal evolution. In him I have found the object of my desires; a personalized universe whose domination secures my personality. And I hold this 'Soul of the World' no longer merely as a fragile creation of my individual thought but as the product of a long historical revelation in which the least believing of men are obliged to recognize one of the master principles of human progress.

There are phrases here that might make a theologian jump; to say that evolution 'made Christ possible' was surely asking for trouble. Étienne Gilson has given his opinion that Teilhard's ideas are innocuous because they are incommunicable. They certainly do not constitute a 'system' which can be taken or left; nor can they be understood without reference to the experience which produced them. They are a way of feeling, a personal vision, irreducible to formula. It was no good, he argued, looking to the universe for a 'picture of synoptic harmony'.[1] We can understand St. Thomas Aquinas without knowing anything about him; we can only understand Teilhard the thinker if we know something about Teilhard the man. He believed himself that the personal tone of the essay would disarm theological objections, and he told Bruno de Solages that he would 'never find it possible to think or to write anything other than these pages contain'.[2]

For all the strength of his affirmations, Teilhard does not pretend that belief is easy:

Sure as I am—and more and more sure—that I must go forward as if Christ was waiting for me at the end of the universe, I have no particular assurance that he exists. Believing is not the same as seeing. As much as anyone, I imagine, I go forward among the shadows of the faith.

The shadows were only one aspect of the problem of evil. God

[1] Letter to Bruno de Solages, 28 August 1934.
[2] 15 September 1934.

allowed us to 'to suffer, to sin and to doubt because he cannot *all at once* cure us and show himself, and because *we* are incapable, at present, of receiving him'. Evil was inevitable in a creation which was developing in time. Our doubts, like our sins and our misfortunes, were 'the price and even the condition of a completed universe'. Here again was Teilhard's struggle to make sense of original sin and unmerited suffering; it was a problem with which he would wrestle, not quite successfully, to the end. Moreover to say that God could not reveal himself 'all at once' and that man was 'incapable of receiving him', was to make nonsense of the history of conversion. It was to forget the road to Damascus—a thoroughfare that Teilhard generally had very much in mind. But *Comment Je Crois* must be read, and welcomed, for its candour:

> In these conditions I accept to go forward to the end along a road of which I am more and more certain, towards horizons more and more drowned in mist. This is how I believe.

Equally important for an understanding of Teilhard's temperament was *L'Évolution de la Chasteté*, composed in the same year (1934). All through his life friendship with women counted for him a great deal. His correspondence, as it is gradually published, eloquently bears this out. On the intellectual plane feminine intuition and sensibility was an indispensable complement to the rational judgment of men. Hence the spiritual power of the flesh. The Church had long approved sexual union for reproductive purposes alone, and held that otherwise it should be reduced to a minimum. Chastity was a transposition of sexual fidelity on to the religious plane, but it had been tainted with a contempt for matter—as the 'virtuosities of asceticism' bore witness. For Teilhard, however, the function of maternity in woman was a small thing beside her spiritual fecundity; and he recognized in the present licence of morals

> the quest for a form of union richer and more spiritualizing than a union limited to the horizons of the cradle. . . . It is in union that man and woman should ascend to God. Spirituality rests upon the human *dyade*, not upon the human *monade*.

Teilhard naturally admitted the corruptive influence of sexuality; of all the forces of matter woman was the most to be feared. But danger was in itself a 'symptom of power'. It was the mountain that created the abyss; and there was no reason to dispense with fire because the flames consumed, or with electricity because it was liable to create explosions. The counsels of prudence had made it appear more important to avoid a risk than 'to place a difficult situation in the hands of God'. Between the two conceptions—above all, avoid mistakes, even if in doing so you are impoverished; and above all, seek enrichment, even if you risk a few splashes of mud—he did not hesitate to prefer the second.

For all this, however, Teilhard did not question the superior value of virginity, if virginity were properly understood. He doubted the wisdom of breaking 'the bonds of moral duty and respectful admiration which human experience has woven, through the centuries, around the ideal of virginity'. Something was lost as well as gained in the ecstasy of physical desire; and in order to attain the limits of spiritual union in their pursuit of God, lovers would have no choice but to 'turn their backs on the body'. Teilhard was looking—far ahead—to a realization of love where everything would be preserved and transfigured:

> At the heart of the noosphere love is in the way of changing its condition; and if the religions are right, it is in this direction that humanity is preparing its collective passage to God, and this is how I imagine the evolution of chastity. All that is needed to bring this about is for the appeal of a *personal* divine centre to be felt strongly enough to master the natural attraction which precipitates human couples on to one another before the time is ripe.... What paralyses life is failure to believe and failure to dare. . . . The mastery of passion in the service of the spirit is a condition of progress, and here we have biology as our witness. And so, sooner or later, and whatever we may believe to the contrary, the world will take this step. . . . Some day or other—after the ether and the winds and the tides and gravitation—we shall capture for God the energies of love. And then, for the second time in the history of the world, Man will have discovered the Fire.

These were high words, and Teilhard admitted that in one important sense he did not know what he was talking about. Yet in another sense he did. Considering the two ways of love, he could write:

> By nature, if I may say so, I was committed to the second, and I followed it as far as I was able to. Of course I had some difficult moments, but I never felt lost or diminished.

By nature, too, everything in Teilhard was virile, just as everything was pure. In a life so largely exposed to secular contacts, and in a vocation—as he continually emphasized—so resolutely directed to 'the Gentiles', he naturally found himself at times in a delicate situation. A vow of chastity, however, scrupulously kept, does not make a man any less of a man than he is already. For Teilhard, friendship was in itself a vocation and he fearlessly claimed its rights. Nevertheless he was acutely conscious of his responsibility, not only to himself, but to other people:

> One knows oneself, and one is master to some extent of one's own suffering. But what does one know about the forces one may unloose in someone else; forces that one cannot satisfy? The only possible friend . . . is one who finds elsewhere, deep within herself, a serious stability in a full life, or in some great ideal.[1]

He was generally fortunate in finding them.

II

Among those attending the Washington Geological Congress in 1933 was Helmut de Terra, a geologist of German origin, then attached to Yale University. He had lectured to the Congress on the geological affinities between the Alps and the Himalayas, and naturally made the acquaintance of Teilhard, who was already known to him through his writings. Teilhard had shown a particular interest in the lecture, because de Terra had discovered a number of stone-age artefacts in Kashmir and the Himalayan foothills. He had subsequently entered into correspondence with Black who was anxious to pursue the researches of the Cenozoic Laboratory into Baluchistan and the eastern borders of Persia. The financial crisis of 1931 had temporarily put an end to these hopes, but he encouraged de Terra to co-ordinate his own work with Pekin, and the result of these exchanges was a letter from de Terra inviting Teilhard to meet him in India during the autumn of 1935. Teilhard warmly accepted the invitation and sailed from Marseilles in the *Cathay* early in September of that year.

In the meanwhile his enthusiasm had somewhat cooled. 'I am not greatly excited', he wrote, 'about the idea of going to India, but I look

[1] Letter to Pierre Lamare, 17 March 1930.

on it as my strict duty to do my best to make the trip.' Now that he was quite fixed in his belief that mankind was carried along by an advancing wave of consciousness, 'does anything', he asked, 'remain to be disclosed in what has been left behind us?' It was an extraordinarily cavalier view of history. Teilhard was so sure that progress was inevitable that he made little allowance for disaster or decline. It rarely occurred to him that, from his own optimistic point of view, the past might be superior to the present and had much to teach it. For all our conquest of the atom we are still trying to catch up with Socrates. Teilhard envisaged progress in a strictly linear development; he did not seem to realize how it could play ducks and drakes with time. It was surely more plausible to conceive the noosphere as an extra-temporal creation, and there were moments in conversation with his friends when Teilhard seemed ready to admit the possibility. But now, as he stood on the threshold of India, he confessed, in a letter to Max and Simone Bégouën, his astonishment that people should consider the past—even the prehistoric past—interesting in itself. This lack of the historical sense—which was quite compatible with palae-ontology—robbed his thought of a dimension that would have enriched it.

He was too professional a scientist, however, for this mood to last for long; and we soon find him in Bombay, the guest of the Spanish Fathers at St. Xavier's College. The monsoon was just over, but the humidity made him eager for Kashmir; and on 23 September he caught the night mail for Rawalpindi. Here he was met by T. T. Paterson, the Scots archaeologist, who drove him to Srinagar where de Terra was waiting for him in a houseboat with his wife and daughter. From Srinagar they explored the Himalayan valleys and Teilhard remembered that it was along one of these routes that Haardt had set out for Chinese Turkestan. As he now wrote to his widow:

I can see the marks of caterpillar-tracks on the mountain passes, and memories of Georges-Marie—that is, really of you—seldom if ever desert me. How time flies, but how vivid events remain! . . . I don't need to describe Kashmir to you, because you know it: a green river valley framed by two snowy ranges. The weather is superb, the rice-fields quite yellow. At the first breath of autumn the huge plane-trees begin to turn red. On the edge of the fragrant forests, beturbanned peasants gather walnuts near orchards full of red apples. It looks like a reflection of Aksu, where I waited for the party at the same time of year.[1]

The Sind Valley, where these traces of the *Croisière Jaune* were found, contained a Neolithic settlement which Paterson had discovered. Teilhard noted a similarity between the geometrical patterns on the ancient potsherds and those which he had seen in the Gobi desert. Near the entrance to the Sind Valley was 'a group of isolated, plate-shaped boulders up to twelve feet in height' which had reminded de Terra of Stonehenge:

The site appeared to have been a temple precinct, possibly associated with sun-worship. When I showed Teilhard the polished stone axes, pestles, mortars and pottery adorned with matting imprints which I had found in the deepest layers of the digging conversation at once turned to the great upheavals that had occurred during the Neolithic period. The fact that no metal objects of any kind had come to light during my excavation of the temple precincts seemed to indicate that it dated from the latter part of the stone age, a circumstance which led Teilhard to speak of the way in which archaeologists currently working in Asia had neglected research into that period.

De Terra noticed how reluctant Teilhard seemed to pursue a discussion about purely factual observations; always he wanted to get behind the fact, once it had been verified; to co-ordinate, compare, and synthesize. For Paterson, on the other hand, 'his mind was a razor, sharp in analytical terms: to argue with him was a delight. He required precision and he liked his arguments (at least in palaeontology) to be as logical as possible.'[2] On 9 October the party moved down to the foothills of the Himalayas in search of fossils from the period immediately preceding the Ice Age. Here among the rock formations of the Salt Range they found

fossil bones and petrified imprints of palm-leaves . . . embedded in stone, like the hieroglyphs which had to be deciphered if we were to follow the evolution of life. The skeletal remains of gazelles, wild horses, mastodons and, last but not least, anthropoid apes all helped to shed light on the problem of man's origins.

[1] 1 October 1935.
[2] Letter to the author, December 1966.

They wandered by camel or by car, sleeping under canvas or in one of the bungalows which the British authorities had put up at convenient intervals. Teilhard had a boy called Simon to look after him; in spite of his youth, he flaunted a formidable moustache. The cracked and stony ground and the thorny trees reminded Teilhard of Egypt or Ethiopia. He was depressed by the sight of the Moslem women under their veils; it made him 'appreciate what our Western civilization has succeeded in winning for their sisters in Europe. . . . All this has got to be swept away, and before very long too.'[1] Teilhard may have been romantic about the cosmos and occasionally naïve about human nature; but where the traditions and taboos of society seemed to him an impediment to social progress—to 'socialization'—he was not romantic at all. He was appalled that a young Bengalese would not sit down to dinner with them because he belonged to the Brahmin caste; and the fakirs, 'squatting beneath the broad branches of mango trees, their naked torsos smeared with ash and their long matted hair piled turban-like atop their ascetic faces', merely reminded him of the bondage to which religious superstition could reduce mankind. Where other visitors have been impressed by the sacral foundations of Indian life, Teilhard was irked by its stagnation. 'The Hindus have been a disappointment to me', he wrote later, '. . . you have to go to India to appreciate the numbing and deadening effect of a religion obsessed by ritualism and outward form.'[2] Or, again, to Léontine Zanta:

> India did not seem to me to have preserved much more of crea-
> tive power than China or Japan. And its religion today is the best
> warning to a Church that would risk allowing itself to be domin-
> ated by ritual manifestations and every form of superstition, how-
> ever veiled. I shuddered sometimes to recognize ourselves in
> them.[3]

Nor was he in sympathy with the eroticism of Indian art. Their Brahmin friend had told them of a temple famed for its phallic sym-bols, where the limestone steps leading to the shrine contained fossils shaped like the creative organ of the god Siva. In all this Teilhard could only see the relics of ancient superstition, the cult of man's re-lationship with the lower forms of life. He did not appreciate the

[1] *Letters from a Traveller*, p. 213.   [2] *ibid.*, p. 216.
[3] 26 January 1936.

assertion of a cosmic unity, which was in many ways analogous to his own ideas.

In the Sohan Valley de Terra had discovered stone-age artefacts—axes, scrapers and splinters—proving that these implements had been fashioned on the spot. Teilhard examined them with the eye 'of a detective permanently aware of his responsibility to some higher authority'—and indeed there was something about his figure and his face, when he was on to a scent, reminiscent of the traditional pictures of Sherlock Holmes. If he had Holmes's method and mien, he also had his memory. This was such that he 'could describe and sketch the precise shape of artefacts which he had found in China ten years before'. After their excursion to the Salt Range de Terra took him to the foot of the Kashmir Himalayas. Here, among the gravel formations, they discovered that the 'strata exposed by an Ice Age river had been folded by intense pressure' and 'the question at once arose as to whether primitive man had actually witnessed the Himalayas' last uplift'. This was answered by Teilhard when he was able to identify as primitive artefacts stones which de Terra dated from 'the close of the second Himalayan glaciation'—thus proving that they were more or less contemporary with Sinanthropos.

A further question was now opened up. 'Was there, both in Asia and Europe, a geological horizon on which could be perceived the first glimmer of human intelligence? It was certainly remarkable that the earliest and most primitive artefacts in both China and India belonged to the Middle Quaternary, and that a similar boundary was discernible in the Palaeolithic period in Europe.' Must these tools be regarded as the earliest records of human intelligence? Might not primitive man have worked on other materials? If so, they would hardly have survived. The fossil remains of anthropoid apes discovered in the Salt Range were geologically separated from the Ice Age gravel; was it in this interval that man had appeared? Teilhard returned to the problem in *The Phenomenon of Man*:

> Between the last strata of the Pliocene age, in which man is absent, and the next in which the geologist is dumbfounded to find the first chipped flints, what has happened? It is our task to divine and to measure the answers to these questions before we follow, step by step, the march of mankind right down to the decisive stage in which it is involved today.

Teilhard came to think the moment of anthropogenesis could not be demonstrated, since he identified it with an emergence of consciousness. This, no doubt, was why he took so little account of environment. Here de Terra disagreed with him.

I felt far more inclined . . . to adduce . . . the geologically demonstrable shifting of climatic belts toward the close of the Pliocene, to account for the decisive changes in fauna and stratum-formation which undoubtedly influenced the evolution of the higher primates. . . . If there was, in Teilhard's sense, a psychogenesis which evolved from general biogenetic processes, I find it hard to believe that it was not influenced by changes in environment. Not to have given sufficient weight to such factors must be regarded as one of the weakest points in Teilhard's magnificent edifice of ideas.

Although geology rather than anthropogenesis was the immediate motive of their research, traces of man might always be round the corner. Here, on the banks of the Indus, were enough fossil bones to fill three packing-cases in a single day; would the site yield the 'remains of higher primates, perhaps even of men'? Teilhard worked with 'suppressed excitement', but 'when the fiery sun sank behind a dust cloud and the hoped-for trophy had not materialized' he did not seem disappointed. He was content to feel that once again Providence had led him

to a critical point at just the psychological moment. I do indeed believe that it is the work in which I'm now sharing that will lay the first serious foundation for the prehistory of India.[1]

And always there was the landscape to enchant him:

In the foreground, deep crevasses exposing under the mimosa growth the striped mass (yellow, violet, pink) of the regularly curved Pleistocene formations; in the middle distance, much further back, the violet mass of Pliocene and Miocene mud almost forming one with the great chains; and finally, floating in the blue sky on the horizon, the white barrier of the Pir Panjal, the last corner of the Himalayan peaks; and lying over the whole scene a golden light playing on the dry, bleached grasses.[2]

Since no human fossils of comparable importance with Sinanthro-

[1] *Letters from a Traveller*, p. 215.
[2] *ibid.*

pos had been discovered in Hindustan, the party moved down to the lower waters of the Indus and spent some time among the ruins of Mohenjo-Daro. These were probably the remains of a city in some way associated with the Mesopotamian empire of Sumer. Teilhard was not an archaeologist but he was interested, with de Terra, to discover how these early cultures of the river valleys were related to those of the neighbouring Iranian highlands. De Terra deduced that 'the extension of agriculture followed certain river networks which favoured hoeing and digging', and that 'the emergence of socialization in the Neolithic period' was dependent on these factors. A 'cosmic sense of life, rooted in fertility-magic' was evident in the pottery of the period. For Teilhard, who regarded the history of culture as 'a special form of zoological development', these observations brought a degree of reinforcement. De Terra noted the difference of Teilhard's biological approach from the tidy schemes of Spengler and Toynbee, but he also noted that it was not so novel as it appeared. A similar interpretation had been worked out by the Munich ethnologist, Friedrich Ratzel. The novelty of Teilhard's thesis lay in its 'phenomenological relationship' to his 'concept of universal growth in psychical powers and their culmination in "consciousness" or self-awareness'. He was certainly quick to relate his impressions of Mohenjo-Daro to the 'thread of Ariadne' which linked one phase to another of his thought:

> In the middle of the tamarisk bush you find a red-brick town, partially exposed since 1922, with its houses, drains, streets, wells and water system. . . . More than 3,000 years before our era, people were living there who played with dice like our own, fished with hooks like ours, and wrote in characters we can't yet read. We live surrounded by ideas and objects infinitely more ancient than we imagine; and yet at the same time everything is in motion. The universe is a vast thing in which we should be lost if it did not converge upon the person.[1]

With a medieval drainage system and a mathematical lay-out of the streets reminiscent of New York, Mohenjo-Daro suggested a discrepancy—to be matched in any twentieth-century metropolis—between mind and technique. Here the bull and the deer, the tiger and the

[1] *ibid.*, p. 216.

rhinoceros, had been worshipped very much as they were worshipped by the primitive cave-men. The two geologists found it 'an incongruous combination ... yet another case where technical progress had outstripped spiritual development'.

Teilhard, who believed in a 'universal dissemination of fossil man in the Middle Quaternary', was anxious to discover traces of an ancient culture in other parts of India. Paterson had reported on Palaeolithic work-sites in the south; might not similar evidence be found in the centre? Starting out from a village near Hoshangabad in the Narbada valley, fifty miles south of Bhopal, Teilhard was able to identify fossil bones from the period of Sinanthropos, and the next day stone tools came to light.

> We had been making our way along the river bank, searching slowly and painstakingly, when Teilhard suddenly called out something in an excited voice from a spur of rock. When I reached him he held out a piece of dark quartzite, a broad-bladed *coup de poing*, similar to those of the Acheul culture, which he had dug out of a layer in the side of a bank, together with a hippopotamus tooth.

This was the first tool of its kind to be found in central India, and beside it were the remains of an animal that primitive man had unquestionably hunted. Other tools—some of them smaller and indicating a more recent culture—were found in the same district. But the artefacts unearthed in the Sinanthropos cave were a good deal more primitive than these, and de Terra agreed with Teilhard that 'the primitive man of India might have been of a different type and date'.

They were taken to see the rock-paintings near Hoshangabad. When Teilhard realized that these probably represented a battle scene from the Indo-European invasion of the sub-continent, he concluded that they were older than generally supposed. Suddenly the fifteen hundred miles separating them from Mohenjo-Daro 'became a bridge... with one of the major events of India's history and one which had radically altered the country's spiritual and social structure'. There were other rock-drawings in the neighbourhood and the path to them lay through thick undergrowth. De Terra feared that at any moment a panther might emerge from it. Turning back to warn Teilhard, he saw him standing quite still, 'his eyes fixed on a thicket from which came a loud sound of snapping twigs'. Involuntarily de Terra seized his arm, but Teilhard was not in the least afraid; or if he was thinking of the panther, he was thinking of it as a fellow-creature. 'This forest', he said, 'is like a sea of hidden life'—and he was conscious only of belonging to it.

One evening, as they returned to their bungalow, they found the village *en fête* in honour of Siva who had brought it rain and left behind some long pebbles as a symbol of his procreative power:

In several houses we glimpsed old men seated at table by candlelight, holding their hands before their foreheads in prayer, Hindufashion, and chanting continuously from books with such devotion that for a moment we felt ourselves carried back in time to the far-off days when the Vedic hymns still formed part of daily worship.

Here, on the banks of the Narbada, was

The real peninsular India: soft summer weather (21 December); golden light; a countryside thickly shaded with mangos and banyans, fine bushy trees like ancient oaks; tall ridges covered with thick forests (tiger jungle); peacocks in the jungle; crocodiles in the river; parrots in the gardens; at every corner frolicking bands of big black-faced monkeys with white ruffs; very gentle, even gracious, people living in big, beautifully clean huts; the women red-veiled, the men in white.[1]

Teilhard had seen something of the Hindu upper classes in Lahore, and he was to see more of them in Calcutta. He found them individually charming but as little capable of self-government as the Chinese. His political judgments were realistic; he was no ideologist. He regretted the hostility to the English, and the desire for total independence, even at a mortal cost; and he thought the English were right not to relinquish their authority. 'The more I get round the world', he told his brother Joseph, 'the more I fear that Geneva (of which I am in my heart a great supporter), numbers of liberal Catholics, and especially my friends the "Missiologues", are making a grave mistake in recognizing the equality of races in face of all the biological evidence. "Universalism" is not democracy'.[2]

He parted from de Terra in Delhi; they had become close friends, Teilhard describing his companion as a *'chic type'*. De Terra left for Bombay and Teilhard for Calcutta, where he embarked on a small

[1] *ibid.*, p. 217.   [2] *ibid.*, p. 220.

British steamer for Rangoon. 'I am glad, once again', he wrote to Madame Haardt, 'that I obeyed life's suggestions and made the "act of faith" of coming to India.'[1]

III

He spent Christmas in Rangoon, where he knew no one, and proceeded to Singapore. Here he was the guest of Collings, director of the Raffles Museum and a prehistorian with interests similar to his own. Three days later he joined a small Dutch liner, the *Ophir*, which was bound for Batavia. Dr. Ralph von Koenigswald, a young, ebullient, and brilliant palaeontologist—'yet another delightful German'[2]—had invited Teilhard to inspect his findings in Java, and Teilhard had responded to the invitation with rather more enthusiasm than he had shown, at first, in joining de Terra in Kashmir. For Teilhard guessed that von Koenigswald's discoveries 'would supply entirely new evidence for his theory of the origin of man'.[3]

It was nearly fifty years since Pithecanthropos had been discovered in Java, and by now the majority of experts were agreed that it was of simian origin. But in 1932 von Koenigswald had found eleven skulls, or fragments of skulls, which he had identified as belonging to *Homo soloensis*—that is to say 'Neanderthaloid in the wide sense of the term'[4]—and in 1935 he had also unearthed the traces of a microlithic industry and a great number of Chelleo-Acheulian flints. In the same year a second and more complete Pithecanthropos skull had been found. This was certified as hominian, of approximately the same age as Sinanthropos and geologically 'perhaps even older'.[5] It seemed possible, therefore, that Java was a junction between two Palaeolithic streams; one from the north-west and the other from the north-east. Teilhard had by now some experience of both, and he was anxious to see for himself how they might be linked together.

He spent ten days on the island, sharing the life of the villages—or *kampongs*—and sleeping in the chief's hut. More than ever he felt himself 'made for the tropics'; he liked the lush vegetation and the heavy

[1] Teilhard de Chardin Album, p. 132.
[2] Letter to Léontine Zanta, 26 January 1926.
[3] *Memories of Teilhard de Chardin*, Helmut de Terra.
[4] Cuénot, p. 191.
[5] *ibid.*, p. 192.

scents. He stayed with von Koenigswald at Bandung in the central and mountainous part of the country where the symmetrical volcanoes rose, like Vesuvius or Fujiyama, from the fields of rice and the forests of coconut palms. In default of drinkable water, the coconuts provided liquid refreshment. When von Koenigswald showed him the Chellean industry, he thought himself back on the Narbada—and one link was clearly established. When they found the floor of a cave littered with the teeth of orang and bear, similar to the fossil-bearing deposits in Kwangsi, the second link was established also. Teilhard confirmed von Koenigswald's view of his latest findings, and thought it providential that he should have arrived—as he always seemed to arrive—just at the right moment. What did they mean—these successive strokes of good luck? 'What', he asked, 'is God expecting of me?'

Indeed throughout the life of Teilhard de Chardin we find this contrasting pattern. Where his scientific researches were in question, the luck came all his way. He met the right people; was on the spot at the right moment; and received his due meed of recognition. It was through no fault of his own, as we shall see, that his career was not crowned by a chair at the Collège de France. But the interpretation of his research—and this was his essential vocation—was muzzled by the 'axe Romain'—the Roman axis—on which he believed, nevertheless, the progress of the universe to turn. His career was a success, while his vocation seemed doomed to failure; and if heroic virtue has any meaning, it surely applies to Teilhard's perseverance in a work which earned, during his lifetime, no visible rewards.

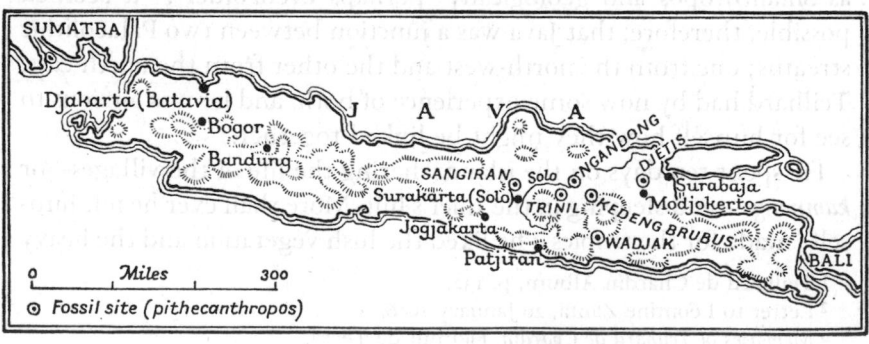

Java

During the twenty days he had spent at sea between leaving Calcutta and steaming outside the muddy estuary of the Yangtse the great question—'What is God expecting of me?'—had not ceased to preoccupy him, and he had given to it many hours of thought and prayer. How could he establish in his own mind, and communicate to others, 'a new religion (call it a better Christianity, if you like) where the personal God will no longer be the great "Neolithic" proprietor of days gone by, but will become the soul of the world that our present stage of cultural and religious development requires and is asking for'? It was no longer a question of 'superimposing Christ upon the world, but of pan-Christianizing the universe'. Teilhard realized that this train of reasoning would lead him

> not only to a broadening of views but to a reversal of perspectives; evil (no longer a punishment for sin, but 'sign and effect' of progress) and matter (no longer a culpable and inferior element) would take on a meaning diametrically opposed to the meaning habitually considered as Christian. Christ emerges from the transformation incredibly greater (at least I think so, and all the worried people I have spoken to think the same). But is it still the Christ of the Gospel? And if it is not he, on whom can we base in future what we are trying to build?[1]

Teilhard admitted that among his colleagues who had preceded or had followed him along the same path of reasoning there was hardly one who understood 'the importance of the step we are now taking'. It was not, after all, so very astonishing. When Teilhard talked about 'a better Christianity' and a 'greater Christ', he was putting his head into the noose. Such ambiguous phrases force one to distinguish—and the distinction is hardly a contrast—between Teilhard and certain of his formulations. This double effect was noted by Étienne Gilson, a great historian of medieval philosophy, and no reactionary thinker. He recalled his first meeting with Teilhard

> in the house of some excellent friends at the baptism of a newborn child. Père Teilhard de Chardin was the officiating priest. I felt immediately the charm of his fine breeding. He baptized the child, if I may so put it, with us; we baptized it, I mean, together. The Father made us part of the ceremony, commenting as he went along, explaining it to us, and taking us into his confidence.

[1] Letter to Léontine Zanta, 26 January 1926.

I never doubted that Père Teilhard de Chardin was an honour to the priesthood, but if I had ever been tempted to think otherwise, the memory of this baptism would have killed the evil thought at birth. I hold his personality in unreserved esteem and profound respect.

Their second meeting was in 1954, at a symposium organized by the University of Columbia at Arden House, near New York. It was only a year before Teilhard's death.

We met on arrival. He had hardly seen me when he came forward to greet me, his face lit up by a candid smile, and grasping my arm with both his hands, said, 'Can you tell me who will give us at last the meta-Christianity we are all waiting for?' I have hesitated for a long time before reporting these words. They seemed to me incredible, impossible from the lips of a priest; and as far as I know, although he may have written something like them, he never wrote that. I am publishing them now because, after reading his works, I think at last I understand them. But at the time this brusque coming to the point left me nonplussed. I think I muttered something or other confused, to the effect that Christianity was already plenty, and enough, for me, and that I should wait till I saw what was the end of it before trying to leave it behind. The Father saw clearly that we were not on the same wavelength, and had the charity to change the subject. His antennae were sufficiently sensitive to feel my embarrassment, and we never referred to the subject again.

But on the same day, during the afternoon, in a passage where a crowd of people were incessantly moving to and fro, I happened to pass in front of a priest seated in an armchair. He was completely oblivious of what was going on around him and absorbed in the reading of his breviary. It was the Reverend Father Teilhard de Chardin of the Society of Jesus. This double image sums up for me what I call 'the case of Teilhard de Chardin'. Even if he was really waiting for a 'meta-Christianity', it was in Christianity itself that he had already found it.[1]

[1] *Seminarium*, no. 4.

CHAPTER XII

BEFORE THE DELUGE

TEILHARD had written to his brother that he would be 'very glad to see brooding old China again'; but when he returned there China was not only brooding but boiling. The Government—and the head-quarters of the Geological Survey—had moved to Nanking, and Pekin, under a Parisian surface of smiles, was echoing to the hobnailed tramp of the Japanese. 'It is impossible', Teilhard wrote, 'to imagine such serenely immoral brutality',[1] but he still thought—and with good reason—that the Chinese might have the last word. It would not be the first time that the stubborn elasticity of a huge population, spread over an immense expanse of territory, was finally able to withstand the *force de frappe* of a highly organized invader. Already, in April 1936, the Japanese seemed a little less sure of themselves.

Teilhard would have his word to say about the general political crisis of which the Japanese aggression and the hopeless internal divisions of the Chinese were only a part. But he was not really interested in politics, and on the voyage from Batavia to Shanghai he was at work on his *Esquisse d'un Univers Personnel*. 'Nothing', he wrote here, 'is more blissful than the attainment of union; neither is anything more painful than its pursuit.' Union was the theme of his essay; union of the sexes, because only through woman can man 'escape the isolation in which his very perfection may too easily imprison him'; union of the couple with humanity; union of humanity with the cos-mos. Nevertheless Teilhard admits the vapidity of a diffused affection. It was true that 'he who loves everything loves nothing', unless the 'everything' is a personalized figure, a precise and recognizable term to the manifold activities of love. Teilhard, of course, identifies this figure with Christ who is 'everything in everybody'; the Pauline Christ incarnate to the dimensions of the universe. The risen Christ

---

[1] *Letters from a Traveller*, p. 223.

had no competitor as a magnetizing force. Teilhard, like any other Catholic, believed in the Resurrection on the authority of the Church; and if he had set out as an unbeliever he might well have believed in it, less on the evidence of history than as a necessity of cosmic evolution. He would have believed in the Church because the Church guaranteed his intuition. He was not very much bothered about 'who moved the stone'; he was very much concerned with who moved the universe.

The temperature of the time, however, compelled Teilhard to come down to earth—although he would have claimed that, in his own understanding of the word, he had never left it:

> I can hardly stand the turmoil of humanity any longer, [he wrote] and many of my friends feel the same. It distresses me to see so many men allowing the pressure of events to force them back into the old-style conservatism. It seems to me the time has come to make a clean break with the old stuff. Fascism, Communism, democracy have ceased to have any real meaning.[1]

Sauvons l'Humanité, La Crise Présente was published in *Études* (October 1937), but Teilhard must have been working out his ideas for it ever since his return to China in the previous year. As usual, he refused the escape of an apocalyptic pessimism. He thought it was too easy to waste one's breath in deploring 'the decrepitude of civilization', and he did not believe that the world would come to an end tomorrow. The history of Egypt, Rome and Athens had shown that civilization was invulnerable to partial catastrophe. We were going forward all the time. 'Futurism, Universalism and Personalism' were 'the three columns of the future'. The instinct of society to merge itself in larger units, and the instinct of the individual to discover the real meaning of his personality, were two expressions of the same movement. Democracy, 'daughter of the Revolution', had confused 'the individual and the person, the crowd and the whole'. A 'ruinous and impossible egalitarianism' was threatening 'any serious construction of a new world'. Communism could only lead to a 'soulless collectivity', in which 'spirit was obscured by matter, and love destroyed by a pseudo-determinism'. Fascism was the 'reaction to revolution', and was therefore favoured by those who had no trust in the future, but for all that it might be taken as 'a fairly successful

[1] *Letters from a Traveller.*

model of the world of tomorrow. A necessary phase during which men would learn, like an exercise, their *métier* as human beings.' This reads naïvely in retrospect, but Teilhard insisted that whatever was good in Fascism would only come to fruition when nationalism had been expelled from its *mystique*. He was not alone among men of high intelligence in thinking that the close organization of the corporative state was superior to the chaos of capitalist democracy. He had seen, and was disposed to admire, the beginnings of the New Deal in America; and although this was a far cry from Fascism, it was only feasible through the assumption of semi-dictatorial powers.

Teilhard looked out on a world struggling for unity—on a crisis of birth, not of death—even though it was preparing to tear itself to pieces in the process. There was a certain validity in all the competing myths; in the democratic sense of personal rights, in the Marxist vision of the powers of matter, in the Fascist ideal of organized *élites*. It might well be that 'the myths of social equality, of racial election, and of empire' were 'the only concrete forms under which the present generation can express its highest earthly ambitions'. These were the days of the Front Populaire, but what was needed was a front at the same time 'spiritual and human'. Why, Teilhard asked, was there an opposition between those who believed in God and those who believed in progress? Because, no doubt, 'in the Church, as elsewhere, the high administration represents the right wheel of the tank, difficult to budge'.[1]

Christianity is universalist, but Christians cling to a medieval cosmogony. Christianity is futurist, but Christians cling to an extraterrestrial ideal. Christianity is personalist, but Christians present the gospel as a moral and juridical precept at the expense of the organic and cosmic splendours included in the Pauline doctrine of Christ recapitulating everything in himself.

'Let us return to Paul', Teilhard had exclaimed in his *Essai d'intégration de l'homme dans l'univers*[2]; it was a journey that he could not take too often.

II

Life in Pekin proceeded smoothly enough for those who were not politically involved. Chaliapin came to sing: 'a fine tall white-haired

[1] Letter to A. Vandel, 31 May 1936.   [2] 1930.

old man, most moving in the decline of his power'.[1] Teilhard went over to Chou-Kou-Tien when digging was resumed in April. The apricot and peach trees stirred into blossom under the clouds of whirling dust. Later he paid his first visit to Shantung, the granitic peninsula jutting out towards Japan—reminiscent of Brittany, but without the gorse and heather; geologically interesting but uncomfortable going in Chinese carts and at night the 'horrors of Chinese inns'.[2]

In the same year (1937) Teilhard suffered two bereavements. On 7 February, shortly after his return to Pekin, he learned of the death of his mother; and on 17 August 1936 his sister Marguerite-Marie died after ten years of incurable illness, borne with heroic and saintly fortitude. In quick succession, now, the shadows were falling over Sarcenat.

The death of Madame Teilhard de Chardin, coming fairly soon after that of her husband, was in the natural order of things. Teilhard owed her, as he often said, '*le meilleur de moi-même*'; indeed of the objects at Sarcenat which had oriented his whole life—the stones which he brought back from the Puys de Dôme, and the picture of the Sacred Heart in the salon—it may be said that he owed the first to his father and the second to his mother. But his debt to Guigite was at once more intimate and more complex. Their destinies could hardly have been more different, but their natures were alike. The title given to her posthumous writings—*L'Énergie Spirituelle de la Souffrance*—was wholly Teilhardian; it enshrined the meaning she had given to her own sufferings, and the meaning that her brother had derived from them. Teilhard had put it in his own way—which was also hers—when he wrote that the Christian's task was 'not to swoon in the shadow of the Cross but to climb in its light'; that Christian resignation was a positive, not a negative, virtue.

As Teilhard came to write the preface to his sister's book, he faced the problem of evil more personally, and more painfully, than he had faced it elsewhere. He had been able to abstract himself—almost inhumanly, some had thought—from the torment of the trenches. He could never abstract himself—nor did he wish to—from the knowledge and the spectacle of Guigite's sufferings. Her death, when it came, might be welcomed as a deliverance; but it created nevertheless 'a sort of universal wilderness around me; it affects every element of an interior world of which I had gradually made her a partner. The

[1] *Letters from a Traveller*, p. 223.   [2] *ibid.*, p. 224.

two of us thought together in everything that makes up spiritual activity and the interior life.'[1] These were his immediate emotions, and their poignancy was not lessened with time. Fifteen years later he placed himself in the situation of one looking at the earth from an immense height. To such a man

Our planet would appear in the first instance blue with the oxygen that envelops it; then green with the vegetation which covers it; then luminous, and ever more luminous, with the thought intensified on its surface; but also dark, and ever more dark, with a suffering which grows in acuteness and in quantity according to the mounting rhythm of consciousness, from one age to another.

As Teilhard drew up his balance sheet between 'physical torture and moral anguish' on the one hand and 'all the joy in the world' on the other, he wondered on which side the heavier weight would fall. The more human man became, the more surely would the problem of evil be found encrusted in 'his flesh, his nerves, and his spirit'; and the evil must be endured and understood. A partial answer was given by the 'complementary mechanism of good and evil'. This was the law of creation, and experience confirmed it. But it was one thing to recognize a law and another to accept it. Only the Christian revelation had the power to transform suffering 'into an expression of love and a principle of union':

Suffering treated first of all as an adversary to conquer; suffering vigorously combated to the bitter end, and yet, at the same time, suffering rationally and cordially accepted in the degree to which it wrenches us away from our egotism, compensates for our faults, and makes us capable thereby of centring ourselves upon God.

This was the 'spiritual energy', the 'increase of spirit born from a defect of matter', which Guigite had expressed in her life before she expressed it in her writing. Teilhard turned to her in the final passage of his Preface:

O Marguerite, my sister, while I was rushing across land and sea, dedicated to the positive forces of the universe, passionately concerned with the sight of all the colours of the earth, you were lying immobile; silently, and in the secret depths of your being, changing the darkest shadows of the world into light. Tell me, in the eyes of the creator, which of us had the better part?

[1] *Letters from a Traveller.*

III

On 25 February 1937 Teilhard left for the United States, travelling via Seattle and arriving shortly afterwards in Philadelphia for a congress of prehistorians. De Terra, von Koenigswald, and Dorothy Garrod were all there. Teilhard stayed with de Terra and his wife in their house on the outskirts of the city. On 19 March he delivered a lecture on the Quaternary period in China, showing how Sinanthropos had used fire and fashioned tools, and estimating that he had lived several hundred thousand years ago. De Terra noted how carefully Teilhard kept to his scientific brief; he never aroused the hostility of his audience by branching out into philosophy or metaphysics. He did, however, take the chance of doing so when he received the Gregor Mendel Medal from Villanova University. This was a Catholic college, and the medal was awarded to Catholic scientists for contributions to biological research. A banquet was given in his honour, and this was the first opportunity to come his way of addressing American ecclesiastics of his own persuasion. He spoke briefly, and without referring to his notes, in his usual rather literary style; and de Terra had the impression that his thought moved too quickly, and on ground too unfamiliar, for the guests to understand what he was getting at. The ground was also tricky, since American Catholics were still touchy about evolution—and Teilhard spoke with his habitual candour.

Shortly afterwards he rashly gave an interview to a representative of the *New York Times*. His remarks were sensationally and misleadingly reported, and given a Darwinian slant which was quite contrary to Teilhard's evolutionary thesis. Anxious to correct the misrepresentation, which he realized—and with good reason—might damage his prestige in the circles he was anxious to convert and seldom had the chance of addressing, he gave a second interview to a Canadian reporter. The result was only slightly less sensational, and when Teilhard arrived at Boston College to receive an honorary degree he was informed that it could not be given him. Boston College is a Jesuit institution, and it looked as though the authorities had been warned, or had taken fright. Times have indeed changed. At Gonzaga University in the state of Washington—also run by the Jesuits—one of the students' hostels is now called Chardin Hall, and a large photograph of Teilhard presides over their comings and goings.

He sailed for France early in April and remained there until 5 August. In July he was laid low with a fever and spent a fortnight recuperating at Murol with his brother Victor and his wife. This was an old hunting ground, and Teilhard wrote to de Terra:

> I try to recognize and number the Pleistocene terraces, which are very clearly shaped in places, but much intricated, as if they were affected by a lot of sub-stages. No Palaeolithic artefacts in the gravels; pebbles mostly lava and quartz—this latter only in the high terraces.[1]

In Paris he caught the sharp whiff of the Front Populaire, but foresaw its failure and found its operations 'rather disgusting. And yet *they have* the spirit of hope and movement—and the others not.'[2] Fascism and Communism were both 'dreadnoughts' and they would not be conquered by 'our medieval galleys'. Unfortunately the Church favoured Fascism 'for exactly the wrong reasons'; for its 'reactionary appearances'[3] rather than its *élan vital*.

On his return to China Teilhard found cholera raging in Hong Kong, and war in Shanghai, where fires were burning and bombs exploding in the suburbs. Many of these were dropped by clumsy Chinese pilots who scored a number of hits on masses of helpless refugees. The ship was painted with the tricolour and was escorted by a French cruiser. There was no question of landing in Shanghai, so the *D'Artagnan* proceeded to Kobe and from there Teilhard was able to reach Tientsin. It had been a six-week voyage from Marseilles.

Teilhard had not wasted it. The long, uneventful days on the seas which by now he knew so well provided an excellent opportunity for his annual retreat; and this, in turn, had stimulated his latest essay—again with its characteristic title—*L'Énergie Humaine*. He began by pointing out that modern science had been exclusively concerned with what it imagined to be the object, as if the scientist were independent of the world he was investigating. Kant—and the great scholastics before him—had clearly perceived the solidarity between the subject seeing and the object seen; and it was only now that the dogmatic objectivity of scientists was being called in question by the scientists themselves. Their 'fine architecture' of waves and particles contained as much of the architects as of the architecture. The 'old

[1] 3 July 1937.   [2] *ibid.*
[3] Letter to Valensin, 25 May 1938.

realism of the laboratories' was developing into a 'scientific idealism' where matter was seen as 'plastic beneath the intelligence informing it'. This reversal of perspective was yet another example of the Teilhardian opportunity; of the law, as he had himself pointed out, that any thinker depends on what is being thought around him, even when he appears to be saying something for the first time.

One is not surprised to find the *phénomène humain* recurring in the first paragraphs of the essay, for this ran like a refrain through Teilhard's mind, and everything he wrote was now leading up, in one way or another, to the work in which his originality first broke upon the world. The science of man must replace what was still no more than men working scientifically. Where was the difference between a machine made by a natural member of the body and a machine obtained by an artificial extension of the same member which had fashioned it—'between the wing of a bird and the wing of an aeroplane'? And if a spiritualized energy could dominate physical and chemical forces, it must necessarily contain them. Each individual was a nucleus of cosmic vitality, and it was here that the *énergie humaine* was united.

Teilhard asked himself whether the noosphere was a kind of 'stationary wave' in which the spiritual energies of the world were perpetually consumed, without leaving a trace behind them. Had evolution come to a stop with man? Teilhard replied—here speaking as a geologist—that the idea of fixity was in itself absurd. He had seen for himself how 'a seismic tremor or a re-formed strip of earth could demonstrate the persistent vitality of a Himalaya'. Mountains had risen, continents had been displaced, the stars had modified their courses, during the millennia of the earth's development. 'Why then should the most essential current of life alone remain fixed? No man of science today questions that humanity appeared, carried forward by an evolution. By what improbable exception to the general laws of the universe should this evolution, of which we are born, come to a halt?' Moreover was not humanity, as we see it today, already suprahuman compared with the men of the Neolithic age?

Teilhard had never held that progress was possible without pain; and here he took an example from the current crisis of unemployment. This might be due to economic mismanagement, but it also represented a 'mass of human energy suddenly liberated by an internal adjustment of the noosphere'. Such an analysis would have brought small comfort to the Rhondda Valley, and Teilhard was the first to admit that unemployment called for its remedies. But for all that, it seemed to him 'as inevitable (and as beneficent) as the march of the universe itself'; a symptom both of material progress and social crisis which demanded that the energies of mankind should be considered and organized as a whole.

This led him to consider a problem which has always exposed him to criticism, and certainly to misunderstanding. It was a problem that he could not, in our ignorance of the future, wholly resolve. How were the rights of the individual, and the acquisitions of personality, to be reconciled with the convergence of mankind towards a superior unity? The consideration, in the first place, of biological energy 'craved wary walking'. Teilhard did not raise with any precision the delicate and explosive topic of birth control, but in the following passage he posed a number of questions to which the laboratories of the Third Reich were already giving an unhesitating answer. The task confronting biology, physiology and medicine was

> not only to master scientifically the maladies and phenomena of counter-evolution (sterility and physical weakening) which undermine the growth of the noosphere—but to produce by various means (selection, control of the sexes, action of hormones, hygiene, etc.) a superior human type. . . . Caught in an obscure complex of reasoning, our generation still looks with distrust upon any effort on the part of science to lay its hands on the springs of heredity, of sexual determination, and of nervous development. As if man had the right and the power to influence the conduct of the world in everything except in what constitutes his own being.

Such experiments would be delicate, to be sure, but they should be 'healthily, respectfully and religiously undertaken'—no longer merely in the sense of one man experimenting on another, but in the sense of 'humanity as a whole feeling its way forward to a new acquisition of vitality'. Writers like Wells and Aldous Huxley had painted their satirical pictures of what such a brave new world might be. Nevertheless the idea behind it was a noble one and it need not, in practice, coarsen into caricature. Eugenics were not only a matter of selective reproduction:

What attitude should the advancing sector of humanity adopt towards static and decidedly unprogressive ethnic groups? . . . Up to what point should the development of the stronger—always supposing that this can be clearly defined—take precedence over the conservation of the weak? How shall we reconcile with a maximum of efficiency the care we expend on the wounded with the superior necessities of the attack? In what does true charity consist?

These were dangerous questions, but Teilhard had gone some way to answer them by his own conduct in the trenches, where he had served as a stretcher-bearer, not as a combatant. Indeed, now that he looked back on that time, he was bound to admit that most people could still understand the meaning of force—and force was the 'symbol and key of greater being'—only in the shape of war. But in the world of the future Teilhard prophesied a 'collective act of perception . . . a fusion of races leading directly to the establishment not only of a common language, but of a common morality and common ideals . . . a community of effort and struggle for the same objectives, accompanied *ipso facto* by fighting comradeship'. In this way, and under the stress of these affinities, the organization of human energies was leading to the emergence of a 'common human soul'.

The technicians of the brave new world would naturally ask whether this organized and reflective life would maintain, or even increase, its power. Teilhard reaffirmed that 'reflective action and total extinction' were 'cosmically incompatible'. Either spirit, seeing itself tricked, would retire from the struggle; or death would take on the lineaments of life. The absurdity of a universe which had brought man to the point of reflective consciousness only to confess its incapacity to satisfy it, forced one back upon the second alternative. Moreover death, if it were no longer to be the death of total extinction, must assure the continuity of what was most precious in ourselves—in other words, our personality. And just as the totality of a sphere was more contained, and more closely concentrated, in its centre than in its surface, so the apotheosis of the *énergie humaine* could be defined as an 'organized plurality whose elements discover the consummation of their respective personalities in a paroxysm of mutual union and transparency; the whole Body depending on the unifying influence of a *centre distinct* from supra-personalization'.

This was the Omega point to which Teilhard's thought consistently led him forward, and once again he found his analogy in the operation of human love:

> When a man loves a woman with nobility, and with the vigorous passion which lifts a human being above itself, the life of this man, his power to feel and to create, his whole universe, are distinctly contained at the same time as they are sublimated in his love for this woman. And yet the woman, however necessary she may be to reflect, reveal, communicate, and 'personalize' the world for him, is still not the centre of that world! If the love of one element for another has such power to fuse—but without confusing—the multitude of our perceptions and emotions in a unique impression, what will be vibration caused by the meeting of our beings with Omega?

In the concluding pages of his essay Teilhard once more identifies the Omega point with the cosmic Christ of St. Paul, and his gospel with the Johannine counsel to 'love one another'. It was not necessary to choose between 'the Charybdis of collectivism and the Scylla of anarchy'. The servants of material progress or racial entity would inevitably be absorbed by their own determinisms; they would become 'mechanized by their own machines'. Only Christ, understood in the plenitude of his Incarnation, could provide a personal centre for the forces which otherwise would petrify in a sterile impersonality. The *phénomène humain* demanded the *phénomène chrétien* as its complement. The intensity of love to which the Christian—and the cosmos—were summoned had already been attained by a St. Paul, a St. Augustine, or a St. Thérèse of Lisieux; the world was now ripe for its radiation. But the risen Christ of the Gospel would only keep his place in the consciousness of the believer if he were seen to incorporate the evolution which was so often opposed to him. From the *noosphère* we should emerge into the *théosphère*—and Teilhard underlined in his final paragraph that 'Christianity, taken in the cold and rigorous sense that Catholicism demands ... has never claimed to be, at bottom, anything less, or other, than that'.

IV

Teilhard finished *L'Énergie Humaine* as he arrived in Shanghai. Some people were disappointed that he did not take a determined stand—

by which, of course, they meant that he should have stood shoulder to shoulder with the Western democracies; or more exactly, with the anti-Fascist front, since the democracies were divided against themselves. The Catholic *avant-garde* in France, and elsewhere, taking their cue from Jacques Maritain's *Humanisme Intégral*, had shown no hesitation in so committing themselves. Maritain was a pure philosopher, which Teilhard was not; and although their approach and formulations could hardly have been more different, their conclusions about the decent ordering of human affairs were not dissimilar. Maritain was psychologically and geographically close to the European crisis; Teilhard was remote. He was no adherent of General Franco's crusade, but the Spanish Civil War touched him less immediately, and his references to it are surprisingly few. Moreover it was not so easy for Catholic ecclesiastics to 'take a stand'; and any stand that Teilhard took would be subject to hostile scrutiny. The French Dominicans, grouped around the review *Sept*, who had strongly opposed the Abyssinian adventure, had been suppressed by the Master-General of their Order—some said at the instance of Mussolini himself, in return for Italian help in the restoration of Santa Sabina. Where Teilhard was on the spot—as he was in China—his sympathies were unequivocal. It was difficult to understand, he wrote, how the Japanese could 'persist in trying to ingratiate themselves with the Chinese by dealing them blow after blow; in fact, if they had made up their minds to get themselves detested, they couldn't have chosen a better way of doing so'.[1]

Teilhard's own difficulties were increasing every day. The Geological Survey in Nanking was trying to withdraw its personnel from the Cenozoic Laboratory where the reconstruction of Sinanthropos was still proceeding. Lucile Swan, a talented sculptress and close friend of Teilhard, resident in Pekin, had an important hand in this. It was finally agreed that the complete head, with mandible, had belonged to a female, whom they christened 'Nelly'—a less cumbersome appellation than Sinanthropos or Pekin Man. To make matters worse Teilhard was still recovering from a severe bout of malaria which had been wrongly diagnosed in Paris. He was now almost alone in the laboratory, and he devoted what leisure he had to writing the first pages of *The Phenomenon of Man*. De Terra was expecting him in Burma

[1] *Letters from a Traveller*, p. 235.

towards the end of the year, but it seemed unlikely that he would be able to go. At last, Pei offered to take his place, and on 15 December Teilhard sailed from Tientsin in a small cargo boat bound for Hong Kong. He picked up a second vessel at Swatow which took him to Singapore in four days, and from there caught a steamer to Rangoon. De Terra met him off 'an antiquated paddle-steamer at the landing-stage of a small township north of Mandalay'.[1]

They drove up from the Irrawaddy valley to the Shan plateau through tropical forests, abounding in deer, rhinoceros, tiger, buffalo and crocodile, where the cries of anthropoid apes came at them from the trees. Teilhard had been advised not to return so quickly to the tropics, but de Terra had noticed the warm tan on his features when he arrived. The nights were cool and the skies unclouded, and Teilhard felt as if he had 'found a new youth. I can walk indefinitely without getting tired, just as I did in India.'[2] He could also stretch out in the shade and fall asleep immediately at any time of the day.

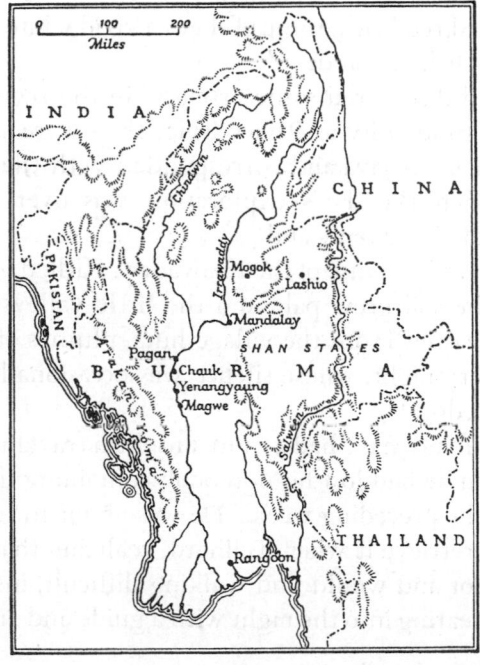

Burma

Proceeding to the district of Mogok in January 1938, the party of five
—Teilhard, de Terra and his wife, with Dr. and Mrs. Movius—stayed
in a bungalow set in an

> idyllic garden where *Poinsettia* blossoms, roses and hibiscus flowers
> glowed amid the green of huge bamboo clumps in which colibris
> and parakeets fluttered to and fro. Above the broad canopies of
> mimosa bushes and palm-trees, the pale blue sky swarmed with
> brown birds of prey, the garadu of Indian mythology, soaring tire-
> lessly and uttering sinister screams.[1]

They visited the local mines in search of fossils but were not unnatur-
ally taken for the agents of European jewel merchants, since the soil—
like the river beds—was rich in precious stones. Teilhard, however,
was anxious to look for Palaeolithic tools in the Irrawaddy valley, so
the party made their way down to Pagan, staying in a bungalow built
for King George V when he was Prince of Wales. Pagan, the ancient
capital of Burma, was 'now only a picturesque bazaar, lost among the
palms and mimosa', but surrounded by a 'forest of pagodas, some of
them dilapidated red brick, some of them a vivid white or even gilded,
like the dome of the Invalides'.[2]

De Terra had discovered some artefacts in the region which Teilhard was able to identify as Palaeolithic; they were similar to tools
which he had seen in Java and corresponded with the age of Pithecanthropos. When the day's exploration was over, the travellers
would sit outside their tents and

> survey the broad expanse of the Irrawaddy. Bathed in moonlight,
> the red of the soil grew pale and the little valleys turned into
> yawning crevasses. From the village huts, plumes of smoke rose
> into the silvery night, whose silence was occasionally broken by
> the bark of a dog.[3]

De Terra could not have had a more unselfish travelling companion.
On one occasion he had lost his notebook containing the record of all
his finds over the preceding weeks. He was about to retrace his steps
in the dark to retrieve it when Teilhard, realizing that de Terra had
blistered his foot and would find walking difficult, insisted on going
instead. Disappearing into the night with a guide and an electric torch,

[1] *Memories of Teilhard de Chardin*, p. 86.
[2] *Letters from a Traveller*, p. 236.
[3] *Memories of Teilhard de Chardin*, p. 90.

he returned some hours later with the recovered notebook and 'beaming with delight'.[1] Both his seniority and his prestige would have entitled him to certain comforts in the field, but he never asked for or availed himself of them. He did not know the meaning of professional jealousy and he never complained. 'If you want to know what jealousy is', the saying ran, 'you must live among artists.' The same could be said of scientists and scholars—perhaps with even greater reason; but Teilhard walked all his life, unscathed, through the Mafia of the museums.

For three weeks they skirted the Arakan-Yoma range between the Irrawaddy and the Bay of Bengal. The mountains, with their blanket of elephant-grass, were impenetrable; and on their lower slopes you could only get about by bullock-cart at the rate of ten miles a day. So, at the end of February, they returned to the northern highlands, travelling along the completed section of the Burma Road from Mogok to Lashio, close to the borders of Yunnan. Here the impossible terrain frustrated them, but one of the miners from Mogok brought Teilhard a human mandible which he had discovered in a cave. Teilhard ran his tongue over it and declared that it was still too porous to be classified as a fossil. They pushed on from the watershed of the Irrawaddy to the headwaters of the Salween. The forests were superb in their 'purple mantle of flowering *Bauhinia*',[2] but the roads were crowded with caravans and evidence of a European front building up against the Japanese was plain to see. The trees were shedding their leaves, brittle from the heat, as they shed them in Auvergne during the late September days; but Teilhard could not shut his mind, or perhaps altogether quiet his conscience, when grimmer reminders pressed in upon him of the continent to which he really belonged. The Burma Road was an uncomfortable extension of the *Route de l'Ouest*, and the tensions of China—visible now as Teilhard looked over into Yunnan—were not to be separated from the European crisis:

> You may well imagine (he wrote to his brother) that I am not too pleased at being a deserter. Still ... it seems to me more important to create a new concept of human activity than to plunge into the feverish intoxication of a political drive which already has its leaders and will never lack followers. .... The emancipation of the Far East disturbs me because I have no confidence in the

[1] *ibid.*, p. 91.   [2] *Letters from a Traveller*, p. 239.

human qualities of the Japanese; they will turn out, I fear, to be false shepherds.[1]
The admission is implicit here that in some respects the Chinese were sheep.

Teilhard felt 'physically consolidated' by three months 'in the jungle and the fresh air', and considered himself 'once again spoiled by Providence' in having been able to make the trip:

> Whenever I emerge from my social and religious milieu for any length of time, I realize acutely the fundamental—and native— differences which separate me from the current conceptions and expressions in the matter of religion. All that does not lead me to envisage a personal future particularly calm. But this has no importance if I succeed, however little, in hastening the birth of the new Christianity which the world needs.[2]

Already, the same words which so took Étienne Gilson aback when he heard them fifteen years later; as time goes by we shall find them constantly on Teilhard's lips.

v

On 24 March the party, assembled in Rangoon, embarked for Singapore, stopping off at Malacca where Teilhard spent some time in visiting the church of St. Francis Xavier—another Jesuit missionary whose vocation had beckoned him to the Orient. The church 'stood silhouetted against the glassy sea in the midday heat like some grotesque crag in an ancient Chinese painting'.[3] Teilhard may well have compared the methods of conversion thought suitable to the sixteenth century with those appropriate to the twentieth. On 1 April they caught a Dutch boat for Batavia, and spent Easter aboard with 'a great tropical storm receding from us, and around us a calm and luminous sea'.[4] The voyage above the submerged causeway which had once linked Java with the Malay peninsula was a kind of 'geological introduction'[5] to the island. Teilhard spent a short fortnight on Java. He was especially interested to examine the eleven *Homo soloensis*

---

[1] *ibid.*, p. 238.
[2] Letter to Madame Haardt, 16 March 1938.
[3] *Memories of Teilhard de Chardin*, p. 101.
[4] Letter to Madame Haardt, Easter 1938.
[5] *Memories of Teilhard de Chardin*, p. 108.

Teilhard and Abbé Breuil
at the Ming tombs, 1935

Teilhard,
Ralph von Koenigswald,
and Helmut de Terra.
Bandung, Java, April 1938

Tea with Lucile Swan in Pekin during the Second World War

Pekin Union Medical College
where the palaeontological collections were housed

skulls, unearthed by Dr. Oppenoorth in 1932 and 1937; these had certain features suggesting a resemblance to Pithecanthropos. Equally important was to discover the geological age of the formation out of which the fossils had been extracted; and this was difficult because the fossils older than *Homo soloensis* had been excavated by natives and not by experts.

Based at first on Bandung, they visited Surakarta, the former capital of the Javanese princes, where 'dancers were rehearsing for a performance in the palace. It was like some old oriental fairy-tale, with young dancing-girls in heavy brocaded costumes gliding beneath the mango trees in the palace courtyard to the strains of a gamelan orchestra.'[1] But more exciting for Teilhard was to stand on the site at Trinil where the Dutch doctor, Eugene Dubois, had made his discovery in 1891. De Terra took a photograph of Teilhard 'his face hot and flushed beneath his tropical helmet'[2] as he contemplated the Dubois memorial. Dubois, a pupil of Haeckel at Jena, had found the remains of Pithecanthropos in those tropical latitudes where Haeckel had foreseen their discovery. Later the party were taken to the place on the Solo river where *Homo soloensis* had been found. Teilhard assumed that the artefacts he gathered that day were of a similar antiquity to the three thousand bones of vertebrate land animals which had come to light during the excavations. He also saw the new Pithecanthropos skull, and its bed, at Sangiran, and found it as well preserved as Sinanthropos. But he had no time to visit the site of von Koenigswald's latest discovery—the brain-case of a baby, not more than one year old, unearthed in the Modjokerto district of Surabaja.

Teilhard concluded that Pithecanthropos represented a human type at least as old as Sinanthropos, perhaps older. Observing that both skulls showed the same simian characteristics, some anthropologists held that they belonged to the same species. In the light of later discoveries on Java Teilhard rallied to the alternative hypothesis; that Pithecanthropos came from a related but not identical branch of hominids which proliferated independently 'at the beginning of the Quaternary in southern China and Malaysia—on the margin of other more central and perhaps already more "hominized" human groups.' There were no stone tools discovered in association with Java Man, and this led some people to suppose that he had not reached the stage of

[1] *ibid.*, p. 113.   [2] *ibid.*, p. 113.

reflection. Teilhard pointed out, however, that whereas Sinanthropos had been found 'at home', with hearth and workshop close at hand, 'the remains of Pithecanthropos were picked up from the mud left by a very ancient Pleistocene lake'.[1] Most probably they had been carried there by a river, and it was not surprising, in these circumstances, that the workman should have been found separated from his tools.

The expedition, though it was brief, had its share of discomforts— nights spent on a straw mat in a thatched hut, with village elders chatting and smoking outside, curious to see how a party of European prehistorians got to sleep; mosquitoes that resisted the fumigation of Dutch cigars; dogs that barked incessantly; painful treks in the jungle through morasses of mud. During these forest marches even Teilhard's figure 'lost its wonderful poise and his face betrayed physical exhaustion', but 'not a word of criticism or complaint escaped his lips'.[2] Nevertheless his second visit to Java was worth its occasional fatigues. He had now concluded that the fossil types found on the island belonged, with Sinanthropos, Meganthropos and Giganto-pithecus, 'to an offshoot of the human race . . . represented by similar forms in Africa',[3] which he had not yet seen. Java, he wrote, was an 'ideal country', and he was reluctant to leave it; but had booked his passage on a Messageries liner, the *Félix Roussel*, which would take him direct from Singapore to Shanghai.

On arrival in Pekin, early in May, he found that the Japanese occupation had reduced Chou-Kou-Tien to a no-man's land and that further digging there was impossible. The European colony was now much smaller, but they were 'closing their ranks to preserve the traditions and spirit of the old gaiety of Pekin. It must have been much the same with the "*ci-devants*" on the eve of the French Revolution.'[4] But the city was beginning to have a Japanese look; the geisha girls appeared in brilliant contrast to the military lorries scattering the rickshaws before them as they thundered through the streets. The Japanese were clearly bent on destroying the Kuomintang which, as a natural and patriotic reaction against invasion, was 'becoming more and more absorbed into the very blood of China'. But what would

[1] *The Appearance of Man*, pp. 103–6.
[2] *Memories of Teilhard de Chardin*, p. 116.
[3] *ibid.*, p. 117.
[4] *Letters from a Traveller*, p. 240.

happen afterwards? Teilhard was doubtful whether Tokyo or Chiang Kai-shek would have the last word.

The Commission for Higher Studies at the Sorbonne had now offered Teilhard a position in the Institut de Paléontologie Humaine. He described the appointment as 'chiefly nominal and honorific', but he asked permission to accept it since the nomination had been virtually unanimous. The authorities in Rome took eight months to decide whether he could accept it or not, and in the meantime the Sorbonne made a public announcement. In face of this, Rome had no option but to acquiesce; but 'it is not I', Teilhard wrote to Madame Haardt, 'who will have forced their hand.'[1] At the same time the Abbé Breuil was elected to the Institut de France. Meanwhile Licent had been recalled to France, and Teilhard was actively behind a plan to reorganize the museum at Tientsin. He hoped that it would develop into an institute of biological research for the whole of Asia, with a new and younger staff. Now that the Rockefeller Foundation had appointed a successor to Black, Teilhard's presence at the laboratory was less indispensable and the Paris appointment made it necessary, as well as agreeable, for him to return to France. He looked forward to his departure with a schoolboy's glee—'I can still hardly believe it's true.'[2] Public recognition by his own countrymen, in however specialized a field, was timely compensation for the disappointments of the past, and it would do something to mitigate the frustrations of the future. For many years now his life had oscillated between Paris and Pekin, with China claiming the larger share of it. From now on, he hoped, Paris would assert its rights.

On 21 September 1938 he sailed from Kobe—five days before the signing of the Munich agreement. Travelling across America he spent a week with friends in Worcester, Massachusetts, and at Harvard. He also attended a staff meeting at the Museum of Natural History in New York before catching his boat for Le Havre. On board was the distinguished physicist, Lecomte de Noüy, and the two men found themselves in immediate sympathy. As the title of de Noüy's book— *Entre Savoir et Croire*—suggested, he was trying to reconcile knowledge and belief, and he was now in sceptical mood about the humanizing influence of science. Here Teilhard's optimism came to his support.

[1] 16 March 1938.
[2] *Letters from a Traveller*, p. 244.

Optimism was in short supply and large demand as they returned to a Europe still dishonourably at peace.

VI

The next few months take on a particular importance in view of the enforced absence that was soon to follow them. Teilhard now settled into his own laboratory at the Institut de Paléontologie Humaine. Breuil was next door and Boule still came in twice a week, repeating his familiar 'stories about the Golden Age of prehistory'—an age to which he was close to belonging himself. His mind, as ever, was 'terribly sharp and full of good sense in scientific matters'.[1] On the surface it was a period of deep discouragement, but behind 'the ridiculous political stage' Teilhard found 'the birth, or at least the expectation, of the new creed of man in a spiritual evolution of the world'. France seemed 'tremendously alive inside', and he saw a great many people of various *milieux* and very mixed opinions. We find him addressing a group of sixty artists—sculptors, painters, writers and musicians—organized by the French engineer Jean Coutrot in association with Aldous Huxley, and telling them that art was the 'expression of the exuberance of human energy' to which it gave a 'personal character' and an 'intuitive . . . almost instinctive shape'.[2] The definition—one may suggest—did not go very far; the same thing might be said of other human activities, some of them a good deal more questionable than art.

After speaking to some young Catholic workers Teilhard concluded that 'we are taking part in one of the most revolutionary movements in man's history, a movement . . . with *not a trace* of any sort of bitterness or hate: simply love—but love founded on the conviction that the world is converging towards *some one*, someone equally loving and well defined'.[3] This was either a naïve 'extrapolation' of Teilhard's own convictions, or a very remarkable degree of charity must have reigned in the circles he was addressing. The French Catholics were, in fact, bitterly divided on the issues of the hour. Between Massis on the extreme right and Mauriac left of centre there was opposition to the point of enmity; Bernanos, outraged by the Munich agreement, had left for Brazil; Maritain, nailing his colours to

[1] Cuénot, p. 219. [2] *ibid.*, p. 220. [3] *ibid.*, pp. 220–1.

Christian democracy, had seen the Spanish Civil War turn many of his closest friends into fierce opponents. Teilhard would not have expected to find much sympathy in the Thomist circles which had gathered round Maritain at Meudon until politics split them up; but he was now at odds with Gabriel Marcel, a Christian existentialist who did not share Teilhard's faith in *l'homme communautaire*, and was not prepared to sacrifice the individual for some supra-personality, very uncertainly defined. Reading Teilhard's impressions of his return, one is forced to the conclusion that he was so far *au-dessus de la mêlée* that he did not always see what the *mêlée* was about. The political stage may have been 'ridiculous', but it was peopled by actors in a play whose tragic *dénouement* was at hand.

He spent a few days in Cambridge where Paterson—de Terra's assistant on the Indian expedition—was now a Fellow of Trinity College and Director of the University Museum of Archaeology and Ethnology. Teilhard had not been in England for some years, but he had kept his links with scientific circles. He was a member of the London Zoological Society, an Honorary Life Member of the Society of Vertebrate Palaeontology, and in 1937 he had been elected an Honorary Fellow of the Royal Anthropological Institute. He also had English friends in Paris. Harper Kelley was in charge of the prehistoric department at the Musée de l'Homme. He and his wife lived at 52 Avenue de la Motte-Picquet, in the same block of apartments as the Abbé Breuil, and every Wednesday evening *couverts* for Teilhard and Breuil were laid for dinner. Teilhard may have been optimistic about the world; he was far from optimistic about himself. He would often discuss the idea of leaving the Society—not as an intention, or even as a temptation, but in the abstract, weighing the pros and cons.[1] Some of his Dominican friends in Belgium were strongly urging him to do so, but something—the thought of his colleagues in the Society—Valensin, Charles, Leroy; an instinct of military honour, perhaps; or respect for the *grande dame*—held him back. On 26 February 1939 he was speaking to the Philosophy Society at the Institut Catholique of Toulouse on man's place in nature and the structure it gave to evolution. The following day he was at the Faculté des Lettres of the University lecturing on Sinanthropos; on 28 February he was again at the Institut

[1] In fact, a Jesuit who has taken Solemn Vows is only free to leave the Society after due canonical process.

speaking on the geology of the Quaternary in China and the Far East; and on 29 February in the great hall of the Institut and before a very large audience, he lectured on prehistoric research in Burma. Archbishop Saliège presided at this session, and although the subject was a scientific one the presence of the archbishop, the stimulating friendship of Mgr. de Solages, and the unimpeachable auspices of the Institut, gave a kind of imprimatur to Teilhard's personality and ideas. But he was not deceived by these genial appearances. On 10 February the long pontificate of Pius XI came to an end. With the 'burning sorrow' of *Mit brennender Sorge* Achille Ratti had gone far towards burning his boats, and this had chased the earlier accommodations with Fascism from the public mind. Teilhard was not reassured by the election of his successor; he discerned, more clearly than most, the writing of *Humani Generis* on the wall.

On the occasion of a lecture with lantern slides at the Musée de l'Homme, during this same month, he made the acquaintance of Jeanne Mortier who was later to become his secretary, and who now handled (or occasionally mishandled) the slides. It was a meeting pregnant with consequence, for it was through Jeanne Mortier that Teilhard's more important writings were eventually given to the world.

He spent three weeks in London during the early spring, and in March his essay, *La Mystique de la Science*, was published in *Études*. He did not claim to be an historian of science, but the conspectus was here so lucid and, within its broad framework, so complete that one wishes he had given as much of his thought to the history of science as he had given to the history of Sinanthropos. The situation of scientific studies at the time of writing could not have been more precisely outlined. Events, once again, had given Teilhard his cue. Before long, he thought, the 'streams of energy and gold' still being lost in the gulf of armaments and war ... 'the monstrous cannons and huge battleships' would seem an irrelevance beside 'the giant telescopes, the ultra-powerful electro-magnets, and the industrial machines designed to split the atom.' Research was 'no longer an amusement of the nursery; it had become the serious, central, and vital occupation of adult man.' This was a fact far more important 'than all our political disorders and our social unease'.

The experiments of the deep-sea diver and the aviator already reaching out towards the stratosphere had the virtue of a 'disinterested passion'; research was already taking on the character of a *mystique*. Teilhard traced its development from the esotericism of the Egyptian *magus*, 'fascinated and terrified like some primitive Faust, by the forces he set free', to the rationality of an Aristotle or an Aristides, mapping out 'the clear geometry of a landscape without distances, fixed in light. If a *mystique* depended, at root, on imprecise and limitless expectations, then the Greeks, taken as a whole, seem to have been the least mystical of men. . . . Their innumerable myths were all related to the past or to an eternity already defined.' Curiosity, supplanting the alchemy of the Middle Ages, came in with the Renaissance; but the mind of the Renaissance had been profoundly affected by the 'Christian revolution'; indeed the Greek Fathers of the Church, St. Irenaeus in particular, 'basing themselves . . . on a mystical perspective rather than factual experiment, had anticipated in an astonishing way our modern views of progress'. Speculation now became discovery, and from the beginning of the seventeenth century history asserted its rights. Teilhard quoted Fontenelle: 'Mounted on the shoulders of the men of old, we see farther than they'; and Pascal: 'The successive generations of mankind can be regarded as a single man who will continue to live and learn'. Out of the infinite abyss which terrified Pascal the new conception of anthropogenesis was coming to birth and, with it, the consciousness of progress and the religion of science. Research became a 'sacred duty' and excited the devotion of a *mystique*. Teilhard, remembering no doubt his conversations with Lecomte de Noüy on the boat, energetically countered the prevailing pessimism. The war between science and religion—commonly interpreted as a war between reason and faith—was really 'a struggle between two opposing *mystiques*'. There was every reason, Teilhard pleaded, why the adversaries should be reconciled in a 'new *mystique*', where Tertullian's '*anima naturaliter Christiana*' should discover its consummation in Christ. Here, for the first time, Teilhard used the term *Christogenesis* to distinguish the Christ of the historical Incarnation from the Christ of the Pleroma. Humanity was no longer conceivable without science, but no more was science conceivable without some religion to animate it. Of this religion *within*[1] science Christianity was 'an exemplary form . . . No *mystique* can live without love. The religion *of*[1] science thought that it had found a faith and a hope, but it

[1] My italics (author's note).

died because it was closed to charity.' And between the lines of the following passage we may read the record of Teilhard's dual vocation:

For the evolutionist who has become a Christian, the barrier which seemed to separate the sacred and the profane can be left behind. In a universe where everything works together for the gradual formation of the spirit that God is raising towards a final union, every work acquires, in its tangible reality, a value of sanctity and communion. In a true sense, the labour which consists in developing through knowledge our awareness of the world is linked to the operations of the priesthood, because it prepares an object on which those operations can work; it can further, under the action of creative forces, the progress of a universe at the heart of which God comes to take his place.

Before returning to Pekin, Teilhard left behind him with the editor of *Études* an important essay which may be read as his last word to a Europe hanging on the precipice of war. *Les Unités Humaines Naturelles* was published in the July issue of the review. Teilhard described it as an *'essai d'une biologie et d'une morale des races'*. Looking back twenty years to his hopes in the League of Nations, he realized that his optimism had been premature. Without begging any burning question of *Lebensraum* he saw that not every nation was ready for the movement of brotherly convergence which was the direction in which humanity was inevitably moving. Mankind constituted 'an animal group prodigiously spread out where branches were continually crossing with each other', and this phenomenon coincided with 'the establishment, ever more clearly marked, of a common psychological atmosphere'. The different branches were uneven in their growth and vigour. The more advanced owed their superiority not only to qualities of blood and spirit, to economic resources and climatic conditions—although these were all important. 'The most fully humanized of the human collectivities always appear, finally, as the product not of segregation, but of synthesis'. And Teilhard discovered in his own country—and he could have found the same thing in Britain or the United States—an example of how the more progressive groupings used their diversity to reach, through intelligent combination, higher forms of consciousness.

He compared the evolution of human society to a sphere in which every grouping derived from the same inferior pole. These were now at the widest point of self-assertion—hence the present crisis—and were caught up in the tensions of a new attraction which was forcing them together into a superior unity. This would be achieved by confluence, not by confusion; Teilhard applied to races the maxim which he applied to individuals—'union differentiates'. But the union would only be complete when each nation had reached a stage of 'fullest consciousness'. Even the divisive agonies of war had a unifying effect:

> The experience of 1914, with the extraordinary impulse it gave to wireless and aviation, for example, is a demonstration of this. The arms, so desperately forged by one nation to defend itself and keep itself apart, immediately become the property of all the rest. They are transformed into links which fortify still further the solidarity of mankind. The same thing is true of the industrial inventions—sometimes revolutionary—which every country is driven to make in order to maintain its economic life, although it asks no help from outside. And finally it is true of the social and psychological adjustments by which each nation thinks it has found for itself... the spiritual supremacy that will make it unique among all the others. Whatever is progressive and valuable in these discoveries of awakenings of consciousness is contagious, and is shared to the profit of the entire human family.

An international ethic, in Teilhard's view, could only be based on the admission that the confluence of national and ethnic groupings was biologically essential for the expansion of human consciousness. Once again he took his stand against a dogmatic egalitarianism:

> Let us be careful not to revive, by a sentimental ideology, the mistakes of the first feminists and the first democrats. A woman is not a man, and that is just the reason why the man cannot do without her. The mechanic is not the athlete, nor the painter, nor the financier; and it is because they are different that the national organism is able to function. In the same way the Chinaman is not a Frenchman, nor the Kaffir a Japanese; and this is a very fortunate thing for the total richness of man, and for his future.

As a scientist, Teilhard had no illusions about the brutal laws of biological competition, but these were inapplicable to the evolution of mankind. Here the law of brotherly emulation must take their place. 'The future of the thinking world is organically bound up with the transformation of the forces of hate into the forces of charity.'

There was little prospect of their doing so when, on 23 June, Teilhard sailed for America in the *Champlain*. While he was in New York he sat for his bust to Malvina Hoffman; and afterwards proceeded to Berkeley where he spoke twice at a geological convention. He then caught a boat from Vancouver, arriving in Pekin on 30 August—just five days before the outbreak of war.

CHAPTER XIII

WAR IN EXILE

TEILHARD at once took up his residence at Chabanel Hall in the northern quarters of Pekin. This was a hostel for Jesuit students of any nationality who were studying Chinese, and it had taken its name from a seventeenth-century Jesuit martyr. The rigorous discipline enforced within its walls matched their forbidding aspect; moreover the rooms were so thinly partitioned that any conversation could be overheard. Teilhard could not have found a more uncongenial lodging. 'By temperament and occupation I am a little out of place in this sort of milieu, but I am managing well enough. I recognize that this ordered and recollected existence from which I have been cut off for a long time even has certain advantages'.[1] Chabanel Hall was a large building and no doubt the temperature varied from one room to another. The students were eager for Teilhard's company, when they could be sure of not being overheard; but the superior lost no time in telling him that his presence was unwelcome because he was both a Communist and an evolutionist, and requested him to return to France as quickly as possible. Teilhard denied that he was a Communist, to which the superior replied that if he was an evolutionist he was *ipso facto* a Communist. It is not recorded how far Teilhard was able to help this naïve ecclesiastic make up his intellectual arrears.

The round of prayer and study, although it interfered with Teilhard s working hours and social obligations, was a certain support at a time when activity in the field and patriotic service of any kind were alike impossible. His routine varied very little with mornings at the laboratory, except when the winter cold dissuaded him, and afternoons at Lockhart Hall, followed perhaps by a cup of tea with Lucile Swan. On Wednesday afternoons—Teilhard always liked to have special times for special people—he would call on another friend, Laure

[1] Letter to Bruno de Solages, 10 March 1940.

Dorget, who remembered 'the wonderful honesty of his conversation'. The war, he reassured her, simply reflected the 'disorganization of multiplicity'—and that proved nothing. It could not reverse 'the great evolutionary thrust towards the consummation of the world in God'.[1] Out of consideration for the rules of the house he never went out in the evening, except to celebrate the seventieth birthday of Dr. Grabau, a particularly valued friend, whose health he had been asked to propose. Teilhard regretted this interruption of social contacts, to which he attached a more than social importance. Besides, the situation of Chabanel Hall—half an hour by rickshaw from the laboratory and a quarter of an hour from the Geological Survey—was inconvenient, and Teilhard would have been much happier in Tientsin where Leroy had replaced Licent at the museum. Very often he dispensed with the rickshaw and walked to the laboratory through the imperial park. Most of the material was safe under seals, but the actual Sinanthropos skulls mysteriously disappeared in December 1941. Writing to Wong two years later, Teilhard still thought they had been mislaid and was relieved that casts had been carefully taken. In fact, Sinanthropos had apparently been ground to pieces and used for medicine, for the Chinese still had a belief in the curative properties of pulverized fossils.[2] Meanwhile he sensed from afar the unreality of the phoney war:

At this distance [he wrote to Breuil] it is hard to get a clear picture of the way things are going or of the general feeling and conditions of life in France. All one gets is the impression that things are very different from 1914 and that both sides are rather holding back and fighting with some reluctance. . . . Should I do better to go back to France? On the one hand I wonder whether I am not cutting myself off from the real life of my generation by not taking part in what is going on; on the other hand I cannot quite see what I could do in Europe. I'm too old for any active service. And I find it hard to work up any enthusiasm for this war, no doubt because I'm out of touch with the general atmosphere in Europe. I must wait till I can see things more clearly.[3]

It was not in his nature to wait for long, and by Christmas 1939 he

---

[1] *La Table Ronde*, June 1955.
[2] Walter J. Ong, s.j., in *The Jesuit Bulletin*, February 1967.
[3] *Letters from a Traveller*, 5 November 1939.

had set out in a short paper what he believed to be the true significance of the Second World War. He regarded it very much as he had regarded the first. 'I find in what is happening now a paradoxal occasion for calm and recollection'[1]—and this was written long after the war had ceased to be phoney. It was 'a magnificent function of man', he assured another friend, 'to resist despair by one's very faith in being. After that you will understand, maybe, that you can throw yourself into the formidable human struggle we are entering, as you might throw yourself into a new and higher life.' Distance may well have lent him a larger, a longer, and a more sanguine insight. To those who could only see the war as a mortal illness Teilhard replied that it was a crisis of growth; and that the Christian, more than another, should recognize that life never increased its vitality except through suffering and the conquest of evil. Its way was the way of the Cross. Teilhard was too intellectually fastidious not to fight shy of current propaganda, even when it was enlisted for the defence of much that he valued. Force, rightly understood, was at the heart of his gospel— the force that emptied the tomb on Easter morning—and there is a sense in which he converted the *Übermensch* of Nietzsche into the cosmic and resurrected Christ.

Since the notion of attack was central to Teilhard's thinking, he was the right physician to detect the feeble pulse of the Maginot mentality:

In what state of mind, deep down, are we using our army? In a spirit of immobility and repose—or in a spirit of conquest? We could, I am afraid, choose a dangerous and inferior method to make war upon war. We could defend ourselves without attacking—as if we had no need ourselves to grow and to change, if we want to become more fully human. We could fight in a mood of mere inertia; fight in order to be left in peace; fight 'to be left alone'. Surely this would be an evasion of the essential problem which the present stage of humanity compels us to face? I am just as convinced as anybody else that 'the others' are mistaken in the violent methods they are employing to unify the world. But they are perfectly right in feeling that the moment has come to think about a new earth; and they are formidably strong precisely because this is how they see things. . . . Unless the dynamism at

[1] Letter to Bruno de Solages, 11 July 1941.

work within us is as powerful as the dynamism to which we are opposed, we shall not be fighting with equal weapons and we shall not deserve to win. For them, war is a principle of life; what are we setting against it as an effective *riposte*?[1]

It might well be, he thought, that 'Rousseau and the pacifists' had done more mischief than Nietzsche, and that talk about 'mankind getting together' would only raise an indulgent smile. And yet, even for the modern world, there could be no more realistic purpose. The democracies should no longer waste their thoughts on the maintenance of a 'static justice' and a 'docile respect for existing frontiers with no better knowledge of each other than strangers living on the same landing'. The war must be waged not in a spirit of resignation—as men fight against 'fire, tempest or plague'—but for 'something fine to discover and to construct'.[2]

The reader may object that Teilhard was too far removed from the realities of the European scene, and too superficially informed about them, to appreciate the enormity of the Nazi menace. Neither in the first war nor the second was he moved by the *mystique* of French nationalism. He was a patriot, but he was also a citizen of the world. He was naturally predisposed towards the more developed nations, because he believed the future to lie with them—and he would sooner have disbelieved in his own existence than disbelieve in the future. Teilhard took peoples, as he took persons, very much as he found them; and the German achievement in science was too considerable for him to regard the *furor teutonicus* as anything but a temporary aberration. Germany, if she were fought in the right way, would return to her senses; there were other nations with fewer senses to return to.

He agreed with his cousin that the awakening of Russia, manifested by the attack on Finland, was the bigger danger; and he wrote in the same sense to Breuil. It was not in the least that he was afraid of Marxism or the Third International (which was now 'no more than a name'); what he feared was the 'constitution of a national group, hostile, water-tight, completely ignorant of what lies outside itself, and so incapable of being included in the far-reaching combination of mankind we need. I am rather frightened when I feel that I can read between the lines of Allied literature the objective of a dismembered

---

[1] '*L'heure de choisir*', in *L'activation de l'énergie*.   [2] *ibid.*

Germany or of some sort of return to a pre-Napoleonic Europe. . . .[1] Naturally he was bewildered by the French collapse, and the first initiatives of Vichy—'*travail, famille, patrie*'—filled him with misgiving. Its 'copy-book maxims for good children' seemed to him 'entirely to lack the fire which alone can bring out the virtues so rightly advocated'.[2] He wanted to be sure that this conversion had 'its roots in the people', and that beneath so much pliancy and discretion there was 'a will to march forward' to something more inspiring than a collective Confiteor. Renaissance must not be confused with restoration; everything would depend on the Anglo-Saxons; England had celebrated her 'finest hour'; and Teilhard looked forward to what he believed would be her 'greatest day'.[3]

He had been invited to attend a Congress in New York at which Einstein and Maritain were both speaking; but Rome would not allow him to go. Meanwhile the Armistice brought a French Embassy to Pekin. Henri Cosme and his wife became close friends, and when they had been moved to Indo-China the photograph of Madame Cosme, which was left standing on the little occasional table beside the sofa where she used to receive, was a reminder of Parisian conversations. Roland de Margerie—a diplomat of wide culture—was appointed Consul-General in Shanghai, and Teilhard delighted in his company and in that of his wife. These, and others, brought into an international colony much reduced in numbers the breath of a France now muted by the occupation. But it was a very ingrown society—more especially after the Americans had left in 1943, escorted by the fanfares of the Salvation Army. Letters came fitfully through the censorship and Teilhard learnt next to nothing of a clandestine renaissance whose watchword was not restoration but resistance. After the total occupation of France he received practically no letters at all; he could only listen to a generally hostile radio and pick up occasional scraps of inside information from his friends in the Embassy. Even the Overseas Services of the BBC were not always to be relied upon; they announced, in terms of flattering regret, that 'we have just learnt today of the death of Father Teilhard, who was assassinated by brigands in Tibet'. The war had been, in sum, a tedious parenthesis, and only a

[1] *Letters from a Traveller*, 16 December 1939, p. 254.
[2] *ibid*, to Max and Simone Bégouën, 20 September 1940, p. 267.
[3] *ibid.*, 11 December 1940, p. 273.

few days before the liberation of Paris we find Teilhard looking forward, with many of his countrymen, to radical solutions in Church and State:

> Without wanting—far from it—any social cataclysm, I wonder whether the new faith of which I catch a glimpse does not require for its establishment an earth violently stripped of the old social and ecclesiastical bark which inevitably shuts us in after two thousand years of Christianity. Only when we have rejected the last traces of a Neolithic framework shall we cease to think and to pray like Neolithic men.[1]

II

He did not have to endure for long the monastic rigours of Chabanel Hall. In the summer of 1940 the Geo-Biological Institute in Tientsin was transferred to comfortable quarters in the Rue Labrousse adjoining the French Embassy on the southern boundary of Pekin. These were too far from Chabanel Hall for Teilhard to make the daily journey without fatigue and inconvenience, and since he was closely associated with Leroy in the transformation of Licent's old museum, and had spent some weeks in Tientsin organizing its transfer, the obvious solution was for him to live there. Leroy was a man of Teilhard's own stamp, and the arrangement was congenial to them both. The new house had its own courtyard, fruit-trees and chicken-run, and a third Jesuit Father—young and sympathetic—was there to look after their material needs.

At one moment, in 1943, there was a threat to make the Fathers eat and sleep at Chabanel Hall—seven kilometres away. This would have ruined the proper functioning of the Institute, and it seemed to Teilhard 'as if the devil, in the person of certain devout superiors, was at work on our unfortunate house'.[2] The threat, however, was averted; and when Leroy was in hospital after an operation on his knee, the suspicions of authority were disproved:

> No missionary would have drawn such a flow of visitors, and this was not the result of purely social friendships. In a sense, it justifies our attitude as religious, and is a great comfort to us.[3]

In November 1942 Teilhard spent three weeks in Shanghai. This

[1] Letter to Eleanor Tafel (Gräfin von Alvensleben), 13 August 1944.
[2] Letter to Claude Rivière, 25 July 1943.   [3] *ibid.*, 21 January 1944.

Teilhard at Sarcenat
in 1950, still convalescent
after his first heart attack

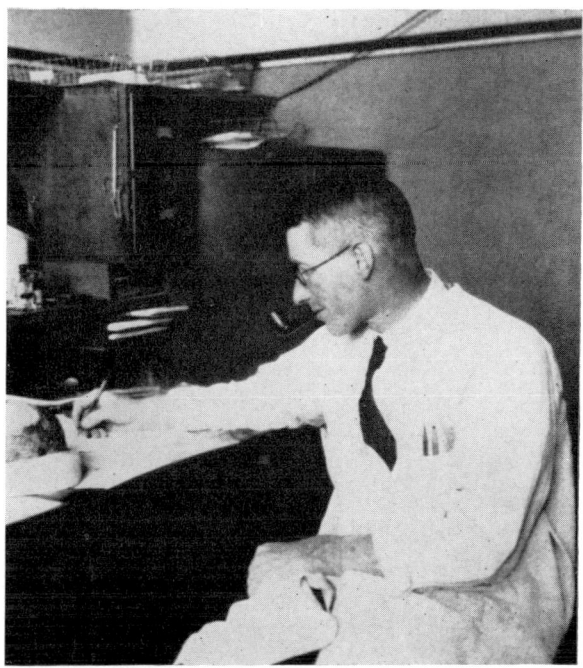

Davidson Black in
his laboratory shortly
before his death

Teilhard at Sterkfontein, 1951

was stimulating after the 'terribly rarefied'[1] atmosphere of Pekin where he sometimes felt like 'a fish in a glass jar'.[2] Further stimulus came from the friendship of Claude Rivière, a talented young Frenchwoman who gave literary talks on the radio. Richelieu, as seen by Sainte-Beuve, was fairly remote from Teilhard's personal line of thought, but he could always go a long way towards 'being all things to all men'. What mattered was the pursuit of a particular vision:

This is a question, above all, of prayer and patience and right intention, under a certain light; this is the vision that we must try to develop, in common, each of us in our own way. For myself, I find my support in a certain passionate perspective of matter which—as I told you—naturally attracted me. You rely, rather, on a certain lyrical and aesthetic perception of the world. Remain fully yourself, and consider that the sum of your past experiences is the stuff capable of spiritualization. . . . Only keep from the past (but keep them well) the multiform impulsions which push you forward. From this point of view nothing in the past is useless, or empty, or regrettable, provided that you gather and remodel everything in an act of forward-looking 'communion'.[3]

But the visit to Shanghai had one unfortunate consequence. Bitter experience had not yet taught Teilhard the danger of leaving his papers behind in strange drawers. An essay of a theological and philosophical kind, written ten years previously, had been discovered, and he was formally forbidden to return to Shanghai. It was the old story; they found him 'dangerous and contagious'.[4] The local superior was sympathetic, but higher authority intervened.

Claude Cuénot in his biography, and Père Leroy in his introduction to *Letters from a Traveller*, have described how Teilhard spent his day. He said his Mass at seven o'clock and after breakfast he would talk with Leroy for twenty minutes or so over a cigarette. Then he would write down in a notebook any thoughts that had come to him during the night. At nine o'clock he would go to the laboratory and work on a scientific article till twelve-thirty. After lunch he either returned there to busy himself with the fossils from Chou-Kou-Tien, or accompanied Leroy to the Pekin Union Medical College to study its palaeontological collection. Later, when Japan had entered the war, this

---

[1] Letter to Claude Rivière, 3 March 1943. [2] *ibid.*, 16 April 1943.
[3] *ibid.*, 8 December 1942. [4] *ibid.*, 30 May 1943.

was closed with all other foreign institutions, and most of Teilhard's working hours were spent at home. At 5 p.m. he visited his friends and was back at the Institute by eight o'clock when the Procurator locked the doors. The routine was varied on Sundays when he often joined a party from the French colony for a picnic in the Western Hills or among the abandoned temples near Pekin. Having ascertained the hour of luncheon, he would go off in search of fossils, hammer in hand—a tall and still athletic figure in his khaki trousers and felt hat—with a red armband denoting, after the attack on Pearl Harbour, his status as an 'enemy alien'.[1] The result of these Sunday excursions was an important article, *The Genesis of the Western Hills*,[2] in which Teilhard argued that their 'flexuration',[3] exhibited on an elementary scale and in a very pure form, would probably throw a valuable light on continental geology. He believed the rock formations to be three million years old.

It was in casual conversation among friends that Teilhard's personality shone out. Occasionally his remote Voltairean blood sharpened a *riposte*, but the irony was softened with good humour. He was simple, candid and gay, appreciating a good meal or a good joke. At times his frankness could be embarrassing:

> Once, forgetting no doubt whom he was talking to, he embarked on an explanation that might have placed him in an awkward position. I was sitting beside him, and to attract his attention I nudged him gently with the tip of my toe. You can imagine my embarrassment when I heard him exclaim with a laugh: 'Whose was that tactful kick?'[4]

Respected as a palaeontologist, he was revered as a priest. There is the evidence of Mme Arsène-Henry, wife of the French ambassador in Tokyo, who declared that 'whoever has not seen Teilhard say Mass has seen nothing'; of Mme Henri Cosme, who has said that it was impossible to make an uncharitable remark when Teilhard was in the room; of his superior in Tientsin, Père Charvet, to whom he had said: 'Don't hesitate to give me orders. I'm a Jesuit and I'll obey.'

[1] See Cuénot, p. 240, and *Letters from a Traveller*, Introduction.

[2] *Geobiologia*, vol. I.

[3] 'The zone where the envelope of the land-masses and the ocean beds changes the direction of its curve' (J. Bourcart, *Géographie du Fond des Mers*, p. 74); see Cuénot, French edition, p. 285.

[4] *Letters from a Traveller*, Introduction.

On one occasion he was invited to Chabanel Hall to meet the apostolic delegate, Archbishop Zanin. The archbishop, wishing to say his office, asked to borrow a breviary, and the superior of the house lent him one that was lying close at hand. It happened to belong to Teilhard and was stuffed with bits of paper on which he had jotted down his points for meditation. 'This book certainly belongs to a man of high spirituality', observed the archbishop as he gave it back. When Teilhard was speaking to what he called the Gentiles, he would sometimes refrain from bringing God into the argument; he would halt at the 'Omega point' without further precision. But if Leroy teased him about this, he would constantly repeat: 'God is a person, God is a person. We must think of him as we do of a person. A God not a person would not be God.' No doubt the jottings that fell under the eye of the apostolic delegate had made the point just as clearly.[1]

Teilhard sent to Rome a short memorandum on the work of the Geo-Biological Institute which he described as a 'laboratory of scientific mysticism where they would religiously define the methods of scientific research, and at the same give a practical demonstration of them'. The Roman authorities sent a vague reply to this, which Teilhard thought rather calculated; they would have been happier if he had announced the inauguration of a new pilgrimage. In the meanwhile, slowly, at the steady rate of two pages a day, he was completing *Le Phénomène Humain*. He had been at work on it for two years and now it occupied the greater part of his time. 'Basically', he told Bruno de Solages, 'what does more than anything else to justify my present retreat is the use I am making of it to finish the book I was telling you about.'[2] By 25 January 1946 half was finished; and the second part, since the lines of its development were already clear in his mind, was written more quickly. At Easter three-quarters was done; by 9 May he had reached the last sub-chapter; and the essay was finished in June, a month earlier than he had expected. Teilhard, optimistic as ever, hoped that it might be published. Yet he knew, with an accurate prescience of the criticism which he never lived to hear, that he would have against him 'the pure scientists as well as the experts in pure metaphysics, but . . . I don't know what else you could say if once you try to work out to its conclusion a coherent place for man in this

[1] See Cuénot, pp. 242–4. [2] 10 March 1940.

universe of ours'.[1] The MS was flown to America, through the kind offices of a friend, in March 1941, and thence to Rome by the diplomatic bag. The censors sat on it for three years and on 6 August 1944 Teilhard learnt that they forbade its publication.

The face that Teilhard presented to the world was not always the face that he presented to his closest friends. The bracing companionship of Leroy was all he had to lean on in these years of exile and rejection; and no doubt it was the interdiction of *Le Phénomène Humain*, among other frustrations, that Leroy had in mind when he wrote of Teilhard that

> He bore with patience, it is true, trials that might well have proved too much for the strongest of us, but how often in intimate conversation have I found him depressed and with almost no heart to carry on. The agonizing distress he already had to face in 1939 was intensified in the following years, and he sometimes felt that he could venture no further. During that period he was at times prostrated by fits of weeping, and he appeared to be on the verge of despair. But, calling on all the resources of his will, he abandoned himself to the supremely Great, to his Christ, as the only purpose of his being; and so hid his suffering and took up his work again, if not with joy, at least in the hope that his personal vocation might be fulfilled.[2]

In the seclusion of his room at the Institute, with a painting of the Yangtse gorges on the wall, and in the depth of his plush armchair, Teilhard had ample time for reading, and the mere list of what he read indicates the depth and range of his curiosity. In fiction—Sartre and Santayana, Koestler and Graham Greene, Camus, Tolstoy and Dostoievsky. In general, historical and scientific philosophy—Gobineau and Toynbee, Gerald Heard, Aldous Huxley, and John Dewey, Jean Rostand's *Thoughts of a Biologist*, James Burnham's *The Managerial Revolution*, Spengler's *Man and Technics*, Nietzsche, Novalis and Condorcet. It will be noted how carefully Teilhard kept himself in touch with thought very different from his own. Among the authors mentioned here, Jean Rostand has since shown himself one of Teilhard's severest critics. The fideism of Barth, the mystical syncretism of Aldous Huxley, the tragic agnosticism of Camus, the existentialism of

[1] *Letters from a Traveller*, to Max and Simone Bégouën, 9 May 1940, p. 263.
[2] *ibid.*

Sartre—these were all competitors for the mind of twentieth-century man, and Teilhard would have to meet them on their own ground as well as on his.[1] He was particularly enchanted by a return to the *Timaeus* of Plato:

> We perceive today very differently from Plato the music of the cosmos. This no longer excites us by the supposed 'harmony of numbers' which we have replaced by an aesthetic of rushing movement. But it remains true that the higher form of knowledge consists ... in hearing everything like a single note, rich and full. And it is because Plato heard this note confusedly that he is so close to us, and so inspiring after 2,400 years. What are the theologians waiting for to sound, fully and cosmically, the 'chord of Christ'?[2]

Teilhard was in immediate sympathy with Steele's *Anatomy of Frustration*—a subject with which he was not at all unfamiliar. He thought the book

> a magnificent act of faith in the 'New Beginning' we are hoping for. What has interested and moved me at the end of these pages is Steele's appeal to a face (that is to say, a personal form) of humanity which he sees as the only value and interest of the individual life. Just that 'communion of love' with evolution that we were talking about together.[3]

Teilhard was much in demand for lectures and informal addresses. Three of these were given during November and December of 1940—the first for the College Women Association, the second for a Protestant circle of theological studies, and the third at Yenching University. In March 1941 he was speaking on 'The future of man, seen by a palaeontologist' at the French Embassy; and in 1942 his public at Aurore University, Shanghai, was so stunned by the originality of his ideas that they begged him not to come back! In 1943 he was invited to address the Catholic University of Pekin on human fossils—a safer subject than human beings—and in December of the same year he was giving his thoughts on 'happiness'.[4] Not many of his listeners can have realized how hardly won was his right to do so. Mankind, he

[1] For a full account of Teilhard's reading at this time, see Cuénot, pp. 236–7.
[2] Letter to Claude Rivière, 22 January 1943.
[3] *ibid.*, 20 October 1943.
[4] '*Réflexions sur le Bonheur*' in *Cahiers Pierre Teilhard de Chardin*, vol. 2.

argued, might be compared to a party of would-be mountaineers. Some regret that they ever left the inn at the foot of the valley and quickly return to it. Others get half-way up and are content to admire the summit from afar, stretched out on the grass, exploring the lower slopes, and waiting till it is time for the picnic. The true alpinists go forward with their eyes fixed on the peak they have vowed to climb.

In the first category Teilhard included all those for whom existence was a muddle or a mistake. 'Carried to an extreme, and systematized into a doctrine, this attitude leads to the wisdom of the Hindu, for whom the universe is fetters and illusion—or to the pessimism of Schopenhauer.' In common parlance, it led to the resignation of 'what does it all matter? Mightn't one as well be dead as asleep?' This was as much as to say that it was 'better to be less than more, and that best was to be nothing at all'. In the second category were the neo-Epicureans—a Paul Morand or a Montherlant—for whom wisdom consisted in the pleasure of the present moment. These could always return to the inn when they had had enough of the view. Going back on his previous admiration for *Les Nourritures Terrestres*, Teilhard put André Gide in the same company—for Gide's ideal was 'to drink without ever quenching one's thirst, but rather to intensify it'. In the third category were those who found happiness in some object greater than themselves.

In the course of a similar lecture, not long before, Teilhard had spoken of Joliot and Eve Curie 'possessed by the demon of research'. Now he evoked other names—Nansen and Shackleton in the Arctic, the climbers of Everest who had not yet reached their goal, the pioneers of aviation. He quoted a phrase from Bertrand Russell, whom he described as 'one of the most acute and least spiritual minds of modern England', that 'the greatest joy is a deep and instinctive union with the total current of life'; and this, as Teilhard understood it, was an adequate definition of the Christian humanism in which Russell's 'quest for happiness' alone could discover its fulfilment.

In *L'Atomisme de l'Esprit* (1941) Teilhard saw man poised on the equator of a universe which looked very different from its respective poles. Since there were about 'a thousand billion cells in a human body' and '25 million atoms in a single grain of virus', man represented an abyss, not of magnitude or pulverization, but of synthesis. It was not possible to incorporate consciousness and thought in the construction of science because physics insisted on building its universe on a spatial axis where there was no appearance of life. But if we imagined a transversal operation from above, we could perceive the organization of life around the axis of 'complexity-consciousness'. Consciousness was an effect of complexity. 'To see, to feel and to think' was to be 'inwardly centred'; and the depth and simplicity of the centre was 'in proportion to the density of the sphere and the extent of the radius at the heart of which it was formed. . .'. Genetically speaking, man was a particular, but a provisional, term to molecular development; 'the youngest and thus the most complicated and most perfectly centred of the molecules'.

Here we are at the core of Teilhard's doctrine, since he held that, through man, the cosmos was struggling towards a further stage of complexity-consciousness. One form of this was socialization—not a collectivism which mechanized or an individualism which disintegrated. He conceded that finally the person existed for the whole, and not the whole for the person; but this was because, in the climax of synthesis, the whole had become personalized. The conclusion, in the eyes of all who are not collectivists, was a trap from which Teilhard could only extricate himself by an act of faith. If the 'whole'—the Omega point—was seen as the incarnate and risen Christ, in whom all things had their being, then the individual need fear no loss of personality. Moreover the act of faith was linked to an act of hope—for without hope in its irreversible progress human and cosmic activity would biologically cease to function. And when love was seen as its dynamic, charity could no longer be confused with resignation; it was an 'extraordinary plenitude in which force was purged of violence and emerged as the paroxysm of gentleness and goodness'. Sympathy became an upward thrust of energy, and morality a *mystique*. But of course Teilhard's vision met the twin obstacles of the problem of evil and the problem of human inequalities. Once again, his answer to the first seems curiously inadequate, not only to the orthodox theologian but to the average observer of human affairs:

> Provided that the summit exists, and that it is worth the climb, what mountaineer is surprised or complains if he is hurt, or even if he risks a serious fall? Considered in static isolation, pain and perversity are absurd. Considered dynamically, in a groping and moving system, they are justified and transfigured.

This is hardly a satisfactory reply to the gas chambers of Auschwitz, or to the Pauline dilemma—which is a commonplace of conscience— of doing the thing that one should not and omitting to do the thing that one should. Teilhard's answer to the problem of human inequalities was more reassuring. If the universe were

> moving to its climax under the form of isolated and divergent consciousness, there could be no consolation for a man who had neither the health, nor the gifts, nor the social opportunities which were the lot of others... but the case is altered if the various thinking elements of the earth only form a single convergent mass, destined to share in an equal and ultimate success. In the heat of attack what soldier thinks of being jealous of the officer who is leading the assault?

With his own country officially *hors de combat* Teilhard could afford a detachment which Frenchmen officially engaged would doubtless have found irritating if they had read what he was writing. The war, as he viewed it, was less an evil than a phenomenon. We may ask ourselves what exactly he meant by an '*axisme universalisé*', since the whole *mystique* of the Axis powers was narrowly racial and nationalist; but he did insist that a 'new order' was being born, and that its nature was in some way universalist. As the war proceeded, the Atlantic Charter and the United Nations Organization confirmed his intuitions from the democratic side; so, more violently, did the spread of Marxist ideas. Teilhard looked beyond the immediate prospect of two hostile blocs in the Allied camp to an interpenetration of ideas and a subsequent thawing of hostility. The war was total not only in its impact and its ruthlessness, but in its cosmic direction, so to speak, and in its concentration of human energy. Teilhard took the example of a bomber pilot in his machine; the various metals which had gone to its construction, the mines from which they had been quarried, and the factories which had refined and shaped them; the oil with its background of wells, pipelines, and prospections; the political and financial interests which assured or disputed its production; the delicate interior mechanism—the result of minute calculations; the body of the machine, and the weight of destructive power which it carried. And then there was the pilot himself:

> When he is at rest, a marvellous human instrument, selected and trained, physically and morally, from among the finest of his

race, but now super-humanized by his flight. Let us try to appreciate the inward tension of this man, who carries and personifies the passions, the pride, and the ambitions of millions of his fellow-men. See him intoxicated by the vast forces which a pressure of his hand commands; excited by the mission on which he is sent; wholly consenting to the sacrifice of his own life; fulfilling himself in an action where the whole of that life is materialized to the point of paroxysm.[1]

Reading this passage, one is not surprised that some of Teilhard's roneoed writings should have been found among the papers of Antoine de Saint-Exupéry. For both men love was not a sentiment but an activity.

Teilhard had his critics in that closed-in society of Pekin. To those who foresaw the future as a monstrous and mechanical collectivism, he replied that there would be no such thing as an ant-heap if ants knew how to love; and when Teilhard spoke of love, he knew what he was talking about:

Time and again, life has brought me in contact with men whose activities and convictions placed them in a camp generally considered to be the opposite of my own. Between them and me, according to the recognized conventions, there should have been defiance or hostility. But instead of this coldness, a deep sympathy sprang up from the first moment of our meeting, one of those growing and lasting sympathies that you find between comrades in arms. Labelled as enemies, we at once recognized that we were brothers. And why? Simply because all we were trying to do, on either side, was to magnify and unify the earth. What does it matter if our methods were still at variance in achieving the same result? We knew that these divergences were only secondary and provisional; one day they would correct each other and be resolved. The essential thing, in waiting for this, was to be able to meet in the atmosphere and light of the same ideal.[2]

What Teilhard saw, beyond the convulsions of the Second World War, was a dual movement in the universe—the growth of the noosphere contradicting and overcoming the disintegrating forces of entropy. Human relations were becoming human bonds, whatever a

[1] 'L'Universalisation et l'Union', in L'Activation de l'Énergie.
[2] ibid.

selfish individualism might desire to the contrary. We were like passengers on board a ship. The bolder spirits had climbed up on deck and taken the measure of the vessel on which they were embarked:

They realized that there was a furnace to stoke and a rudder to hold. Above all they saw the clouds floating in the sky, and breathed the perfume of the isles beyond the horizon's rim. The agitation of men and women was no more—the vessel was no longer adrift. Now there was just the *Voyage*.[1]

III

On 29 October 1941 Teilhard's brother Gabriel died after an illness of several months; he had been mobilized on the staff of the French Air Force at the outbreak of war. Marcellin Boule, Henri Bergson and Léontine Zanta had all died before the war was over. One by one the links were being severed. But Teilhard's thoughts were still questioningly turned to what was happening in his own country. He was particularly shocked by the anti-Semitic legislation of Vichy, for—as he wrote to Breuil—'in France my best friends are Jews'. The grandparents of these people had served in all the French armies, and their persecution was not only odious in itself but 'dangerous for the future'.[2] Two months earlier he had been unable to 'make up his mind'[3]; events had done much to clear it for him. In March 1945, when everyone else was talking about the end of the war, Teilhard was talking about the end of the world—although he did not believe, like the more apocalyptic pessimists of that time, that it was likely to occur in the near future. Was it not conceivable, he argued in a lecture at the French Embassy, that humanity would reach a point of development when it would detach itself altogether from the earth and unite with Omega? 'A phenomenon outwardly similar to a death, perhaps; but, in reality, simple metamorphosis and accession to the supreme synthesis.'[4] He never lost sight of his personal apocalypse. But when the Japanese surrendered five months later, the first intelligence officers of the American Forces to arrive in Pekin found him escaping from the social round and bicycling over the hills to talk with the

[1] '*La Montée de l'autre*' in *L'Activation de l'Énergie*.
[2] *Letters from a Traveller*, 12 July 1941, p. 284.
[3] *ibid.*, 19 May 1941, p. 283.
[4] '*Vie et Planètes: Que se passe-t-il en ce moment sur la terre?*', *Études*, May 1946.

Communist guerrillas. He found their conversation much more interesting.

On 30 September he learnt from the Gaullist authorities that he could return to France, with an intimation that they wished him to do so. Place in an aeroplane was found for him. But with an allowance of only 25 kilos for baggage and with small prospect of buying clothes in a country where they were in such short supply, he preferred to wait for a ship. No reason for urgent departure had been given him, and none reached him as he began to organize the affiliation of the Geo-Biological Institute with the Geological Survey, which was now resuming its activities. It was not until the early months of 1946 that he received permission to return from his new Provincial, Père Décisier, a particularly valued friend from Ore Place. Père d'Ouince, lately released from captivity and equally sympathetic, was his immediate superior and Teilhard wrote to him asking for a room at the Rue Monsieur. On 1 April he embarked at Shanghai on the s.s. *Strathmore*, a P & O liner whose lower decks had been converted for the transport of troops. The passengers—all expatriates—had still to sleep in hammocks. The voyage was gregarious but not intolerable, with 'simple and solid food'. Work, however, was 'practically impossible',[1] and for the first time Teilhard looked forward to his landing without regret. He spent three days in England; crossed over to Dieppe by the Newhaven route; and reached Paris on 3 May. He was never to set foot in China again.

[1] *Letters from a Traveller*, 5 April 1946, p. 290.

CHAPTER XIV

PARIS AND ROME

TEILHARD described his first few months in Paris as 'the most exalting' of his whole life. His return to Europe coincided with his sixty-fifth birthday, and he had reached an age when most men have their important work behind them. The first war had not only put his 'feet in the stirrups'; it had taken him a good distance on his way. The second had seen the completion of the synthesis towards which he had been moving, at the same time as it cut him off from the human contacts that he cherished. 'I work', he had told Père d'Ouince, 'for Paris and for tomorrow.'[1] Now Paris was waiting to welcome him, and he had little thought for anything but the morrow. His hair had turned white and he knew that his physical strength was no longer what it had been. 'In my life', he said, 'it is now five o'clock in the evening.' The years of exile and relative inactivity had formed a kind of parenthesis from which he now emerged inwardly fortified, curious as ever, and anxious only to clarify and communicate those aspects of his doctrine which he felt able to define more exactly.

The first euphoria of the Liberation had given way to a corrosive cynicism, and the disciples of Sartre were celebrating the death of God from the Café de Flore. The Church was in ferment, with Cardinal Suhard issuing the encyclicals which others thought should have come from Rome, if they came from anywhere; the Dominicans in the Boulevard de Latour-Maubourg doing their best to talk across the barricades; and the worker-priests exercising their desperate apostolate in Aubervilliers and Montreuil. Physically Paris was unchanged by the war and the occupation; psychologically it had changed a great deal. One intrepid journalist actually called for the abolition of the Académie Française.

Teilhard may well have been astonished by the publicity which

[1] 1941.

attended his return, for this was greeted with headlines in the literary journals. He could not have known how widely his roneoed brochures had circulated, not least among the prisoners of war. The Marxists, intellectually ascendant and still popular as the *parti des fusillés*, found in his theories of '*l'homme communautaire*' a useful reinforcement. Gabriel Marcel, from the standpoint of Christian existentialism, was among the first to take issue with him. The two men would meet at the house of Roger Lévy, professor at the École Nationale d'Administration and a specialist in Pacific problems. They also debated publicly, under the chairmanship of Père Dubarle—a brilliant Dominican scientist—on the subject of 'Science and Consciousness'. Teilhard was inquiring how far 'the material organization of humanity leads man to the point of spiritual maturation'. Marcel's reply was very sceptical:

I ask myself why such a consciousness should necessarily produce a spiritual value. By 'spiritual' I understand a reference to certain values which are very precise. Let me take the example of the doctors at Dachau. On this level, can one be optimistic? What is the integrating consciousness of these scientists worth? I see nothing hominizing there.

Teilhard replied that 'man, to be man, must have, as a man, tried everything to the very end'—an assumption that seems morally questionable in the highest degree, and one that Teilhard himself would have been the last to follow through to its logical conclusion. He argued that to have an integrating vision was in itself a spiritual activity, to which Marcel replied that this was a Promethean, not a Christian, conception. But Teilhard maintained that 'what makes a man Promethean is his refusal to transcend his deeds'; and that what confronts Prometheus is 'total death'. The Christian, by contrast, realizes that he must transcend himself. There is a sense, as we have seen, in which both Marx and Nietzsche were at Teilhard's elbow, although neither succeeding in annexing him. Marcel was too aware of this proximity ever to be comfortable with Teilhard; and he had been himself in too close proximity to the Gestapo for Teilhard's explanation of the monstrous perversity of man as a necessary accident of evolution to appear as anything but seriously inadequate. The dialogue between Teilhard and Gabriel Marcel illustrated not only two radically distinct ways of looking at Christianity, but also the psychological gulf between a man who had spent six years cheek by jowl with diabolic evil, and one who had not.[1] The 'eclipses of God'[2] left Teilhard surprisingly undisturbed.

Another Christian thinker to whom he found himself opposed was Louis Lavelle. In May 1947, before an audience of 250 at the Catholic Centre for French intellectuals, Lavelle argued that although man depended on the world for the discovery and expansion of his powers, he must disengage himself from external reality in proportion to his spiritual growth. Teilhard reacted strongly against this view of the world as an instrument and an intermediary; the destiny of the world was its consummation, not its abandonment. Lavelle was an idealist philosopher in the classical tradition; Jean Hippolyte was a disciple of Heidegger, and a professor of philosophy at the Sorbonne. Teilhard met him at the house of Madame Romain Rolland in June 1948 with three Marxist professors. They discussed 'the future of man'. Hippolyte was struck by Teilhard's optimism, generosity and openness of mind, but found him far removed from politics. Teilhard noted that the non-Christian found it as difficult to understand the Christian idea of love as many Christians found it to understand the scientist's faith in matter.

But of all the minds that were then meeting in a passionate dialogue probably Emmanuel Mounier, with his philosophy of Personalism, was the closest to Teilhard. Mounier, it is true, was concerned with politics, and also with psychology, in a way that Teilhard was not; but Mounier's militant engagement in political causes was in many respects an illustration in the concrete of what Teilhard was preaching in the abstract. Generally speaking, Teilhard's mind was made up; it never stopped moving, but it was not easily influenced. He was anxious, as ever, to persuade; but his means of doing so were limited. He was forbidden to address large public meetings, and on one occasion, when he saw the size of the audience, he refused to go on to the platform. He was allowed, however, to attend meetings sponsored by the Jesuits, and it was at one of these—on 19 January 1947—that he accompanied Père Dubarle, who was to introduce the discussion. Teilhard repeated his thesis that God permitted evil because a price must be paid for order, and that in creating the multiple he had at the

[1] See Cuénot, pp. 251–3. M. Cuénot suggests that the later thought of Gabriel Marcel has developed in a Teilhardian direction.
[2] Martin Buber.

same time created a resistant. For Teilhard the evil of sin, as distinct from the evil in nature, was the form of disorder corresponding to the conscious state of the multiple; and he admitted that with the increase of consciousness the evil became more serious and left the success of the universe in suspense. This, at least, was some kind of answer to the physicians of Auschwitz. But when Dubarle intervened to say that a comet could destroy the earth, Teilhard replied that such a thing could never happen. 'That', answered Dubarle, 'is the answer of a theologian, not of a philosopher'—to which Teilhard, with his customary leap of faith, replied that 'our life should be only a life of believing'.[1]

In the summer of 1946 he spent a fortnight at Les Moulins, his brother Joseph's house in the Puys de Dôme. It stood, four hundred metres high, at the foot of the mountains on the edge of the Limagne —the wide plain which extends to the east of Clermont-Ferrand. It was not far from Sarcenat, but Sarcenat was too haunted by its dead for Teilhard to wish to return there. Nevertheless, his heart was still in Auvergne:

> Those long years in China had given me the impression that I no longer cared for Auvergne. Now I see very well that this was only an illusion.[2]

In September of this year, and again in 1947, Teilhard spent some days with Bruno de Solages and Père de Lubac s.j., at the Château de Carmaux in the Tarn. This belonged to the Marquis de Solages, who lent it to his cousin for theological meetings; their present purpose was to decide how the objections raised by the Roman censors against *Le Phénomène Humain* could be met without dishonesty. In the event, as we shall see, their efforts were unavailing, and the essay remained unpublished during Teilhard's lifetime. It was, however, the first of his writings to break upon the world, and the one upon which his reputation has largely rested. To discuss it fully would be to discuss his total synthesis—a synthesis, moreover, which had already been adumbrated in several previous essays. But it may be useful to assess its impact on certain critical, yet sympathetic, observers. For Father John Russell, s.j., Teilhard's system was a context for a philosophy rather than a philosophy itself. His conception of a 'within' and a

[1] See Cuénot, p. 258.
[2] Letter to Madame Haardt, 14 September 1946.

'without' of matter eliminated the sharp dualism between matter and consciousness introduced into philosophy by Descartes. Teilhard had restored the unity between science and the philosophy of nature. If all matter had some intrinsic property of consciousness, metaphysical objections to evolution disappeared. In tracing a unity of orientation in the world of phenomena Teilhard proved himself, once again, a better Thomist than his scholastic adversaries supposed. For St. Thomas matter had 'within itself an intrinsic natural tendency or orientation towards the reception of progressively more perfect forms and . . . the ultimate form to which all matter tends is the human soul'.[1]

Père Dubarle, looking back no doubt on their previous discussions, and with St. Thomas very much in his mind if not at his elbow, equated the Angelic Doctor's '*désir naturel*' with Teilhard's '*désir cosmique*'; and St. Thomas's proof of God's existence from the argument of the Prime Mover could lead to Teilhard's argument from 'the natural necessity of a real end'. Teilhard's personal experience lent support to this, for St. Thomas's argument that 'everything that moves is moved by another than itself' implied a connection between potency and act—and Teilhard's philosophy was essentially a philosophy in action. Dubarle also claimed that evolution was implied in Aristotelian physics as it was in scientific cosmology, and he described Teilhard's attempt, in facing quite new aspects of the problem, as in itself Aristotelian. But Aristotle had a 'conceptual reference for his phenomenology, leading to an autocriticism, which Teilhard had not'. Teilhard's system was 'a thought partially inhabited by a dream', and his mind was 'too little analytical, operating rather by an intuitive fusion of elements than by a precise conceptual articulation'. It was certainly a creative method, but it was not the one best calculated to secure the truth of its propositions. Teilhard's greatness was to have opened the way to a projection of the dynamism inherent in nature— a dynamism which was not present in Aristotle—'towards ever higher fulfilments of being, and postulating a divine fulfilment of the universe through the operation of nature itself'. *Le Phénomène Humain* already sketched out, however confusedly, 'the path by which theology might coherently make contact with the experience of mankind today'.[1]

---

[1] *Heythrop Journal*, 1961.   [1] *La Vie Intellectuelle*, March 1956.

It was Dr. Joseph Needham, writing in the *New Statesman*,[1] who introduced Teilhard to English readers unlikely to have heard of him, and unlikely to be prejudiced in his favour. They had met in Paris at a session of Unesco, shortly after Teilhard, with Père de Lubac and Bruno de Solages, had put the finishing touches to *Le Phénomène Humain*. Needham was a Cambridge man, but he was captivated nevertheless by what Marcel Brion described as 'that kindly and ironic grace, that sharp and yet benevolent refinement, and that Oxonian distinction which makes you think of some English scholar—Newman and Darwin rolled into one'.[2] Needham hailed *Le Phénomène Humain* as 'the work of a first-rate evolutionary biologist who knew his facts'. He saw Teilhard as a lonely thinker; only Bergson seemed to have influenced him, although he 'could have gained much from Whitehead's organic philosophy'. As a great historian of science, Needham put his finger on Teilhard's want of historical sense. It was particularly curious that a man who had lived so long in China should have received so little impression from Chinese culture—'the most historically-minded of all'.

> To say of a civilization to which we owe the technology of cast iron and the first development of the mechanical clock that it remained throughout the centuries persistently 'Neolithic', and to insist that 'during historic time the principal axis of anthropogenesis passed through the West' is simply to perpetuate a vulgar error still capable of doing great harm.

Needham also thought that Teilhard undervalued the power of religions older than Christianity to adapt themselves to scientific knowledge; but these reservations in no way diminished his admiration for the book or his veneration for its author.

Dr. Needham was not the only British scientist of international repute to give his attention to *Le Phénomène Humain*; in the January 1961 issue of *Mind* Sir Peter Medawar subjected the book to eight pages of sustained invective. Already, in his Reith Lectures, he had referred to 'mopings or exaltations of poetistic prose' and many listeners might have guessed that he had Teilhard in mind. Now, the 'poetistic prose'—not a happy epithet—became 'tipsy, euphoric prose-poetry'. In his later Herbert Spencer Lecture Medawar declared

[1] 7 November 1951.
[2] *Les Nouvelles Littéraires*, 11 January 1951.

that 'Teilhard . . . was in no sense a serious thinker. He had about him that innocence which makes it easy to understand why the forger of the Piltdown skull should have chosen Teilhard to be the discoverer of its canine tooth.' One may well retort that this was not serious criticism, and on the continent it would hardly have been taken seriously. As Dr. Bernard Towers, an anatomist of high distinction, pointed out in his broadcast reply[1] to Medawar, both Piveteau in France and Dobzhansky in America regarded Teilhard as 'a seminal force of great significance to science'. Sir Julian Huxley, whom Teilhard had also met at Unesco and who wrote the preface to the English translation of *Le Phénomène Humain*, was of the same opinion. Ved Mehta[2] concluded that, 'Unless a philosopher finds for us an acceptable faith or synthesis . . . we remain becalmed on a painted ocean of controversy.' It was just such a synthesis that Teilhard, using the tools of science and sustained by the impetus of faith, was constructing.

Dr. Towers reminded his listeners that 'the initial opposition to Copernicus and Galileo came, not from theologians, but from university professors . . . from the scientific establishment of the period'. Darwin had been opposed by 'the most knowledgeable anatomist of his day' and had confessed to the fear 'that his ideas would not be tolerated by entrenched scientific orthodoxy'. The last word was not always with the professors against the pioneers—as the scientific honours which came to Teilhard in his lifetime and the obituaries in the scientific journals after his death abundantly demonstrated. Teilhard's 'fundamental pioneering achievement'—codified, so to speak, in *Le Phénomène Humain*—was to have made sense 'out of the two most famous, but apparently contradictory, scientific ideas to come out of the nineteenth century . . . the theory of biological evolution on the one hand and the second law of thermodynamics'—or the law of increasing entropy—'on the other'. The latter held out no better prospect to mankind than ultimate annihilation. Against this, Teilhard's law of increasing complexity-consciousness—his perception of an alternative trend in evolution—was 'far more than an unreasoned hope for the future'; it was scientifically verifiable—and its verification from a strict observation of phenomena was the theme of *Le*

[1] 8 March 1965.
[2] Author of *The Fly and the Flybottle: Encounters with British Intellectuals*, 1963.

Phénomène Humain. Dobzhansky had ended his study of *Mankind Evolving* with a quotation from Teilhard:

> Man is not the centre of the universe as was naïvely believed in the past, but something much more beautiful—Man the ascending spearhead of the great biological synthesis. Man is the last-born, the keenest, the most complex, the most subtle of the successive layers of life. This is nothing less than a fundamental vision. And I shall leave it at that.[1]

But Medawar's article had done its damage and Teilhard's reputation in England has not yet recovered from it. It is true that his vocabulary, and his insistence on capital letters, present difficulties and irritations to the English reader, for English favours the concrete where French favours the abstract. Moreover Teilhard was straining the muscles of language to find new words for original ideas. As a friendly critic pointed out:

> He had a natural and disarming indifference for the verbal police. . . . He created a vocabulary for himself and was incapable of entering into that of his opponents. . . . He tailored afresh for his own use the language of other people. Like Péguy, he made himself a suit to fit his thoughts as they came to birth. He never put on the frock coat of his ancestors; he piously left it in the cupboard.[2]

It is most unlikely that Teilhard had ever read a line of Dr. Johnson, but he might have taken comfort from the Doctor's dictum: 'Difference of thought will produce difference of language. He that thinks with more extent than another will want words of larger meaning.' What would Johnson have said to 'poetistic'?

On 20 August 1947 Teilhard addressed an international meeting of the Society of Jesus on the importance of research, but he generally confined himself to smaller gatherings and private contacts. He was living at the headquarters of *Études* in the Rue Monsieur and here, as he sat talking in the garden after luncheon, the younger priests might be seen with their necks craning out of the windows and hoping to catch the drift of his argument. Sometimes, as he turned back into the house, he would remark: 'Of course, I may be wrong'—and then add,

[1] Dobzhansky's translation.
[2] M. de Nédoncelle: 'Un Prophète des Convergences Humaines', *Revue des Sciences Religieuses*, 31 (1957), pp. 293–8.

with an ironic twinkle, 'but I don't think so.' The present writer recalls one such occasion in the summer of 1946. Teilhard had only just returned from China and he spoke of what was happening there —a crude reversal of the mandarin tradition, but also a genuine awakening. Then the conversation turned on the atom bomb. If the gas chamber and the Gestapo were one challenge to his optimism, the atom bomb was another. His essay on the subject had recently appeared in *Études*.[1] Whereas hitherto man had used the natural forces of matter—fire, steam and electricity—he now had his hand on the levers of matter itself. He was 'a new being' who hardly as yet 'recognized himself', conscious of a power capable of indefinite development. Teilhard believed that the 'spectre of bloody conflicts' would be exorcised by the 'rays of some mounting unanimity', and that the effect of the atom bomb might well be that war would 'be doubly and definitively put an end to'. The excess of power in our hands would make all strife impossible; in comparison with the possibilities of conquest opened up by science, the romantic trappings of war would seem tedious and old-fashioned; and men would grow together in sympathy by 'looking passionately, and together, at the same thing'.

> In spite of their military apparatus, the recent explosions at Bikini would give the signal for the coming into the world of a humanity inwardly and outwardly pacified. . . . In the last analysis the final effect of the light projected by the atomic fire in the psychic depths of the earth is to bring to the surface the ultimate and culminating question of an end to evolution—in other words the problem of God.

These were brave words in the Paris of 1946 and if you questioned them as you sat with Teilhard in the garden of the Rue Monsieur, he would reply—as he had replied to Père Dubarle—'*Il faut croire.*'

II

Teilhard was confidently hoping to join Breuil in South Africa during the July of 1947. The necessary permission had been given, and the financial arrangements had been made. Breuil had been in Africa since 1942, engaged on important prehistoric research, and it was at

[1] September 1946.

the instance of Field-Marshal Smuts that Teilhard received the invitation. Dr. Camp, an American palaeontologist from the University of California, was to lead the expedition. On 31 May Teilhard was speaking on the mystery of the Ascension—one of his favourite feasts—at the home of Madame Solange Lemaître, a Protestant who had gathered round her a group, belonging to all denominations or none, known as the '*union des croyants*'. Teilhard used occasionally to address them. The following day he baptized an adult, whom he had instructed and received into the Church. During the night of 1 June he suffered a severe heart attack and was removed to the hospital of the Brothers of St. John of God in the Rue Oudinot. For two weeks he remained dangerously ill, with a high fever, and hardly able to speak to such friends as came to see him. As soon as he was well enough to move, he was taken to the clinic of the Augustinian nuns of the Immaculate Conception which adjoined the Forest of St.-Germain. Here his strength slowly returned to him and he delighted to walk among the trees. He remained there until 1 December.

He had not suffered excessively; only a 'rheumatic pain, with attacks of nausea, but no breathlessness'.[1] Nevertheless he knew that he might have been 'sent to Jesus',[2] and he realized that he had come to a turning point in his life. The renewal of Catholic thought in France, and in particular the 'new theology', had already provoked a lively reaction in Rome. Teilhard was not a professional theologian, but his influence was greatly feared because so much of it could not be directly counteracted. An important article by a theologian, 'well thought of in Rome',[3] urged that the writings of five religious should be placed on the Index, and Teilhard was asked to write no more philosophy lest he too might be condemned. The news reached him while he was still recuperating at St.-Germain, and he accepted it with his usual serenity, replying to the General in the following terms:

> The Father Provincial has recently communicated to me your letter concerning me of 22 August. I have no need to say that, with God's help, you may count upon me. I am too surely convinced—and more so day by day—that the world can only be fulfilled in Christ, and that Christ can only be found through an interior submission to the Church, for me to have been able to

[1] *Letters from a Traveller*, to the Abbé Breuil, 15 July 1947, p. 293.
[2] Cuénot, p. 263. [3] *ibid*, p. 266.

feel the slightest hesitation at the news of your decision. I only hope that the Lord will help me faithfully to find my way in a situation which is psychologically difficult. Fortunately I have around me, here, in the Society great and reliable friends whom you know, and who will help me on the road.

Allow me to add, in all simplicity and filial trust, that, as far as I judge, a kind of mistake or misunderstanding has arisen in the matter of my personal situation which will eventually, I am sure, by the sheer force of fidelity, be cleared up. Since 1939—and I think that all the papers which have been brought in accusation against me date from before that time—I have made great progress towards the correct explanation of a point of view which (given my experience of the 'Gentiles') really seems to have a chance of being of service to the Kingdom of God. This is the opinion of the authorized theologians who follow my thought. Don't you think it would be a pity to reject without examination a fruit which is perhaps on the point of ripening? And don't you think that the best reparation for what I may have done less well in the past would be for me to produce at last something that no one can gainsay?

Whatever happens, never doubt that for a long time my only passion has been to spread the glory of Christ Jesus; and you may always rely, in all circumstances, on my very respectful and complete devotion in him.[1]

Among Teilhard's defenders was Mgr. de Solages, who had boldly taken his part in an article appearing in the *Bulletin de Littérature Ecclésiastique* (April–June 1947). This was entitled 'Pour l'honneur de la théologie'. Bruno de Solages argued that since everything in the universe evolved, the thoughts of men evolved with it, and that the problem for theology was how to maintain transcendent values in the midst of this perpetual flux. Truth was immutable, but its expression changed. He then paid his tribute to Teilhard:

It is the deep Christian significance of this great scientist's work— of worldwide fame—of this powerful thinker, of this enchanting writer, and, I add, of this *gentleman*, Teilhard de Chardin, to have succeeded in showing, more than any other man, that evolution itself can only be finalistic, that it is advancing towards the spirit,

[1] 25 September 1947.

that it can be explained only by the spirit, and that it postulates at the beginning because it postulates at the end, a transcendent God.[1]

Teilhard now reconciled himself to certain physical restrictions. Something of a chain smoker, he was forced to abandon cigarettes; coffee was forbidden; and he would not be allowed to fly. Future work in the field was extremely doubtful. He was bitterly disappointed at the cancellation of the South African trip, but resolved to take the shock 'as a touch of the spur rather a tug on the bridle'.[2] In December he again spent a fortnight at Les Moulins and by the end of the month he was back in Paris already lecturing to the student-inspectors at St.Cloud and at the students' hostel in the Rue Vaugirard. 'I have seldom felt so on top of things', he told the Bégouëns, 'or that I spoke so clearly.'[3]

He had previously entertained the idea of returning to Europe by way of America where he had by now so many friends, and by the early spring of 1948 he was well enough to make the journey. It was a turbulent crossing, during which Teilhard and his bed were carried bodily across the cabin. He was met in New York by Rhoda de Terra and Lucile Swan, and lodged at the Jesuit house of St. Ignatius Loyola in Park Avenue, where he was given a 'rough and cordial welcome'.[4] The superior, though elderly, was open-minded. Teilhard also had the use of a top-floor study at the headquarters of the Viking Foundation[5] on East 71st Street. Here George Barbour seized every opportunity to visit him:

> Teilhard occupied a small room on the fifth floor, reached by an elevator, and lit only by a dormer window and a desk lamp. There was room for a small desk, Teilhard's desk chair, and two seats for visitors separated by a low table, usually with an ashtray and a pile of books. The slope of the roof and the low ceiling made the quarters seem cramped, and one could stand comfortably only in the window embrasure and the inner half of the room. It had no doubt been designed as a servant's bedroom—which

[1] Cuénot, p. 267.
[2] *Letters from a Traveller*, to the Abbé Breuil, 15 July 1947, p. 293.
[3] *ibid.*, 29 December 1947, p 296.
[4] Letter to Père Leroy, 1 March 1948.
[5] Later to be re-named the Wenner-Gren.

Teilhard smilingly agreed was an anachronism that proved the fact of social progress! The hide-out was secluded, yet accessible to his friends, and an extension telephone in the laboratory next door was handy for those who knew the unlisted number, 'REpublic 7.2400'. An oblique view to the extreme left caught the tree-tops in Central Park and the buildings across the street did not entirely block out the sky.[1]

Teilhard went round to the Museum of Natural History every day, but did no work there. He now confessed to a 'sort of nausea for the past', except for continental geology. If people were surprised at this, he replied that 'life has its seasons'.[2] For the rest he visited his friends —Mrs. de Terra who lived near by; Frick, the millionaire, with whom he spent a week-end on Long Island; Malvina Hoffman, for whom he sat again for his bust. The previous cast, destined to be cast in bronze for installation at the Musée d'Art Moderne, had been broken on the quay at Cherbourg. The sculptress was better pleased with her second attempt than with her first. 'This time', she said, 'even I felt that somehow a bell had been rung and a door closed, with a certain definite thankfulness that I had been able to catch the elusive expression that had evaded me in the earlier attempts.'[3] Teilhard made useful contacts with the authorities of Fordham University, and they have since been conspicuous in a recognition of his work. Father Gannon, the President, and some of the staff entertained him at the Century Club. He went down to Washington where he met a number of old friends from China, including Barbour and Le Fèvre, and was given a friendly welcome at Georgetown University. The woods of Virginia were still dark, shot through with transparencies of green and red. In general he was depressed by the 'hysterical anti-Communism' which then coloured the political temper of the country. 'Who can tell whether, in the very interests of the Kingdom of God, a good dose of Marxism is not the thing to save us?'[4] He went up to Boston, although some projected lectures at Harvard had fallen through. In New York his most important appearance was at the Viking Foundation where he spoke on anthropogenesis. This, he claimed, would be

[1] *In the Field with Teilhard de Chardin*, p. 121.
[2] Letter to Père Leroy, 1 March 1948.
[3] *In the Field with Teilhard de Chardin*, p. 123.
[4] Letter to Père Leroy, 1 March 1948.

the new science of anthropology—no longer the study of man as he had been in the past but as he might be in the future. In May he passed through a period of depression, when every obstacle became 'a mountain',[1] but 'all in all', he wrote to Barbour, 'I feel I have gained a lot by this last contact with America. Not much to do with fossil man, but a great deal on the subject of living man. You know that the best part of myself is focused on that.'[2]

Teilhard returned to France on the *New Amsterdam*, and in August was again staying at Les Moulins. Here he made his annual eight-day retreat, walking alone among the plantations of firs and oaks. In a letter to his cousin he summed up the direction of his thoughts in words that were movingly prophetic:

> For the moment, my chief concern (increasingly so, for a long time now) is not to know what sort of beginning I have made, but how to *end well*: and by that I mean ending my life in the spontaneous attitude and the providential circumstance which best bear witness to the sincerity and value of the vision for which I have lived.[3]

Or, again, to Solange Lemaître:

> After a certain time it is not so much that one's thoughts are new; but one thinks more deeply.[4]

When he was not in retreat he was visited by his widowed sisters-in-law and their children. The château was isolated in the middle of deep woods—not very comfortable since there was no running water and the lavatories were primitive, but it was charged with memories and redolent of a long past. Not all the recollections were happy ones, for it was in a pond near by that Teilhard's nephew had been drowned only a year earlier:

> His memory hovers all around, like a shadow at the same time gentle and sad—like the presence, as I was telling some friends, of someone who seems just to have left the room when you enter it.[5]

Teilhard was not so lost in his vision of the future that he was insensitive to the *loi de naissance*: but Auvergne had now become a cemetery, and the *loi de naissance* was not to be distinguished from the *loi de mort*.

---

[1] Letter to Père Leroy, 23 May 1948.
[2] *In the Field with Teilhard de Chardin*, p. 123.
[3] *Letters from a Traveller*, p. 280.
[4] 20 September 1948.   [5] Letter to Père Leroy, 28 August 1948.

III

In 1947, at the instance of the Ministry of Foreign Affairs, Teilhard had been promoted to the rank of Officer in the Order of the Légion d'Honneur

> for outstanding services to the intellectual and scientific influence of France, through a body of work mostly written and published in China, which has established him as a leading authority in international, and particularly in English-speaking scientific circles. He may now be regarded, in the fields of palaeontology and geology, as one of the chief ornaments of French science, whose international standing he has done much, by his personal contacts with foreign scientists, to maintain and exalt.

He became director of research at the National Centre for Scientific Research; was elected a corresponding member of the mineralogical section of the Académie des Sciences; and was now being pressed to pose his candidature for the chair just vacated by Henri Breuil at the Collège de France. He had a firm assurance that he would be elected unanimously if he agreed to stand, but his candidature could not go forward without the permission of the Jesuit authorities. He must give his answer by the beginning of November. This, and the prospects for *Le Phénomène Humain*, were in his mind when he obeyed the invitation of the General to go to Rome in October 1948. 'I shall be glad to see the big chief', he wrote to Père d'Ouince, 'and I shall tell him everything I have in my heart. You take my meaning: I said, *in* the heart and not *on* the heart, for on the heart I have nothing.' What Teilhard had in his heart was, of course, his vision of the universe:

> Absolutely nothing [he told Pierre Lamare] will make me change my mind or hold my tongue on this essential point. They must take me as I am, or not at all. . . . I am going to Rome, but not to Canossa.[1]

Teilhard had never ceased to believe that Rome was the 'axis' of human progress, whatever appearances might suggest to the contrary, but this was his first visit to the capital of Western Christendom. It gave him no shock whatever, either aesthetic or spiritual:

> I'm inoculated against the past, and after the great East the

[1] Letter to Pierre Lamare, 17 September 1948.

picturesque has no further astonishment in store for me. On the other hand I felt immediately at home in the southern and colourful surroundings.

In St. Peter's, although nowhere else, he felt

the paradoxical and humbling assurance of representing the earthly extremity of an arc springing out between man and what is beyond man—the great affair beside which the inflated baroque of the churches, and the penitential wands in the confessionals, and the most bewildering display of ecclesiastical accoutrements that you can imagine, all disappear.[1]

Here, in Rome, were concentrated in a simultaneous equilibrium everything to which Teilhard was attached and everything to which he was opposed. The Gesù, in particular, gave him a sense of repatriation, recalling him—though he had no need of recall—to his Jesuit allegiance, with the altar and relics of St. Ignatius and the chapel of the Madonna della Strada. 'All the great names that have prayed before that picture . . . family memoirs . . . impressions of a religious childhood . . . and, there too most of all, a feeling that the Order is something very great.'[2] One of the things that most delighted him were the immemorial ilex trees in the Borghese Gardens; if only human life were as long as theirs! He liked to sit in Rosetta's Glaceria in the Piazza del Popolo and wonder why it was thought necessary to put a cross on top of the obelisk. Obelisks could stand on their own pagan feet.

He made only one excursion outside the city—to the promontory of Circeo, where a young prehistorian friend, Baron Alberto Blanc, had found a Neanderthal skull among the bones of hippopotami and hyenas on the floor of a cave accidentally opened up by Mussolini. Teilhard lodged in the Borgo Santo Spirito adjoining the Piazza of St. Peter's, with a mixed community—rather too reminiscent of Chabanel Hall. It was a heavy modern building, backing on to a pretty garden with palm-trees, mimosas and tangerines. He had an interview with the General, Father Janssens, who immediately won him over—'honest, direct and human'.[3] And at a cocktail party given at the house adjoining San Luigi dei Francesi he espied Père Garrigou-Lagrange, the formidable Dominican theologian, who was among his

[1] Letter to Père Leroy, 15 October 1948.
[2] Cuénot, p. 269.   [3] *ibid.*

principal adversaries at the Holy Office. 'There is the man', Teilhard remarked to a companion, 'who would like to see me burnt at the stake.' When they were introduced they 'smiled and talked of Auvergne.'[1]

He did not, however, see the Pope, who was still at Castel Gandolfo. It was a pity he did not do so, since to meet Teilhard was to go a long way towards understanding him. About this time a friend of Teilhard's, to whom Pius XII had given a private audience, spoke of his influence in Pekin. The Pope listened carefully and then replied:

> I know that Père Teilhard is a great scientist, but he is not a theologian. In one of his essays he speaks of 'resolving the problem of God'. But for us there is no problem.

This answer from a man of unique authority, and also exceptional intelligence, demonstrates the difficulty Teilhard always found in piercing the ecclesiastical sound-barrier. How strange that the Pope should not have seen that a man may firmly believe in the existence of God and yet admit that his existence raises problems with which the human mind is eternally wrestling! Yet it should be remembered to the credit of Pius XII that he assured a French politician that Teilhard would never be condemned while he was on the papal throne; and that he kept his word.

On the last day of Teilhard's visit permission was refused him to accept the Chair at the Collège de France. It was not that the Jesuits were frightened of palaeontology, or that they were unsympathetic to Teilhard. They were merely afraid of the open pulpit that he would have for the preaching of his ideas, and that the Society as a whole, at a time of acute theological tension, might be involved in the ensuing controversy. Teilhard was not unduly depressed by the decision; he would have been able to occupy the chair for only two years before reaching the age of obligatory retirement. The question of Le Phénomène Humain and Le Milieu Divin was left in suspense. 'Nothing from Rome' echoes like a refrain in his letters about this time. A second report on Le Phénomène Humain was more favourable and even recommended publication. Teilhard had added an epilogue and a number of footnotes which had gone far to satisfy the censors' previous objections. But Cardinal Ruffini had brought out a book against evolution, and Cardinal Ruffini was regarded as papabile. So

[1] Cuénot.

the answer, when it came, was blandly and blankly negative; Teilhard must neither publish nor teach. The visit to Rome—Teilhard's first and his last—had been fruitful in only one sense; it had given him an awareness of the extraordinary focus of spiritual radiation concentrated by the two thousand years of history these places have witnessed. In these days it is here in Rome that we find the Christic pole of the earth; through Rome, I mean, runs the ascending axis of hominization.[1]

[1] *Letters from a Traveller*, p. 299.

CHAPTER XV

THE FUTURE OF MAN

SHORTLY AFTER HIS RETURN from Rome Teilhard received a letter from his old friend and fellow novice, Father C. C. Martindale, who had been marooned in Denmark throughout the war. Teilhard sent him in reply one or two of his brochures, and promised him a copy of *Comment Je Vois*, on which he was then at work. 'I seriously believe that it is orthodox', he wrote, 'but you will know how to make a discreet use of it. The people high up are not so keen on my circulating these things, and after all one must preserve a little obedience.' He went on to speak of his sadness at the prospect of no longer being able to work in the field, 'all the more so as they don't leave me much freedom to speak or to write. . . . I spent October in Rome at the formal request of the Father General. I think this contact was bene-ficial in one way and another, but it has not sensibly improved the situation as far as my liberty is concerned. It was very convenient, before 1940, to be able to go back to China and be forgotten for a while.'

In a word, Teilhard was now paying a price for the publicity which surrounded his name and the eagerness with which he was listened to. In the concluding paragraph of his letter he expressed the convictions that lay behind everything he wrote during these post-war years in Paris:

I remain extremely optimistic about the way our world is going—on a long run [*sic*]—and radically hostile to our existentialists (Christian or non-Christian) and to our eschatologists. But I am more and more convinced that our century will only give itself *en bloc* to a Christian faith powerfully warmed and impregnated with 'human fervour'. This 'human coldness', this agnosticism, or scepticism rather, of the 'official' Catholics when there is any question of an ultra-development of the spiritual forces in human nature seems to me the direct cause of the dechristianization of the masses (and of the *élites*!) And this vexes me all the more since we have everything, in a Christ fully understood, to animate the world exactly as the world is asking to be animated. To baptize the neo-humanism of our time—that is the precise goal that we must reach.[1]

In all his essays of this period Teilhard was haunted by the opposition between Marxism and Christianity, and—less acutely—between Marxism and Democracy. He did not believe that either opposition was necessary or, still less, likely to endure. At the meetings of Unesco, which had its headquarters in Paris, he watched the dialectic at first hand. On his return from Rome he was at work on *Le Cœur du Problème*,[2] in which he faced the first of these oppositions clearly. Moved, perhaps, by the *non possumus* which was all he had brought back from the Borgo Santo Spirito, he wrote more personally and candidly than usual. As one who had spent more than fifty years 'in close and intimate professional contact, in Europe, Asia and America, with what was and still is most humanly valuable, significant and influential—"seminal", one might say—among the people of many countries', he felt he had the right not only to speak but to 'cry aloud' what he had seen and felt; and this was 'the obsessive impression, everywhere around us, of an irresistibly mounting atheism—or more exactly a mounting and irresistible dechristianization'. Christianity had lost nothing of its power to attract, but it was no longer attractive. That was the heart of the problem.

Looking and listening around him in Paris, Teilhard detected the signs of a renaissance, and indeed he could hardly have done otherwise. But these movements were 'subterranean', as he himself—in a sense—was subterranean. He illustrated the contemporary religious crisis by a diagram in which three lines started from the same point of faith, although the faith was not faith in the same things. One line went vertically upward; this was faith in God to the neglect of everything else. One went horizontally; this was faith in man. And a third went between the two, upwards and also outwards; this was the faith in God and man together, and it was the only direction which, in Teilhard's belief, mankind could profitably take. He was careful to

[1] 11 December 1948.
[2] 1949: *The Future of Man*, pp. 266–70.

point out that it represented a synthesis, not a compromise. The second line was the route of neo-humanism, either in its Marxist or its liberal form, and it was the most immediately favoured of the three. Yet it offered no 'escape from total death, no supreme centre of personalization to radiate love among the human cells'; only a heartless and purposeless universe; a 'frozen world that in the end must disintegrate entirely'.

But if the 'distinctive function of the Church' was to know how to 'christianize all that was human in man', and to have the power of its knowledge, what was likely to happen, Teilhard asked—what indeed was happening already—if at the very moment when the *anima naturaliter Christiana* was ready to receive the Christian illumination, 'the authorities of the Church should ignore, disdain, and even condemn, without trying to understand', the new aspiration which it was their business to meet? Because Christianity was 'momentarily subhumanized' it no longer completely satisfied its own adherents; was less able to attract the unbeliever; and less able to resist its enemies. Why was there so much spiritual anxiety among priests and religious? A stream of missionaries had been sent to China; why had they made so few conversions? Why was the Church so powerless to win over the working masses? Simply because the Church, for all the splendour of its charity, had failed to achieve the *human* faith and the *human* hopes without which any religion would, in reason and in fact, appear 'colourless, cold, and incapable of assimilation'. These were strong words, but many other people were feeling the same way; many more would express the same feelings just as strongly at the Second Vatican Council. But fifteen years of internal crisis had yet to pass before the Roman 'axis' was ripe for *aggiornamento*. In the meanwhile a whole population of 'spiritual expatriates' was equally repelled by a Marxism which robbed them of their personality and a Christianity tepid in its human appeal.

When Teilhard spoke of Marxism, he knew what he was talking about; Marxists might be mistaken, but they were not monsters. Teilhard had met them in China, as he had met them in France. He measured their strength and respected their sincerity. He did not believe that the future belonged to them exclusively, but he could not imagine a future in which they would not have a considerable say. He was closer to them by far than he was to the existentialists because he could foresee a point at which the Christian hope and the Marxist optimism would meet. The vertical line and the horizontal line were each capable of inflection because each sprang from an impulse of faith. But where there was no faith there was no hope; and without faith or hope there could be no *élan* in any direction whatever.

The Church, however, maintained her dogmatic opposition to Marxism, and Teilhard did not underestimate the practical reasons for her attitude. But he looked beyond the political issues of the day. Madame Simone Beaulieu—a Canadian painter of outstanding gifts, married to a Canadian diplomat then in Paris *en poste*—was among those to whom he opened his mind:

In Rome they see in Communism nothing more than a product of social 'dissatisfaction', and they think they can bring it to heel with a little more comfort and justice. But (unless I am mistaken) the essence of Communism (a very bad word for what is really a neo-humanism) is the expectation of an 'ultra-humanity' in every domain. It corresponds with a *new* faith and a new hope in man; and it can only be mastered and balanced by a Christianity where faith in God will have incorporated and sublimated this new faith of man in the future of humanity on earth. As I intend to say in a 'filial' report to my General, the situation can be summed up in a few lines: 'Some (the old-style Christians) say: Let us wait for the return of Christ. Others, the Marxists and the people with Marxist leanings, reply: Let humanity fulfil itself. The third group (the neo-Christians) think: Let us fulfil humanity here on earth, so that Christ can come back.' But in Rome they don't yet see that 'faith in man' is a definitely new element in the human soul; they don't feel it; they only see a 'fashion' (my General told me this, word for word); there's the drama. And in the meanwhile those who are deeply convinced that awaiting us in the future are not only *men* but *man*—these are caught between a Stalinism which makes life impossible and a Catholic authority which doesn't understand them. So they group themselves into a mass—growing larger every day—of 'expatriates' and 'straying sheep' for whom the Lord certainly has a great pity. I say all this without a drop of bitterness, and with the optimism that you know; I am more and more convinced that we are seeing the first manifestations of a Christian renaissance destined to spread through the world as completely (or more completely?) than after the first expansion of the Gospel two thousand years ago.[1]

In believing, as he did, that the Christian and the Marxist ways must eventually come together because 'in the nature of things everything that is faith must rise, and everything that rises must converge', Teilhard might have remembered that there had also been a Fascist faith capable of rising very rapidly indeed. Was there any guarantee that such a faith might not rise again? What the statesmen of the world did about the deadlock was a matter Teilhard did not feel competent to discuss. If one suggests that politics were beneath him, one implies an Olympian stance which he would have been the last to assume. But he was looking over the heads of the politicians to the people, not always inarticulate, behind them. He could not believe that men and women capable of working together for scientific research were incapable of doing so for purposes of government. Here we must remember that Teilhard was a man limited by his experience in one way, although he was broadened by it in another. If he had been a parish priest, spending hours in the confessional, would he have felt that Newman's 'vast aboriginal calamity' was no more than a mysterious flaw in the universe which paradoxically both helped and hindered evolution?

When his opinion was officially asked for, as it was by Unesco in 1947, he gave it. What exactly, they wanted to know, was meant by the Rights of Man? These were a legacy of 1789—a time of fierce individual and national self-assertion. Any new definition must take into account 'the conditions under which the inevitable totalization of mankind may be effected, not only without impairing but so as to enhance, I will not say the autonomy of each of us but (a quite different thing) the incommunicable singularity of being which each of us possesses'. The individual, he claimed, had 'no right to remain inactive', since upon his development depended 'the perfection of all his fellows'. This, one may deduce, implied the approval of compulsory education. Society, in return, must be so organized as to favour a development which was in its own interest. And, thirdly, the forces of collectivism must never compel the individual to be untrue to himself; they might persuade, but they must not coerce.[2]

[1] 7 August 1949.
[2] *Quelques réflexions sur les Droits de l'Homme* (*The Future of Man*, pp. 193-5).

A similar questionnaire asked for a new definition of democracy—a word not quite so large as the Rights of Man but just as loosely applied. There were the old democracies and the new democracies, and they were at loggerheads. De Tocqueville had opposed democracy and socialism; Teilhard refused to oppose democracy and socialization.[1] Biologically speaking, he maintained, there could be no true democracy except through 'a balanced combination of two complementary factors which respectively found their pure expression in liberal and authoritarian régimes'. What was needed was 'a judicious mixture of *laissez-faire* and firmness', and an understanding that democratic ideals could only be realized by way of 'countless experiments and probings'. This was the way of life itself, for mankind was still composed of elements very unequally developed despite 'the compressive and unifying conditions' to which it was now subject.

The word 'compressive' should here be noted. Teilhard was not given to cries of alarm, but the population explosion—coupled with the erosion of arable land—filled him with profound misgiving. Were we not wasting our reserves? Would not human progress come to a halt simply through lack of food? How long would it be before chemistry was able to feed us directly from carbon, nitrogen, and other simple elements? Would it ever succeed in doing so? From a total of 400 millions in the seventeenth century the population of the world was likely to reach a figure of two and a half milliards before the end of the twentieth. The compression and unification of mankind, an excellent thing in itself, must not be allowed to 'exceed an optimum beyond which any addition of numbers would only mean famine and suffocation'. The time had been when the command 'to increase and multiply' made scientific sense; it made sense no longer. Teilhard admitted that the problem was not easy of solution. There were technical and psychological difficulties in the way of a healthy eugenics. But we had come to a dangerous turning point; we still had 'feet of clay'—should we be able 'to round the corner'?[2] Even the *Osservatore Romano* admitted that in seventy-five years' time there might be a corner to round, although in the same article it talked about 'colonies of virgins' and 'currents of continence' in marriage.

[1] *L'Essence de l'Idée de Démocratie*, 1949 (*The Future of Man*, pp. 238–43).

[2] *Les Directions et les Conditions de l'Avenir* (*The Future of Man*, pp. 227–37), *Psyché*, October 1948.

Teilhard thought that one could not 'play more frankly with the limits of psychological forces, nor rely more absolutely on the power of a faith that one was doing everything possible to make anaemic'. But at least it was a good sign that someone had recognized that '"increase and multiply" was no longer the supreme rule of sexual morality'.[1]

Teilhard did not look out upon the world created by technology with an eye blind to its defects. He had known—none better—'the poetry of the Neolithic fields', and he saw them vulgarized and defaced by industry. He admitted 'the frightful menace ... of the totalitarian states', in spite of a war which had claimed to reduce them. He looked back at the long history of animal creation and saw it victim to the same servitudes which now threatened the world of men. Were we 'lapsing into a kind of senescence'? This was 'one way of explaining the irresistible movements of concentration that has us in its grip: the quick answer, the simplest and most morbidly fascinating to sensibilities as shaken and bruised as our own at the present time'. It was the answer that satisfied conservatives and existentialists alike, for prophets of disaster not only enjoy—like some other prophets—the sound of their own voices, but they also enjoy the echoes of their own fear. The difference between Teilhard and his existentialist opponents was the difference between one who could perceive, in spite of disconcerting appearances, a sense and a direction in life, and those who could only see its incoherence and absurdity; between those for whom the world was broken and those for whom it was merely cracked. Teilhard could sympathize with people who complained of the 'gregariousness and stupidity of the masses', but he stressed that this was the result not of complexity but of numbers inadequately organized. We were in a situation as crucial as that which faced the contemporaries of Galileo:

> Following the moment when a few men began to see the world through the eyes of Copernicus all men came to see it in the same fashion. A first flash of illumination, intuitively accepted despite the risk of error; and as the intuition was increasingly confirmed by observation and experiment, it came to be embodied in the inherited core of human consciousness. ... May it happen ... that our descendants four centuries hence, being faced with some

[2] Letter to Père Leroy, 6 July 1950.

new parting of the ways that we cannot yet foresee, will look back and say: 'In the twentieth century they saw clearly. Let us seek to follow their example.'

Where others were talking of pluralism as a *modus vivendi* for a divided world, Teilhard was talking of unanimity as the condition of survival for a world that was inexorably drawing closer together.[1] For Teilhard unanimity was not only essential but inevitable in proportion as men allowed themselves to be pulled from in front as well as pushed from behind. It must come from a 'total community of desire'. Invention and research and mutual effort were not enough, for scientists might hate each other in their hearts even when they agreed in their conclusions. This gap between heart and head must be bridged. The newly recovered 'sense of species', which was now asserting its rights over the atomic individualism of the humanist and liberal centuries, must discover 'a veritable *Ego* at the summit of the world . . . needed for the consummation, without confounding them, of all the elemental *egos* of earth'. Camus, the most humane of the literary existentialists, had written that 'If man found that the universe could love he would be reconciled'; and the biologist Steele in Wells's *The Anatomy of Frustration* had sighed for a 'universal lover'. There was never any doubt that Pierre Teilhard de Chardin had found him.

Early in February 1949 Teilhard began a series of lectures on anthropogenesis at the Sorbonne, but these were interrupted by a severe chill which developed into pleurisy. He remained in hospital until 18 April, and afterwards convalesced with the sisters of the Immaculate Conception at St.-Germain-en-Laye. He used this time of inactivity to finish *Le Groupe Zoologique Humain*, working up the material of his lectures into what was in effect a restatement of *Le Phénomène Humain*. If the second book lacks the flame and *élan* of the first, Teilhard himself thought it a more exact presentation of his ideas. When he had dated the last page '4 August 1949', he again retired to Les Moulins:

Everything is so calm here—and the view over to the chain of the Puys is so lovely. In the evening the sun sets splendidly behind them. But why is it so dry? We spend our time looking to see if by

[1] *Comment concevoir et espérer que se réalise sur terre l'unanimisation humaine?*, 1950 (*The Future of Man*, pp. 281–8).

chance any cloud formations are in sight. But there is nothing. Fortunately a spring, close by the house, has not dried up. But the land is so thirsty. If our wine has no sugar in it this autumn, what should we do about it? We have been to see some friends over in the Haute-Loire; they have a charming seventeenth-century château, entirely of the period—down to the bedspreads. And the château is lost among the woods in one of the remotest corners of Auvergne. Green, and almost humid, in spite of the season.

I stay in my room, looking at the view.[1]

George Barbour, with his son, came to visit him:

We spent two unforgettable days, strolling down the avenues, sitting in the garden, listening to him talking about his childhood with Marguerite . . . and could I, in two years' time, visit Africa again?[2]

In October Teilhard was lecturing to the International Congress on the Philosophy of Science with a paper on 'The Vision of the Past'; and in the winter of 1950 he gave five lectures at the Sorbonne on the Pleistocene of the Far East. He also addressed the students at the Cité Universitaire. In March he took part in an international symposium on the sociology of animals. It required more than the Holy Office—it required incapacitating illness—to keep Teilhard quiet for very long.

At the beginning of May 1951 he was invited to stand as a candidate for the mineralogical section of the Institut de France. Opposing him was Guyénot from Geneva. If he should fail at the first attempt, he would be certain of election in three months' time when another vacancy would be open. Since there were no ecclesiastical objections to his doing so, he yielded to the insistence of his friends and agreed to stand. Membership of the Institut might, he thought, 'shield me from some attacks; or, to change the metaphor, give an armour-piercing skin to my projectiles'.[3] He was elected on 22 May, and the event was celebrated with champagne at the Rue Monsieur and several Academicians among the guests. Teilhard thought—not without reason—that his election was a compliment to his philosophy rather than to his science. It was certainly a laurel wreath for the Jesuits, and it was followed by invitations to lecture for them in Brussels and Liège.

[1] Letter to Solange Lemâitre, 17 August 1949.
[2] *In the Field with Teilhard de Chardin*, p. 128.
[3] Cuénot, p. 276.

M. Cuénot suggests that certain of the authorities in Rome took it in the sense that Teilhard took it himself, and were correspondingly displeased. At about the same time he was elected to the Linnean Society in London.

Nevertheless, for lack of work in the field, Teilhard's scientific activities were considerably reduced; it was this, no doubt, that projected his thoughts on to the future of man. He made close friends with René Grousset, the historian of the Crusades and an eminent orientalist. Conversation with Grousset led him to compare the spiritual contributions of the West and the Far East. Beyond the superficial and unsightly materialism of the West he discerned a latent mysticism capable of mastering the earth and offering it to God. This was Teilhard's 'mysticism of research'. By contrast, the Hindu had the metaphysical sense of God whose existence was much clearer than the existence of the world, and needed less justification. 'Be silent if you want to hear the fundamental note. Bury yourself gradually in the depths of your own self, if you want to escape the turmoil of plurality.' The Chinese, by contrast, placed their emphasis on the tangible; but theirs was a 'taste for the human rather than a faith in humanity'. Neither Confucius nor Lao-tze were troubled by the spirit of Prometheus; the roof above their city was impenetrable. The aim of Chinese civilization had been to achieve 'a fine and static equilibrium between the earth, society, and the stars. To pacify rather than to conquer.' In Japan the individual was the servant of society. His mysticism was a mysticism of war; 'Zen Buddhism remoulded into a code of violence and chivalrous abnegation . . . a practical spirit of service and sacrifice impermeable to the supreme detachment of the Hindu and the supreme common sense of the Chinese.'

To all these oriental mystiques Teilhard proffered once again the 'route de l'Ouest'. When he had first analysed his reasons for doing so, orientalism was à la mode. Henri Massis—a spokesman of the French 'Right', who stood for an intellectual and political immobility radically opposed to Teilhard—had written his Défense de l'Occident precisely to counteract these tendencies. He and Teilhard were strange allies. Did the neo-theosophists of Europe realize, Teilhard had then asked, that the Buddhist and the Brahmin, with their 'refined and pessimistic solution' of the mystery of being implied 'the complete death of constructive activity and the fundamental inanity of the experimental universe'? Their Western followers, in Teilhard's experience, were 'generally pessimists or snobs'.[1] Resuming his theme in 1947, he went forward to welcome the new humanism of the West, 'young, original and forceful; still badly formulated in theory and context, but absolutely clear in its principal axes, the hidden spring of the whole modern movement'. Here was the expectation of a God who should be at once 'centre and summit; a God of tension'. Here was the road to a true collectivism, which should be a free union of minds. The West would not be leading the world in science, if it were not 'the spearhead of a creative religious effort'. The advent of Marxism in China, with the humanism of Tagore, showed that the East was turning westward; and Teilhard was not original in describing Marxism as a Western—and illegitimately materialist—*mystique*. There was every reason to believe that the three streams of Oriental thought would converge through the breach opened by the Christian humanism of the West.

We have seen that Teilhard's opinion was tolerated in the Rue Chanez, but Unesco was not always pleased with his answers. He was sometimes mistaken for a racialist because he stated the obvious fact that not all races were biologically and culturally equal. Just as 'to produce a beautiful picture, you must have a wide range of different colours on your palette', so the 'biological richness of mankind' owed much to its 'generic diversity'. It was natural that, in the general advance of mankind, certain groups should emerge as leaders; there should be nothing here to shock racial sensibilities. 'In sociology, as in physics, there are laws we cannot trifle with.'[2] The varying capacities of ethnic groups were part of the phenomenon of man, and Teilhard was too scrupulous a phenomenologist to pretend the contrary.

Whatever objections the ideologists of Unesco might raise, Teilhard was not necessarily misunderstood by the coloured people themselves. Léopold Senghor, President of Sénégal, is at once the philosopher and the poet of *négritude*—and no narrow racialist. Converted to Catholicism by a reading of Teilhard, Senghor was able to see where his thought rejoins the mind of Islam with which Teilhard's own contacts were minimal. For several decades already Moslem reformers had been constructing a parallel synthesis between scientific

[1] Letter to F. Richaud, 12 June 1950.
[2] *ibid.*, p. 301.

socialism and religious faith. How did a Moslem or an animist react on reading Teilhard? Senghor replied:

like the Protestants, among whom a number of eminent minds are *Teilhardistes*. The essential problem, here, is the problem of God; and the question, posed at this level, demands a positive response. The God of the Moslem, like the God of the animist, is definitely *personal*. He is the centre and the love in whom particular centres and loves converge.[1]

Senghor stressed that *négritude* must not be based on a single race, but on the facts of geography and on history, political and economic. He echoed Teilhard's plea that 'a total earth requires fully conscious nations'. Africa must awaken its dormant energies; there, as elsewhere, man must be saved and perfected 'intellectually with Descartes, morally with Pascal, integrally with Teilhard'.[2]

The establishment of Unesco in Paris brought Teilhard one of the most valued friendships of his later years. Already, in 1944, he had corresponded with Julian Huxley after reading *What I Dare Think*, and they met in 1946 when Huxley was appointed the first director-general of Unesco. As early as 1941 Teilhard had found in Huxley's collection of essays, *The Uniqueness of Man*, a line of thought very close to his own, although God was not recognized at the end of it; and Huxley's tribute to Teilhard in *Encounter*[3] showed how far the scientific examination of phenomena could bring a mystic and a rationalist along the same path:

From the moment of my first meeting with Père Teilhard in 1946, soon after I had gone to Paris as head of Unesco, I realized that I had found not only a friend, but a partner in the intellectual and spiritual adventure. Though he had approached the problem of human destiny from the standpoint of a Christian and a Jesuit Father, and I from that of an agnostic and zoologist, we had been thinking along the same lines and had come to astonishingly similar conclusions. This was because we had both been determined to look at human destiny (that is to say, man, his cosmic

[1] 'La Négritude comme voie africaine du socialisme' in *Cahiers Pierre Teilhard de Chardin*, vol. 3.

[2] Allocution on receiving an honorary degree at Laval University, Quebec, September 1966.

[3] April 1956.

background and home, and the relation between them) as a phenomenon, not as a metaphysical, an ethical, or theological problem. In such an approach, man is seen not as a creation alien or separate from nature, but as a part (and a very essential part) of the phenomenon of evolution. And mind and spirit appear not as an irrelevant epiphenomenon nor as a supernatural injection, but as highly important natural phenomena.[1]

Nevertheless, in all these scientific contacts, Teilhard was careful to preserve his independence. When Joliot-Curie invited him to sign the Stockholm Appeal he refused, not for confessional reasons, but because he thought it 'pacifist rather than pacific' and 'oversimplified in its anti-Americanism'. He did not wish to compromise himself with men 'holding an inadequate view of the evolutionary reserves of humanity'.[2]

III

Teilhard now felt that he would soon be strong enough to undertake the African journey. Moreover he realized that he was becoming an embarrassment to the Church authorities, and he wanted a 'shelter out of France'. Pius XII's encyclical, *Humani Generis*—in which the circulation of Teilhard's MSS was implicitly reproved—had dismayed the more progressive minds in the Church, and Teilhard was writing a good number of letters to reassure them. 'For an encyclical entitled *Humani Generis*', he told Solange Lemaître, 'it would be difficult to present a narrower view of humanity.'[3] In so far as the aim of the encyclical was to prevent dogma from 'evaporating into symbolism' Teilhard wholly approved of it; the opposition was not between the encyclical and science but between 'science and the *language* of the encyclical'. The Thomist theologians in Rome, under whose persuasions the Pope had acted, did not seem to realize that 'a way of thought that takes account of cosmogenesis is infinitely more capable of expressing the Creation, the Redemption, the Incarnation and the Communion than Aristotelian Thomism'.[4] The encyclical had 'a strong smell of *intégrisme*', and Teilhard wondered whether a good psychoanalyst

[1] Quoted by Cuénot, p. 303
[2] Letter to F. Joliot-Curie, 16 June 1950.
[3] Letter to Solange Lemaître, 17 August 1949.
[4] Letter to Gérard Soulages, undated.

would not see in it the clear traces of a specific religious perversion —the masochism and sadism of orthodoxy; the pleasure of swallowing, and making others swallow, the truth under its crudest and stupidest forms. I am resolved to continue quite simply along my own way in a direction which seems to me to point exactly towards the dogmatic realism that Rome wants and is asking for.[1]

In a letter to Simone Beaulieu Teilhard presented his usual optimistic face to discouraging events:

The theological atmosphere is extremely tense just now. A large-scale *intégriste* (that is to say, fundamentalist) offensive which doesn't frighten me (nothing can stop the march of the neo-humanism, and consequently of the neo-Christianity, now in full swing) but which obliges us to take to the *maquis* and work more than ever underground. How curious that the theologians have so much difficulty in understanding that man's realization of the biological movements of life, and the principle of relativity, are at least as important for our religious attitude to God (and for our very conception of God) as the definition of some new dogma.

When Teilhard spoke of 'some new dogma', he was referring of course to the dogma of the Assumption that Pius XII was expected shortly to proclaim. 'In itself', he wrote later to Leroy, 'this event does not displease me. I am too conscious of the bio-psychological necessity of the "Marial" (to counterbalance the "masculinity" of Jehovah) not to feel the deep need for this gesture. But won't it be taken as a challenge to all our physics and all our biology?'[2]

In retreat at Les Moulins Teilhard returned to the Spiritual Exercises of St. Ignatius. As a scheme they were splendid, but the cosmology seemed to him so childish that he literally stifled in it:

What we need is a complete transposition of the Ignatian theme for an organic universe . . . and I think this transposition is perfectly possible.[3]

It would not have been possible just then. The atmosphere in ecclesiastical circles was reminiscent of the worst years under Pius X. Five professors—men of great distinction—had been forced to leave the

[1] Letter to Père Leroy, 29 August 1950.
[2] 18 August 1950.
[3] Letter to Père Leroy, 29 August 1950.

Lyon scholasticate, and Teilhard's own writings were being indiscriminately—and sometimes inaccurately—circulated. He could not understand how they had got into the hands of the nuns! Cardinal Feltin—who was wholly sympathetic to the Jesuits of the Rue Monsieur, and had been to lunch with them—advised the preachers of his archdiocese to be '*against* Communism, *reserved* for evolution, and *for* Thomism'. It was 'the mixture as before', and Teilhard had no wish to swallow it. So it was now that Barbour's original proposal gave him the opportunity for escape he was looking for:

I feel [he wrote to him] the moment has come for me to disappear for a time from Paris, where things are getting 'too hot' for me personally. For the last six months the press has been speaking too much about me and my indiscretions. From that point of view, it would be better to give Rome the impression that I am delving back into what people down there call 'pure science'.[1]

Teilhard had known for some years of the first Australopithecus skull which had been discovered to the north of Kimberley in 1924. The full importance of this, however, had only been revealed in 1946, and Breuil, who had been closely connected with the subsequent diggings, near Johannesburg, had of course kept Teilhard fully informed about them. *Australopithecus* was not recognized—and has not yet been recognized—as hominian; the cerebral capacity was too small, the muzzle too elongated, and there was no evidence that he used fire. But in his bone structure he was closer to man than any other known hominid; and his discovery gave Teilhard a *raison d'être* for work in a field which was specifically his own.

When he informed the Roman authorities that he intended to busy himself with the Australopithecines, they were visibly reassured. In the meantime, the Viking Foundation in New York raised a subsidy of 2,500 dollars for the voyage, and Teilhard was invited to draw up a plan of research for the expedition. It so happened that Rhoda de Terra had reasons of her own for visiting South Africa at the same time, and it was arranged that she should travel with Teilhard to look after his practical needs. They met in Paris and crossed to London where Barbour had already arrived. Teilhard stayed with the Jesuit Fathers at 114 Mount Street, where he would have found Father Martindale eager to revive memories of the Aix novitiate, and Julian

[1] 11 November 1950, *In the Field with Teilhard de Chardin*, p. 132.

Huxley gave a dinner for him. Among other scientific friends he saw were Kenneth Oakley at the British Museum and Tindall Hopwood with whom he was able to discuss the Kenya primates. On 10 July Barbour said good-bye to the two travellers at Waterloo Station, and they embarked on the s.s. *Carnarvon Castle* from Southampton two days later.

Teilhard's friends in the Society were well aware that his hold on life was as precarious as his appetite for it was unabated, and shortly before his departure Père Jouve, the director of *Études*, urged him to secure the future of his writings. A canonist was consulted and replied that ecclesiastical law was in two minds as to whether a man who had taken a vow of poverty had the right to dispose of his own manuscripts. At the instance of Père Jouve, and in perfect accord with his own conscience, Teilhard chose the more favourable of these interpretations, and appointed his devoted secretary, Mlle Jeanne Mortier, as his literary executrix. After he was dead the censors of the Holy Office might do as they liked; the *odium theologicum* would have no further power to hurt him. His cause would no longer be debated *in camera*—and before a packed jury.

CHAPTER XVI

LAST DAYS IN THE FIELD

TEILHARD arrived in Cape Town on 31 July, and in Johannesburg a day later. Barbour, who had flown from London, was there to meet him. Teilhard—obedient to his doctor's orders but restive under the leash—stayed quiet for a few days and then drove with Dr. van Riet Lowe to Krugersdorp, and on to the Sterkfontein excavations. Later they proceeded to the Makapan site, beyond Pretoria, 180 miles to the north. This was the real African bush, with the aloes and euphorbias in flower, and the round huts of the natives reminding Teilhard of the Harar. At other times he could hardly believe he was not back in northern China and, as circumstances required, he took to saying over to himself *La Messe sur le Monde*, polishing and deepening the text as he went along. Most of the fauna had disappeared, except for an occasional springbok, and the monkeys and baboons. At the end of August he spent a week round Kimberley where the diamond diggers had exposed a number of stone implements in the gravel beds of the Vaal. The landscape, under its canopy of unchanging blue, was monotonous but impressive—'great expanses, with barely an undulation, of tall yellow grasses and thorny mimosas in which less than a hundred years ago elephants and giraffes still roamed'.[1] In September Teilhard was taken up as far as Taungs on the edge of the Kalahari desert. Here the first Australopithecus had been found in pockets similar to the caves at Chou-Kou-Tien. Early in October he returned to Capetown, lodging at an hotel on the slope of Table Mountain. It was already spring, with the bright red flowers of the Kaffir trees in bloom.

Such was the bare itinerary of his visit. What he was out to investigate was a 'true wave of hominization forming somewhere in the region of Lake Victoria or Tanganyika . . . which progressively shed its centrifugal sheets from age to age, until towards the end of the

[1] *Letters from a Traveller*, p. 310.

Australopithecus sites in South Africa

Quaternary it covered the entire surface of the earth'.[1] The researches of Dr. R. Broom had given him the data of the problem even before he set out, and he had examined them in an article for *Études* (June 1950):

> For hundreds of miles on the Transvaal border and in the north of Cape Colony a dolomitic platform, formerly eroded by underground streams, contains thousands of caves or fissures more or less full of fossil-bearing deposits of different ages (Pliocene or more recent). It is in one of these pockets, at Taungs (in the southeast Transvaal) that the first skull of Australopithecus was recognized (in 1924) and immediately described as 'hominid' by Dr. Dart of Johannesburg.[2]

Between 1936 and 1949 Dr. Broom had added a number of remarkable finds—fifty specimens belonging to at least fifty individuals. He believed that upon this evidence he could establish a continuous zoological link between the anthropomorphous apes and the hominians. Teilhard had doubted, from the start, the validity of Broom's argument. There was no proof that a jaw which, in Europe, would have been attributed without question to Neanderthal Man, belonged to the series which Broom had discovered. Moreover the anatomy of Australopithecus and his family was much more simian than human. Broom thought he had laid his finger on the 'missing link', but Teilhard suspected—without, of course, having as yet been on the spot—that Australopithecus represented 'an attempt at man' rather than man himself. He returned to his old simile of overlapping branches or interlapping scales. Australopithecus belonged not to 'the main trunk' of humanity; he was a 'peripheral branch.'[3]

These preliminary suggestions were confirmed by the African visit. It was certainly true that Australopithecus differed from all known anthropomorphs. His dental formation was hominid, and his pelvis indicated an upright stance. He must also have possessed considerable skill to have survived in a country where so many powerful animals disputed his sway. Nevertheless—Teilhard was careful to point out—'hominid' was not the same thing as 'human'. No traces of fire or hand-fashioned implements had been found in association with the Australopithecines, and neither their cranial capacity nor the reduced

[1] *The Appearance of Man*, p. 197.   [2] *ibid.*, p. 126.
[3] *ibid.*, pp. 128–30.

structure of their faces indicated that they had 'crossed the boundary separating anthropomorphs from hominians'.[1] This agreed with what was known or suspected about their geological environment. The fossil-bearing deposits in which the Australopithecines had been discovered were quite different from those containing human tools. The two had not yet been 'found in juxtaposition or one above the other in the same bed'; and the Australopithecines seemed to represent 'a particularly progressive population of large anthropomorphs occupying southern Africa just before man appeared on the same territory to displace and replace them'.[2]

But if they could not be identified as the 'actual root of the human phylum', they indicated a type morphologically very close to humanity; and since it was becoming more and more certain that Africa had been 'the principal centre of anthropoid development', this was 'an additional argument in favour of the thesis that the human group originated there'. After his second visit to Africa in 1953, Teilhard summed up as follows:

In South Africa it seems evident that the Australopithecines did not give birth to man. He quite simply took over from them. For all that, however, the overlapping of the two types does not diminish the singular anthropological importance of the great extinct apes of the Transvaal . . . in some way or another, their existence entails and announces the imminent if not immediate proximity of man in the same region.[3]

There was further evidence for this in the Pebble Industry. The use of stones flaked at the edge at one or more points had been proved by African prehistorians, and this was so widespread as to mark a recognizable archaeological terrain. Teilhard had no doubt whatever that these pebbles had been flaked deliberately, and they had been collected in great quantities from beds more ancient than those in which the first two-faced tools appeared. The stone industry in Africa was not only more complete but, in its initial products, more primitive than anywhere else—not excepting Chou-Tou-Kien. A certain *Man X* had unquestionably lived in Africa at the dawn of the Quaternary, although we possessed no fragment of his bones:

We must perhaps imagine him as Pithecanthropine in form, but with much more progressive, much more adaptive features than

[1] *ibid.*, p. 182.   [2] *ibid.*, p. 183.   [3] *ibid.*, p. 200.

those of any Pithecanthropine. For it is from him, after all, that the particularly vigorous form of humanity which, as we can see, occupies the whole of the world today, must certainly have sprung (and perhaps much earlier than we think).[1]

Taking into account the abundance of two-faced implements in the same countries, Teilhard was led to postulate a second, and particularly progressive, wave of humanity—*Man Y*—and it might be that here would be found the 'roots of *Homo sapiens* himself'.[2]

It was no longer the indefatigable Teilhard of the *Croisière Jaune* who visited the 'Cave of Hearths' at Makapan, so called from the traces of ashes which were found there. From the cockpit of a small aeroplane Barbour had detected a track passable for jeeps; and Teilhard was thus able to climb down to the cave and so to the field laboratory on the floor of the valley. Moreover, these expeditions were spaced in order to spare him fatigue. In the intervals he would relax in an hotel and work at whatever essay he happened to be writing. Several photographs show him in the company of Dr. van Riet Lowe, through whom the invitation to visit Africa had originally come. He reminds one now, in his shirt sleeves and pullover, or wrapped in a dark overcoat, of a benevolent headmaster. In one of them, where he is clasping a fossil at Sterkfontein, his eyes look out into the infinite distances of his thought—for his mind was still fixed, more and more intensively, upon the future of man.

In the middle of October he left Johannesburg by way of Durban, where the Curator of the Museum took him to see the face of a quarry exposed for a length of 100 metres. He was particularly interested in the huge rounded boulders which had slipped down into the quarry. These seemed to represent an old, and possibly Pliocene, river level. 'The white sand-dune calcareous deposits, capped with red sands, were beautifully exposed, overlying a pocket of the large boulders you told me of.'[3] On the way down to Capetown by boat—the same *Carnarvon Castle* which had brought him out—he saw the famous Crossopterygian fish[4] at East London—a survivor from the armoured fish from which the amphibian had seemingly emerged—and the

---

[1] *ibid.*, p. 202.   [2] *ibid.*, p. 204.
[3] Letter to Van Riet Lowe, 5 October 1951.
[4] *Crossopterygii*: a family of fish whose respiratory system and skeleton 'foreshadow' the land vertebrates (*Letters from a Traveller*, p. 313).

Pleistocene fauna at Elandsfontein. From the Mount Nelson hotel in Capetown he made several excursions, meeting at Stellenbosch University a teacher of geology called Tilyaard, descended—like many others of the name—from the same Pierre-Louis Taillard who had come to South Africa in the eighteenth century. It was a satisfaction to know that 'stones' ran in the blood.

Before sailing for Buenos Aires Teilhard wrote the following letter to the Father General of the Jesuits:

I feel that the moment has come for me to let you know in a few words what I'm thinking and where I stand—without forgetting that you are 'the General', but at the same time—as I did three years ago during our too short conversation—with that filial candour which is among the most precious treasures of the Society.

Truly (and by reason of the very structure of my thought) I feel myself today more irremediably bound to the hierarchical Church, to the Christ of the Gospel than I have ever been at any moment of my life.

Of course I cannot (save at the cost of interior catastrophe) stop searching for myself. But I no longer (and this has been the case for several months) busy myself with the propagation of my ideas (only with a personal deepening of them).[1]

Teilhard spent a week in Buenos Aires, where he made the acquaintance of Dr. Menghin, a well-known German prehistorian. He saw the local collections in which there was nothing dating further back than ten thousand years. For Teilhard this was recent—'the other terminus of the human expansion' whose origins he had been studying in Africa. For the rest, he saw little except 'Evita' and 'Peron' scrawled up in hysterical hero-worship on the walls of the city. He left Buenos Aires in the s.s. *Uruguay*, of the Moore-MacCormick Line, towards the middle of November. It was a large ship in which the few passengers were entertained by a 'conjuror, a Broadway singer, and a pair of dancers of incredible suppleness'[2]; and the boat bringing Teilhard from Capetown to Buenos Aires had included a pair of hyenas—so he had not wanted for company. 'My African journey', he told Bruno de Solages, 'seemed like a dream. This diving

[1] 12 December 1951.
[2] *Letters from a Traveller*, p. 318.

back into the great biological and geological realities has made me young again.'[1]

II

Having learnt 'from a sure and friendly source that Rome has no wish to see me in Paris at the moment, or for the moment',[2] Teilhard now arranged to stay with the Jesuit Fathers in New York, in their house adjoining the Church of St. Ignatius at 980 Park Avenue. For this he had to thank the good offices of Father John LaFarge, a remarkable priest known and respected for his courageous stand on the colour question. The only room available was of infinitesimal proportions, but Teilhard could always expand, both physically and intellectually, in his quarters at the Wenner-Gren. He had as his immediate superior Father Gannon, who had recently retired from the Presidency of Fordham University. The Jesuits have a rule—more honoured in the breach than the observance—that wherever they may happen to be they should go once a month to their superior for spiritual advice. Father Gannon did not feel himself qualified to tell Teilhard much about the spiritual life that Teilhard did not know already, and he was impressed by the punctiliousness with which he made his monthly visits. Teilhard could not help feeling 'something of a parasite', and he missed the electrical atmosphere of Paris 'so rich and so dense'— but the American Jesuits showed him every kindness even when they did not understand (or approve) what he was talking about. Moreover they raised no objections when Dr. Fejos, director of research at the Wenner-Gren Foundation, asked him to join it as a research associate. This would have 'the great advantage of keeping them quiet in Rome and putting me in touch with all the interesting people that I shall want to meet'.[3] The foundation was only a quarter of an hour's walk from 980 Park Avenue, and the Museum of Natural History was no further away on the other side of Central Park.

Teilhard envisaged his work on three planes, the last of which could hardly be described as strictly scientific; to organize research on fossil man and the origins of mankind; to discover and verify a 'convergence' in man of evolution turning in upon itself; and to 're-think Christology and Christianity' in terms of this convergence. He clarified

[1] 2 February 1952.   [2] *ibid.*   [3] *ibid.*

these aims in a letter to Bruno de Solages, wishing to see anthropology 'finally emerge from literary humanism and medical anatomy to become a true science of man'. The problem, as he saw it, was as follows:

Do the peculiar mental (or affective) attractions, and tensions operating (in a conscious way) between highly complex corpuscles (a) merely represent some peculiar transformation (interioriza-tion) of thermodynamic energy; or (b) on the contrary correspond to the emergence of some new type of energy (escaping the statistical laws of conservation and entropy), the two forms of energy being interconnected by the increase or decrease of internal complexity?[1]

Where the reform of Christology was concerned, Teilhard spoke of the 'radical impossibility, for me, at the present moment of believing, loving and adoring in any other way. (I and a crowd of others with me. I meet them at every corner, even over here—except the Irish, of course).'[2] The Foundation promised to put him in touch with the 'intellectual cream'[3] of such minds as were then in New York—and the cream was pretty thick. He addressed the New York Academy of Sciences on the Australopithecines, and the Wenner-Gren Foundation itself on the prehistory of South Africa. He also took a session on anthropology at a seminar for the Museum of Natural History. In Washington the Catholic University—not always noted for its liberal outlook—gave a cocktail party for him. By the spring of 1952 he was fairly in the swim, with visits to Harvard and Yale and a week-end with Frick on Long Island. Fairfield Osborn, director of the Bronx Zoo, was there and the three men 'had a great deal of talk . . . in a series of enormous rooms packed with flowers'.[4] Teilhard may have been missing Paris, but he sometimes wondered whether he were not getting too fond of New York.

When important visitors from France came through he often met them. Jules Moch was trying to do business with the Russians over disarmament, and Teilhard found conversation with him 'like a wel-come breath of fresh air'. Untouched as he was by the anti-Communism

[1] Letter to Dr. John Q. Stewart, 29 February 1952.
[2] Letter to Bruno de Solages 26 November 1952.
[3] *Letters from a Traveller*, p. 320.
[4] *ibid.*, p. 326.

à la mode, Teilhard was amused by the suspicion with which his residence in New York was at first regarded by the State Department. It was dangerous to have lived so long in China, even if you were a Jesuit. Teilhard saw that the trouble with the Russians was the Soviet 'morality of deception'. Whatever new thoughts he may have had about Christian dogma, he had none about Christian morals. When he had occasion to give advice to people in difficulty—and this happened much more often than appeared to those who only knew him as 'scientist and seer'—his words were carefully weighed and the thought behind them was based not on his own experience alone, but on the traditional wisdom of the Church. We have seen how he had consoled his family in their cruel bereavements; here he was speaking as a son to parents who shared his faith. But when this faith was not fully shared, he always took account of such common ground as he found and delicately trod on it. Early in 1953 Barbour's son, Freeland, whom Teilhard had known as a boy in China, died during his third year of training at the Harvard Medical School. Teilhard knew that he could count on Barbour's discernment of the *milieu divin*:

> I am convinced that . . . what looks like a meaningless catastrophe will transform itself into a kind of blessing. And my wish and hope is that, despite the blow, you will still find (purified, maybe, but still intact) the taste for activity and work—and that, because you will know how to recognize and *adore* a higher form of love, in what has just happened to you.[1]

It was not always to important or 'interesting' people that Teilhard offered his advice: and to all who did not believe as he did, he tried to communicate something of his faith in life. He urged a friend—not a Christian—who was seriously ill:

> not to *strain* against suffering. Try to close your eyes and abandon yourself—as it were to a great and loving energy. This is neither a weak nor a silly attitude . . . it's still too soon for you to get up; try to 'sleep'. Sleep with the active sleep of trust—the sleep of the seed in the winter fields.

Or again:

> The death of selfishness is understanding that we are an element in a universe which is becoming personal—if I may so put it—

---

[1] *In the Field with Teilhard de Chardin*, p. 147.

through union with God. (I don't say in becoming God.) So the self that we love in ourselves is no longer ourselves.

I hope that life may become for you, not merely a sort of blind and favourable fatality, but a kind of presence and animated benevolence on which you can not only rely but to which you can entrust yourself.

What matters is not to do remarkable things, but to do ordinary things with the conviction that their value is enormous.

In writing of Edmund Campion, Evelyn Waugh referred to the 'profound and accurate piety of the Society of Jesus'; in these maxims of Pierre Teilhard de Chardin its echoes are plain to hear.

III

On 3 July 1952 Teilhard left for Chicago where he arrived on the eve of the Republican Convention. His native optimism could hardly have matched the optimism with which the supporters of General Eisenhower flaunted his candidature from their buttonholes and the bonnets of their cars. Teilhard remained only for the night in a city which he may well have found hotter—in every sense—than New York. He proceeded to the more salubrious plateaux of the Rockies and spent a couple of days with Dr. Simpson, a palaeontologist friend, who had a house near Albuquerque. From there he went on to Berkeley, where he installed himself for the better part of four weeks. The Golden Gate was visible from his window, and he reflected that this was the first time that it was not to open for him. The nearest he came to China were the Chinese restaurants of San Francisco, little though he liked Chinese cooking. These put him straight back in the atmosphere of Pekin or Shanghai, and into a phase of his itinerant existence at once so familiar and so far away.

The chief interest of Berkeley was a visit to the nuclear energy research centre in the hills above the city. Here, in the power and complexity of a single gigantic cyclotron, everything Teilhard had divined about the significance of atomic energy was dramatically apparent, although not immediately to be understood; 'mathematical speculation, laboratory research, the wide scope of industrial enterprises, military ambition, medical hopes of therapy—and even the secret hope of finding the ultimate explanation of things'.[1] And all

[1] *Letters from a Traveller*, p. 331.

this was the result of unanimity between a hundred different minds bent upon a single task. The contemplation of the monstrous engine moved Teilhard to a flight of apocalyptic prose. It was as though, in his mind,

> another group of images gradually took the place of the atomic accelerator which I was looking at. My guide went on talking to me about interlocking fields, and all the time I could not help feeling, and perceiving, beyond and around this electromagnetic whirlwind, the concentric afflux of another and no less formidable radiation—that of the Human sucked in on me in a vast wind from the four corners of space. Before my distraught eyes the Berkeley cyclotron had completely disappeared, and in its place my imagination saw the whole noosphere, which, coiled in upon itself by the breath of research, formed a single and enormous cyclone, whose property it was to produce not nuclear energy, but psychic energy in a continually more reflective state, in other words the ultra-human itself. And what was remarkable was that, faced by this colossal reality that should have made my mind reel, I experienced on the contrary a calm and joy—a *deep-seated* calm and joy.[1]

On 8 August Teilhard went up to Montana where he spent a week investigating the geology of Glacier Park. With two other geologists he stayed in the chalets on the shores of Lake McDonald close to the Canadian border. He was interested to study the Pre-Cambrian Collenia; to compare these with what he had seen in South Africa and the Far East; and to ascertain how far the elements of biology, chemistry and geological developments which he observed in them had reacted one upon the other. He then crossed the continent to the north of Maine, close to Mount Desert Island. Here he lived in a cabin, deep in the forest, on the edge of a fjord, and made excursions to Bar Harbour, Mount Cadillac, Beaver's Bay and Porcupine Island. What he studied particularly were the moraines and the granite formations of the rock. It was a great pity, he thought, that no one had yet written about the 'granitization' of America, for traces of this were everywhere. He had written of China that 'Asia has never been, since the beginning of time, as vast, as wide, or as high as it is at the present moment'. The same was true of Africa and America; Teilhard did not believe that

[1] Cuénot, pp. 342–3.

the continental masses of the earth would collapse. It was time, he thought, for the geologists to synthesize. They were 'so busy counting the waves that they did not notice the tide'.[1]

During the winter of 1952-3 Teilhard did not leave New York. Like many others, he shed a tear for Stevenson's defeat at the November elections, and he was disturbed by the appointment of Foster Dulles as Secretary of State. A 'strong line' with Moscow seemed a 'risky game', for the only way for humanity to increase its force was to reduce the tendency to violence among its members. The French visitors came and went—Jean-Louis Barrault and his company; Madame Georges Bidault, whom Teilhard had known in Paris; and Louis Massignon, the great Islamic scholar. Massignon had been converted to Catholicism in dramatic circumstances, and after meeting his Christ on the road to Damascus had become the spokesman—and indeed the prophet—of a Mariology which Teilhard might have found unbalanced. On learning that Massignon was *en route* for Bethlehem, Teilhard neatly described him as 'the wandering knight always in quest of his Lady'.[2] When they met in New York, he found him 'gay and almost sparkling, as I had never seen him before. I greatly enjoyed talking to him.'[3] Other Frenchmen, living in or near New York, were Maritain and the novelist-diplomat Romain Gary. Some readers have seen a portrait of Teilhard in Gary's Père Tassin,[4] but the likeness is a very distant one—if it is a likeness at all.

Teilhard was steadily at work on articles which were published in the *Revue des Questions Scientifiques* and the *Revue Scientifique*; and he was anxious to write a short book on 'the future of the human species'.[5] He thought he might do this 'without coming under fire from the theologians'.[6] As winter turned into spring, he made his annual visit to Frick on Long Island where, as usual, the azaleas had been brought out of the green-houses to decorate the rooms. He had friends in plenty; notably Rhoda de Terra who was his 'great resource (and source of calm)'.[7] But he was homesick for Paris; nothing in New

[1] Letter to Henri Termier, 11 November 1954.
[2] Letter to Solange Lemaître, 17 August 1949.
[3] *ibid.*, 11 January 1953.
[4] *The Roots of Heaven.*
[5] Letter to Solange Lemaître.
[6] *Letters from a Traveller*, p. 337.
[7] Letter to Bruno de Solages, 26 November 1952.

York was comparable to the ferment of French Catholicism—although he was delighted by a meeting with the priests attached to *America*, and flattered to take part in a symposium on evolution at Fordham University. Meanwhile both in France and in Rome,

> the right-wing reaction continues to be superficially felt, but it does not appear to have deep roots. I'm getting very comforting information from over there (even from certain highly placed superiors).[1]

Teilhard's optimism and good sense preserved him from impatience—more certainly now, maybe, than in earlier years:

> But perhaps one shouldn't go too fast ... the Church is a large body, unequally developed. American Catholicism, extraordinarily alive at the present moment, is still childish—intellectually speaking. Maybe it can only evolve slowly.[2]

He was greatly impressed by a reading of Father Langmead-Casserley's *The Retreat of Christianity from the Modern World*. The author was an Anglican and had written that 'the only issue for religion today is in a Christianity which surpasses itself'. The expression, Teilhard commented, 'is perfect. It makes me jealous; I ought to have found it myself.'[3]

But if there were no immediate prospect of Paris, plans were afoot for a second visit to South Africa. Diggings—financed by the Wenner-Gren Foundation, mainly at the instigation of Teilhard himself—had been started north of Pretoria, and he had been given the task of organizing anthropological research in the whole of Africa south of the Sahara. The initial aim was to examine the human bones, including a skull, and tools recently discovered by Hopefield near Capetown; to inspect more thoroughly the 'Cave of Hearths' at Makapan; and to classify the fossil-bearing deposits lately identified or explored in the Transvaal and, if possible, in Rhodesia. Teilhard was not particularly excited at the thought of the journey, but he felt he needed 'this humble platform to make people listen to me'. He left New York by the Farrel Line on 1 July 1953—eighteen days of uneventful voyage with nothing in sight but Ascension Island and St. Helena—and arrived in Capetown on 18 July to find the hibiscus, camellias and aloes everywhere in flower. During the next few days he examined

[1] Letter to Pierre Lamare, 23 December 1952.
[2] *ibid.*, 23 December 1952.
[3] Letter to Solange Lemaître, 11 January 1953.

Hopefield's latest find—the cap of a skull unearthed from the consolidated sand-dunes. This seemed to indicate that the African men capable of fashioning two-edged tools formed part of a complex—Teilhard again used his simile of overlapping scales—where a man who might be classed as Proto-Sapiens was existing side by side with another man of Neanderthal type—to which Hopefield's skull had evidently belonged. Teilhard next proceeded to the diggings north of Pretoria. Already he envisaged a five-year plan to establish a depot at Makapan where the geological layers from the Pleistocene to the Upper Palaeolithic could be shown one above the other. He hoped to see an international team of experts working in Africa similar to the group with which he had co-operated himself in the Far East.

In defiance of doctor's orders, he flew up by Comet to Lusaka—still a skeleton capital—in Northern Rhodesia. Desmond Clark, director of the Rhodes-Livingstone Museum at Livingstone, showed him Freeman's Hole where they found a number of pebbles broken *in situ*, and Teilhard, writing to Kenneth Oakley at the British Museum, described their discovery in the opening by Twin River of the missing half of a tool which Oakley and Clark had come upon a few months earlier. This might enable one to bridge the gap between the Australopithecines and the Pebble Industry. Here was the central problem for palaeo-anthropology; the other question raised by the discovery of hand-axes was less important, even if it were more spectacular, and easier of solution. Nothing in the monotonous and burnt-up landscape seemed to have changed since the days of Livingstone, but the end of the dry season was approaching and here and there, above the yellow grass of the limitless bush, a few trees were turning green. Upstream from the Victoria Falls—where they spent a couple of days —the hippopotami were bathing in the Zambezi, and the crocodiles emerging from the slime. To the end of his days Teilhard had the eye of a naturalist, but if he had been travelling in Rhodesia today he might have found the Zambezi river less interesting than the Zambezi dam.

Returning south, he was disappointed to learn that no further human remains had been discovered at Makapan—although it seemed possible that the most promising section of the cave had not yet been excavated, and in fact important evidence of the Pebble Industry was found there in 1954. It was in the hopes of this that Teilhard advised the Wenner-Gren to concentrate their resources on the work that van Riet Lowe was doing. The two men had become fast friends, and Teilhard was soon addressing him by his Christian name—a familiarity taken more easily for granted in New York than in South Africa. It was known that Teilhard was in Africa as something more than an observer, and that he had the power to recommend the allocation of considerable funds. His help was naturally solicited from many sides—very often from friends or respected colleagues. But he refused to allow such aid as was feasible to be dispersed. His native— and occasionally naïve—candour was balanced by a certain diplomatic finesse which enabled him to refuse without offence. In his own life he had had many difficult waters to navigate, and he tried to manage others as he would that others would manage him.

He saw nothing on his second African visit to modify his previous conclusions—provisional as all such conclusions must be in a matter where so much evidence is lacking. He believed that there were two poles of anthropogenesis. One was in Asia, and this was abortive because it had not led to *Homo sapiens*. The other was in Africa where hominization had been pushed to the limit. It looked as if there had been two centres. But Teilhard did not believe that there had been more than one phylum of human development; he thought that the original phylum had thrust out a second branch in the immediate neighbourhood of its origins—and that these were in Africa. It seemed probable that *Homo sapiens* had been born in the Uganda–Kenya area —which, for reasons of health, Teilhard had not been able to visit; that he had then expanded to the north; and that the black race of the Bantus, in themselves a mutation of *Homo sapiens*, came in to fill the gap. In fine, the monophyletic theories of Teilhard—though resting essentially intact—became a little more elastic as a result of what he had seen in Africa. It remained to discover, as Claude Cuénot has pointed out, whether 'certain races such as the Bushmen were marginal survivors to one side of the monophyletic *Homo sapiens* group or whether they are marginal forms of this same phylum'.[1] But this was a question which Teilhard did not discuss. He was very much aware of being a watcher where others were workers, and as far as possible he left others to do the talking.[2]

[1] Cuénot, p. 338.
[2] For an exhaustive discussion of Teilhard's second African visit, see Cuénot, pp. 327–46.

The excursion into Northern Rhodesia had been the chief excitement of his visit and on his return to the Transvaal early in September he found the bush 'rather impoverished'[1] by comparison. The Tritonia flowers covered the hillsides, as they used to cover the *puys* above Sarcenat, but the aloe blossom had faded and the mimosas had not yet come out. After a further stay at Pretoria he was back in Capetown on 21 September. Here, at the medical school of the university, he examined the latest results of Hopefield's findings. He also visited the museum of Bloemfontein in the Orange Free State, and had conversations with T. F. Dreyer who, in 1932, had discovered the fragment of a fossilized skull twenty-five miles to the north of the city. In the last week of September he embarked on the *Tijsedam*, the little Dutch cargo boat which had taken him from Batavia to Shanghai in 1936 and now plied between Tokyo and South America. The Chinese crew and stewards were a further reminder of his long Far Eastern exile. It was an eighteen-day voyage to Buenos Aires with nothing to see but the albatrosses and the grey sky.

Teilhard had hoped to cross the Andes and come up the western coast of South America; but a bridge had collapsed in the mountains, and the sailing of the boat he counted on catching from Valparaiso had been cancelled owing to a dock strike. So he took a Moore-MacCormick liner from Buenos Aires, which called at Rio and Trinidad on the way to New York. It was wholly characteristic of Teilhard that although, as a priest, he was entitled to a reduction of his fare he preferred not to avail himself of the privilege. This return from his last days in the field was crossed with an embarrassing reminder of his first, when the forgery of Piltdown Man was finally attested. He was invited to give his views in an article, but he preferred to make no public statement. Dawson had died during the First World War, and Teilhard had too fond a memory of their excavations to believe in his bad faith. In answer to a letter from Kenneth Oakley announcing the exposure, he replied:

> No one would think of suspecting Smith-Woodward. I knew pretty well Dawson—a methodical and enthusiastic character. When we were in the field I never noticed anything suspicious in his behaviour. The only thing which puzzled me, one day, was when I saw him picking up two large fragments of skull out of a

[1] *Letters from a Traveller*, p. 346.

sort of rubble in a corner of the pit (these fragments had probably been rejected by the workmen the year before). I was not in Piltdown when the jaw was found. But a year later when I found the canine, it was so inconspicuous among the gravels which had been spread on the ground for sifting that it seems to me quite unlikely that the tooth would have been planted. I can even remember Sir Arthur congratulating me on the sharpness of my eyesight.

Don't forget: the pit at Piltdown was a perfect dumping place for the farm and cottages. It was flooded in winter, and water in the wealden clay can stain at a remarkable speed. In 1912, in a stream near Hastings, I was unpleasantly surprised to see a fresh-sawed bone (from the butcher's) stained almost as deep brown as the human remains from Piltdown. Had a collector possessing some ape bones thrown his discarded specimens into the pit? The idea sounds fantastic; but, in my opinion, no more fantastic than to make Dawson the perpetrator of a hoax.

If there had been a hoax one would normally expect to see a rise in the tempo of the discoveries: something still better than the jaw and canine. But this was not the case.[1]

In a further letter Teilhard confirmed that, on his second visit to the second Piltdown locality in late July 1913, the pieces of skull and a tooth had already been found. He remembered Dawson pointing out the little heaps of raked pebbles as the place of the discovery. Oakley maintained that it was no accident that the ape's jaw was found at Piltdown; the grinding of the teeth and the chemical stains were sufficient evidence of fraud. It was also discovered that the pointed flint, found in the layer just overlying the dark gravel, had been stained with dichromate; and it was curious that not until 1915 had Dawson said anything to Smith-Woodward about the specimens found on the second site. For the rest, a distinguished prehistorian was to write five years later: 'The discovery, in the same bed of soil, of the skull of a man unquestionably *sapiens* and of a jaw no less unquestionably simian faced the palaeontologists with a particularly thorny problem.'[2] Teilhard himself wrote an ironic epitaph to the story when he expressed his surprise that *Homo sapiens* should have made his first appearance on English soil. Others went so far as to say that as there was a Jesuit mixed up in the affair, he must have been the author of the forgery.

[1] 28 November 1953.   [2] F.-M. Bergounioux, *Encore la Fraude de Piltdown* (1958).

CHAPTER XVII

ET POST HOC EXILIUM

TEILHARD was subject to moods of deep depression during the winter of 1953–4. He was seventy-three years old, and he knew from his precarious heart condition that he might not have long to live. On 11 December the death of Père Valensin in Nice was a further reminder of mortality. Hearing at one moment that he was getting better, Valensin had exclaimed: 'What a pity! I was so ready to die. Doctor, you're going to make me miss my death.' It was a belittlement of God to think of him as a judge—'but to go to one's Father, to love and tenderness and goodness—what happiness!' When Teilhard learnt that his friend and confidant had died, his grief was touched with envy: 'now he *sees*—when will it be my turn?'[1]—and for Teilhard it was always more important to see than to explain. Their two lives had followed very different paths since they first tried their hands at preaching in the novitiate at Aix-en-Provence, where the great Maurice Blondel used to call to see Valensin in the parlour. Valensin had scarcely moved from Lyon or Nice—a sedentary and literary figure as much at home with an unbeliever like Roger Martin du Gard as Teilhard was at home with Julian Huxley. He had remained the pure philosopher and at the same time had advanced so far along the mystical way that, while he held fast to dogma, he no longer believed in theology—and Teilhard was disposed to agree with him. Their minds, like their temperaments, were complementary to an extraordinary degree, each correcting what was lacking or one-sided in the other. Valensin was a humanist in the classical understanding of the word; Teilhard was a humanist in a sense that he spent a lifetime attempting to explain.

In January 1954 the crisis of the worker-priests came to a head, causing much more popular dismay than the publication of *Humani*

[1] *Letters from a Traveller*, p. 348.

Generis, to which it was in some ways a sequel. Teilhard freely admitted the defects and dangers of the first experiments but deplored that in the eyes of Rome 'work is still regarded, at bottom, as a punishment, and research—whatever verbal blessings they may bestow upon it—as an accessory, an addition and a convenience'. Teilhard thought the vocation of the worker-priests eminently a task for the Society, and their suppression moved him strongly:

> The sin of Rome (for all its casual benedictions on technique and science) is not to believe in a future, and an achievement (for heaven) of man upon earth. I know it because I have stifled for fifty years in this sub-human atmosphere.[1]

He was now at work on *Les Singularités de l'Espèce Humaine*, and he was glad to find his projects for the Wenner-Gren—a virtual reform of anthropology—favourably received. The idea was mooted of a centre, not too far from New York, where these problems could be quietly studied and discussed. Teilhard had in mind the Centre Culturel, founded by Henri Gouin at the Abbaye de Royaumont, which he had visited during his last stay in France. It was shortly after his first heart attack and they had fixed him up a bed on the ground floor to save him from climbing the stairs. The director of the Centre, Gilbert Gadoffre, described himself as '*médusé*' by the radiance of Teilhard's features, worn as they were by illness, as he sat at table talking to the technicians who had come to listen to him. These were the contacts—the friction of minds mutually engaged—which were more frequent and more stimulating in France than in America. It was not that Teilhard was not listened to in America—he was listened to very carefully in a restricted circle of experts—but in France people hung upon his words.

He continued to see his compatriots who came to New York—notably Malraux, with whom he had two long conversations and whom he was surprised to discover well acquainted with his unpublished writings. Owing to building operations at St. Ignatius, he now moved his quarters to the Lotos Club on East 66th Street, and instead of celebrating his daily Mass in the Chapel of the Sacred Heart in the Jesuit Church, he said it in the Dominican Church on Lexington Avenue. But Teilhard knew that his time was getting short; and he wanted to see Paris and die. There was already talk of a scientific

[1] Letter to Bruno de Solages, 17 January 1954.

congress at which the question of 'integration' would be studied on the interrelated planes of sociology, biology, and physics. Two of Teilhard's friends—Jean Piveteau from the Sorbonne and Théodore Monod from the Museum at Dakar—were active in the promotion of this, although the date of the meeting had not yet been agreed upon. Teilhard's presence would have been as welcome as his absence would have been deplored, and it was with this in mind that he obtained permission from his Provincial, who was in Rome at the time, to spend three months in France during the summer of 1954.

There was a further reason for his wishing to go. He had been profoundly disturbed by a reading of Jean Rostand's *Ce que je crois*, which he thought poor in argument and likely to be harmful in effect. Rostand was a scientist of note and Teilhard was eager to rebut his pessimistic conclusions. He also wished to correct the views of other scientists for whom he had more respect—Simpson's *The Meaning of Evolution*, Julian Huxley's *The Future of Man*, and Galton-Darwin's *After a Million Years*. Here, he thought, was a work of apologetics which he was well qualified to undertake; a work which could fortify the faith of those who still believed that science and Christianity— even 'neo-Christianity'—were incompatible. 'Perhaps', he wrote, 'the people high up will realize this time that the moment has come to let me publish.'[1] Accordingly, he applied to Rome, through his Provincial, for the necessary permission, and embarked on 3 June in the *Flandres*.

The visit was not a success. Teilhard was visibly overtired, and his return was greeted with embarrassing publicity. His lecture on 'L'Afrique et les origines humaines' at the Hotel des Sociétés Savantes was naturally crowded, with many Jesuits unconvincingly disguised *en clergyman*. But his presentation of the slides lacked its usual expertise and he seemed to be under considerable strain. When he had finished speaking, the applause was noticeably lacking in warmth.[2] Fatigued by a succession of visits and interviews, he left Paris for Lyon where his Provincial, Père Ravier, received him with every mark of sympathy. The Lyon scholasticate is perched high up on the Montée de Fourvière, close to the basilica which overlooks the city. It was then a nursery of the 'new theology', and a number of its theologians— men now wholly restored to favour—had not escaped the discipline

[1] To Bruno de Solages, 17 January 1954.   [2] Cuénot, p. 365.

which all nurseries must expect. High as it stood above the city of gastronomes and silk merchants, Fourvière had in a sense gone underground. Among Teilhard's own contemporaries only Victor Fontoynont, now mortally ill, was there to welcome him; but here was the Society of Jesus at its best and its broadest—the Society as Teilhard wished it to be, and to which he indissolubly belonged.

If Fourvière spoke to him of his vocation in one way, Sarcenat spoke of it in another; and Teilhard now felt the desire to revisit the house where his first 'stones' were laid out under their glass case. He wanted to see the pointed *puys* which had seemed like volcanoes when he set out to explore them, and which of recent years he had only seen from the distance of Les Moulins. The house was now occupied by the widow of his brother Victor, and her family. Of all Emmanuel Teilhard de Chardin's eleven children, only Pierre and Joseph were still alive. From Lyon to Clermont-Ferrand is an easy journey, but when Teilhard came to Sarcenat he stayed there for only a quarter of an hour. Quick as ever to exchange emotion for curiosity, he expressed a wish to visit the recently discovered caves at Lascaux. The authenticity of these prehistoric paintings—an obvious celebration of fertility—had been guaranteed by Breuil, and it was here that the two friends, with Leroy joining them, met for the last time. And it was in this way that one vision of the past was completed by another.

On his return to Paris at the end of August Teilhard lodged at his old headquarters in the Rue Monsieur. Père d'Ouince was no longer the superior, and Père Jouve was dead; so Teilhard had none of his closest friends at hand when he received the reply from Rome in answer to his request to be allowed to publish a reply to Jean Rostand. The answer forbade him to publish and ordered him to return to New York as soon as possible. The harsh refusal had reached him, by a cruel irony, on 31 July—the feast of St. Ignatius. It so happened that on this day Père d'Ouince called to see him. Teilhard opened his door and advanced towards his friend with arms outstretched. 'Ah! you have come to see me today,' he exclaimed, 'what a lovely feast of St. Ignatius!'

It was the ultimate test of obedience. Ignatian he had always been, and Ignatian he remained to the bitter—though not embittered— end. *Contemplatio ad amorem* had been the mainspring of his spirituality and also of his research. The limits of his obedience can only be properly understood by those of his own spiritual family, and none understood them better than Père d'Ouince:

The obedience of Teilhard was, as I see it, exemplary; neither reticent nor timorous; at once generous and free. He accepted without bargaining the sacrifices imposed upon him; and on the other hand he always behaved to his superiors with that openness of mind which is the antidote to servility and complements the religious discipline of the Society. His superiors could count upon his absolute docility, but he never left them in any doubt of whatever he thought unduly rigorous in their decisions, and right up to the end (the last letter to his Provincial is dated a few days before his death) he asked for the revision of a policy of prudence which seemed contrary both to his own interior vocation and to the interests of the Church.[1]

Teilhard admitted that there were 'many occasions when the duty of a son was to leave his mother in order to be more truly a son'; but to those who begged him to take a freedom always open to him, he would borrow the words of St.Exupéry: 'In order to have an effect upon the house, you have got to live in it.'[2] To all such impulsive well-wishers Teilhard emphasized that he was 'not a prodigal son'; that 'a revolutionary attitude would be pleasant but suicidal'; that it would mean 'the killing of everything that I want to liberate, and not destroy'. When somebody compared him to a 'young swan fighting among ducks', he replied that he would 'stay with the ducks'.

Would it be logical for me [he wrote to Père d'Ouince] in breaking with the Church, impatiently to force the growth of the Christian trunk in which I am convinced the sap of tomorrow's religion is at work? I am held prisoner to the Church by the same views which lead me to discover its insufficiencies. Don't you find that rather dramatic?

Max Bégouën asked him if he were not consoled to see the growing influence of his teaching; to which Teilhard replied that his mission would only be fulfilled when others had gone beyond him.

The Roman theologians, Teilhard thought, were less important in themselves than for what they represented; and he met their intransigence with serenity. 'I am prepared to go on to the end,' he said,

1 *L'obéissance du Père Teilhard de Chardin.*
2 '*Pour agir sur la maison, il faut être dans la maison.*'

'and with a smile if possible.' What put him out of patience, and momentarily out of temper, was the invitation of an ex-religious to join a small and dissident community of freethinkers. If people said to him, as they sometimes did: 'Your religion is admirable, but it is not the Catholic religion', he would answer severely: 'Do you think me mad enough to want to found a new religion, or to imagine myself a second Jesus Christ?' There are still Catholics who doubt whether Teilhard's religion was the religion of the Church which he claimed to serve; but if the authorities of that Church are alarmed by the expansion of his ideas, they have very largely themselves to thank. The *consensus fidelium*—and *infidelium*—does not, in the case of Pierre Teilhard de Chardin, amount to unanimity, but it has given a pretty reverberating answer to tribunals who pronounce, in secret, sentences against which there is no appeal.[1]

II

Three days after hearing his sentence Teilhard was writing to Bruno de Solages: 'You know that all this doesn't worry me very much. I am so sure of the final triumph. . . Pray for me that I may stand firm to the end.'[2] He said much the same thing to Père de Lubac, who twice came to visit him in the Rue Monsieur and was himself under a similar cloud. De Lubac found him 'as simple and brotherly as ever, and as thoughtful of the other person. But there was something a trifle constricted and at the same time over-confident in the organization of his thought—the natural effect of age and ill-health. In any case, not a word of bitterness, or the slightest complaint about his troubles.'[3]

Teilhard left Paris for London on 5 August and five days later—after meetings with Kenneth Oakley and Dr. Loriot, treasurer of the World Congress of Faiths—he embarked on an ocean liner for the last time. It was not that he had minded the incessant migrations of an Odyssey that was nearing its end:

We have the duty, up to a certain point, to look for a fixed

[1] For the foregoing I am indebted to Père d'Ouince's *L'obéissance du Père Teilhard de Chardin*, and to his introduction to *Letters from Teilhard de Chardin* (Perspectives in Humanism).

[2] 3 August 1954.

[3] Letter to the author, 30 March 1967.

anchorage, but if life keeps tearing us away, without allowing us to settle anywhere, that is perhaps an appeal and a blessing. It may be that the world will only be saved by those who have not where to lay their heads. Personally I ask God to let me die (metaphorically at least) at the side of the road.[1]

For the immediate future—and there might be no other future—he was resigned to working 'in darkness and exile'[2]—and the resignation did not come easily. If only he could see France once more! For this tireless traveller and intrepid visionary of cosmogenesis, the world was less precious, in the last resort, than the corner of it which had never ceased to be his home. There seemed, indeed, in the late autumn of 1954 a chance that he might, after all, have an opportunity to return to France. Jean Piveteau was organizing a conference on palaeontology for April 1955, in which Teilhard was officially invited to participate. He took soundings from his Provincial, but was advised not to apply for permission. As a further irritation—no doubt the Roman censors found it easier to hit a man when he was ageing—he was forbidden to publish a German translation of his articles which had appeared in *Études*.

In October, however, he did take part in a symposium organized by Columbia University in celebration of its bicentenary:

There were about seventy of us, in a wonderful countryside, about two hours from New York. The place[3] has been given to Columbia University by the Harrimans to try out as a conference centre. It lies in the outlying foothills of the Catskills, covered just now with fantastic gold and purple mantling of sycamores. The company was very varied and representative, ranging from physicists like Niels Bohr to poets like Macleish, via naturalist philosophers like Julian Huxley and theologians like Van Dusen (leader, with Niebuhr, of the new American Protestant Movement).

The subject for discussion was the unity of human knowledge. In my section a deep and vital cleavage plane became apparent between the humanists and scientists, which turned, ultimately, as I said at the last meeting, on the new Galileo question: Is man still moving biologically upon himself? With Huxley and the majority of the scientists, I, of course, vigorously attacked the

---

[1] Letter to Père d'Ouince, 1939.
[2] Cuénot, p. 366.   [3] Arden House.

immobilist position taken up, alas!, by the more Christian-thinking members of the section, such as Gilson, Malik (Lebanese representative at the United Nations) and Battaglia, lay rector of the University of Bologna, and even Van Dusen. I was greatly taken by Van Dusen, in spite of some traces of Barthian pessimism, and I expect our paths will cross again.[1]

The weight of these oppositions should not be underestimated. In Barth Teilhard had against him some very considerable theologians, and in Gilson perhaps a most erudite historian of philosophy. Not an historian in the dry, academic sense, but a mind which had counted for a great deal in the renaissance of Catholic thought; deeply versed in scholasticism, but well able to look beyond it. For Gilson—as for St. Augustine whom he quoted in support[2]—theology was 'the most exact of sciences', and Kant had admired the scholastic method. Gilson criticized Teilhard's transposition of the Christ of the Trinity into the Christ of the cosmos, and his generalization of Christ the Redeemer into a motor of evolution. The Alexandrian Fathers to whom Teilhard appealed had assimilated the Logos to the Redeemer —not, as Teilhard claimed, the other way about; just as it had been the error of the Gnostics to 'cosmify' the Redeemer at the same time as they 'christified' the universe. For St. Irenaeus 'the true gnosis' was 'the teaching of the twelve apostles'. Gilson maintained that the historical Christ was not 'the concrete germ of Christ Omega'; and he denied that the masses had deserted Christianity for scientific reasons. Moreover the cosmic Christ was a Christ in whom no scientist believed. There was 'too much para-science in Teilhard for too little true Christian wisdom', and as for his style—'what a fall is there when one deserts the naked rigour of the old masters for the gelatinous prose of our contemporaries'. But when Gilson criticized Teilhard's ideas, he did not forget the priest sunk in his breviary while the *savants* passed to and fro in the corridor:

> There is nothing shady about the origins of Père Teilhard de Chardin's celebrity; everything in him was pure. Under the continual flow of scientific or other alluvions he kept intact and miraculously preserved the nugget of pure gold which was the piety and faith of his childhood.[3]

[1] *Letters from a Traveller*, p. 354.
[2] '*nobis ad certam regulam loqui fas est.*'   [3] *Seminarium*, no. 4.

To whatever extent one agrees or disagrees with Gilson, this relation of Teilhard's thought to Teilhard's life is of capital importance. Equally interesting would have been the confrontation with Barth's pessimistic fideism—two Pauline spirits passionately at loggerheads over St. Paul. Here, too, Teilhard had made up in his life—and never more painfully than now—for the tragic dimension which is generally lacking in his ideas. He had experienced to the full the existentialist *Angst* which he condemned. He had felt it, intolerably, on his last visit to Sarcenat. The death of Louise in girlhood, of Albéric in the prime of life, and of Gonzague in the field of battle; the death of Françoise in Shanghai and the sufferings of Marguerite; the death of Gabriel in 1943; the passing of Davidson Black and of Georges-Marie Haardt at the height of their vigour and achievement—all taken prematurely from the world that Teilhard loved; if life were indeed absurd, could there be a stronger proof of its absurdity? And his own thirty years of exile and frustration—the seeming failure of the axis to support the spiral—what could be more absurd than that? Let it be granted that Teilhard walked with his eyes so resolutely fixed upon the light that his vision lost in depth what it gained in length; but let it also be understood that he walked in the shadows to which he refused his introspection.

At the same time he was corresponding with a philosopher far younger than Gilson and more responsive to the wavelengths of contemporary thinking. Claude Tresmontant was among those who had read such of Teilhard's essays as had been circulated *sous le manteau*, and he had in mind to write a book about him. Teilhard insisted that he was 'essentially pantheist in temperament and thought', emphasizing that there was 'a true pantheism of union'—the 'pan-Christic' union which he had long ago discovered with Rousselot and Blondel. Tresmontant objected that all Teilhard's thought was anti-pantheist in the classical understanding of the word; and in a long letter whose candour does not conceal its admiration he placed a friendly finger on what seemed to be lacking in Teilhard's biblical and theological formation:

> I wonder how far you understand the revelation upon which you base your thought. Your theology is only distantly related to the thought of the Church. If you were versed in the Bible, it is there that you would have discovered your own ideas. You are still more orthodox than you imagine.

Teilhard seemed only to have read the Gospels and St. Paul, and his lifelong battle had been with the old Manichaean dualism:

But if [Tresmontant continued] it pleased God to speak to us over a certain number of centuries, perhaps it is a little cavalier to want to listen only to the last sentences of his discourse and to treat all his previous publications as anthropomorphic and childish. . . . The Jews were no more primitive than the Greeks. You have not recognized your adversaries because you have not known the mind of the Church; her adversaries were the same as your own, even when they were within the Church—as heretics so often are.[1]

Of all those men whose minds had once met in rigorous encounter— Valensin and Blondel, Maréchal and Charles—only Teilhard and Le Roy were now living; and with the death of Le Roy on 1 December 1954 Teilhard looked back—as he so often did—with a particular affection to the friendships that were knit on the fifth floor of the house in the Rue du Vieux Colombier during those difficult post-war years of creative thinking:

I still think something was born there, and even though it's buried under several feet of earth, the seed will germinate.[2]

and he now wrote to Le Roy's widow:

You know how deeply he influenced me; both in urging me forward to go on 'daring', and in teaching me to stay faithful, just at the time when I needed it most. If I have preserved the passion of my vocation, I owe it very largely to his magnificent love of God and the truth. I have always thought that instead of seeking its subjects for canonization in the depths of monasteries, it is saints like Édouard that the Church should hold out to us in these times: Christians who christianize the whole of their humanity.[3]

'In order that ideas may triumph, many of their defenders must die in obscurity.' To this obscurity, as we have said, Teilhard was now resigned. In January 1955 he was at work on two papers—one for a Symposium which the Wenner-Gren were holding in June; the other for his 'personal archives'.[4] *Le Christique* was his testament and he would leave it, as another might leave his will, in a drawer. It was a *résumé* of his mystical vision—a 'natural' mysticism, some have called it, and he would not have minded the abridgement—as he had first

[1] 17 January 1954.　　　　[2] Letter to Père Jouve, 6 July 1934.
[3] December 1954.　　　　[4] *Letters from a Traveller*, p. 358.

tried to formulate it in *Le Milieu Divin* and *La Messe sur le Monde*. The vision is no longer new, and the manner is less exuberant; but the sense of wonder and the impetus of passion are the same. And the problem was the same, too. For the Christian there was 'a deepening sphere asking for a centre'; if Christianity gave each what they were seeking, could this be 'a coincidence and an illusion'?

He went through the familiar arguments offering, here and there, the customary hostage to the theologians. (In what sense could one say that Christ was 'saved' by evolution?) His mind went back to those first days with Licent in the Gobi desert, when he had neither bread nor wine, and only the earth for an altar; and he spoke again of that

> universal transubstantiation where the words of consecration fall not upon the sacrificial bread and wine alone, but upon all the pain and joy engendered by the progress and convergence of the world; and where the possibilities of a universal communion follow in their wake.

To the classical Christianity where the Cross was a symbol of failure and the Parousia a distant catastrophe, Teilhard opposed the 'diaphanie' of a cosmic Christ which, for him, had transfigured the whole phenomenon of man, and the '*divine matière*' from which man had sprung and to which he must ineluctably return. And yet how came it, he asked himself, that

> looking around me, and intoxicated with everything that has appeared to me, I should be almost alone of my kind? The only one to have *seen*? And thus, incapable—when people ask me—of quoting a single author or book, where the marvellous 'diaphanie' is recognizable and clearly expressed. And how can it be, when I have 'come down from the mountain', in spite of the magnificence I have seen, that I should be so little better, so little pacified, and so impotent to translate into acts, and thus communicate effectively to others, the wonderful unity in which I feel myself engulfed? For all the ambitious splendour of my ideas, I am still, in practice, disturbed by my imperfections. In spite of my claims to formulate it, my faith does not produce in me as much real charity, or calm confidence, as the children's catechism produces in the humble person kneeling at my side. But I know, too, that this faith . . . of which I make so poor a use . . . is the only

faith that I can entertain, the only one that satisfies me—and even (for of this I have no doubt) the only one that will satisfy the coal-heavers and charwomen of tomorrow.

And so, as he took a second look around him, there vibrated the sound-waves of a future unanimity. Teilhard was not as alone as he had thought. The love of God and faith in the world were 'in the air' though rarely—as yet—combined in the same person:

In me, by the chance of temperament, education and environ-ment, the proportion of one and the other are favourable, and the fusion has spontaneously come about—too feebly as yet for an explosive propagation—but still in sufficient strength to show that the reaction is possible and that, *some day or other, the two will join up*. A fresh proof that the truth has only to appear once, in a single mind, and nothing can ever again prevent it from invading everything and setting it aflame.

These last words of *Le Christique* have stood, among many others, for Teilhard's epitaph. They ring with the confidence of a prophecy soon to be fulfilled, but they must be read in a context of humility. Jacques Maritain, one of Teilhard's most rigorous critics, has described him as a '*grand imaginatif*'.[1] The proportions of imagination, mystical insight, and scientific perception in his writings are not to be debated here. Nor can we predict how far 'classical' Christianity will assimilate or reject his views. But behind the prophecies and avowals of *Le Christique* there echoes the simplicity of his invocation:

'*Seigneur de mon enfance et Seigneur de ma fin*.'[2]

III

The end was not far off, and the presentiment of death was strong in him. Over and over again, he repeats to his correspondents: 'Pray that I may end well.' Shortly before Easter he went into retreat, and the notes that he made during this time have come down to us. All through his life Teilhard had jotted down anything that occurred to him:

The youth that we draw from the risen Christ is the best 'apologetic'.

[1] *Le Paysan de la Garonne*, 1967.
[2] 'Lord of my childhood and Lord of my ending.'

May he keep me young (for the greater glory of God)
1. Because trials and age come from him
2. Because trials and age lead to him
3. Because trials and age will only touch me as measured out by
   him.
Accept death as it comes to me in Christ.
The difficulty in old age is to fit one's interior life to a life without
   future for oneself. (One has one's face to the wall.)
If a crowd of immediate interests vanish (career, sympathy, influence) some higher interest must take the place of them all.
Find a place, and an *elevating* place for the approaching end, and
   for the decline of life (within the limits of God's will).
'To be ready' has never seemed to me to signify anything else
   than 'to be stretching forward'.

On Good Friday, 8 April, Teilhard wrote a long letter to his Provincial and friend, Père Ravier. It was thirty-three years since he had
last written to him about the meaning of the Cross, and he found
nothing to add now to what he had said then:

What the world expects from the Church of God is a generalization and deepening of the meaning of the Cross. . . . In a universe
which is in the way of unification with God, the Cross (without
losing its expiatory and compensatory function) becomes, even
more surely, the symbol and expression of evolution as a whole
. . . That is what I believe, and that is what I so long to confess
publicly before I die.

This may well have been the last letter that Teilhard wrote, and it
was his last word to the Society.

On Saturday, 9 April, he made his confession to a Jesuit friend,
Père de Breuvery. Not long before, he had told a diplomat cousin,
Jean de Lagarde, that he would like 'to die on the day of the Resurrection'. On Easter Sunday he said his Mass as usual and then attended
Pontifical High Mass in St. Patrick's Cathedral. He was no lover of
ecclesiastical pomp, but it seemed as if he could not have enough of
the Resurrection. He was in particularly good health and spirits. In the
afternoon he walked through Central Park in the clear spring sunshine, attended a concert, and then called in for tea with Mrs. de
Terra, whom he called his 'Providence' and who had watched over
his needs so carefully. He had just put down a piece of paper on the

window-sill and was about to sip his tea when he 'suddenly fell full length on the floor, toppling over like a stricken tree'.[1] It was clear that he had had a heart attack, and a doctor was sent for. Realizing the gravity of Teilhard's condition, he urged that a priest should be summoned. Père de Breuvery was out and an American priest came in his place. By the time he reached the apartment Teilhard was dead, but he anointed him and gave him absolution.

The body was embalmed and lay in the chapel of St. Ignatius Presbytery. It was vested in a white chasuble, with the hands clasping a crucifix and rosary. On the Tuesday in Easter Week a Low Mass of Requiem was celebrated by Père de Breuvery, and the almost perfunctory simplicity of these rites seemed to emphasize the obscurity in which Pierre Teilhard de Chardin believed that he was destined to die. For Valensin the cathedral at Nice was crowded and the Bishop officiated; but for Teilhard not even the *In Paradisum* was sung, and there were only a handful of people present. Père Leroy, who had flown in from Chicago, and a priest from St. Ignatius accompanied the coffin to the Jesuit novitiate at St. Andrew's on the Hudson, sixty miles up-river from New York, where the burial was to take place. By a strange irony the 'matter' which Teilhard had adored for its consistency was too hard to receive his body. So it remained in a temporary vault until the ground grew softer. When it was finally buried alongside his brothers in the Society of Jesus nobody was present.

But it was not long before the audience had begun to gather.

[1] Père Leroy, quoted by Cuénot, p. 387.

GLOSSARY

BIBLIOGRAPHY

INDEX

Short glossary of scientific and other terms which occur in this biography

ACHEULIAN: Refers to the lower Palaeolithic age in the Old World, from the early second to the third inter-glacial period. Name taken from Saint-Acheul in France.

ALLUVIAL: Applied to land formed from deposits from rivers.

ANTHROPOGENESIS: The science of man's development, taken as a whole, and not divided into separate spheres of study.

ARSINOTHERIUM: A genus of extinct mammals (Order Embrithopoda) of the Oligocene of Egypt, having limbs resembling those of the elephant and a pair of large horns.

BIOSPHERE: The area of whatever life on the earth is incapable of reflection.

BRECCIA: A rock formed of angular fragments embedded in a matrix of similar material; rocklike deposit of debris on prehistoric site inhabited by man.

CENOZOIC: Designates the span of geological time from the beginning of the Tertiary era—i.e. about 58 million years ago—to the present day.

CHELLEAN: An early stage of Palaeolithic culture in which stone implements of the rougher type were fashioned. The name is taken from Chelles in France.

COLLENIA: Fossilized deposits of calcareous algae, which form layered mounds with a knobby surface. The individual mounds are 2 to 3 feet in diameter; the grouped mounds form hills covering many acres.

COMPLEXITY–CONSCIOUSNESS: The correlation of psychic energy to a proportionately greater concentration of matter.

COSMOGENESIS: The movement of the universe to its evolutionary goal.

DEVONIAN: The oldest period of the Upper Palaeozoic era. Usually dated about 300 million years ago.

DINOSAUR: A Mesozoic reptile, usually of enormous size.

DIPLODOCUS: A giant herbivorous dinosaur of the Cretaceous period, i.e. from 70 to 140 million years ago.

DOLOMITIC: Carbonate rocks having the double carbonate of calcium and magnesium, thus differing from ordinary limestone which is essentially carbonate of calcium.

ENERGY, RADIAL: The cosmic energy which produces bodies increasingly complex and increasingly centred upon themselves.

ENERGY, TANGENTIAL: The energy that sets up external relations between the material bodies of the universe.

ENTROPY: A measure of the gradual dissipation of physical energy, which occurs spontaneously and inevitably in any closed thermodynamic system.

EOCENE: The first period of the Tertiary era; about 68 million years ago.

HOMINIZATION: The process leading to reflective life in mankind.

HOMO SAPIENS: The only surviving species of the genus *Homo*. Walks upright and has hands capable of fashioning and using tools.

ICE AGE: See PLEISTOCENE.

IGUANODON: A duck-billed dinosaur.

LOESS: A buff-coloured, wind-blown deposit of sandy material. In the central Asian deserts the accumulation of these has been attributed to the binding power of grasses, shown by a network of narrow tubes, the grasses having in the course of time lost all their organic matter.

MAGDALENIAN: Period of the late Palaeolithic which takes its name from the rock shelter of La Madeleine on the river Vezère in south-west France where the typical artefacts of the culture were first found in abundance. In addition to flint implements these included a great number of tools made of bone and ivory, e.g. harpoons, hooks, needles, borers. Many of the polychrome cave paintings in southern France and northern Spain belong to this period which is sometimes referred to as 'l'âge de rennes' (the reindeer age).

MAMMIFEROUS: Pertaining to a vertebrate animal that suckles its young.

MASTODON: An extinct animal of the elephant type.

MEGALOSAURUS: A gigantic carnivorous dinosaur.

MESOZOIC: The age of the reptiles. Lasted from perhaps 195 to 70 million years ago.

MIOCENE: Last but one period of the Tertiary era. Miocene sedimentation began approximately 35 million years ago, and lasted for about 15 million years. It was during this time that apes and ancestral gibbons made their appearance.

MONAD: A centre of individual consciousness.

NEANDERTHAL MAN: A race of palaeanthropic men, not directly ancestral to man as he is today, with its origins far back in the Pliocene era. Takes its name from a cave in the Neanderthal gorge of the valley of the Düssel, a tributary of the Rhine.

NEOLITHIC: Pertaining to the later part of the Stone Age, notable for the production of highly finished stone implements. A period dating from 3,500 to 7,500 years before historical times.

NOOSPHERE: The envelope of reflective life embracing the biosphere, though still dependent on it.

GLOSSARY

OBSIDIAN: A natural glass resulting from the quick cooling of lava.

OMEGA: The point at which the universe will ultimately centre upon itself and the climax of evolution, identified by Teilhard with the risen Christ of the Parousia.

ORANG-UTANG: A large ape found in Borneo and Sumatra.

ORDOVICIAN: A period of the Palaeozoic era which began approximately 440 million years ago and lasted for 60 million years.

PALAEOLITHIC: A period lasting from 500,000 to one-and-a-half million years ago during which artefacts were produced by the chipping of stone or the bones of animals.

PALAEOZOIC: The era of invertebrate animal life, lasting from approximately 500 to 300 million years ago.

PHYLUM: One of the 12 major subdivisions of the animal kingdom. Man belongs to the Phylum *Chordata*, which includes organisms with an internal skeleton and a segmented backbone, or—in more rare cases—only a spinal chord. Teilhard, however, tends to apply the term to any recognizable group-system.

PLEISTOCENE: The ice age and first period of the Quaternary in the geological time-scale. Probably began 2 million years ago.

PLIOCENE: The last major division of the Tertiary. It dates from some 15 million years before the beginning of the Pleistocene, and was marked by the appearance of apes of modern type.

PRE-CAMBRIAN: The period of geological time during which the earth was formed. Approximately 3,000 to 520 million years ago.

PRIMATES: Men, apes, monkeys, marmosets, lemurs and related forms.

QUATERNARY: The geological period which followed the Tertiary, and the last principal division of the Cenozoic. Roughly speaking, the last million years of the earth's history.

SOLUTREAN: A stage of Palaeolithic culture marked by a refinement in the making of flint implements, about 70,000 years ago. The name is taken from Le Solutré in France.

SYMPHYSIS: The fixed articulation of two bones.

STONE AGE: Preceding the Bronze and Iron Ages, i.e. before 3,500 B.C.

SAURIAN: The snake and lizard group of reptiles.

TERTIARY: The earlier subdivision of the Cenozoic, or last, geological era.

TRANSFORMISM: To be distinguished from evolution since it only applies to the transformation of one living species into another.

TRILOBITE: Extinct group of transversely segmented invertebrates. They occur among the oldest known fossils of the Cambrian era, i.e. 520 to 420 million years ago.

Bibliography

Titles listed in order of publication

WORKS BY PIERRE TEILHARD DE CHARDIN IN ENGLISH TRANSLATION

The Phenomenon of Man (London, Collins, and New York, Harper, 1959; revised edition, 1965; Fontana edition, 1965).

Le Milieu Divin (London, Collins, 1960; Fontana edition, 1964); *The Divine Milieu* (New York, Harper, 1960).

Letters from a Traveller (London, Collins, and New York, Harper, 1962; London, Fontana edition, 1967).

Hymn of the Universe (London, Collins, and New York, Harper, 1965).

The Appearance of Man (London, Collins, and New York, Harper, 1965).

The Making of a Mind (London, Collins, and New York, Harper, 1965).

Letters from Egypt 1905–1908 (New York, Herder & Herder, 1965).

The Vision of the Past (London, Collins, and New York, Harper, 1966).

Man's Place in Nature (London, Collins, and New York, Harper, 1966).

CRITICAL AND BIOGRAPHICAL WORKS ON TEILHARD DE CHARDIN

Dialogue with Teilhard de Chardin, Olivier Rabut, O.P. (London, Sheed & Ward, 1961).

Teilhard de Chardin: Scientist and Seer, C. E. Raven (London, Collins, and New York, Harper, 1962).

Memories of Teilhard de Chardin, Helmut de Terra (London, Collins, and New York, Harper, 1964).

Teilhard de Chardin: Pilgrim of the Future, Essays edited by Neville Braybrooke (New York, Seabury Press, 1964; London, Darton, Longman & Todd, 1965).

Teilhard de Chardin: A Biographical Study, Claude Cuénot (London, Burns & Oates, and Baltimore, Helicon Press, 1965). *Note:* This is slightly abridged from the French. Contains full bibliography of Teilhard's writings.

In the Field with Teilhard de Chardin, George Barbour (New York, Herder & Herder, 1965).

The Faith of Teilhard de Chardin, Henri de Lubac, S.J. (London, Burns & Oates, and New York, Hawthorn, 1965).

Teilhard de Chardin and the Mystery of Christ, Christopher Mooney, S.J. (London, Collins, and New York, Harper, 1966).

Teilhard de Chardin, Bernard Towers (London, Carey Kingsgate Press, 1966).

Teilhard de Chardin Album, ed. Mortier & Auboux (London, Collins, and New York, Harper, 1966).

The Religion of Teilhard de Chardin, Henri de Lubac, s.j. (London, Collins, and New York, Desclée, 1967).

Teilhard de Chardin: A Guide to his Thought, Émile Rideau (London, Collins, and New York, Harper, 1968).

Among works not translated into English, the following should be noticed.

BY TEILHARD

Cahiers de Pierre Teilhard de Chardin (Paris, Éditions du Seuil, 1958).

L'Énergie Humaine (Paris, Éditions du Seuil, 1962).

L'Activation de l'Énergie (Paris, Éditions du Seuil, 1958).

Lettres à Léontine Zanta (Paris, Desclée de Brouwer, 1965).

Science et Christ (Paris, Éditions du Seuil, 1965).

Écrits du temps de la Guerre (Paris, Grasset, 1965).

Lettres d'Hastings et de Paris (Paris, Aubier, 1966).

ABOUT TEILHARD

Maurice Blondel et le Père Teilhard de Chardin, Henri de Lubac, s.j. (Archives de Philosophie, vol. xxiv, Jan.–Mar. 1961, pp. 123–56).

Essais sur Teilhard de Chardin (Paris, Fayard, 1962).

Initiation à Teilhard de Chardin, Jacques Madaule (Paris, Éditions du Cerf, 1963).

Bergson et Teilhard de Chardin, Madeleine Barthélemy-Madaule (Paris, Éditions du Seuil, 1963).

Pierre Teilhard de Chardin ou la Foi au Monde, Jean Onimus (Paris, Plon, 1963).

La Carrière Scientifique de Pierre Teilhard de Chardin, Louis Barjon et Pierre Leroy (Monaco, Éditions du Rocher, 1964).

Éléments du Bâti Scientifique Teilhardien, Louis Barral (Monaco, Éditions du Rocher, 1964).

La Vision de Teilhard de Chardin, Pierre Smulders (Bruges and Paris, Desclée de Brouwer, 1964).

Le Père Teilhard de Chardin Savant, Jean Piveteau (Paris, Fayard, 1964).

Teilhard de Chardin et la Pensée Catholique, ed. Claude Cuénot (Paris, Éditions du Seuil, 1965).

Teilhard, Missionnaire et Apologiste, Henri de Lubac, s.j. (Toulouse, Éditions Prière et Vie, 1966).

Index

PERSONS

PLACES

GENERAL

TEILHARD DE CHARDIN, PIERRE—WRITINGS BY